Ray Corrigan

Digital Decision Making

Back to the Future

Springer

Ray Corrigan
Open University in the South
Oxford, UK

British Library Cataloguing in Publication Data
A catalogue record for this book is available from the British Library

Library of Congress Control Number: 2007923183

ISBN 978-1-84628-672-8   e-ISBN 978-1-84628-673-5

With thanks to the Open University for kind permission to include extracts from Open University
course T182 Law, the Internet and Society: Technology and the Future of Ideas

Printed on acid-free paper

9 8 7 6 5 4 3 2 1

Springer Science+Business Media
springer.com

For Nicholas, Jack and Gillian

Contents

Acknowledgements

Over the course of the past year during which this book was developed and in the many years leading up to it, the number people to whom I am indebted has grown to unmanageable levels. I hope I can be forgiven, therefore, for singling out a few for a special thanks and for failing to mention many others without whose help the book could never have been written.

I am indebted to the governing body of Oxford University's Harris Manchester College, which kindly elected me to a year-long Visiting Fellowship between 2005 and 2006, during which time most of the research for the book was conducted. Thanks in particular are due to my friend and colleague, Mark Rogers at Harris Manchester, who regularly reminds me of the important things in life and whose support, encouragement and advice have been invaluable.

If it was not for the good folks at the British Library, the Open University Library and Oxford's Bodleian Library, most notably Sue Killoran, the wonderful chief librarian at Harris Manchester College, I would never have had access to the literally hundreds of books and articles I have needed as part of the research for this book over the past year or so.

Ley Robinson and Ian Eiloart read complete drafts, heroically wrestling with an entire manuscript's worth of undiluted Corrigan prose and providing gratefully received in-depth and honest feedback. Bernard Coen, one of the smartest and most decent people I have ever known, not only went through multiple complete drafts but encouraged me to keep going when times were tough and the book would never have been completed without him. Others, including David Crabbe, Mark Rogers, Dick Morris, Jo Davis, John Naughton, Peter Suber, Geoff Aldridge, Martin Weller, Andrea Berardi, Iain McKie, Jennifer Davis and Peter Butcher have read drafts of parts of the book. To the degree that I have managed to incorporate all the sound advice I have received, the final work has been immeasurably improved. Dick's suggestions, indeed, completely transformed Chapters 5 and 8. Bernard's had a similar effect on Chapters 1 and 7 and John tried valiantly to save me from the worst excesses of my original, very long, draft of the Colmcille story. Needless to say, any remaining errors, omissions, solecisms, malapropisms or lack of clarity remain the responsibility of the author.

Cathleen Blackburn of Manches LLP, which manages the Tolkien Estate, very kindly assisted in providing some factual information. However, where I make statements about the law or about the cases in which the Tolkien Estate has been involved, I alone am responsible for the accuracy or otherwise of these statements. What I say is not endorsed by Ms Blackburn, the Tolkien Estate or Manches and such endorsement cannot and should not be inferred.

Thanks to Kees Schouhamer Immink, the inventor of the CD and one of the unsung heroes of the digital age, for his advice and encouragement to write this book in the wake of my keynote talk at the IEEE International Symposium on Consumer Electronics in Reading in 2004. Thanks also to Ian Sherman for his insider's advice on publishing and publishers.

I owe a debt of gratitude to Open University colleagues Geraldine Kirby, Tina Armstrong and Bob Clark who have generously undertaken the burden of my day job whilst I took a year out to write a book. The Open University has given me the privilege of working with some absolutely amazing people, colleagues and students, and of pursuing a diverse range of academic interests spanning the gamut of technology from environmental decision making to Internet law. I have learned vastly more from my colleagues in these enterprises than I fear I have contributed and the cognitive fingerprints and influence of Dick Morris, John Naughton, Ray Ison, Chris Blackmore, Pam Furniss, Martin Weller, Tony Nixon, Sue Betteridge, Geoff Aldridge and Susan Carr in particular, sprinkled liberally throughout the pages of this book, will be familiar to anyone who knows their work.

My thanks to the Open University for permission to use materials from my Open University course, *T182 Law, the Internet and Society: Technology and the Future of Ideas*, including some of the wonderful cartoons drawn by the talented Tony Seldon. Thanks to Katie Meade for arranging said permissions and to Sue Betteridge, Robin Kyd, Gary Hills, Bryan Waddington, Geoff Aldridge and his systems support team, for rescuing me from my last minute formatting woes when my Microsoft Word software and the templates from Springer-Verlag were stubbornly refusing to communicate as I thought they should.

The people who have most influenced my thinking in the subject area of this book are Colm Reilly, James Boyle, Bruce Schneier, Peter Drahos, Larry Lessig, Peter Checkland, Bernard Coen, Dick Morris and John Naughton, Dick and John being the primary architects of the platform of ideas and opportunities at the Open University from which this book has emerged.

My greatest debt, however, is to my family. Thanks to my children, Jack and Nicholas, who have anticipated with such excitement, the 'real book' that dad has been writing ["Does this mean you're going to be a *real* author dad?!"] as well as tolerating, with inordinate patience, my tapping away at the computer keyboard when I should have been outside kicking a football with them. Thanks finally to Gillian, who, whilst I have been pretending that this authoring business is tough, has been quietly getting on with the real work of looking after the two boys and without whom none of it would be worthwhile.

Chapter 1 The battle of the book

"We learn from history that we do not learn from history." Georg Wilhelm Friedrich Hegel (1770 – 1831)

Colmcille and the battle of the book

In Ireland in the mid-6th-century AD, power depended on connections and access to and control of information. Not a great deal has changed in fourteen hundred years. The short story of Colmcille and the Battle of the Book[1] at Cooldrumman[2] goes something like this –

Colmcille[3] copied another monk's manuscript. The other monk, Finnian, objected and they settled things the way they did in those days. Three thousand were killed at the resulting battle.

The political landscape at the time was in pretty much constant turmoil, with about 150 warring tribes vying for power, territory and revenge for some earlier wrongdoing perpetrated by their neighbouring foes. In the thick of these skirmishes, the factions did coalesce, occasionally, into loose transient alliances under the toughest leaders and there was a fierce rivalry for overall dominance of the land between the northern and southern branches of the strongest clan, the O'Neills.[4]

As a boy Colmcille O'Neill was a larger than life, intellectually gifted, charismatic, fiery young redhead, who thoroughly immersed himself in the teachings of the Christian church, ably cultivated[5] by his mentors, local priest, Cruithnechan, and a monk called Finnian, whose school he attended at Molville in County Down.

Colmcille's sporting prowess and big, generous, open (if quick-tempered) nature earned him a lot of friends when he was growing up. He apparently had a booming, melodious voice and a very sharp sense of humour, which led him into many mischievous escapades. Being a devoted member of a church that was so integral to community life meant also being actively engaged in local society. He ran, chased, rode, hurled,[6] hunted, fished, sailed, and fought with great skill, energy and often savagery, as was fitting and expected of royalty.[7] He also delighted in Celtic culture and the natural environment and had a magical touch with plants and animals of all kinds.

A prolific scribe, Colmcille was made a deacon[8] before the age of twenty. He then spent some time with a Christian bard called Gemman. Over the next couple of years, he received an unparalleled education in Celtic folklore, politics and human nature, though the young deacon was already a shrewd student of all of these. Gemman taught him that learned men often lost touch with ordinary people because of their disconnected academic way of communicating. He needed to stay immersed in communities, their folklore and their lives. The idealistic, ambitious student, full of his own destiny and keen to spread his influence far and wide, learned the psychology of trading and negotiating and the mechanics of power dynamics and integrated these lessons into his own ongoing observations of the world around him. He already knew of the power of the bards to make or break public figures. The importance of perceived status to the influence of each tribal chief cannot be overstated. And it was the bards that created and spread tales, myths and legends about the strength and great deeds of kings.

At the age of 25, a newly ordained priest, he began travelling round the country on a missionary quest, eventually setting up 36 monasteries[9] in the space of 15 years. Colmcille was a shrewd politician, a hard-nosed negotiator and a gifted administrator, without being blindly devoted to arbitrary rules.

Trailing around the country reconnoitring the latest prevailing political landscape and badgering local kings for land to build the monasteries involved significant personal risks to him and his followers. Not all of these kings were Christians, neither were they prepared to hand over hard-earned territory willingly to some missionary who just happened to ask for it, especially one widely known to be a prominent member of an increasingly ambitious northern O'Neill clan. That, along with his ever-growing power and reputation within a growing church, itself engaged in a struggle for dominance over hearts, minds and souls with paganism, was more than enough to get somebody killed.

Amongst the tasks he attacked most passionately was the transcribing of biblical manuscripts. A devoted scribe himself, he recognised the shortage of books as one of the critical paths restricting the growth of the scholarship of the church, as well as of his own band of followers.[10] Wherever and whenever he could get access to the materials he would copy and encourage his monks to copy, study and disperse the copies of books to spread the teachings of the church. He was one of the earliest in the tradition of Irish monks committed to such a philosophy, credited with saving the church's literary treasures during Europe's Dark Ages,[11] when book burning was a common practice amongst religious zealots.

When he learned that Finnian had got hold of a copy of the 'Vulgate',[12] Colmcille decided to visit his old teacher in order to see it. This was sometime between 557AD and 560AD. Finnian, delighted to see him, willingly showed him the book, though he was generally very protective of it. Given that by then he had probably had many visitors intent on getting a glimpse of this treasure it would have been natural for him to be careful about the degree of access he allowed to the manuscript.

Whatever the circumstances of Colmcille's initial encounter with the book and any conditions Finnian might have placed on his handling of it, it is fairly clear that Colmcille decided to make a copy surreptitiously by night. Finnian discovered what he was up to and was angry that someone he trusted so implicitly could have done such a thing behind his back. He asked that Colmcille give him the copy he had made when it was finished.

Colmcille was not impressed at his former mentor's attitude. He was enraged that an old man should presume to act as such a reluctant gatekeeper to a book, the sharing of which, he believed, was crucially important to the future of the church in Ireland. Finnian suggested they resolve the issue by referring it for arbitration to the Diarmaid, the High King of Ireland and his court at Tara. Colmcille readily agreed, feeling he could not lose both because he was in the right (acting for the greater good of the church) and because he felt the king was an ally, who also happened to be related to him.

At the High Court Finnian claimed ownership of the copy of the book based on what he believed to be legal precedent and on the moral grounds that a visitor and a friend, to whom he had extended an open welcome and hospitality, had betrayed him by secretly copying his property. He was also concerned that, if the book was to be copied and widely distributed, this had to be done carefully and through appropriate channels and procedures. He was concerned to maintain the integrity of the manuscript and ensure there were no errors introduced through hasty copying processes, the like of which Colmcille had secretly engaged in. Colmcille, by that time, had something of a manuscript production line operating at his monastery at Durrow, a group of monks transcribing manuscripts in order that these might be made widely available. It's interesting to speculate on what Finnian's views would have been about this activity and the quality of the work thus produced. Perhaps he felt any copying of his precious copy of the Vulgate should be done at Durrow? On the other hand, if his perception was that even a small fraction of the work there was sub-standard, he would have felt completely justified in demanding that any copying of the manuscript could only be done under his personal supervision.

Colmcille, by now used to being revered in public circles, was disturbed to have his pristine reputation attacked in public at Tara. After a hearing which reportedly went on all through the night and where many questioned Colmcille's integrity, it became clear that there was an undercurrent to the proceedings that went way beyond a dispute over a book. Part of it was to do with the perception amongst some that the monk had become too powerful and needed to be taken down a peg or two. This jealousy would have been politically motivated and could have counted on factions within the Christian church, the pagans and the political establishment who saw him as a powerful agent of change in society. The increasing tensions between the church and paganism, the church's increasing intolerance of the king's accommodation of the pagans and the political battle lines between the most powerful tribes in the land gave this arbitration hearing on a much wider significance. In any case, as the dawn broke Colmcille made his closing address to the court:[13]

"My friend's claim seeks to apply a worn-out law to a new reality. Books are different to other chattels (possessions) and the law should recognise this. Learned men like us, who have received a new heritage of knowledge through books, have an obligation to spread that knowledge, by copying and distributing those books far and wide. I haven't used up Finnian's book by copying it. He still has the original and that original is none the worse for my having copied it. Nor has it decreased in value[14] because I made a transcript of it. The knowledge in books should be available to anybody who wants to read them and has the skills or is worthy to do so; and it is wrong to hide such knowledge away or to attempt to extinguish the divine things that books contain. It is wrong to attempt to prevent me or anyone else from copying it or reading it or making multiple copies to disperse throughout the land. In conclusion I submit that it was permissible for me to copy the book because, although I benefited from the hard work involved in the transcription, I gained no worldly profit from the process, I acted for the good of society in general and neither Finnian nor his book was harmed."[15]

When he had finished, King Diarmaid, sought the advice of his Supreme Court counsellor Bec MacDe.[16] Then he made his famous ruling:

"I don't know, Colmcille, where you get your fancy new ideas about people's property. Wise men have always described the copy of a book as a child-book. This implies that someone who owns the parent-book also owns the child-book. To every cow its calf, to every book its child-book. The child-book belongs to Finnian."[17]

Now nobody rose to the prominence of a high king's counsellor without significant political skills and MacDe would have had his own agenda in considering how to advise Diarmaid. As a druid this included the welfare of the pagan religion and concerns at the success of missionaries like Colmcille in spreading the Christian faith. He was well acquainted with the big monk and can scarcely have believed his good fortune in having this opportunity to influence the reputation of the high profile evangelist. In addition he was simultaneously able to inhibit the distribution of copies of a book which he understood to be the purist form of the Christian doctrine available in the country.

In the immediate aftermath of the ruling, Colmcille was a man in shock. So convinced was he of the righteousness of his cause that he had never even considered he might lose the case. Furious that his integrity had not only been publicly questioned but now, in the decision, found wanting and also that these important scriptures were to be locked away from a church in desperate need of them, he cursed Diarmaid, turned his back on the king and left.

Shortly thereafter Diarmaid was responsible for the murder of a young prince, Curnan, who had been granted sanctuary by Colmcille. The vengeful warrior in Colmcille took hold. He made his way to his family, the Northern O'Neills, who were already considering that they had the strength to challenge the high king. They just needed an excuse. By the time he got home he had probably rationalised his rage and considered that his cause – the defence and greater glory of the church as well as revenge for the injustice he had suffered – justified the battle he intended to catalyse. His family and their allies went on to defeat Diarmaid's forces at Cooldrumman in 561AD.

Though it came to be known as the 'Battle of the Book', the carnage at Cooldrumman, in common with most complex events, had multiple causes, albeit that the copying of that single manuscript was one of the key triggers. Colmcille, though sorry so many men had to die for it, still felt after the battle that his cause had been just. Spreading copies of and access to the knowledge contained in the precious book was, in his view, a holy cause and a key strategy in building the power of the church.

Three ideas

The Colmcille story is about a struggle over access to information. Access to information underpins the themes of this book which is about decision making related to and involving the development, deployment and regulation of complex information and communications technologies (ICTs).[18] For the purposes of the book I am going to use the shorter term 'digital decision making' or DDM (or ddm), to represent this concept. Digital decision making is not a commonly used/recognised jargon phrase in the industry or academia; nor should it be confused with some kind of artificial intelligence or the idea of machines making decisions. It is simply, in this case, a literary device to hopefully make life easier for me and for the reader. DDM, even though it might sound like a toxic chemical, also saves a few trees.

Information systems which have a considerable impact on public welfare are being created, deployed and regulated often without a fundamental understanding about what these systems are required to do, how they might actually work in practice or what their limitations might be. Electronic voting systems, childcare worker databases, terrorist and other criminal suspects databases, genetic profiling, DNA databases, national identity cards systems, national health information systems, information systems in education, air passenger profiling, motorist and mobile phone tracking systems, CCTV and communications data retention schemes are being deployed at a phenomenal rate. The whole area of information related laws is changing rapidly. All this is happening in piecemeal fashion without a genuinely coherent overall view[19] or a sound understanding of what the technology can and, almost more importantly, *cannot* do.

That is something which strikes me as a problem for society in response to which I offer three basic ideas:

1. Firstly, people who make decisions about the deployment and regulation of information systems of considerable significance to public welfare should *base action upon an understanding of the systems,*

technology and environment within which they operate. They should also have *a clear idea of exactly what they want* these systems and regulations *to do*.

2. Secondly, ordinary people (or 'stakeholders') and 'experts'[20] working together can facilitate the development of this understanding. Indeed it is often ordinary people who contribute the true expertise.

3. Thirdly, in a knowledge society[21] the default rules of the road are the laws governing the flow of information and the restrictions built into the architecture of technology. These laws and technologies are shaping up to be a bottleneck, particularly for decision making and education. It might be reasonable to stick a digital lock on an electronic version of some educational material and make it a crime to bypass the lock, but *people need to be aware of this*.

The first idea – the simple thesis that people should understand what they are dealing with when making decisions – seems so patently obvious it hardly seems worthy of being the core idea in a book. As we shall see in Chapter 2, however, there are a multitude of things which get in the way of that understanding in the context of information systems. Contrary to popular belief that it is highly sophisticated, for example, the information technology industry is actually only in its infancy and even just understanding the difference between *'information systems'* and *'information technology'* is not something we can be confident that decision makers are aware of. There is a tendency to focus on the computing components of an information system, rather than the multifaceted system as a whole, including importantly, the human factors. Moreover a focus on *having to use the computer* rather than *doing what we need with the aid of a computer where it is useful*, can actually blind us to the real exciting possibilities of the technology.[22]

In the context of environmental decision making, there has been a considerable and, in theory at least, very positive movement towards facilitating stakeholder involvement in decision making processes; as well as encouraging every individual to take an active role through considering the impact of their lifestyle choices on the environment. Contrary to prevailing fashionable theories, however, stakeholder involvement is not the holy grail of decision making in or about complex systems, though it is a crucial element. If stakeholders have neither access to the appropriate information to pursue informed decisions nor real influence in decision making processes, then stakeholder involvement is a mere public relations exercise. By the same token, the notion of leaving decision making about complex information systems solely to the experts[23] is not to be recommended. The reality of information systems deployment is that when no account is taken of user needs the system nearly always fails. The second central claim in this book, therefore, is that the far-reaching implications for commerce and society, of decisions in hitherto invisible or opaque specialist fields regarding the regulation and deployment of large information systems, mean they should be matters of concern for every citizen. Additionally ordinary citizens[24] working together with experts (and regulators) will prove more effective than each group acting in isolation. If the reader was to take only one thing from this book this would be the most important.

As the Internet and other communications technologies become more central to our lives, alterations in their nature or functioning could have consequences for us all. Implicit in the technology, for example, is the capacity to monitor the online activity of every single user – to track every website visited, every e-mail sent (and to whom), and so on. So debates about the future of the Net, and about the legal framework within which it operates, are simultaneously debates about the future of society – just as, say, arguments about press freedom are inevitably arguments about liberty and democracy.

There is a strong connection between developments on and surrounding the Internet that affects something (privacy or access to education, for example) which is normally regarded as a subject for political concern and debate. Yet what we generally find is that debates about the development, regulation and deployment of the technologies tend to be regarded as technical or legal arguments about specialist subjects, rather than as matters which should concern everyone. The viewpoint implicit in this book – and one of the reasons I am writing it – is that this is misguided.

Perhaps if we realised digital decision making is like environmental decision making, we would take a little more notice? If the last remaining trees and hedgerow in my neighbourhood were being ripped up to make way for a waste incinerator, I would feel strongly enough to speak to local people about it, sign a petition or write to my member of parliament. I would do it because I could see the impact it would have on my family's day-to-day quality of life. But we do not realise the effect of new technologies because they are not always so obvious or immediate. Neither do we know what powers we have to engage in decisions related to these new technologies. It is all too novel and we don't know enough about them. The little we do see are warnings against pirating DVDs and CDs or high profile cases with CCTV pictures of terrorists, neither of which engages the ordinary citizen from our own perspective.

A vibrant information ecology is at the core of our knowledge society, just as a vibrant natural environment is at the heart of a healthy society. James Boyle and Larry Lessig have persuasively argued,[25] however, that we could be facing an enclosure of the 'commons of the mind' where the basic raw materials of cultural, scientific and educational discourse get locked behind legal and technical toll booths, controlled by a small number of actors. At a time when we have the capacity to facilitate universal access to a virtual digital Library of Alexandria[26] for our time, we are actually increasingly moving in the opposite direction towards a pay-per-view society.

The third idea in this book is that changes in law and technology could be leading to a kind of 'second enclosure movement'[27] which threatens not only our ability to make informed decisions about those complex information systems, but even something as fundamental as our access to the basic raw materials of education. This is something which has been a problem in the developing world for generations. Relative to average incomes,[28] a student paying $80 for a book in Indonesia would be the equivalent of a student paying nearly $3200 for the same book in the US. This third idea is partly a synthesis of the important work of scholars like Boyle and Lessig but it is also partly an attempt to wrap some of their key ideas in a slightly different context, in the hope of making them more accessible.[29]

None of the central ideas here are particularly radical. Primarily this book is a collection of stories and developments in the regulation and deployment of technology that, taken together, add up to a picture of a developing information society, which we are reacting to rather than actively shaping.

In the final chapter I offer an outline of a theoretical decision making framework for the development, regulation and deployment of communications technologies. It is based on a parallel framework developed with colleagues at the Open University in the context of environmental decision making, an area with a lot to teach us about designing, regulating and managing complex information systems in a knowledge society.

About this book

So we have three ideas:

1. People should understand what they are dealing with and be clear about what they want to do.
2. Ordinary people and experts should work together.
3. The rules of the road are given by the information laws and the technology.

The introduction has already described the story of Colmcille and the battle of the book and for the moment you can think of it as a kind of a historical case study in DDM. The closing arguments in the arbitration hearing at the king's court could almost have come straight out of one of the modern-day intellectual property[30] disputes involving digital technologies. In fourteen hundred years though, despite the dramatically different context, the core issues we see disputed seem to a large degree unchanged. Perhaps the past has more to teach us about handing modern technologies than we might have expected?

Chapter 2 is a whistle-stop tour in how decisions happen and the reasons why the idea that people should understand what they are dealing with is not as simple as it sounds.

Chapter 3 goes on to set out a series of stories that made me stop and think that perhaps we could and should be doing digital decision making differently, particularly when thinking about how the law regulates access to information. There has been a legal dispute over the copyright in silence for example. A music producer, Mike Batt, was threatened with a lawsuit by the estate of the late John Cage for infringing the copyright in Cage's composition '4 minutes and 33 seconds of silence'. We are seeing outcomes of the suing-over-silence variety, often unintended, in the case of commercially successful children's literature, technology in education, and a huge number of other examples of the creation, regulation and deployment of information systems and information flows.

Chapter 4 looks at the central importance of 'intellectual property' law to digital decision making and offers a synthesis of the ideas of James Boyle. Access to information is a fundamental requirement of good DDM. If Boyle and other prominent US scholars like Lawrence Lessig are correct and access to information is becoming controlled to an unprecedented degree, this has implications not just for DDM but for commerce, governance and society more generally.

Chapter 5 then broadens the scope beyond intellectual property with stories of information systems which are set to have a considerable impact on public welfare, such as children's databases. It focuses on the remarkably common lack of clarity of purpose that is often evident when creating or deploying large information systems.

Chapter 6 looks in more detail at the distinction between facts and values mentioned in Chapter 2 and explores power relationships in decision making. It is rarely transparent, for example, that many public arguments involve a confusing mixture of facts, values and agendas. Arguments get presented as if they are disputes only about facts, whereas they are really about conflicts in values and it is the values of the most powerful actors in the decision making process that achieve primacy.

Chapter 7 covers the importance of recognising the limitations of technology as a tool as opposed to a magic cure for ill-defined problems. The failure to understand information systems as multi-dimensional, including human factors, can lead to all kinds of problems. There is a common tendency to focus instead on the technology [computing] element of the information system at the expense of seeing the big picture. The chapter uses two main case studies – the development of radar in Britain in the 1930s and electronic voting systems – to explain how difficult it can be to deploy effective information systems, as well as what can be achieved when systems are developed deliberately and purposefully by experts and users to achieve the desired aim.

Chapter 8 returns to the complex regulatory landscape known as intellectual property law. Picking up where Chapter 4 left off, I suggest that, with a looming global energy crisis, access to cheap and easy copying of electronic materials might not be as ubiquitous as we currently seem to be assuming. Then in the main part of the chapter I look at the story of how intellectual property policy is developed. There is a notable absence of ordinary users of intellectual property materials – readers, entertainment goods consumers, patients, etc. – in the process. Given then my contention in earlier chapters that large DDM systems that exclude users from the decision making process will always fail, the suggestion is that the system is currently not as well balanced as it could be.

Chapter 9 then goes on to look in more detail at the central idea of the role of experts and the value of multiple perspectives in the context of digital decision making. It starts with three stories, the first noting of the value of appropriate expert input when choosing textbooks for schools. The next two are cases where the experts got things wrong with serious consequences for two individuals and their families. I then go on to look at computers in education and the value of university teachers and students working together. The second half of the chapter covers some of the modelling tools used by experts and the power of ordinary people to test the robustness of the use of these models. The message is that ordinary people and competent experts working together can make a potent force.

Chapter 10 finally provides a theoretical decision making framework as one way to facilitate understanding, through the coming together of experts and lay people in decision making processes involving the deployment and regulation of information and communications technologies. I am not suggesting that this framework provides a magic silver bullet of the 'consumer choice' variety, merely that it may prove useful to some as a way of improving prevailing DDM processes. I round off the chapter and the book with my personal 'education wish list' in the context of DDM. This is based on the need for understanding and clarity of purpose, collaboration between experts and ordinary participants, and the facilitation of access to knowledge, without which we do not have an education system.

We are all products of our background and experience and, as I point out in more detail in Chapters 2 and 6, have difficulty thinking outside our personal biases and values. So in the interests of full disclosure here are a few things which you might find helpful to know about the author.

I grew up in a small village in Ireland in a working class family, generations of which earned their living in the engineering and construction industries. After graduating from University College Dublin, where I had some of the happiest years of my life, I spent about 10 years in a variety of manufacturing industries and some local government work, the greater part of which was the 7 years I worked in aerospace development engineering. Testing parts of aircraft structures to destruction can be great fun and I did an MBA at Warwick University whilst there but I never came to identify with the management and formed some strong views about what I considered to be good and bad management.

After that I had some time out of work and went back to university to study law before joining the Open University (OU) in 1995 as a 'Staff Tutor in Technology'. This OU-unique role is sort of a combination of traditional technology academic and director of studies, and I look after the South Region of the UK, overseeing the University's undergraduate technology curriculum.

Coming back to university as an academic was a bit like coming home. I have never spent so long at the same organisation but you never get bored at the OU and there are always opportunities to get right into the thick of interesting new challenges. My colleague, Alun Armstrong, likes to say that there are two types of people in life, complicators and simplifiers. The simplifiers thrive in coping with anything. For the complicators, even the most straightforward problem has to be turned into something impossibly difficult. In my early days at one organisation it took three and a half weeks and 23 people simply to book a computer room for a meeting. Life is too short for that. I like to hang out with the simplifiers at the OU. To the degree that this is possible, it can make it a really fun place to be.

Chapter 2 Introduction to decision making

"When you are face to face with a difficulty, you are up against a discovery."
Lord Kelvin

The maths professor and the government

In an information society the key laws are those governing information and these can be found in unexpected places generating unintended effects.

Following the huge impact of the Bletchley Park code breakers in World War II, many countries imposed strict controls on the export of cryptographic products, for national security reasons. The basic idea is to prevent criminals, terrorists and hostile foreign powers from getting access to codes which they can use to communicate and plot in secret. That seems like a fairly sensible objective but broad-based, complex rules, regulations and laws applied to complex information systems can and often do have a strange and distorted effect at the level of the individual.

In the autumn of 2003 mathematics professor Daniel Bernstein's long running legal dispute with the US government finally ended.   Professor Bernstein had created a small program which could be used to teach some of the basic mathematics and programming of codes.   However, he was unable to use it for teaching or research, without first clearing it with the government.   Otherwise he could be breaking US arms export regulations,[1] especially if there was any likelihood that there might be a foreign student in his class.   Technically he also needed government clearance to discuss his program with other research colleagues at international conferences.

Bernstein's interest in cryptography was triggered when, as a student, someone hacked into his computer.   It was in 1990, whilst still a student, that he wrote the original US government-offending mathematical functions and program.   He became aware of the government restrictions through networking with others interested in cryptography and decided he should ask for permission before publishing his work.

His first problem was tracking down who precisely in government he needed to ask for permission but he eventually found his way to the appropriate office.[2]   Officials informed him he would be risking a stretch in jail if he did make his work public without a formal grant of approval from the government.   His application for such approval was quickly turned down essentially because his mathematical functions and program were considered to constitute dangerous weapons.

Bernstein appealed the decision with no success.   Then by 1995, by which time he was a professor at the University of Illinois in Chicago, he had become so frustrated with the process that he decided to mount a legal challenge with the support of the digital rights campaigning group, the Electronic Frontier Foundation (EFF).   The basis of the case was that computer programs were a form of speech. Communication through computer programming languages should be considered to be equivalent to communication through English, French or any other recognised language and should therefore be subject to protections granted to speech by the first amendment to the US Constitution.   To the surprise of many US District Judge, Marilyn Hall Patel, agreed with this proposition in 1996 and ruled in favour of the good professor, as did an Appeals Court three years later.

The case dragged on for a further four years with attempts to have the arms export regulations relating to cryptography declared unconstitutional but by then there had been a shift in the politics.   Arguably the restrictions had been loosened and the US Department of Justice made an undertaking to the court not to prosecute Professor Bernstein or other legitimate cryptography researchers for publishing their work. Given these assurances that the regulations would not be enforced against Bernstein, the original judge,

Marilyn Hall Patel, sided with the government and technically dismissed his complaint.

Now Bernstein, having innocently fallen into a bureaucratic minefield, then deliberately set out to test and change the limits of the US regulations governing cryptography. This was because he and many other security experts believed those regulations to be ineffective and in many ways contrary to the interests of US national security, by undermining the ability of US researchers to collaborate on cryptographic research, for example. By inhibiting the collaborative work of cryptographic experts the government was inhibiting progress in the field. The striking thing about the case from the perspective of this current study, however, is that a teacher effectively needed to clear the teaching of basic maths and computer programming with the government and the process he had to engage with was complex and opaque, as well as time consuming and expensive.[3]

Introduction to decision making

Everyone makes decisions from the moment they wake up in the morning until they go to bed at night. These range from the simple decisions to brush your teeth or take the usual route to work, to the more complex such as considering whether to change schools or jobs or what our responses to the threat of terrorism should be.

Know-how

In making decisions we go through a set of thinking and other processes consciously or subconsciously. When we go through the automatic routine of scrubbing our teeth it is because we have decided we would rather avoid having preventable dental treatment at some point in the future and are prepared to invest some time and effort each day, along with the money we have spent on toothpaste and toothbrushes, to achieve this outcome. It is a rational decision but to some degree subconscious because it is just part of our daily routine.

In fact, most of what we do is at the level of cleaning our teeth i.e. 'habit' or 'know-how' of one sort or another. Babies learn to walk, talk and recognise their mum and dad through an intense process of trial and error. Young children survive the shock of realising the universe does not revolve around them without reading a library of self-help books, when, for example, they first start having experiences outside of their immediate family, such as starting school. All the time they are making huge numbers of subconscious decisions in an attempt to get their muscles to move in a coordinated fashion or reacting to the feedback supplied via the complex social dynamics of the playground, in order to engage better the next time. They are constantly assimilating knowledge of the patterns of the world around them and developing skilled responses to enable them to survive and satisfy their curiosity and need for e.g. social interaction. Know-how in decision making essentially gets automatically programmed into our brains through experience and it is valuable not just at the level of deciding to put the kettle on to make a cup of coffee but also in much more complex decision making situations.

This is ably demonstrated by the joke of the old engineer being called into to fix a ship's engine when the problem has defeated the most able ship's company personnel. The engineer does a long and thorough inspection of the engine, takes out a small hammer and lightly taps it at one point, whereupon the engine magically springs back to life. He later sends the ship's owners a bill for £5100 which they complain about. All he had done was to tap the engine once with a hammer. [Interestingly enough, in advance of him doing the job, the owners would probably have been willing to offer him significantly more than this to get their ship back in service.] So the engineer itemises the bill:

- Engine inspection £95
- Tapping with hammer £5
- Knowing where to tap £5000

The knowing where to tap is the know-how. It is difficult to articulate what it is and even more difficult to measure it. We tend to know it when we see it – the skilled carpenter or sportsman, the successful business woman, the popular child in the playground – but we do not often think about it as just the ability to get on with the multitude of life's decisions. We all use our own unique know-how all the time, whether we're aware of it or not, in making the decisions large and small that get us through the day.

Rational decision making

There are a large number of different types of decisions and ways we go about making those decisions as individuals or as part of some group. In a rational decision making process we systematically follow a recognised series of steps to identify various options open to us and then choose one.

Benjamin Franklin once wrote to Joseph Priestley:

"When those difficult cases occur, they are difficult, chiefly because while we have them under consideration, all the reasons pro and con are not present to the mind at the same time, but sometimes one set present themselves, and at other times another, the first being out of sight. Hence the various purposes or inclinations that alternatively prevail, and the uncertainty that perplexes us.

To get over this, my way is to divide half a sheet of paper by a line into two columns; writing over the one Pro, and over the other Con. Then, during three or four days of consideration, I put down under the different heads short hints of the different motives, that at different times occur to me, for or against the measure.

When I have thus got them all together in one view, I endeavour to estimate their respective weights; and where I find two, one on each side, that seem equal, I strike them both out. If I find a reason pro equal to some two reasons con, I strike out the three . . . and thus proceeding I find at length where the balance lies; and if, after a day or two of further consideration, nothing new that is of importance occurs on either side, I come to a determination accordingly.

And, though the weight of reasons cannot be taken with the precision of algebraic quantities, yet when each is thus considered, separately and comparatively, and the whole lies before me, I think I can judge better, and am less liable to make a rash step, and in fact I have found great advantage from this kind of equation."[4]

So, when making tough decisions, Franklin went through the rational process of making a list of pros and cons and then weighing these against each other.

Security specialist, Bruce Schneier[5] offers another rational five-step decision making process, which he believes applies universally to any decisions about security, including the regulation and deployment of technology for security purposes. He asks a series of questions:

1. What assets are you trying to protect?
2. What are the risks to these assets?
3. How well does the security solution mitigate those risks?
4. What other risks does the security solution cause?
5. What costs and trade-offs does the security solution impose?

Project managers and engineers are familiar with another rational approach:

1. Survey the situation.
2. Specify the problem.
3. Identify a series of alternative options to tackle the problem.
4. Assess the alternatives.
5. Choose one and implement it.
6. Monitor the outcome and adjust action in accordance the relevant feedback.

7. If the 'solution' works move onto the next problem. If not go back to the beginning.

These approaches represent variations on a theme which most of us will have used at some stage. They all rely on the gathering and assessment of accurate information or facts about a situation in order to make a rational choice about the best course of action. Because the decision situation is usually in a state of flux we often find we have to go through the steps more than once. So if a parent decides to get a child a computer games console for Christmas and a more modern version becomes available, then the decision situation has changed and the decision process needs to be re-visited.

Complexity in decision making: garbage can situations

These rational approaches are much richer than a superficial list of the steps involved will make them appear but they have been criticised as ig-noring or underestimating the complexity and real-world uncertainty and confusion involved in actual decision making.

James March [6] has written[7] that real-life decision situations are often better characterised by the 'garbage can' metaphor than artificially rational steps. Many decision environments display fuzziness, complex interac-tions between the people and machines involved, problems, solutions, op-portunities, changing technologies, social norms, and organisational, legal and economic contexts. These are all mixed up together in a garbage can at a point in time and the relationship between a problem, a solution and a decision maker may have more to do with them coming together in the same place at the same time, than any rational process.

March says[8] that people constantly have a range of issues, professional and personal, competing for their attention. The deadline for contract ne-gotiations on a big project is looming; your partner is suffering from a de-generative illness; one of the kids is being bullied at school; you forgot to put the cat out and it makes such a mess when it's shut in the house all day; your partner has an all-day appointment at the hospital; the car would not start this morning and there is a public transport strike so you were late for work; on top of that you forgot your sandwiches, so what are you going to do for lunch; one of your team noticed a major last-minute hitch with the contract but believes there is a computer vendor with exactly the right system to deal with that; you did not get your caffeine fix first thing this morning because of the problems with the car and it is annoying you, as is that fly buzzing around the conference room; you do not trust lawyers and are not sure that some members of your team have been as thorough as they should have been. In complex decision environments it is impossible to know or shut out everything but the relevant issues, then analyse these through some rational process to come to the 'right' decision. Real life is much messier than that.

Bounded rationality in decision making: satisficing

So if the real world is so messy and there is too much extraneous noise in complex decision making situations to act entirely rationally, what can we do? Well we could apply a rational approach to the limited amount of apparently relevant data we can extract from the situation. If the assessment of a variety of bidders for a government telecommunications contract suggests that two of the companies could meet the requirements within the required budget, then randomly picking one through the flip of a coin would lead to a 'good enough' choice.

You can probably think of a few occasions, in a personal and professional context, where you have made a decision like this. When I got my latest mobile phone, I gave the vendor a clear specification of what I was looking for, was shown two matching that specification and randomly picked one. It does the job I need it to do, most of the time. Occasionally the battery runs out at inconvenient times. Decision theorist, Herbert Simon,[9] coined the term 'satisficing' for this partly rational, just-good-enough approach to decision making.

The British radar technology in World War II was inferior to that of the Germans, so much so that when the Germans captured a British radar set in 1940 it was declared so obsolete as to be useless.[10] The technology, however, was good enough, as part of an integrated system, to collect the raw data on approaching enemy aircraft. This raw data from their chain of radar stations and visuals from the Observer Corps was passed on (via radio telephone and teleprinters) to headquarters and an integrated set of operations centres, where it was assessed, filtered, analysed and turned into useful information at varying levels. This then facilitated the scrambling of the right fighter squadrons and even more specific instructions to be radioed to the RAF pilots once in the air, to enable them to intercept their enemy at the earliest opportunity.

The Germans had better information technology (radar). The British had the better information system (radar, human intelligence, signals intelligence, and an integrated, purpose-developed system, allowing the situation to be viewed holistically, as well as delivering the right information to the right users, at the right levels, in a useful format and in sufficient time to act on it). The better information system prevailed in the Battle of Britain in 1940 and it got built in time largely due to the decision of those involved to use technology that was just good enough to get the job done.

Factors that influence [digital] decision making

Amongst the factors that influence decision making, the personal values and relative power basis of key decision makers are fundamental. The UK government's decision to introduce a biometric identity card system provides an illustration.

Personal values and power

Winston Churchill abolished identity cards in 1952. In the wake of the 11th of September 2001 attacks on the US, the then Home Secretary,[11] David Blunkett, embraced a plan to reintroduce them. He invested a lot of energy in pursuing it, as have his successors, Charles Clarke and John Reid. The proposal for the high tech system came about at a time (2001/2) when the government was facing serious questions on terrorism and immigration. The idea appealed to Mr Blunkett, someone with a strong belief in the need for government to be taking big decisions to tackle complex problems. He was also in a position, at the time, to make it happen. Note that this plus the fact that terrorism and immigration are incredibly complex issues fits the temporal link theory in March's garbage can process.

Values are strongly held personal beliefs about what is important and about how the world *ought* to be.

A value is a belief that something is good or bad. For example, some people believe the music of the Beatles is better than Mozart's or that abortion is morally wrong under all circumstances.

Personal values are critically important when it comes to interpreting information. This is very important to keep in mind in digital decision making (DDM). People can have very strong feelings about technology, particularly when it gets enmeshed in complex issues like terrorism, other serious crimes, immigration, and civil liberties.

If a government minister, or anyone else, strongly believes some action is the right thing to do, it is difficult to get that person to question that belief. The most powerful actors also tend to have the means to act on their beliefs.

There is an extra complication in the context of powerful actors. People like prime ministers, presidents and chief executives tend to be surrounded by people whose jobs depend on keeping the boss happy. They therefore have an incentive to tell the boss what she wants to hear i.e. to reinforce her beliefs. The good ones know this and compensate accordingly.

A friend of mine once worked for a company where the general manager held a production meeting twice a week to check on developments in the factory. The meeting included directors, foremen (they were all men at the time), charge-hands, managers, engineers, finance, operations and logistics people. It always featured the general manager picking a victim and blaming them for anything that happened to be going wrong, that day, week or month. Before every one of these meetings, unbeknownst to the general manager, there was always an informal meeting of the usual victims, at which the participants got their stories straight. They would joke about whose turn it was to be the victim that day and literally make up a story of how things were going in the factory to avoid the abuse in the main meeting becoming too vicious. The general manager liked to know things were going well and he was managing a dynamic, world class factory, so by and large that is the story he got told, even when there were serious production problems.

It is important to understand the power dynamics, the personal values and the agendas of the most powerful actors in any DDM situation. Government ministers have an interest in being seen to be doing something in the wake of a terrorist act, such as the London bombings in 2005, so, for example, will support the creation of extra security at airports.

Thinking traps

The thinking trap can be a barrier to even bounded rationality in decision making. Geoffrey Vickers described it thus:

"Lobster pots are designed to catch lobsters. A man entering a man-sized lobster pot would become suspicious of the narrowing tunnel, he would shrink from the drop at the end; and if he fell in he would recognise the entrance as a possible exit and climb out again – even if he were the shape of a lobster.

A trap is a trap only for creatures which cannot solve the problems that it sets. Man-traps are dangerous only in relation to the limitations of what men can see and value and do. The nature of the trap is a function of the nature of the trapped... we the trapped tend to take our own state of mind for granted – which is partly why we are trapped."[12]

He goes on to note that we can only start to climb out of our self-made thinking traps when we recognise that we are in a trap and start questioning our own limitations and the assumptions that led us there.

When I was in industry I believed that the engineering department was the most important part of every company. It took me a while to realise that everyone thought their own department was the most important and that for the business to function it needed most of those departments working together. It is common for a particularly high level of animosity to exist between the engineering and marketing departments, for example, both unable to communicate with each other because they each use different professional jargon.

I also used to find it hard to accept that lawyers were prepared to act for people or organisations who had allegedly engaged in ethically questionable practices. Yet it is a fundamental tenet of a just society that people accused of even the most heinous crimes are entitled to a fair trial.[13] Both of these thinking frames – 'the engineer is the best'[14] and 'only *good* people should be entitled to legal representation' represented traps in my thinking inhibiting a wider understanding of organisational behaviour and the legal system.

Complexity: the technology

At the heart of computer technologies lie hardware with millions of tiny electronic components and software programs with millions of lines of code, which together constitute some of the most complex machines that have ever been built. That very complexity is a key factor in the success or failure of digital decision making processes involving these machines.

Influential Yale University professor, Charles Perrow, thinks that some complex technologies and the complex systems of which they form a part, such as nuclear power plants, are so prone to failure with catastrophic effect that we should abandon them completely.[15] Perrow describes the partial meltdown of the reactor core at the Three Mile Island nuclear power plant in 1979 as a 'normal accident', the inevitable result of the complexity of the plant system, and the tight coupling of its component parts.

The complexity means no one can fully understand the system and the tight coupling means that failure in one component can have a ripple effect, leading to a string of other components failing like dominoes falling over. The complexity also leads to parts of the system, including the human actors,[16] interacting in unexpected ways (because they are interlinked in unexpected ways) resulting in the emergence of properties of the system which would not have been predicted in advance.

At Three Mile Island part of the cooling system had been isolated for some maintenance. In accordance with standard practice, compressed air was being used to clear a blockage. The blockage proved to be stubborn and difficult to shift and the operation was taking much longer than usual. A small amount of water leaked back through the compressed air pipes into the control instruments triggering a shut down of one of the plant's three main cooling systems and of the electricity generating turbines. A stuck pressure relief valve in the reactor core cooling system then went undetected partly because of misleading and hidden indicators in the plant's control room.[17] Operators in the control room were left with the erroneous impression that pressure was building up dangerously in the reactor core cooling system, which if it failed would leave them with no means of cooling the reactor and preventing a total meltdown. So instead of pumping more cooling water into the system they drained water away, in order, so they thought (and with very good reasons), to prevent the core cooling system failing catastrophically. It is difficult to imagine the stress endured by plant operators faced with a nuclear disaster and a power plant system behaving in ways they could not understand despite their significant combined level of experience.[18]

It was not until more than two hours later, when a new shift supervisor, Brian Mehler, arrived on the scene, that the problem with the valve was discovered and they began to pump more water into the system to prevent a disaster. Mehler modestly says he merely "brought a fresh pair of eyes to the room" but he was able to enter a highly stressed environment and test his theory about the valve to a natural conclusion. His colleagues had also considered the valve as a potential problem but within a couple of minutes of the start of the incident over one hundred alarms were going off in the control room. In the confusion of frenzied activity, a temperature reading on the valve had been either considered to be within the required limits or reported erroneously to the people in charge.

This again was partly down to serendipity. The pressure valve was known to have a small leak which could not be easily fixed, so the computer linked to the temperature indicator on the valve line had been programmed not to give any readings over a specific limit, 280°F. Mehler noted the temperature, still felt it was unnecessarily high and asked for the valve to be isolated. Almost instantaneously the system began behaving in predictable fashion and they were able to bring the water levels up thereby avoiding a disaster.[19] According to a US Presidential Commission report on the accident the nuclear core had been less than an hour from total meltdown.[20]

Complexity: the situation

I have drawn attention above to some of the key factors influencing decisions – personal values, relative power, thinking traps and the complexity of the technology but there are quite a number of others which I would group together under the heading 'complexity of the situation'. These include:

- The decision makers
- Decision criteria
- Time
- Dynamic (changing) nature of the situation
- People affected
- Law
- Decision making models (such as cost-benefit analysis etc)
- Decision environment (organisational, ecological, economic, social, political and physical).

Take the Challenger space shuttle disaster at the Kennedy Space Center at Cape Canaveral in Florida, on 28 January 1986, for example. The technical cause of the accident was the failure of rubber O-ring seals in one of the booster rockets. The freezing temperatures at the launch meant that the rubber was not capable of doing the sealing job required. Escaping gas destroyed one of the key fixtures securing the booster rocket to the main fuel tank and burned a hole in the side of the tank. The out-of-control rocket swivelled around its upper fixture, crashing into the top of the fuel tank and leading to a massive fireball. The space craft broke up. It was just 73 seconds into the flight.[21] Engineers at Morton Thiokol, the company which made the booster rockets had strongly advised against launching in those temperatures and company managers, as well as those at NASA, were later vilified for acting against this advice.

The launch had nearly happened the day before the accident, when technical problems led to it being abandoned during countdown and reset for the following day. Shortly thereafter, at NASA's request, Morton Thiokol engineers had a meeting about possible problems with the performance of the O-ring seals in the freezing temperatures forecast for the next day. There was a history of hot booster gases burning through O-rings, the most significant damage occurring on a shuttle flight in 1985, when the launch temperature had been the lowest on record, 53°F. Morton Thiokol engineers and management agreed they should not sanction a flight below this temperature. At a teleconference later that evening, however, under pressure from NASA to agree to the launch, Morton Thiokol took a 'management decision' to agree it should go ahead, in the face of their engineers' objections.

John Young, NASA's chief astronaut, in an internal memo following the accident said:

"There is only one driving reason why such a potentially dangerous system would ever be allowed to fly – launch schedule pressure."

NASA was regularly criticised and ridiculed in the media and by politicians for launch delays and excessive spending. This particular flight had drawn a lot of media attention from all over the world because it was to include the first teacher in space, Christa McAuliffe. It does seem unlikely, though, with the attention of the world's media more intense than it had been for many years that NASA managers would have risked the flight, if they had any serious doubts about its safety.

Diane Vaughan, in her book, *The Challenger Decision*,[22] characterises this misplaced confidence in the safety of the mission, in spite of the clear technical advice to the contrary, as a 'normalization of deviance'. She tells a convincing story of how, since the Apollo moon landings, the history of NASA has been one of budgetary constraints which led to design trade-offs in the shuttle they would have preferred to avoid. In spite of the fateful decision, which with hindsight proved to be so disastrous, she also discovered many examples of cases where NASA managers had made very expensive decisions purely in the interest of safety. Crew training, launches frequently abandoned on safety grounds in spite of launch schedule pressure, huge numbers of complex procedures and safety checklists and the fact that they talked at length to Morton Thiokol on the eve of the launch point towards an organisational culture which clearly did not neglect safety.

Critically, after previous problems with the O-rings, the booster rockets had been tagged with a formal NASA 'launch constraint'. This meant the O-rings were a recognised safety concern serious enough to prevent a launch. Critically also, NASA had developed a formal 'waiver' procedure – a procedure that allowed NASA personnel to ignore normal rules and procedures, when they needed to. Under the waiver procedure five shuttle missions had proceeded, even though the problems with the O-rings were known.[23]

In these circumstances it is possible to see a false confidence in the safety of the O-rings developing. The argument is that it has not failed catastrophically in the past, so it will not do so the next time either. Hence Vaughan's conclusion that NASA slowly evolved into a state *where they had actual formal procedures allowing crucial safety issues to be ignored*. This she characterised as the normalisation of deviance. That any organisation should draw up procedures to bypass other formal organisational procedures, particularly those involving safety, might seem completely barmy but it is extremely common. It is a well known, ironically *unwritten* rule of every organisation that the way to bring the place to a grinding halt is to work to the letter of organisational procedures. This is why 'work to rule' is one of the standard tactics in the armoury of any union involved in an industrial relations dispute.

The Challenger shuttle type of situation always has multiple causes beyond the immediate technical failure or series of failures (in this case the O-ring, rocket fixture, out of control rocket, disintegration of shuttle). The organisation rationalised, and then tolerated serious safety problems due to launch schedule pressure, arising from the prevailing social, organisational, political[24] and economic environment. The disaster points to the immeasurable importance of informed decision making at the heart of complex systems.

Lessig's constraints[25]

There are a lot of things to consider when making decisions about complex systems:

- Rational approaches
- Satisficing
- Values, relative power and agendas of the decision makers and stakeholders
- Thinking traps
- Complexity of the technology and the situation
- Decision criteria
- Time
- Dynamic (changing) nature of the situation
- People affected
- Law
- Decision making models (such as cost-benefit analysis etc)
- Decision environment (organisational, ecological, economic, social, political and physical).

How is it possible to gather them up in some kind of coherent way in order to make sense of them? Lawrence Lessig uses a fairly simple but powerful model. Lessig says there are four main constraints[26] on the decisions we make about how to behave:

- Law
- Social norms

- Economics
- Architecture or built environment.

To some degree we have already seen the effect of economics and social norms in the Challenger story but it is worth revisiting these in the context of Lessig's model.

Law

Government uses the law to dictate unacceptable behaviour. Law acts as a threat. If we break the law we may get caught and punished. For example, the law says cigarettes should not be sold to children. If someone sells cigarettes to children they can be prosecuted.

Social norms

Social norms dictate that a group of friends will meet in the pub every Friday night or that we should be polite in our dealings with other people. When I first came to the south of England to work I did not realise that strangers do not usually speak to each other on trains or buses. If I did attempt to engage someone in conversation I was often met with surprise or suspicion. Social norms, like the law, punish deviation after the event.

Economics or market forces

Market forces also regulate behaviour. The price of cigarettes should usually make them inaccessible to a child even where there are people prepared to sell them to children. The price regulates the behaviour at the time of the transaction. If children have no money, they cannot buy cigarettes through conventional outlets.

Architecture or built environment

'Architecture' or the built environment – i.e. how the physical world is – also regulates behaviour. If a room has no doors or other openings then we cannot get in or out of it. Architecture regulates behaviour when we are trying to engage in that behaviour. If a building has steep steps at the entrance and no other way in, it is difficult for a wheelchair user to enter the building unaided.

The idea of using architecture to monitor behaviour has been around for a long time. America's Pilgrim Fathers laid out their towns, buildings and town squares in such a way that the Puritan inhabitants could keep a constant watch on each other. For practising Puritans, at that time, allowing friends, family and the rest of the community to pry into their private lives was routine. Good behaviour in private was considered to be essential for society. Religious leaders believed people could not be trusted, however. Good behaviour would only be guaranteed if everyone was kept under constant surveillance and they knew they were being watched.

Combine these values, which still exist today, with the availability of pornography on the Internet and you get yourself a business opportunity. A company called NetAccountability, in the autumn of 2002, set up a service whereby people can have a morally upstanding friend or family member monitor their web-surfing habits. The monitor receives regular comprehensive reports of the websites that person visits. If someone is aware he is being watched he may think twice about visiting inappropriate sites.

Robert Moses was a prolific 20th century New York City planner.[27] He probably would not have had a great deal of time for one of the core messages of this book – the need to involve ordinary people in decision making about technological infrastructure. Moses was committed to getting things done and if that meant demolishing certain neighbourhoods to build roads then so be it.[28] He built highway bridges along roads to parks and beaches in Long Island which were too low for buses to pass under.[29] Hence certain parks and beaches were accessible only to car owners, many of them white middle class or wealthy. Poor people without cars, mainly African Americans, Latinos and other minorities, were obliged to use other parks and beaches accessible by bus. Hence social relations between the poor and the affluent were regulated – regulation through architecture.

It should be noted that Moses categorically denied that there was any racist intent on his part.[30] I make absolutely no claims here about his personal values but in one sense his intent is irrelevant: the architecture regulated behaviour, whether he intended it to or not. Complex systems often have unintended emergent properties. Changing things in complex systems also results in unintended consequences, sometimes negative, sometimes positive. Irrespective of the intent of the architect, therefore, architecture can regulate behaviour in ways not originally envisaged.

Constraints of the context – the built environment or the architecture – change or regulate behaviour in all these cases. Architecture is also self-regulating – the steep steps get in the wheelchair user's way because they are steep and they are steps. Once the architecture is in place it does not need someone to enforce constraints on behaviour. It does so by default. Laws, norms and markets, on the other hand, can only punish or regulate behaviour deemed unacceptable when a 'gatekeeper' chooses to use the constraints they impose.

Law, norms, economics and architecture regulate behaviour

Lessig's four forces – law, norms, market forces and architecture or built environment – operate together to limit or enable what we can or cannot do. In this model these four devices determine how individuals, groups, organisations or states are regulated. The four interact and can compete, just like the components in any system. One can reinforce or undermine another. If the price of cigarettes dropped to 10 pence a packet tomorrow, then more children would get access to them, regardless of what the law says.

Lessig's is a relatively simple but fairly powerful model for looking at decision making situations.

Proxies in decision making

Because it is impossible for us to do everything or understand every complex situation we face, we often employ proxies to make decisions for us. A proxy is a person or an organisation or a machine that acts on our behalf in some way.

We vote for politicians who subsequently sit in parliament where our laws are passed. The English Football Association appoints the England manager to pick the team to play in the World Cup. Organisations have proxy computers that act as gatekeepers between the company network and external networks connected to the Internet. The chef at the restaurant sources the ingredients in the food customers are served. Law enforcement authorities and intelligence services are our proxies in fighting serious crime.

Proxy decision makers present us with a problem, however. Even though they are making decisions on our behalf, we may or may not trust them. If the Irish team manager fails to get the team through to the World Cup finals we may lose confidence in his ability to choose the right team and employ the right tactics. Governments are often reported as being untrustworthy in the eyes of the public, especially in the wake of political scandals, such as political favours granted in exchange for financial donations to parties in power. Proxies have to earn our trust through success, transparent decision making, third party audits, experience, know-how and recommendations of people we do trust. Trust in governments for example is fundamentally dependant on transparency and the more a particular government resorts to secrecy, as in the case of Bernstein's cryptography program, the more likely it is that the general public will not trust their actions.

Proxies will not necessarily make the decisions we ourselves would have made faced with the same circumstances, since they have their own complex agendas, motivations and constraints.

Social technologies

NASA's procedures allowing a shuttle launch to proceed in spite of clear safety concerns could be considered to be a subset of what my 'systems thinking' colleagues at the Open University think of as 'social technologies'. Social technologies involve people, organisations and practices and mental and administrative frameworks and models for understanding situations, including language and numbers. They are often invisible and followed without question or awareness of their origins, or the need for contextual understanding because they form the fabric of our daily routines. I spent a proportion of my early days in industry, as a graduate trainee, documenting production processes. I would regularly ask why some procedure was carried out in a particular way. By far and away the most common answer I got was: "Because we've always done it like that." NASA bypassed their safety procedures because it was routine, so routine in fact that they had established a formal process for doing it.

Social technologies include laws, organisational procedures and rules to regulate behaviour. They can structure how we think and act and therefore determine how decisions are made. A hugely widely deployed (used and abused) numeric social technology is cost benefit analysis which we will look at later in Chapter 9. In the context of language, control of the language used in a decision process can be the key to controlling the outcome of that process. Language is rarely neutral in complex decision making situations. 'Intellectual property',[31] which is at the heart of some of the most contentious decisions in this book, is something of a misnomer, which might be more accurately described as 'temporary and limited intellectual monopoly'. Describing someone as a 'citizen' or a 'consumer' subtly defines their role. Social technologies therefore include the mental structures through which we view the world and hence we come full circle again to the personal values that shape our thinking.[32]

The Rio and the copyright lawyers: a DDM situation

In the mid-1990s Karlheinz Brandenburg's team at the Frauenhofer Institute in Germany invented the MP3 digital audio standard.[33] Then in 1998 Diamond Multimedia launched a hand-held digital music player, about the size of a pack of playing cards, called the 'Rio'. The Rio could be used to copy and subsequently play music (or other MP3 audio files) from the Internet. There wasn't much high quality music available on the Net at the time but this state of affairs was just about to change dramatically with the arrival of Napster, the peer-to-peer file swapping software. The Rio could also be used to record sounds directly in budding rock stars' bedrooms or from CDs. The Apple iPod music player is often referred to as the 'modern Sony Walkman' but the iPod's true digital ancestor is the Rio and it seemed to be a fairly uncontroversial innovation in the consumer electronics market.

The Recording Industry Association of America (RIAA) and the Alliance of Artists and Recording Companies (AARC) thought differently. To them this little electronic gadget was a threat to the future of the music industry and so they immediately deployed their lawyers to get the device outlawed by the courts. The theory was that if something like the Rio became widely available, it would encourage people to engage in widespread illegal copying of songs over the Net. Thus it had to be outlawed or at least hamstrung and delayed by legal action until the industry could work out what to do about it. They were right to be worried. Some years on there is a massive amount of illegal swapping of copyrighted songs over peer-to-peer networks like Grokster or Morpheus or Bittorrent.[34]

The Rio case was brought under a rather obscure US law,[35] which stated that companies selling 'digital audio recording devices' needed to pay a levy on each unit sold which would be distributed to copyright owners by the appropriate collecting society. The law also required that these devices should be designed and manufactured in such a way as to inhibit multiple serial recordings of the same source – so the machine could not be used to copy a copy. Diamond Multimedia had not paid the levy and the Rio did not incorporate copy-of-copy prevention technology, so the industry lawyers felt they had a pretty strong case.

Surprisingly, however, they lost the case in the appeals court on a legal technicality. According to the letter of the law, neither the Rio nor a computer hard disk[36] qualified as a 'digital audio recording device' and hence the music player was perfectly legal.[37]

This furore over the Rio was what first drew my attention to an obscure, complex and increasingly important area of legal doctrine for the digital universe, with the eye-glazing title 'intellectual property'.[38] Intellectual property covers things like copyrights, trademarks and patents. As we come to live in an information-dominated economy, the legal regulations governing the flows of information, like intellectual property laws, are becoming increasingly important. Yet these laws, despite their direct effect on increasing sections of the population, remain in the esoteric domain of influence of a small number of trained professionals, lobbyists and businesses dependent on intellectual property for their revenues. That story forms a large part of the subject matter of the next two chapters and Chapter 8.

Chapter 3 Harry Potter and the full-blooded lawyers

"You claim you own Casablanca and that no one else can use that name without your permission. What about Warner Brothers – do you own that, too? You probably have the right to use the name Warner, but what about Brothers? Professionally, we were brothers long before you were." Groucho Marx

Sometimes [imprecisely] called the 'copyright wars', disputes over the developing landscape of a complex but increasingly important area of law, called 'intellectual property', form a prominent battleground to decision making about modern digital systems, systems which in turn have an increasing impact on the knowledge society.[1]

The phenomenon that is J.K. Rowling's *Harry Potter* series, like all such commercial success stories in film, music or publishing, attracts not just a legion of fans but also a variety of other associated commercial enterprises, legitimate and otherwise. The worldwide black market[2] in *Harry Potter* related items is huge and, unsurprisingly, has triggered something of a job creation scheme for intellectual property lawyers, acting to protect Rowling's, her publishers' and associated rights.

In the summer of 2003, within weeks of the launch of the fifth Harry Potter book, rough Spanish translations were being sold on the streets of Caracas, in Venezuela, for about $25 each. Nearly every page of these unauthorised copies of *Harry Potter and the Order of the Phoenix* carried apologies from the translator for not being able to understand parts of the text and leaving them in the original English. Yet they sold like hot cakes, partly because the official Spanish translation was not due to be released in Latin America for some months to come.[3]

Just prior to the publication of the sixth Potter book,[4] a British tabloid newspaper alerted the police that they had been offered an unauthorised copy of the manuscript in exchange for a large sum of money.[5] On Friday, 3 June 2005, a man threatened a reporter with an imitation pistol, as the deal was taking place. Fortunately no one was hurt. Shortly before the sixth book was released on 16 July 2005, some booksellers accidentally sold a handful of copies in Indianapolis, New York and Coquitlam[6] (on the west coast of Canada). The Canadian publishers, Raincoast Books, sought and obtained an order from the Supreme Court of British Columbia:

"(i) restraining … anyone … from copying or disclosing all or any part of Harry Potter #6 or any information derived therefrom including without limitation the story, plot or characters of Harry Potter #6 to any person prior to 12:01 a.m. local time on July 16, 2005 …

(ii) restraining … anyone who is given notice of the order from displaying, reading, offering for sale, selling, exhibiting in public or without the express consent of the Plaintiffs possessing Harry Potter #6 prior to 12:01 a.m. local time on July 16, 2005;

(iii) subject to paragraph (iv) below, restraining … anyone … from making any use of, or destroying or concealing, or … parting with possession, power, custody or control of any copy of Harry Potter #6 or any part of it or any copies thereof or any notes or descriptions of it prior to 12:01 a.m. local time on July 16, 2005;

(iv) compelling … anyone who has directly or indirectly received a copy or any other form of disclosure of Harry Potter #6 from John/Jane Does to deliver to the plaintiff Raincoast Book Distribution Ltd. any and all copies of Harry Potter #6 in their possession..."[7]

In other words the early buyers were not supposed to read or to reveal any part of the plot and had to return their copies to the publisher. That is quite a wide-ranging order from a provincial supreme court – banning the reading of a children's book – and many complained that it was disproportionate.[8] The publisher engaged with that criticism and robustly defended their actions as a reasonable response to the possible early leaking of details of the book:

"Despite some wonderful editorial cartoons, there were no police raids on Harry Potter fans, no charges laid, and, although many journalists asked, no private details offered about the people who came forward...

The legal controversy might 'be remembered long after the latest Harry Potter plot twist is forgotten', but Raincoast believes that most fair observers will judge our actions as being far more benign than the controversy suggests. They will remember the millions of avid readers from around the world who gathered together on July 16th to celebrate the magic of one author and one extraordinary book. How we as a publishing community can sustain this immense outpouring of goodwill and popular enthusiasm towards reading should be the common goal of publishers, booksellers, librarians, and yes, civil libertarians, in the months and years to come."[9]

As a question of principle, regardless of what the law might technically allow in this case on the grounds of protection of confidential information or copyright, I believe that there can be no justification for banning someone from reading a children's book that they have bought in good faith. Publishers and copyright lawyers tell us that real life and the law are not as simple as that, however. Raincoast had to have a sound legal basis for their claims otherwise the Supreme Court of British Columbia would not have granted the injunction. Practical lawyering is also about acting reasonably within the spirit of the law in the interests of your client and not about blindly applying arbitrary rules out of context. Spinning the rules to suit your case is, however, one of the many tactics in a good lawyer's armoury. There have been many intellectual property disputes surrounding commercial success stories in children's literature and the people dealing with these on a day-to-day basis are obliged to take a pragmatic approach to resolving them.

The author of some books about characters called 'muggles', Nancy Stouffer, wrote to J.K. Rowling's US publishers, Scholastic, in 1999 saying that the first Harry Potter book breached her copyrights and trademarks, relating to works she claimed to have written in the 1980s. This initial approach did not mention another Stouffer character, Larry Potter, which became part of the subsequent legal dispute when Scholastic, J.K. Rowling and Time Warner Entertainment Company sued Ms Stouffer for 'declaratory and injunctive relief'. They basically wanted a declaration from the court that they had not infringed Ms Stouffer's intellectual property rights and an injunction banning her from claiming that they had done so. They also asked for sanctions against Ms Stouffer. Forensic tests showed that some of the words on the title pages, submitted in evidence by Ms Stouffer, could not have been printed until the 1990s and a US federal judge supported the action in September 2002, granting a summary judgement in favour of Scholastic, Ms Rowling and Time Warner. Ms Stouffer appealed and the appeal court issued a summary order in January 2004 supporting the original judgement.[10] Faced with this kind of case it is easy to imagine how a lawyer acting for Rowling and her publishers might take a cynical hardnosed attitude to other similar challenges.

Sometimes, however, busy lawyers churning out legal threats as a matter of routine can create unnecessary angst for their targets, their clients and themselves. Warner Brothers' lawyers scared a teenager running a Harry Potter fan website[11] in the UK by threatening to sue her. Lawyers representing Vladimir Putin were rumoured to be considering suing Warner Brothers over rights to publicity, following claims that the house elf Dobby in the second film, *Harry Potter and the Chamber of Secrets*, was modelled on the Russian leader. Even J.K. Rowling herself inadvertently stepped on the toes of her legal representatives when she informally gave her approval for a school[12] to produce a play based on her novels. That probably generated a lot of furious behind the scenes activity in Harry Potter lawyer-land, which led to the permission being withdrawn on the basis of avoiding setting a precedent for other schools.[13]

One of my favourite Potter copyright disputes is one that never actually happened. The satirical website, the Watley Review,[14] created a story about a disgruntled fan who released a 'corrected' version of the sixth book, supposedly because she did not like the way the narrative developed. There is, in fact, a vast reservoir of real Harry Potter fan and imitation fiction, some informally approved of [15] by the author and her representatives and some, of the adult or commercial variety,[16] which they furiously object to. That there are now parodies of these copyright disputes is an indicator in itself of how big an associated industry the Harry Potter intellectual property arena has become.

Law lord of the rings

J.R.R. Tolkien is another author whose work attracts both a huge and intense fan base and its own related commercial ecology, spanning the whole legitimate to illegal spectrum. Cathleen Blackburn, a partner at Manches LLP in Oxford, manages the legal side of the Tolkien estate's navigation through the issues created.[17] On a regular basis she has to deal with requests such as that of someone wanting to produce a series of coffins named after Tolkien characters,[18] to others who publish and sell editions of Tolkien's books without permission,[19] or just post the entire text on the Internet.

The Hobbit was published for the first time in 1937 and the Lord of the Rings trilogy originally appeared in the mid-1950s. Tolkien died in 1973, which means his creations are protected by copyright in the UK until 2043 (i.e. 70 years after the author's death).

Tolkien invented a whole new world in Middle Earth, its history, geography, languages and culture. Indeed some of his more fervent admirers have been accused of seeming to inhabit his imaginary universe more than the real world. That in itself, before even thinking about commercial spin-offs, can cause a few headaches for someone engaged in protecting the intellectual property interests of the Tolkien estate.

Harper Collins UK holds the worldwide publishing rights to Tolkien's books and handles the sub-licensing of publication of the work outside the UK.[20] That and the pursuit of publishers of unauthorised versions all over the world is a big task, arguably made easier with the implementation of the World Trade Organisation (WTO) international treaty on Trade-Related Aspects of Intellectual Property Rights (TRIPS) in 1994.[21] Harper Collins can now, with the backing of the WTO, at least theoretically, call on the national authorities in signatory countries to deal with serious breaches of Tolkien copyrights in those countries.

Stage, film and merchandising rights in The Hobbit and the Lord of the Rings, at the time of writing, reside with 'Tolkien Enterprises', a division of the Saul Zaentz Company run by film producer, Saul Zaentz. Tolkien sold these rights to United Artists in 1969 for US$250,000 plus a royalty on exploitation of the rights sold. United Artists sold these rights to Saul Zaentz in 1976. Zaentz produced an animated film version in 1978,[22] which did badly at the box office.[23] In 1997, he licensed Miramax to create a film. Peter Jackson was chosen as the director. Miramax sold its licence to New Line Cinema, when Jackson insisted on making three films. Miramax figured that unless the first film was a big success, the whole enterprise could fail catastrophically. The films eventually went on to win multiple Oscars and other international awards.

New Line Cinema has extensive rights to merchandising e.g. trademarks in characters and names, though there was a major legal dispute with Tolkien Enterprises over unpaid royalties in the autumn of 2004. The two companies settled out of court in August 2005. The Tolkien name and signature are trademarked by the Tolkien estate.

It would appear the Tolkien estate has a couple of guiding principles in administering and managing the Tolkien literary assets, namely:

- To protect the copyright and maintain the integrity of the works of J.R.R. Tolkien as works of literature[24]
- To prevent misrepresentation or inappropriate use of them (e.g. the coffin manufacturer's request to produce Tolkien-related coffins was refused permission)

whenever possible and practicable.

In practice, since the estate is focused on maintaining literary integrity, rather than commercial exploitation, this means it will generally not allow abridgement of the works and will consider carefully the question of new illustrations.[25] In dealing with the estate's business, Manches arguably try to take a sensible, balanced approach in their work and in most of the cases I am aware of, the solicitors succeed in this regard.[26] No doubt those who have found themselves on the opposing side of the legal arguments would dispute that point of view. Cathleen Blackburn has certainly earned the respect of thousands of Tolkien fans and it seems that she gets regular emails from people alerting her to potential infringements of copyright.

In the US, Michael W. Perry wrote a book called *Untangling Tolkien: A Chronological Reference to the Lord of the Rings* which was a retelling of the story in chronological diary form. He applied to the publisher for permission to quote from the original assuming there would be no problems.[27] So he was shocked and angry when Manches brought a lawsuit against him on behalf of the estate in Seattle and US District Court judge Barbara Rothstein issued a temporary restraining order preventing publication. Given the constitutional protections afforded to speech in the US it is quite unusual for a US court to issue this kind of temporary restraining order.

The author was convinced his first amendment rights were being abused but he was at least able to characterise the dispute in the wake of the court case as a 'misunderstanding'. He has since denounced the estate's lawyers for putting him through "fifteen months fighting one of the most deep-pocketed literary estates on the planet, that of J.R.R. Tolkien".[28] He did, however, manage to negotiate a settlement whereby he was able to publish his book with agreed amendments.

In Peru an abridged version of the *Lord of the Rings* story, 'El Senor de Los Anillos', was published and a few hundred copies sold. Since the estate policy is not to allow abridgement, as they feel it undermines the integrity of the work, Manches engaged Peruvian lawyers to stop the sales.

A website in Russia run by Askar Tuganbaev contains the entire text of Tolkien's novels. Manches tried to have them removed but it is difficult in certain jurisdictions. In Russia the copyright theoretically ran out on the *Lord of the Rings* before 1973, when Russia signed an international agreement called the Berne Convention for the Protection of Literary and

Artistic Works. So possibly Mr Tuganbaev felt he was operating within the law anyway. Manches wrote to him asking that he take the material off his website but he refused. Manches then engaged a law firm in Russia to pursue the case but they also failed to encourage the site owner to remove the offending text. Eventually it was widely reported that the Russian lawyers concluded that it would be inadvisable to pursue the case through the courts, because even if they won they probably could not enforce the judgement in Moscow.

There have been cases in the UK and Poland of publishers with a good faith belief that they had acquired legitimate licences to publish versions of the books only to find out when contacted by the estate's solicitors that the licence was not valid.

David Colbert has written a number of books about the myths and legends from which authors like Tolkien and Rowling have derived parts of their stories.[29] I have picked up and browsed copies of these in bookshops, where they are promoted and sold alongside the original *Lord of the Rings* and *Harry Potter* books. They do not infringe on the copyright of the originals but there can be little doubt that the main selling point is the explicit connection to the titles of the original works. I am not aware of any formal legal complaints about these books by the authors' representatives, which some might believe implies tacit approval of an enterprising effort to cash in on the market for extra information about these publishing phenomena. The legal issues in these cases are highly complex, however, bringing into question not just copyright law but trademark law and the law of passing off. So we should not infer from the lack of reported cases that there is any approval of these types of spin-off works, tacit or otherwise, by the estates or authors concerned.

There have also been numerous parodies like *Bored of the Rings*,[30] *The Soddit*[31] and the Barry Trotter books.[32] Author A.R.R.R. Roberts rounds off *The Soddit* with the kind of adverts sometimes found at the back of popular novels:

"Have you enjoyed the Soddit? Why not read the three volumes of A.R.R.R. Roberts's magical sequel *The Lord of the Dancings*."

He goes on to encourage readers to buy books like *Hairy Potsdam* by J.K. 'not from Jamiroquai' Rollinint and *The Spuddit*:

"Read this hilarious, light hearted, thoroughly respectful, not-cashing-in-at-all *Parody of A.R.R.R. Roberts's classic The Soddit.* There's a laugh in every sentence or your money back!"

I suspect even the lawyers saw the funny side, though copyright law in the UK, unlike the US, does not explicitly condone parodies.

I have two points to make by telling the Harry Potter and Lord of the Rings copyright stories.[33] The first is that the day-to-day legal protection of the rights of popular authors and their publishers can be a time-consuming, messy and no doubt occasionally frustrating job for the lawyers involved. It can involve stepping into the middle of people's hobbies or creative endeavours in ways that are rarely welcome. The second point follows from the first. Given the impact it can have on people's lives, it is important that the *balance* of both the letter and the practice of intellectual property law respects the interests of the creators, publishers[34] and users of the fruits of creative endeavours.

The following stories are mostly illustrations of where I believe that balance has been lost.

Professional focus on how silence is [golden] profitable

One of the perils of professional training and experience is that, at the very least within the context of their work, professional people like doctors, engineers,[35] scientists, lawyers and others just don't see the world like ordinary people do. To some extent that is a big advantage because it gives them the skills and perspective to diagnose illness, build planes, understand the universe or protect the legal interests of their clients. In another sense it can lead to unnecessary traps in thinking of the type mentioned in Chapter 2. For the moment let me illustrate the point with an example.

A copyright lawyer will consider it perfectly reasonable to sue somebody for infringing the copyright in silence.[36] It has happened. Well almost – the case was settled out of court. The rules of intellectual property say that if someone holds the copyright in a piece of music and someone else copies that music without permission they are breaking the rules. If someone is breaking the rules, the lawyer wants to protect the interests of their client...

One of US composer John Cage's best-known compositions is a piece of musical silence of 4 minutes and 33 seconds, first performed at a concert in Woodstock in New York, in 1952. It was delivered in three parts of 33 seconds, 2 minutes 40 seconds and 1 minute 20 seconds,[37] by pianist David Tudor and caused a lot of controversy. Mr Tudor identified the beginning and end of each section or movement by opening and closing the lid of the piano. Sometimes called John Cage's 'silent piece', the Musical Score reads on an otherwise blank page:

"4' 33" silence for any instrument or combination of instruments"[38]

In 2002 music producer Mike Batt included a minute's silence in a CD by a popular classical music group called the Planets.[39] He gave it the title 'A One Minute Silence' and suggested it was composed by 'Batt/Cage' on the CD packaging.

This was the cue, after the album had proved very successful, for m'learned friends, lawyers representing John Cage's estate and publishers, to contact Batt over the matter of infringing their clients' copyrights. Leaving aside the question of the artistic merit of the Cage and Batt silent pieces,[40] the lawyers believed it was reasonable to threaten someone with legal action over infringing the copyright in silence, because that silence constituted a musical composition. John Cage had apparently been given credit for the work on Batt's CD and within the confines of the copyright lawyers' worldview, that 'One Minute Silence' could be argued to be a performance of part of Cage's work. I wonder if the sticking point in court might come in establishing which specific part of the silence was infringed.

In 1993 Frank Zappa had recorded an *authorised* version of 4' 33" silence, for which he paid royalties, on an album in tribute to Cage.[41] So the lawyers had previous custom and practice to guide them too.

This all sounds completely ridiculous. How can someone corner the market on silence? However, no behaviour is inherently ridiculous. It only becomes so in relation to some set of social norms or a particular context. This particular ridiculous state of affairs – suing someone over the copyright in silence – is brought about by a complex and arcane set of legal rules and narrowly focused professional lawyers' abilities to exploit those rules in the economic interests of their clients.

This is not, at this point, a criticism of the rules or the lawyers. Remember that lawyers do not see the world as ordinary people do. Society might well judge it ridiculous that someone could get sued over the copyright in silence but intellectual property lawyers operate within the context of a specialised set of social, legal and professional norms. They refer to legal precedent and prior custom and practice in interpreting the law. If Frank Zappa paid royalties for recording silence, then they reason that the next person should too.[42] They are paid to protect the interests of their clients in the context of the rules and regulations of their professional area of expertise. In the wake of this case it is even possible to suggest that the estate's legal team may have done a good job, at least as far as their clients were concerned, because Mike Batt agreed to pay a one-off undisclosed fee, reputed to be tens of thousands of pounds, to settle out of court.

Following the settlement Batt decided to register the copyrights in every period of silence between 1 second and 10 minutes, except for 4 minutes 33 seconds and now figures he's got Cage's estate caged in. He has threatened to sue anyone performing Cage's work that over-runs or under-runs the 4 minutes 33 seconds.[43] John Cage died in 1992, which means his estate retains copyright on 4 minutes 33 seconds silence until 2042 in many parts of the world and in the US until 2062.

So the experts are acting in the best interests of their clients and the clients are getting a satisfactory deal but there is something important missing – the public interest. Copyright experts and vested interests may well be able to rationalise and settle a dispute over copyright in silence but most people can see that it is idiotic. So the involvement of ordinary people in such scenarios enables important questions to be asked.

- If it is really the law which facilitates such situations, should that law be reviewed?
- How can anyone believe any rules allow someone to make money from copyrighting silence?
- Has this really got anything to do with copyright law at all or just someone chancing their arm?
- What role does intellectual property law have in such disputes?
- Perhaps the law in practice is significantly different to what law schools teach, meaning case and textbooks are of little use in the real world?
- Is the kind of 'perfect protection' of intellectual property that James Boyle[44] and Larry Lessig[45] believe is sought by intellectual property industries realistic or desirable?

The point is that ordinary people can bring a sensible general perspective to complex decision making situations, whereas experts often take the narrow approach of just working the system because that is the way it is. This is problematic in individual cases like the copyright in silence dispute and also in the policymaking process. As discussed later in Chapter 8, intellectual property laws all over the world have, for a long time, been written by experts and lobbyists representing the copyright industries. The result is that we have a mass of detailed and complex intellectual property laws targeted at particular problems, as perceived by the affected industries and lacking in overall coherence or balance.

Law protecting digital fences intended to protect copyright

Executives in companies lucky enough to possess commercial success stories like Harry Potter will rightly want to protect those assets and maximise the profits arising out of them. It is their legal duty to maximise the returns to their shareholders. But just because they control the copyright and their own market in a particular copyrighted work does not necessarily mean they can extend that control to associated markets such as consumer electronics.

I would like to think we have come a long way since people were killed over a copy of a painstakingly manually transcribed manuscript 1400 years ago at the Battle of the Book. Sadly I wonder when I listen to some of the extremist rhetoric that passes for debate in the modern-day copyright wars. That applies both to the people who want to abolish copyright at one end of the scale and to those who want to further strengthen copyright in favour of existing large institutional copyright holders at the other.

In 1983, Jack Valenti, head of the Motion Picture Association of America (MPAA) described the video cassette recorder as follows:

"I say to you that the VCR is to the American film producer and the American public as the Boston strangler is to the woman home alone."[46]

Yet by the time the DVD came along the film industry were earning significantly higher revenues from the sale of video cassettes than from cinemas. DVDs are still huge earners for the industry, though sadly video cassettes are being phased out.

In 2002 Jamie Kellner, head of Turner Broadcasting, said that anyone who recorded a programme for later viewing and then fast forwarded the commercials whilst viewing was 'stealing the programming'. He claimed that viewers have a contract with the broadcaster to watch the adverts. Complete nonsense.

One US congressman, when talking about a particularly draconian piece of copyright law[47] he wanted to introduce, went so far as to suggest he was actually doing copyright 'pirates' a favour by not including the death penalty as a sanction for copyright infringement.[48] A US Senator[49] introduced a bill[50] which, if it had passed into law, would have inadvertently resulted in the need for aircraft intercoms, digital church bells and electronic sewing machines to contain built-in anti-copying devices.[51] Tony Blair is keen to extend the term of copyright in the UK because his friend, Cliff Richard, tells him it is not long enough.

'Piracy' is in reality something that happens at sea rather than when copyright is infringed. Would Disney have got a large audience for a movie called the *Copyright Infringers of the Caribbean*?

We need to be careful about the use of language in the copyright context. Just as losing your voice is not the same as forcible removal of your larynx, copyright infringement is not theft. We have to be careful about the choice of language biasing the debate.

The publishing and entertainment industries have, however, got legitimate concerns about digital technologies and the Internet. These concerns for their future have led them to lobby hard for changes in law and technology.

'Digital rights management' (DRM) technologies[52] are being built into digitised copyrighted works such as music CDs and film DVDs. Think of DRM as a digital fence or a digital strait jacket, locked inside which resides the film, song or other digital file. Then only someone with an approved DVD or CD player or electronic book reader, containing the key to the digital lock, can access the file.

Copyright law changed significantly over the latter part of the 20th-century. It now covers more things in more ways and for longer than was originally anticipated when it provided 14 years' protection for maps, charts and books in 1710.[53] Important changes affecting technology have been the introductions of the Digital Millennium Copyright Act (DMCA) in the US in 1998 and the European Union copyright directive (EUCD) in 2001.[54]

The intention behind 'anti-circumvention' laws like the DMCA and the EUCD[55] was to stop people defeating copy protection systems wrapped around digitised copyrighted works. These laws also ban devices intended to bypass or break these digital fences.[56]

The law protects the digital fences surrounding the works, which in turn are protected by copyright. It is a kind of law and technology sandwich, with the technology as the filling. The act of bypassing the digital fences is criminalised regardless of the intention of the person doing it or their right to access the work behind the fence.

If you put a digital fence – a DRM access control – around a copyrighted work, it is illegal to bypass or break or find a way through that digital fence. It is illegal to make a tool that breaks or bypasses or finds a way through that digital fence. It is illegal to tell someone how to make that tool. In the Universal v Reimerdes Hacker 2600 case in the US, the court even held it illegal to link to a website telling someone where she can find out how to make that tool.[57]

The DMCA led to a whole host of court cases in the US surrounding the decoding of the copy protection system on DVDs.[58] Jon Johansen,[59] the Norwegian teenager who originally posted the code[60] on the Internet, had the prospect of a jail term hanging over him for 5 years as his case played its way through the criminal justice system. It is a crime in Norway, punishable by up to two years in prison, to bypass technological controls to access data one is not entitled to access. Acquitted in January 2003 Johansen had to suffer a re-trial following an appeal and was acquitted again in December 2003. He had bypassed the digital fence on a DVD he bought in France, so that he could watch it on his Linux computer. The judges said that someone could not be prosecuted for breaking into their own property. On 5 January 2004 the Norwegian Economic Crime Unit (Økokrim) announced they would not be appealing the case further. Johansen is now suing Økokrim for damages and legal costs. The Motion Picture Association of America (MPAA), who had pressurised the Norwegian authorities into bringing the case in the first instance, were disappointed that Johansen did not go to jail.[61]

On 17 July 2001, the FBI, following a tip off from Adobe, arrested Dmitry Sklyarov, a Russian PhD computer science student, for an alleged violation of the Digital Millennium Copyright Act. He had presented a paper at the DefCon hacker convention in Las Vegas entitled: *'eBook Security: Theory and Practice'*.

He talked about the Adobe eBooks security and how it was relatively trivial to bypass, if you happen to own an eBook. Bypassing the security allows the eBook owner to backup their eBook,[62] read the eBook on a platform other than Microsoft Windows and is useful to the blind because it allows an audio version of the book to be switched on.

Sklyarov spent a month in jail and had his passport confiscated for 6 months, preventing him returning to his young family in Russia until the New Year. He faced a further 25 years in jail before the US prosecutors eventually agreed to drop the case in return for Sklyarov's agreement to testify in a case against his employer, software company Elcomsoft. A jury threw out the charges against Elcomsoft in December 2002.

In the wake of the case the Russian foreign ministry issued a general warning to computer scientists about the US being potentially hostile territory due to the nature of US copyright laws like the DMCA.

In the same summer that Sklyarov was having difficulties, Princeton computer science professor Edward Felten and his colleagues found themselves on the receiving end of a threat of DMCA-based legal action by the music industry. The Princeton group had taken up the challenge of the music industry to crack their new digital watermarking technology.[63] They defeated all four watermarking technologies and Felten agreed to present a paper on the work at a conference. Felten and the conference organisers received the legal threats before the conference and withdrew the paper. Following adverse publicity the music industry denied that they had intended to threaten Felten and he eventually presented the paper: *'Reading Between the Lines: lessons from the SDMI challenge'* at the 10th USENIX Security Symposium in August 2001.

In 2003, SunnComm threatened to sue one of Felten's PhD students, Alex Halderman, for $10 million. Halderman discovered he could bypass the company's latest copy protection technology, 'MediaMax CD3', simply by pressing down the 'shift' key on the computer when loading the CD. SunnComm quickly backed off the threat in the face of adverse publicity. However, Halderman's discovery still meant that the shift key on a computer keyboard became a device

"for the purpose of circumventing protection afforded by a technological measure that effectively protects a right of a copyright owner"[64]

which potentially made the manufacture or sale of computer keyboards illegal.

Fortunately the law has some protection from such a scenario. It requires that prohibited technology is "primarily designed or produced for" and should have "only limited commercially significant purpose or use other than" the purpose of bypassing copy protection systems.

Blackboard and the technology students

All of the above DMCA cases bothered me as a member of a university devoted to open access to education. The one which hit closest to home, to someone involved in the industrial-scale deployment of communications technologies in higher education, however, was a lesser-known case involving a company called Blackboard, which dominates the market in supplying digital platforms, sometimes called 'virtual learning environments'(VLEs), to universities.

In 2003, two students decided to publish a research paper on an electronic security problem. The two, Billy Hoffman of the Georgia Institute of Technology and Virgil Griffith of the University of Alabama had discovered a security hole in Blackboard's university ID card system. They decided to publish a paper on the problem at a security conference in Georgia but Blackboard's lawyers stepped in wielding the DMCA, trademark and computer hacking laws and got a court to issue an injunction preventing the disclosure of the details of the problem.[65]

The students eventually reached an out-of-court settlement with Blackboard, apologising to the company for their actions and agreeing to "refrain from any further unauthorized access to or use of the System", including "any transaction designed to better understand or determine how the System works". They also agreed to do 40 hours community service.

Now Blackboard got their injunction preventing these students from presenting their research, so they had an arguable legal case. However, the builders of one of the most widely deployed platforms for the creation and delivery of higher education digital content were prepared to go to court to block the publication of inconvenient research. They were also prepared, by threatening criminal sanctions, to extract a settlement whereby a couple of technology students agreed to refrain from any action that would enable them to understand a piece of technology. Blackboard may have been acting in the interests of its shareholders as a business is obliged to do but the case sets, for me, a very worrying precedent for the education sector.[66]

Universities should think carefully before locking themselves into propriety virtual learning products like Blackboard's. The corollary of that is that the architecture of the platforms for open content needs to be:

- based on open standards
- modular
- flexible and
- expansible
- interoperable with other systems.

If a small number of players come to dominate the market for digital platforms for universities, in the long term we could face restrictions on information development and distribution which we take for granted today: restrictions built into the architecture of the systems we use backed up by the force of law.

This whole area of electronic learning materials and open content in education cuts right across the natural territory of intellectual property lawyers. Most universities and most academics sadly will remain unaware of this until something like a DMCA or EUCD case hits them unexpectedly.[67]

What seems strange is that we appear to have come to a state of affairs where someone can be threatened, arrested or jailed for pointing out a flaw in electronic security or DRM technologies. That does not bode well for an education system which is fundamentally based on facilitating access to knowledge.

Control through technology

Now, not too many years ago people were predicting the demise of the traditional publishing industry with the advent of e-books. It has not happened. The thing about e-books is that they come with 'permissions' or licences written by a lawyer, in lawyer-land.

The first edition Adobe e-book version of *Alice's Adventures in Wonderland*[68] came with a license which read:

"This book may not be read aloud."

Is any sensible person who has purchased this expensive piece of kit going to take any notice of such a provision? Probably not. The chances are they will not even read the licence so will remain blissfully unaware of it. It is easy enough to ignore the daft demands of such a license and still read the book to your children. However, someone who is blind or has a visually impaired child cannot use the audio feature of their e-book reader to listen to the audio version of the book. The e-book's audio reader is disabled by the software instructions built into the digital file containing the story. The restrictions preventing this are built into the technology.

The control is built into the technology.

Sony used to make a range of robotic dogs called Aibos.[69] Some Aibo enthusiasts set up a website called aibopet.com to share ideas on how to hack their dogs and program them to do tricks like dance to jazz and other music. The owners of aibopet.com got a letter from Sony's lawyers:

"your site provides the means to circumvent the copy protection protocol of Sony's Aibo™ memory stick™ to allow access to Sony Aibo-ware software"

The lawyers were alleging a violation of the anti-circumvention provisions of the DMCA. Aibo enthusiasts were telling other Aibo enthusiasts how to program their expensive toys to dance and this was illegal.

Leaving aside all notions of the rights or wrongs of copyright laws, and the legality or otherwise of particular kinds of dancing, it does not actually strike me as a very good idea to threaten to sue your most enthusiastic customers. Yet the lawyers, acting within the rules of intellectual property and with the narrow focus of apparently protecting Sony's interests still thought the action was appropriate.

Larry Lessig and James Boyle[70] argue that to a significant degree, copyright industries have been dictating to regulators, the personal computer and consumer electronics industry what laws and technologies should be allowed. They are leveraging control over one market to gain control in other associated markets. The 'DVD Copy Control Association', a trade body set up by the Hollywood movies industry, controls the market for DVD players by deciding who gets a licence to manufacture approved equipment.

Why should the US film industry get to decide the kind of DVD player someone gets to buy in Europe or Japan? Why in addition can they dictate that those European or Japanese machines should have built-in region coding restrictions (DRM or digital fences) which mean they will not play a DVD disc that is bought in the US? This is an example of what I am talking about more generally with intellectual property and associated technological developments. Decisions which have a direct impact on ordinary people – e.g. what kind of DVD player I can buy and what DVDs that machine is allowed to play – are made in less than transparent ways in unexpected places.

Lessig says at the behest of copyright industries and their claims of irreparable damage facilitated by new technologies, engineers are building restrictions into the technology. Yet we have been here before, repeatedly.

When player pianos were introduced in the early 1900s, the music publishing industry was up in arms. This upstart industry were recording music by punching holes in rolls of paper, allowing the pianos to play it automatically and making money out of the music publishers' and composers' creations.[71]

The record industry which we know today was accused at the time of:

"sponging upon the toil, the work, the talent and the genius of American composers."[72]

It was arguably born a 'pirate' industry.

Similarly the film industry in Hollywood was built by 'pirates' or as they preferred to call themselves 'independents' like William Fox. Fox and others moved to California to avoid the patents of Thomas Edison and the strong-arm tactics of the Motion Pictures Patents company set up to protect those patents. California was still sufficiently remote that Hollywood could ignore Edison's patents without sanction. By the time effective legal regulation reached out West the patents had run out and a new industry was thriving.

Similar stories of copyright owners resisting new technologies played out through the 20th century – radio, TV, photocopiers, cable TV in the 1970s[73] and digital audio tapes in the early 1990s.[74] Then came the World Wide Web, the Rio, Napster and the drive for DRM digital strait jackets and laws to protect those technical restrictions.

DRM security theatre

DRM presents a problem for copyright owners who see building restrictions into technology as the solution to protecting the interests of their shareholders in a digital world.

The problem is that DRM, according to Professor Felten at Princeton, is like an impregnable armoured car transferring supermarket takings to the bank at the end of a busy day. The money is safe as long as it is locked inside the armoured car. But the money is useless unless you open the car doors to get it out. The money is vulnerable when it has to be transferred to the car and when transferred from the car to the bank.

To stretch the analogy a little further, the suspected criminals are in charge of the bank. In the copyright context, the people you want to access your digital music file (the money) are the same people whose access to that music you want to restrict (the suspected criminals) by locking the music file in DRM, the digital equivalent of an armoured car. They cannot play the music (use the money) unless you give them the key to the digital armoured car. The armoured car doesn't solve your problem because it doesn't provide 'end-to-end' protection. As Ed Felten says:

"The same is true for encryption-based DRM. End-to-end protection requires that the material be protected all the way from the performer, to the customer's eyes and ears. If you leave the content unprotected anywhere along that path, it's vulnerable. And encryption can't protect the entire path, in the same way that the armoured truck can't protect the money's entire path. You can't seal the content inside its envelope of encryption until after it has been recorded, and you have to unseal it before you can play it for the customer."[75]

DRM systems are not widely believed to be effective against sophisticated pirates but are designed as a road bump for the average user to avoid exposing them to the temptation of copying. Yet average users are going to get irritated by the restrictions of these DRM digital fences.[76] If a new CD refuses to play in their new Volkswagen's CD player for example they may possibly turn to the other nemesis of the copyright industries, song swapping on the Internet. DRM I think will eventually fail because of the problems of interoperability.

People will get fed up with their music players deciding whose music they will be allowed to play, and with the music industry having a veto over the design of digital music players. It's what economist Milton Friedman would call a 'no brainer'.[77] In the days of the vinyl LP record,[78] a record player would play a record regardless of where or who you bought it from. The record player was a universal music player. Likewise audio tape and CD players. Now there is no guarantee when you buy a CD that it will play on your home CD player because of the digital fences built into the CD. iPod owners can only buy downloadable music from Apple iTunes stores. The need for a universal digital music player is a no brainer. Who really wants to buy several different music players, just so they can buy music from different suppliers? The music industries will eventually figure out, as similar copyright industries have done in the past, that it can make more money out of licensing their works to the digital technology innovators like Apple, than in paying lawyers to delay the innovation.

RealNetworks v Apple

Take the dispute between Apple and RealNetworks in the summer of 2004. In response to RealNetworks developing some software called 'harmony' that allowed iPod owners to buy and play music from Real Music Stores on their Apple iPods, Apple announced:

"We are stunned that RealNetworks has adopted the tactics and ethics of a hacker to break into the iPod, and we are investigating the implications of their actions under the DMCA [Digital Millennium Copyright Act] and other laws."

Until RealNetworks bypassed Apple's digital fence there was only one source from which to buy and download songs for the iPod: Apple's iTunes service. Temporarily then there were two sources. I figured this would benefit iPod owners but Apple was not happy that their captive audience could find their online music somewhere else. Yet Apple allegedly does not make any money on their iTunes service because they do not hold the copyright on the songs they are selling. Yet they do make money on their sales of iPods. The bigger the digital music market, the more useful a digital music player like the iPod becomes. You would think Apple would have been happy too.

Notice the rhetoric again about breaking into the iPod. If 'breaking and entering' is the same as figuring out how a technology works and making other gadgets that talk to it, then I am all for that kind of tinkering.

It would be completely daft for a furniture manufacturer to say someone had broken into their table and figured out how to make chairs that might be compatible with it, thereby stealing their customers. But it is apparently easier to swallow this line of rhetoric when used in the context of more complicated digital technologies.

Bob Young of Red Hat says "every business person wakes up in the morning and says 'how can I become a monopolist?!'" Beyond that, though, business people in the entertainment and software businesses want to control the uses of their goods after they are sold. This is not your iPod, it is Apple's iPod. You cannot use that book to prop up a table and you may not under any circumstances read that e-book out loud. Yet, as Larry Lessig says:

"even if they believe this, we don't have to agree."

But Apple is on more solid legal ground than us with one of the unintended consequences of laws like the DMCA and EUCD – they are being used to lock in customers and lock out competition like RealNetworks in this case. It has to be said that RealNetworks are hardly innocent vic-

tims in this instance. The company has a proven track record of supporting propriety technology as long as it is *their* technology.

Napster, Peer to Peer (P2P), Grokster

About 20,000 people have been sued all over the world for downloading[79]
too many copyrighted songs and films from peer to peer (p2p) networks
like Grokster[80] and Bittorrent.

Why did the original Napster[81] have such a galvanising effect both in
the user base it acquired so rapidly and the amount of resources the music
industry were prepared to put into killing it off? Napster was significant
for several reasons:

- It showed how an open platform like the Internet facilitates
  technological development. Napster was created by a few individuals
  with little more than a simple idea and a personal computer connected
  to the Internet. They did not need the approval of corporate
  management or the owner of the network, since no one really owns
  the Net and they turned the world of commercial music upside-down.
  Within eighteen months Napster had about 60 million users.

- It was disruptive in two senses. Firstly, it challenged the business
  model of an established industry built around the control of a physical
  distribution network. Napster revealed the potential of the Net as a
  distribution medium – something that the music industry had
  ignored[82] up to that point. Secondly, Napster undermined
  conventional ways of protecting the copyright embodied in recorded
  music. Though it was something the industry had complained about
  for decades, friends copying each others CDs or audio tapes
  represented nothing like the scale of the copying that was to take
  place on the Net. Once a song was available on Napster millions of
  'friends' could copy it.

- It showed how the Internet could change – user PCs at the edge of the
  network could provide content as well as request it from central
  network servers controlled by professional entertainment, media and
  publishing industries.[83]

- It was shut down by the courts in 2001.[84]

What should the copyright holder do?

I have been pretty hard on the excesses of certain copyright owners since citing the story of copyright in silence but what can a copyright holder do about someone posting their entire text online? The simplest thing to do is to ask the site owner to remove it. Sometimes they do not even realise they are infringing someone's copyright. A common tactic in the US now is to serve the internet service provider (ISP) with a 'DMCA notice', following which most ISPs act quickly to take down an alleged infringing site.

Barney the purple dinosaur is a well-known children's television character. Barney's lawyers have suggested that entertainment companies may need the right to hack into sites to shut them down, when the site owners ignore a court order to go offline. They went through a tedious process of obtaining a court order relating to a site selling counterfeit goods. The court sided with the lawyers and they informed their clients they won, only to be asked why the fraudsters were still selling counterfeit goods from the offending website.

"Your solution seems obvious, if unconventional: You have to shut down this web site technologically, whether by a denial of service attack or other technological approach. You have to become a hacker with a white hat – and a writ."[85]

But this kind of hacking is a crime, unless the lawyer can get the law enforcement or intelligence services to do the job for him.

It might initially sound like a reasonable suggestion. If a fraudster is ignoring the court the only way to stop them is to digitally and perhaps remotely lock up their computers. But this solution creates some problems and some questions. Other sites on the same server or even the entire ISP's network could be affected by a crude hacking attack. Who then pays for the damage to innocent parties? At what point in the litigation process would a copyright holder be given the go-ahead for such a remote attack? What would be the checks and balances in the system? A responsible ISP, detecting a denial of service attack and recognising the widespread damage it could do, would shut off access to the attacker.

The level of security protecting websites varies enormously and the targeted site may be more robust in the face of an attack than others. The fraudsters could set up lots of mirror sites even if one is taken down remotely. What if the website is hosted overseas and outside the jurisdiction of the court? I suspect the lawyers' answer to the collateral damage question would be for the judge to require assurances that the attack could be carried out clinically and concisely without any such damage, in addition to agreeing to be bound to pay for any damage should the exercise go wrong.

It is one of those situations that you feel technology should be able to help solve. But in practice it would be very complicated and at the current stage of evolution of the technology impractical. It is an interesting idea but technology will not solve the problem if we do not know specifically what we expect it to do, how it works and what other problems it is likely to cause.

So when the courts fail and the technology fails to protect the copyright holders, what then? I suspect the most effective way out is to offer reasonably priced legitimate and secure versions of the copyrighted works. Black markets in all products spring up when the price is set significantly above the marginal cost of production. Legitimate vendors selling legitimate files at a reasonable price and with the guarantee that the product is clean and secure, will always have a competitive advantage over the 'pirates'. The copyright industries say "you can't compete with free" but the bottled water vendors have been doing a good job of competing with tap water for at least a generation on this side of the pond (though I remember, as a boy, laughing at the idea that someone would be able to make money selling bottled water in Ireland).

The magic of Harry Potter

All the Harry Potter legal cases have been interesting stories in themselves, as have those related to Lord of the Rings and lots more.[86] That these popular stories trigger whole societal ecologies and economies is interesting from an academic perspective but, like millions of others, my children love the Harry Potter books and I have to say I enjoy reading them aloud and experiencing the kids' captivation with J.K. Rowling's magical world.[87] My younger son, Nicholas, is particularly tuned into the magic and the occasional slapstick humour and loves the Hagrid character. His spontaneous and infectious giggling at times has us all in stitches with laughter that has a magic all of its own. In the rush to protect the legitimate interests of copyright holders, we need to be careful not to lock that particular magic behind legal and technical tollbooths.

Chapter 4 Infodiversity and the sustainability of our digital ecology

"In our every deliberation we must consider the impact of our decisions on the next seven generations." Ancient Native American Saying

The idea of 'the environment'

James Boyle has written extensively[1] about the degree to which theories on the environment and environmental activism can inform the debate about the regulation of digital technologies. He explains that whilst the duck hunter and the bird watcher might not like each other, they have a shared interest in ensuring that the birds' natural environment or habitat is preserved.

The word 'environment' is used in lots of different ways, by different people, in different contexts and just as part of everyday language. If you pick up a daily newspaper you'll probably see dozens of references to 'abuses of the environment', 'working environment', 'ecological environment', 'political environment', 'business environment', 'school environment' and many others.

Everyone bringing their own meaning to this abstract concept, however, can be useful in bringing together those with different interests – duck hunters, bird watchers, park keepers, families worried about industrial effluent – in a way that would not have happened prior to a widespread use of the idea of an 'environment' which all those people have an interest in protecting. There was nothing that enabled a disparate range of people to see the connections between their various environmentally related interests until this notion of 'the environment' became widely used. As Boyle says, the abstract concept of the 'environment' is an "articulation of a shared interest which calls that interest into being". The 'environment' is an idea which moves our general understanding to a level where we can see the common interests.[2]

My interest in trying to weave a route through this complicated story of intellectual property, commons and enclosure is a simple belief in the idea, shared with Colmcille and given real impetus through the age of the enlightenment, that it is generally good for society when we share knowledge. The intellectual property system, contrary to what some would have us believe, is based on the idea of sharing knowledge to facilitate the enlightened development of society and the personal development of individuals within that society.

Inventors, creators, authors or commercial organisations get a limited monopoly on the product of their creativity, for a limited time, in exchange for sharing their knowledge with society. In the case of the patent system, for example, James Dyson gets a twenty-year monopoly on his vacuum cleaners in exchange for telling us how they work. After the term of the monopoly is completed the invention falls into the public domain. Or that is the theory. If we look at some of the stories in Chapter 2, like Blackboard suing students, it seems as though telling people how technology works has now become unlawful, in some circumstances. Lawyers and industries get trapped in a way of thinking and operating. Focused on the details of the complex rules of the system and exploiting those rules in their own interests, they can end up undermining the original purpose of the whole system, which is to promote progress.[3]

Systems thinking

Like environment, 'system' is another word in everyday conversation which is widely used to mean different things. When using the word system people are usually referring to something complex, with many inter-connected components or subsystems that [should] work together in some coherent way. A computer system, a nuclear power plant system, an in-formation system, an education system, a legal system, an examination system and a health system are common examples. 'Systems thinking'[4] is a way of letting us look at something as a whole. The whole system can be greater than, less than or equal to the sum of its parts.

The England football team does less well than would be expected given the proven abilities of the individual players at its disposal. It does not just apply to footballers either. One example people usually find amusing is that a group of managers, with individual IQs above 120, were found to have a collective IQ below 63, when observed working together on a par-ticular task.[5] The Challenger space shuttle had over a thousand subsystems or components with 'criticality 1 waivers', the failure of any one of which would have been enough to lead to the loss of the shuttle and the death of the crew. The UK government are introducing an identity system not just an ID card.

The idea is that by looking at the whole system we can better understand the complexity and interconnections between the system components and the system's overall effectiveness.

The very act of thinking of something in a different way is often enough in itself to enlighten our perspective of a particular system. A copyright system designed to maximise the income of copyright holders might re-quire copyright to last forever. If the objective of the copyright system was to promote progress in science and the useful arts,[6] however, then never-ending copyright might interfere with the ability to use other peo-ple's work to develop new ideas.

One of my favourite stories illustrating the power of viewing the whole system (in the context of its environment) is the parable of the blind men and the elephant.

It was six men of Hindustan
To learning much inclined,
Who went to see the Elephant
(Though all of them were blind)
That each by observation
Might satisfy the mind.

The first approached the Elephant
And happening to fall
Against his broad and sturdy side
At once began to bawl:
"Bless me, it seems the Elephant
Is very like a wall."

The second, feeling of his tusk,
Cried, "Ho! What have we here
So very round and smooth and sharp?
To me 'tis mighty clear
This wonder of an Elephant
Is very like a spear."[7]

A third thinks it is a snake having touched a wriggling trunk, a fourth goes on to say it is like a tree, after touching the knee, a fifth touching the ear says it is like a fan, and a sixth says it is more like a rope after touching the tail. All six go onto argue "loud and long" and

Though each was partly in the right
and all were in the wrong.
So oft in theologic wars,
The disputants, I ween,
Rail on in utter ignorance
Of what each other mean,
And prate about an Elephant
Not one of them has seen![8]

Systems' thinking was pioneered by biologists who stressed the need to consider living species as integrated wholes. Life is greater than the sum of its component parts. James Boyle is essentially urging the duck hunter, the bird watcher and the family whose water supply is contaminated with industrial waste to use systems thinking or to think 'systemically', when pointing out how the term 'environment' enables them to see their shared interests. Thinking about the environment at different levels facilitates understanding. Getting too deeply immersed in our own particular concerns in our own part of a system can blind us to the wider picture, which itself can suggest connections and help we would not otherwise see.

Whereas I do not propose to go into systems thinking in great detail, it does contain a number of useful concepts that I will be using. So it is worth stating that when using the term 'system' I am referring to something that conforms to the following definition:

- A system is an assembly of components connected together in an organised way
- The components are affected by being in the system and are changed if they leave it
- The assembly of components does something i.e. the system has a purpose[9]
- The assembly has been identified by someone as being of interest.[10]

Take each of those parts of the definition in turn.

A system is an assembly of components connected together in an organised way

A warehouse full of aircraft components piled into a heap will not be a system until those components are assembled together into a working plane. A collection of laws which have passed through parliament in response to heavy lobbying by narrowly focused interest groups may result in a legal system lacking in overall coherence, as the components will not work together in an organised way.

The components are affected by being in the system and are changed if they leave it

Neither I nor my liver will survive too long if the liver is separated from the rest of my body. If the components and the system change once they part company that means the interactions must make a significant contribution to the system's properties. So it will not necessarily be easy to get an understanding of the system by breaking it down into its component parts and studying each independently.

The assembly of components does something i.e. the system has a purpose

A system is dynamic i.e. it changes over time. It also has a purpose. This notion of purpose is incredibly important when dealing with information systems. Many information systems fail for the simple reason that the purpose of the system is never really clarified. Should copyright promote progress or maximise some people's income? Even if you do not know the purpose of a system it is useful to examine it as if it had a particular purpose. The intellectual property system may or may not have grown up over many years into something that favours particular vested interests, as some argue. But it is still helpful to look at it *as if* it had the purpose of increasing access to knowledge.

The assembly has been identified by someone as being of interest

NASA could be considered to be a system for depositing satellites in orbit around the earth or a system for wasting taxpayers' money. The key thing from a systems thinking perspective is that *some person* has identified a system as being of interest.

The fundamental value of systems thinking and practice is that it facilitates the development of different perspectives. Simply thinking about a situation in a different way can be enlightening.

Messes and difficulties

One of the gurus of systems thinking, Russell Ackoff,[11] gave the term 'mess' a particular meaning in the context of decision making:

"What decision makers deal with, I maintain, are messes not problems. This is hardly illuminating, however, unless I make more explicit what I mean by a "mess". A mess is a set of external conditions that produces dissatisfaction. It can be conceptualized as a system of problems in the same sense as a physical body can be conceptualized as a system of atoms."[12]

He means that decision making situations are often unstructured messes (like James March's garbage can from Chapter 2). This contrasts with simple 'difficulties' where it is easy to identify and solve a particular problem. One of the exercises my systems colleagues at the Open University get their students to do is to think about three simple situations they have dealt with and contrast these with three complex and difficult situations. The students are asked to identify the features of the simple situations that distinguish them from the complex counterparts.

People find that messes tend to be bigger, more complicated, involve more people, more organisations, happen over a longer time scale, have more serious impacts, many confusing features which are difficult to grasp, no obvious solutions and no real clarity often about what the problems are. In other words large in scale and involving lots of uncertainty.

By contrast, difficulties are easier to pin down. It is clear what the problem is and which various solutions might be available to deal with it. So when the car has to go into the garage for a service, the driver can cycle or take the bus to work. The problem is bounded, small scale and clear.

Most of the digital decision making situations dealt with in this book are of the mess variety. Yet they are often treated by policymakers as being difficulties. There is a rather touching faith in the magical ability of technology to solve problems in a way which turns a mess into a mere difficulty. This belief is particularly widespread amongst decision makers who do not understand the technology. Yet technology, no matter how sophisticated, is just a tool. It is not magic and will not automatically evolve towards a state where it will comprehensively address an ill-defined mess. Policy makers, however, rarely seem to understand this.

That is partly why we now have laws which protect the digital fences (or DRM) behind which digitised copyrighted works are locked. There is no law which makes it a crime to jump over a real fence. There is a law of trespass which applies to the land behind the fence but the fence is not considered to need its own special legal protection in order to deter someone from jumping over it. Likewise in the digital copyright context there is a law of copyright to protect the work behind the digital fence. Yet the digital fences also get their own special laws and the penalties for breaching the fence are much more severe that those for breaching the copyright the fence is supposed to protect; as the arrest and jailing of Dimitry Sklyarov showed.[13] The state of the copyright system is a mess of the Ackoff variety.

MercExchange v eBay

In the spring of 2006 the eBay v MercExchange patent case was heard by the US Supreme Court.

MercExchange is an online retailer and patent holding company. eBay is the popular online auction website. People familiar with eBay will know that if you pull up a web page with an item you are interested in, it sometimes includes a 'buy now' button which you can click on to say you are happy to pay the price on the seller's price label, instead of getting involved in an auction. Amongst other things MercExchange have a patent for the electronic 'buy now at a fixed price' business method.

No. I'm not joking. Digitise the obvious and you can get a patent on it because it appears, at least superficially when wrapped up in technical and legal jargon, to meet the requirements for patenting, which are that it needs to be:

1. New
2. Not obvious and
3. Useful.

It is one function of the shock and awe that's visited upon society in the face of the magic that is computing technology. The effect of wrapping up a technical description of a simple idea in a further legal description of that idea is to make it appear quite complex. In fairness it is not just the dazzling effect of the technology or legalese that is at work here. Patent examiners, particularly in the US, are underpaid and overworked and the income of the US Patent Office is directly dependent on the number of patents it issues each year. So the system is effectively set up to ensure that the maximum number of patents get granted, regardless of the merit of the individual patent applications.

A jury awarded MercExchange $35 million damages for breach of their patent. The judge reduced the damages and refused an injunction to stop eBay operating the 'buy now' feature. He reasoned there would be no harm done by allowing them to continue. MercExchange appealed. The

Appeal Court said that the original judge's assessment is not a good test – i.e. that there would be no harm done – even if a particular business method patent, like one for a 'buy now' electronic button, might be considered 'unwise'. They then concluded there should be an injunction prohibiting eBay from using the 'buy now' button, even if that injunction could cause harm. So eBay appealed to the US Supreme Court which heard the case in the spring of 2006.

At face value, a dispute over an electronic button is not the sort of thing I would expect busy Supreme Court justices to be dealing with. The case, of course, was really about something more than a simple technical device that happened to have been granted a patent. A lot of money stands behind both sides in the dispute, with the big technology firms backing eBay and the big pharmaceuticals backing MercExchange.

Modern digital systems are immensely complicated and can contain millions of individual components. Technology companies cannot possibly be expected to second guess or check how many or which of those millions of components someone may have patented. They would be spending all their money on lawyers and never get anything done. By the same token, the pharmaceutical sector fundamentally depends on the ability to obtain patents on the tiniest of chemical and genetic components in order to justify their large investment in research and development. Any case that reaches the Supreme Court could result in a shift in the balance of the legal system. In this case two large industrial sectors found themselves concerned about a small shift in the balance of the patent system that could potentially have a large impact on their businesses.

Chief Justice Roberts, recently appointed to the Court by President Bush, was apparently a bit perplexed by the patents that were the subject of the dispute. The MercExchange lawyer said he wasn't a software developer so couldn't explain the technicalities and "I have reason to believe neither is your honour." Hmmm I would not have thought insulting the Chief Justice would be a particularly bright tactical manoeuvre? Apart from that, though, *the lawyer, representing one of the parties in a case before a national supreme court, arguably admitted he did not understand the technology that was the subject of the dispute.* Here we are again at the point where people making decisions about important information systems – in this case the patent system and how it deals with digital technology – do not understand the technology at the heart of the dispute.

Chief Justice Roberts accepted he was not a software expert but thought displaying pictures of goods to let people pick what they want[14] did not seem particularly innovative. Here is the classic case of the intelligent layperson – which Roberts was here in relation to the technology – stepping in and saying maybe we should not get distracted by the flashy buttons and lights; and asking what it is that this technology really does.

It does not make sense for something obvious – buy now at a fixed price rather than take part in an auction, or let someone choose with the help of pictures – to be patentable just because you facilitate it with an electronic button. If Chief Justice Roberts can keep that perspective in the face of all the future complicated technology cases that come his way, the balance of his influence in this area could prove to be quite positive.

The case was decided some weeks later in favour of eBay but what matters is not really who won but that so much time, energy and resources have been poured into a dispute about an electronic button. The final irony was that a couple of days before the Supreme Court heard the case, the US Patent Office finalised their decision to declare one of the patents at the heart of the dispute invalid, stating that it never should have been issued.

This kind of case engenders a worrying culture of disrespect for the law, whereby we ask if it can really be true that someone got a patent on an electronic button. Then we build an argument to suggest the patent system must be stupid if it allows this kind of thing; therefore we should scrap it, ignore it or do what we can to undermine it. That is not a healthy state of affairs for the legal system.

Cases such as the dispute over copyright in silence can trigger the same kind of thinking but my point in telling them is not to encourage disrespect for the law. Rather it is to call for reason and balance in the development of these laws and associated (DRM) technologies as well as their deployment in practice. It is relatively easy to build technology or pass laws. It can be much more difficult (though it does not necessarily have to be) to deploy them in a way and with sufficient resources and intelligence to make them useful to society.

Access to information: the BMJ

In 1998 the *British Medical Journal* (*BMJ*), based on the principle of facilitating free and unrestricted access to scientific information, decided to make the entire contents of the journal freely available on the Internet. By January 2005, due to a drop in income, the journal partly reversed that decision, making some of the contents accessible online only to paying subscribers.[15] In February 2006, the *BMJ* published the results of a survey:

"To determine whether free access to research articles on *bmj.com* is an important factor in authors' decisions on whether to submit to the BMJ, whether the introduction of access controls to part of the BMJ's content has influenced authors' perceptions of the journal, and whether the introduction of further access controls would influence authors' perceptions."[16]

It was a relatively small survey with a little over 200 authors participating but the results suggested free online access was important to a large majority (75%) of them, so the publishers agreed to retain their partial open access policy for the time being.

Other important medical journals, like *The Lancet*, only provide online access to paying subscribers. Hundreds of other science and medical journals offer a variety of access approaches between the *BMJ*'s initial completely open access and *The Lancet*'s closed access policies. Some give you a trial free period after which you have to pay; some offer some articles freely, or for a limited period, or a number of years after the original publication; some sell individual articles separately to non-subscribers. They all require some form of revenue-generating capacity to keep them running.

In recent years the UK government has been very interested in pursuing the concept of 'patient choice' in the National Health Service e.g. choosing your GP or at which hospital you would like to have your operation. To an even greater extent in the US there has been a focus on 'consumer-driven health care', with personal healthcare plans, insurance and saving accounts.

But is putting complex personal healthcare decisions in the hands of the individual a good idea? Well to a large degree that depends on the capacity of the individual to make informed decisions about the management of their health and on the context of the circumstances within which we find ourselves having to make those decisions.

'Consumer choice' is right up there with 'property' as the mantra of our time.[17] It is so taken for granted that it is offered unthinkingly as the panacea to solve all of society's ills. Yet it is no good to anyone without the accompanying knowledge to make an informed choice. Most of us do not diagnose complex illnesses or manage medical emergencies on a daily basis. Neither have we received the formal medical training to do so. We do, however, manage our health quite adequately on a day-to-day basis without constant medical professional intervention. If I do find myself or a member of my family facing a serious medical emergency, I want access to a doctor who has successfully dealt with the condition thousands of times previously, who can make a rapid diagnosis, prescribe the most effective treatment and explain her carefully thought out, tried and tested options for managing the aftercare towards a full recovery, once the worst is over.

What about if I have a bit more time to do some research and find out a bit more about an ongoing chronic condition? A friend of mine with a hip complaint went to great lengths to research his condition and ended up impressing his doctor with the depth of his knowledge on the subject. But supposing the materials he read had not been as freely available as they had been and he had to pay *The Lancet*, the *BMJ* and hundreds of other sources a hefty fee for each article he read. Would he have had the ability to make the decisions he did about his treatment? Doctors could justifiably claim that most lay people are insufficiently well trained to understand even the language of medics or the reliability of the sources, especially on the Internet, from which we might derive much of this medical 'information'.

If the truly reliable peer reviewed sources like the *BMJ* do gradually move towards a subscription-only service, where is the average patient going to get access to important medical information required to make informed healthcare choices? Moreover, even if most of us do not research medical literature to make informed personal healthcare choices, there is a case to be made that the public welfare is enhanced by the information being openly and widely available. The ethos of science dictates that we can only reach a sound understanding when research information is shared and robustly tested by peers e.g. to converge on a scientific or in this case medical consensus of whether a particular medical diagnostic technique or treatment is sound.

Well it looks as though, for the moment, the *BMJ* will remain at least partly open, due to the commitment of the journal's contributors to making medical research freely available. On balance that is a good thing. But even then it is still only of use to those who have access to the Internet and will remain primarily the domain of the medical profession.

The medical profession knows how to treat malaria, cataracts, childhood dysentery; that a saline/sugar solution of 3/1 would save the majority of children suffering famine; that water can be made safe by putting it in plastic bottles and leaving them lying in the hot sun for long enough to kill any dangerous bugs. The rest of us, particularly those communities suffering from these problems, need to know. Here is where technology can get magical. It is no longer beyond the bounds of possibility that someone in a poor community in the developing world might have access to the global network. A member of the community or visiting medic or aid worker with a mobile phone and a cheap Ndyio[18] open network connection in the most remote shack in Africa might well be able to get access to that small piece of information on the global network which could make a difference to the survival of that community.[19]

A second enclosure movement?

The copyright in silence, eBay v MercExchange, Sklyarov, Felten, Apple, Harry Potter and other stories of the past two chapters could just be seen as a string of relatively unrelated intellectual property anecdotes. Taken together, however, from a systems perspective, they do provide strong evidence to suggest that James Boyle's theory about an emerging 'second enclosure movement' requires serious consideration.[20] The enclosure movement in England between the 15th and 19th-centuries led to big changes in the rural landscape. Formally communally shared land was fenced off and through changes in the law given to big landowners, who in turn divided it up further and rented it out to tenants.

To make things we need resources, including intangible resources like information and ideas. Authors, inventors, creators of all kinds, use language, stories, professional skills, musical notes and chords, facts and ideas, building on the work of earlier creators. Many of these resources are free. A public highway, a public park, Maxwell's equations or other scientific theories, or a book on which the copyright has expired are all free to use or copy.

These free resources are part of an 'intellectual commons' which anyone can use. It is Boyle's contention, however, that these raw materials of creative intellectual endeavour are increasingly getting fenced off and divided up amongst private owners. Unlike the grassy commons of old England, though, Boyle sees the modern enclosure of what he calls the 'commons of the mind' as a potentially more worrying development.

The intellectual property system now covers the human genome, business methods, books more than a hundred years old and even collections of facts in a database. These are all things that, for most of the past three hundred years,[21] intellectual property specialists would not have even conceived of coming within the scope of the system.

Myriad Genetics hold patents on the BRCA1 and BRCA2 genes which indicate a predisposition towards contracting breast and ovarian cancers. In the summer of 2001 the company informed the Canadian province of British Columbia that they would be rigorously enforcing their patent on tests for mutations in these genes. The British Columbia Ministry of Health then stopped funding the tests since the costs of continuing with them would have quadrupled.

What we are getting in the Internet age is intellectual property spreading out with the system covering more things in more ways for longer periods, with greater penalties than ever before. We also have a situation where it is now much easier to infringe intellectual property than ever before. Prior to photocopiers you needed a printing press and a manufacturing plant to copy someone's book. Even with a photocopier it would be a tedious and time consuming process to copy a book. A computer, connected to the Internet, however, puts the tools of mass copying and distribution on the desktop.

Surfing the World Wide Web involves copying. Every time we click on a link we copy a webpage or other digital file. The act of copying, something which used to be difficult, is now routine. Increasingly broad and continually expanding intellectual property laws, originally designed to regulate industries like publishing and entertainment, now apply to the individual. That can have unintended consequences, like a young Russian programmer getting jailed in the midst of a trip to the US, simply for having done his job in Russia. National laws can have extra-territorial reach. Incidentally, not only was Sklyarov's program legal in Russia, but Russian law requires users to have the facility to make backup copies of digital files. I thought that was a pretty good idea the first time I heard it, especially since I had just purchased my sixth copy of a CD that my elder son, Jack, was particularly fond of when he was little. Modern CDs, unfortunately, have an irritating inclination to get easily scratched.

Boyle asks us to think about the evolution in copying with a monk like Colmcille at one end of a temporal scale, copying out biblical scripts, on to Guttenberg and his printing press in the middle and then the photocopier, tape recorder, video cassette recorder, the Internet and associated technologies at the other end. As we move from Colmcille to the Internet, copying becomes easier and cheaper. The argument therefore goes that we must have stronger intellectual property rights with tougher penalties, otherwise creators will have no incentive to create. We do not need much intellectual property to guard against Colmcille (though Finnian might have disputed this) because it takes so long to copy a manuscript. There are not many people with the skills and materials to do it anyway. On the Internet, though, everyone is a potential copyright infringer.

Does this argument make sense? To a degree yes, if we accept that tools like the Internet are purely vast efficient copying machines. Copying is easier, cheaper and more widespread. However, as is always the case with new technology, it presents us and the entertainment industries with benefits as well as problems. Intellectual property holders can take advantage of communications technologies to vastly reduce distribution costs and increase the possibility of reaching new markets. A music company's back catalogue of songs can be made available digitally at a very low cost and even low volume sales can become profitable.[22] Printing a book on demand is now economically feasible and many publishers could have the facility to make their entire back catalogue of books available for order via the Internet. Selling merely half a dozen copies of each of 100, 000 out-of-print books could amount to quite a tidy income.

Search engines and other tools can be used to track people engaged in illicit file sharing. Indeed the entertainment industries have investigators monitoring the peer-to-peer file swapping networks, like Kazaa, Morpheus, Limewire, eDonkey, Gnutella or BitTorrent directly. So in deciding whether to expand intellectual property rights to compensate rights holders for some of the downsides of the technology, we should also be looking at the benefits, in order to decide whether they are better or worse off.

Yet with intellectual property, empirical cost-benefit considerations do not feature in the decision making process. No one ever asked the question, when the EU required most member states to extend their copyright term[23] – how long copyright should last – about what the effect on the market for books was the last time the term had been extended. Given that the various member states had different copyright terms, perhaps it would have been worth comparing the markets in different member states prior to introducing the directive. It is slightly over-simplifying the situation, though not much, to say that industry representatives make a case to legislators that 'it is obvious' that they need bigger, better and stronger intellectual property laws and the law gets passed.

The British Phonographic Industry's campaign to have the term of copyright on sound recordings extended, involved prominent media appearances by singer Cliff Richard. Cliff claimed that ageing recording artists were being deprived of their pensions because of the prospect of losing royalties on 50+ year old recordings.

No doubt a retired plumber or teacher would also like to enjoy a continuing substantive income from a day's work done 50 years previously but how likely is that? In any case, when the copyright in a song recording expires, which is likely to sell more copies – a special 50th-anniversary edition recorded by the original artist or an edition recorded by other lesser known artists? Viewed from the right perspective, the expiry of copyright can present a business opportunity, especially since most of the original recordings are just no longer commercially available.

In the US for about the past hundred years, whenever the interested industries have felt the need for a change in the law, e.g. due to the emergence of some new technology, they get together and negotiate an agreement. Their lawyers draft a bill, which gets handed to Congress where it gets passed into law. Jessica Litman describes this process in detail in Chapter 2 of her wonderful book, *Digital Copyright*:

"About one hundred years ago, Congress got into the habit of revising copyright law by encouraging representatives of the industries affected by copyright to hash out among themselves what changes needed to be made and then present Congress with the text of appropriate legislation...

A process like this generates legislation with some predictable features. First of all, no affected party is going to agree to support a bill that leaves it worse off than it is under the current law...

So negotiated copyright statutes have tended, throughout the century, to be kind to the entrenched status quo and hostile to upstart new industries." [24]

This is how the term of copyright got extended 11 times between 1960 and 1998 in the US. A similar process goes on in the European Union. When the EU considered a directive to 'harmonise the term' of copyright, after extensive lobbying by the affected industries, they settled on the longest existing term in an EU country at the time.[25] In Germany copyright in literary works lasted for the life of the author plus seventy years. The harmonised EU term became the excuse for the US to increase their term to 'life plus seventy' in 1998. In 2003, Mexico extended its term of copyright to life plus one hundred years. It will not be long until the need for parity with Mexico becomes the next rallying call for those looking to have the term further extended in other parts of the world.

Neither is the debate about the term of copyright a new one. Thomas Babbington Macaulay made a famous speech on the issue in the House of Commons in 1841, when a fellow member of the House, Thomas Talfourd,[26] was attempting to get the term extended to the life of the author plus 60 years. Almost every important thing we need to know about copyright even more than a century and a half later is contained in that speech. Macaulay said:

"The advantages arising from a system of copyright are obvious. It is desirable that we should have a supply of good books; we cannot have such a supply unless men of letters are liberally remunerated; and the least objectionable way of remunerating them is by means of copyright. You cannot depend for literary instruction and amusement on the leisure of men occupied in the pursuits of active life. Such men may occasionally produce compositions of great merit. But you must not look to such men for works which require deep meditation and long research. Works of that kind you can expect only from persons who make literature the business of their lives... Such men must be remunerated for their literary labour. And there are only two ways in which they can be remunerated. One of those ways is patronage; the other is copyright.

There have been times in which men of letters looked, not to the public, but to the government, or to a few great men, for the reward of their exertions... But these cases are exceptions. I can conceive no system more fatal to the integrity and independence of literary men than one under which they should be taught to look for their daily bread to the favour of ministers and nobles. I can conceive no system more certain to turn those minds which are formed by nature to be the bless-ings and ornaments of our species into public scandals and pests.

We have, then, only one resource left. We must betake ourselves to copyright, be the inconveniences of copyright what they may. Those inconveniences, in truth, are neither few nor small. Copyright is monopoly, and produces all the effects which the general voice of mankind attributes to monopoly...

I believe Sir that I may with safety take it for granted that the effect of monop-oly generally is to make articles scarce, to make them dear, and to make them bad. And I may with equal safety challenge my honourable friend to find out any dis-tinction between copyright and other privileges of the same kind; any reason why a monopoly of books should produce an effect directly the reverse of that which was produced by the East India Company's monopoly of tea... It is good that au-thors should be remunerated; and the least exceptionable way of remunerating them is by a monopoly. Yet monopoly is an evil. For the sake of the good we must submit to the evil; but the evil ought not to last a day longer than is necessary for the purpose of securing the good.

...the evil effects of the monopoly are proportioned to the length of its duration. But the good effects for the sake of which we bear with the evil effects are by no means proportioned to the length of its duration. A monopoly of sixty years pro-duces twice as much evil as a monopoly of thirty years, and thrice as much evil as a monopoly of twenty years. But it is by no means the fact that a posthumous mo-nopoly of sixty years gives to an author thrice as much pleasure and thrice as strong a motive as a posthumous monopoly of twenty years. On the contrary, the difference is so small as to be hardly perceptible.

We all know how faintly we are affected by the prospect of very distant advan-tages, even when they are advantages which we may reasonably hope that we shall ourselves enjoy. But an advantage that is to be enjoyed more than half a century after we are dead, by somebody, we know not by whom, perhaps by somebody unborn, by somebody utterly unconnected with us, is really no motive at all to ac-tion...

Now, this is the sort of boon which my honourable and learned friend holds out to authors. Considered as a boon to them, it is a mere nullity, but considered as an impost on the public, it is no nullity, but a very serious and pernicious reality.

I will take an example. Dr Johnson died fifty-six years ago. If the law were what my honourable and learned friend wishes to make it, somebody would now have the monopoly of Dr Johnson's works. Who that somebody would be it is im-possible to say but we may venture to guess. I guess, then, that it would have been some bookseller, who was the assign of another bookseller, who was the grandson of a third bookseller, who had bought the copyright from Black Frank, the doctor's servant and residuary legatee, in 1785 or 1786. Now, would the knowledge that this copyright would exist in 1841 have been a source of gratification to Johnson? Would it have stimulated his exertions? Would it have once drawn him out of his bed before noon? Would it have once cheered him under a fit of the spleen? Would it have induced him to give us one more allegory, one more life of a poet, one more imitation of Juvenal? I firmly believe not. I firmly believe that a hundred years ago, when he was writing our debates for the Gentleman's Magazine, he would very much rather have had two pence to buy a plate of shin of beef at a cook's shop underground. Considered as a reward to him, the difference between a twenty years' and sixty years' term of posthumous copyright would have been nothing or next to nothing. But is the difference nothing to us? I can buy Rasselas for sixpence. I might have had to give five shillings for it. I can buy the Dictionary, the entire genuine Dictionary, for two guineas, perhaps for less. I might have had to give five or six guineas for it. Do I grudge this to a man like Dr Johnson? Not at all. Show me that the prospect of this boon roused him to any vigorous effort, or sustained his spirits under depressing circumstances, and I am quite willing to pay the price of such an object, heavy as that price is. But what I do complain of is that my circumstances are to be worse, and Johnson's none the better; that I am to give five pounds for what to him was not worth a farthing."[27]

In the EU the list of narrowly focused intellectual property directives, covering special interests like software, rental of copyrighted works, term, databases, satellite and cable broadcasting, digital rights management technologies, and criminal sanctions for breaching intellectual property rights, grows by the year.[28] The result is arguably a system which, in Europe and individual European countries that have implemented these various directives, lacks overall coherence.

So the argument that 'it is obvious' that new technologies will lead to massive intellectual property infringement, with no compensating benefits, turns out to be a weak one. The evolution and growth of science, law and formal education[29] all fundamentally depended on sharing and testing information without the protection of intellectual property.

Though intellectual property plays an important role in providing creators with an incentive to create and innovate, it is not the only thing that provides that incentive. Shakespeare, Archimedes, Rembrandt, Galileo and Leonardo da Vinci all wrote, created, invented and theorised before intellectual property existed as a legal construct. J.K. Rowling wrote the first Harry Potter book without the slightest idea that it would transform her life in the way in did.

People create and invent all the time without the prospect of an economic return directly related to their creations. You only have to look at an enthusiastic toddler with some crayons and paper to see this. Often they don't even care if they have paper – they can always find something to use the crayons on. Creativity has always existed and will continue regardless of the state of the intellectual property system. Part of the value of the Internet in this context is that it allows lots of people geographically remote from each other to network cheaply and engage in collaborative creative enterprises.[30] How we reward creativity and provide incentives for those to engage in creative works is a question for society. It is my view that a strong but balanced intellectual property system has an important role in this.

The purpose of the intellectual property system is to promote progress. It exists to provide creators with an economic incentive to create and thereby increase the global store of knowledge[31] to which we can all have access. That global store of knowledge is also filled with ideas, inventions, scientific discoveries and facts developed without the benefit of intellectual property. We get access to the intellectual property facilitated part of that global store of knowledge initially for a price, in order, theoretically, that creators can get paid. This pay per access situation lasts as long as the temporary and limited monopoly on the items protected by intellectual property lasts. Once the monopoly runs out we get access, theoretically, for free. *So most of the contents of our theoretical global knowledge store should eventually be free or in the public domain.* In practice of course these things will not be free, as we still need intermediaries and aggregators like publishers, libraries and internet service providers to supply the books and electronic content, as well as the indices and advice regarding the information that we want or might be interested in.[32]

Boyle's concern is that we are, however, locking these contents up behind laws and digital fences in a way which will have a hugely detrimental effect on the ability of future creators to contribute to the knowledge store.

Nobel Laureate, Richard Feynman, once said "Our responsibility is to do what we can, learn what we can, improve the solutions and pass them on." If we do not have easy access to the raw materials of creativity, like language, stories, know-how, musical notes and chords, facts and ideas, we will not be able to build on what has gone before. An award-winning documentary about the civil rights movement in the US in the 1950s and 1960s, *Eyes on the Prize*, was out of circulation for many years because the fees required to renew the rights on copyrighted materials included in the documentary were too high.[33] Fox wanted to charge another documentary filmmaker, John Else, $10,000 to use 4.5 seconds of the Simpsons which was accidentally included in one of his scenes, on a small TV playing in the background.[34] Is this really what intellectual property should be about?

Boyle and fellow advocates respond to these developments and personal stories of their negative effects with a call for a shared interest in the public domain of knowledge and information (in culture and science).

About 450 million years ago the earth created rich seams of coal under various landmasses, the fuel of choice of the industrial revolution. About 300 million years later it cooked up the large reservoirs of oil[35] which the world so heavily depends on today. There was a lot of coal and oil but not an infinite amount and nothing like the quantity we need to sustain the current levels of consumption through to the end of the 21st century.[36] The oil, on which 90% of our transportation runs and access to 95% of the goods (including food)[37] in our consumer-driven culture depends, is running out and we are going to need alternative energy sources. It may take a crisis, like the rationing of oil and gas, to make the majority of us really focus on the impact of the oil economy, not just on oil reserves but on the environment in terms of pollution, global warming and climate change. An understanding of the environment can lead us to concentrate on the things that matter e.g. thinking about how high and increasing levels of consumption might affect future generations.

An understanding of the public domain could similarly lead us to consider the impact of our current actions – in the realm of intellectual property and associated digital fences – on future generations' access to knowledge. Boyle believes an articulation of a shared interest in the public domain can lead to a programme of activism and action to protect it, backed up by and intimately related to a programme for scholarship and analysis.

Biodiversity and infodiversity

The Internet and its associated technologies are a complex information system with a complex set of ecologies analogous to the environment. Technical experts and ecologists understand, to some degree, the effect that changes to these systems will have. Most of the rest of us do not. That is not a criticism. It is impossible even for the experts to completely understand the knowledge society or the environment in their entirety.

Experts may have a deep understanding of parts of the system but they never know it all and the models they use are simplified representations of some aspect of reality. We do however need this deep understanding if we as a society are to make informed decisions about information systems, particularly those with wide-reaching effects.

In an information society access to, and control of, information is crucial. Who is to ensure that information technologies and the regulations governing them evolve in progressive or positive ways? What political philosophies will underpin this evolution? How, when, where and by whom will such decisions be made?

Sometimes these issues are left to groups of experts who draft legislation, on intellectual property for example, which potentially has a global effect. Yet intellectual property experts pursue lawsuits over silence and electronic buttons and it often takes the ordinary woman on the Clapham Omnibus[38] to throw some common sense into the mix.

If, as Boyle suggests, we need parallel programmes of activism and scholarship to protect the public domain, do we need a kind of sustainable infodiversity[39] in our global knowledge store, equivalent to a sustainable biodiversity in our physical and ecological environment? In 2001 Edward O. Wilson wrote that more that 99% of the world's biodiversity was un-known[40] and that we should rectify that state of affairs, since our ignorance was contributing to the destruction of the environment. He outlines a five-point plan for doing this.

1. Comprehensively survey the world's flora and fauna. This will need a large but finite team of professionals.[41]
2. Create biological wealth e.g. through pharmaceutical prospecting of indigenous plants. Assigning economic value to biodiversity (e.g. as a source of material wealth as food or medicines or leisure amenities) is a key way to encourage its preservation.
3. Promote sustainable development i.e. "development which meets the needs of the present without compromising the ability of future generations to meet their own needs".[42]
4. Save what remains i.e. being realistic we are not going to halt environmental degradation overnight.
5. Restore the wild lands e.g. through designating large areas of land as natural reserves like Costa Rica's 50,000-hectare Guanacaste National Park.

We could conceive of a parallel plan for that global information store, the infodiversity of which is potentially endangered by Boyle's second enclosure movement prospectors.

1. Comprehensively survey the world's global knowledge store.
2. We already have vast industries built on information wealth and intellectual property but we need to look at whether those industries are operating in a way which is in the best interests of a society requiring access to knowledge.
3. Promote sustainable information development – information production and exploitation which meets the needs of the present without compromising the ability of future generations to build on that knowledge store.[43]
4. Save what remains e.g. seek to nullify developments in law or technology whose primary effect is the privatisation of knowledge and information in the public domain.
5. Restore the wild lands. Perhaps we need information reserves or wild lands, like networks of universities and other public institutions,

where ideas can be allowed to roam in the wild and the people in these institutions can exchange ideas without the need to deal with proprietary intellectual property claims of the commercial world, at least within the confines of the reserves?

Scientific knowledge is currently at a stage of development whereby the popular belief that we can synthetically create biodiversity is a complete pipedream. Wilson suggested that the "search for the safe rules of biotic synthesis is an enterprise of high intellectual daring". Likewise the inter-action of ideas, which creates the kind of infodiversity from which emerges other useful ideas, could be stifled by dividing up that public knowledge store amongst private owners. It would be like trying to recreate the biodiversity of the African continent in Dublin Zoo or someone's garden. Wilson is an advocate of using the law to protect biodiversity: "The wise procedure is to use the law to delay, science to evaluate and familiarity to preserve. There is an implicit principle of human behaviour important to conservation: *the better an ecosystem is known, the less likely it will be destroyed.*"[44] We could justifiably ask the question of whether intellectual property law, and indeed the whole portfolio of information and communications regulations, could play a similar role with our global information ecosystem.

Ultimately, the success or failure of what Boyle has called a second enclosure movement, rests on the evolutionary battle for dominance between two competing memes – the idea that knowledge should be shared and the idea that it should be controlled. They both have staying power.

When I first read James Boyle's and Larry Lessig's work it left me pretty gloomy about the future of the knowledge society, as a natural 'glass half empty' kind of guy. In spite of a number of the negative developments since then in the direction of Boyle's enclosure, though, I am now fairly optimistic about the power of the simple meme that sharing information is a good idea. The trick will be to continuously manage the balance between the competing (and simultaneously complementary) notions that:

- information should be shared and
- information should be controlled

– in the best interests of society as a whole.

Chapter 5 Canaries in the mine

"The greatest dangers to liberty lurk in insidious encroachment by men of zeal, well-meaning but without understanding." Louis Brandeis

Government systems: the canaries in the mine?

For some years now the UK government has used a lot of resources building up what they have come to call 'e-government', by which they mean government services facilitated by computing technologies. Unfortunately, if reports[1] about government information systems failures are to be believed, their record of designing, building and managing these systems is not encouraging. There have been a range of problems, for example, relating to the national DNA database, the Criminal Records Bureau Database, a variety of children's databases, the Child Support Agency (now scrapped), the Police National Computer (PNC) system, the Department for Work and Pensions system,[2] the scanning and creation of a digital population database (outsourced to India), the Passport Agency computer system, the Immigration and Asylum system, a £100 million Violent Criminals Database (scrapped in 2000 after being criticised by police and probation services as a disaster);[3] and more recently the national identity card system and the National Health Service (NHS) information system.

The Department of Health has a special information technology agency, *Connecting for Health* (CfH), to manage the commissioning and deployment of the NHS system. From their website:

"NHS Connecting for Health is delivering the National Programme for IT to bring modern computer systems into the NHS which will improve patient care and services. Over the next ten years, the National Programme for IT will connect over 30,000 GPs in England to almost 300 hospitals and give patients access to their personal health and care information, transforming the way the NHS works."[4]

So every GPs surgery is due to be linked to every hospital, facilitating remote, as well as on-site access to the medical records of over 50 million patients. The immediate concern of many doctors on learning of the proposals was the security and privacy of medical records and the British Medical Association has officially raised these concerns with the government. By April 2006, 23 leading professors from Oxford, Cambridge, Edinburgh, the Open University, the London School of Economics and other universities were sufficiently concerned about developments to write an open letter to the House of Commons Health Select Committee questioning the viability, security and management of the system.

By the summer of 2006 multiple problems with the electronic appointment booking system were being reported, though only 12 of 176 major hospitals had implemented the system. This included regular systems crashes and failure to record patient details, described by one NHS manager as 'a potentially significant clinical risk'. By July 2006, the system, installed by ten of the primary health care trusts in London, to track child vaccination rates, led to eight of those trusts being unable to provide vaccination records on about 50,000 children. The Health Protection Agency[5] described this as a "major public health threat". These problems largely arose because the system had to be implemented at short notice because the supplier of the old system "withdrew support for its ageing system from the market".[6] By August 2006 the £1 billion system supporting eight large hospitals in the West Midlands crashed heavily, leaving everadaptable and dedicated NHS staff to return to pen and paper to track patient appointments and movements.

For about 75 years miners in the UK relied on canaries to detect the presence of poisonous gases like carbon monoxide or methane. Everyone passing the canary cage would check on the bird's condition and if it was showing signs of distress or swaying on its perch the alarm was raised for the miners to get out. The catalogue of failures in the NHS National Programme for IT have been mirrored in many of the other major technology based information systems the government have been attempting to implement since the advent of the World Wide Web[7] and before. It makes you wonder if these failures represent the canaries indicating that perhaps government is not the best place to be constructing and piloting some of the largest and most complex information systems the world has ever seen. Yet there is every indication that the private sector is just as prone to failures in information systems management. Anyone who has changed their address regularly, such as university students, has horror stories about getting utilities and financial institutions to register the change.

The staff involved in the government projects are amongst the most dedicated and professional you could hope to find anywhere in the public or private sectors. Officials in charge such as Richard Granger at the NHS IT programme and Ian Watmore who was the government's chief e-government official for 18 months between 2004 and 2006,[8] are amongst the most highly respected in the field of information systems. And inevitably the big IT failures are the ones that get publicised rather than routine success stories. 'Government information system works' doesn't stimulate headlines. The Passport Office have transcended their initial problems with their computer system introduced in the late 1990s and are operating efficiently again.[9] The Government Gateway website allowing registration for online government services has also been praised by users.[10]

Yet ultimately it is the failures that give rise to concerns and ministers that make the final decisions on these systems, ministers who admit themselves that they have no in-depth understanding of the systems.[11] Ministers operate in an adversarial political system that uses failures to score points and often do not have the time or capacity to develop the level of understanding or perspective required to manage these systems. It is also the failures we need to pay attention to if we are to avoid building those failure modes into more ambitious information systems projects in the future.

To some degree this chapter is aimed at helping provide that perspective, using Bruce Schneier's 5-step approach[12] to evaluate the proposed UK identity card system and other large government database projects. It is eminently possible, even for inexperienced policymakers like new junior government ministers, to grasp the essence of complex information systems, if they are prepared to examine their proposed systems with the requisite degree of critical thought.

Firstly, though, I would like to consider the nature of risks, hazards and uncertainties that lead us to consider deploying these types of information systems.

DDM: risks, hazards (threats) and uncertainties

In so far as it is possible, bearing in mind the Ackoff-messy nature of DDM in the real world, I believe we should use rational, transparent, objective processes, backed by solid evidence when making decisions about the deployment and regulation of large-scale information and communications technology projects. The UK, the US and many other governments formally require the use of 'cost benefit analysis' when considering large-scale projects, a principle that is arguably rooted in rational decision making.[13] The UK government define cost benefit analysis as:

"Analysis which quantifies in monetary terms as many of the costs and benefits of a proposal as feasible, including terms for which the market does not provide a satisfactory measure of economic value."

Money is the main driver but the government definition recognises that there are other things of value that are not easily assigned a monetary value. One of the reasons the government give for introducing a biometric identity card system, for example, is to fight terrorism. They estimate the scheme will cost about £6 billion.[14] The claimed benefit of fighting terrorism, however, is very difficult to value in pure monetary terms and it is not clear that the government have fulfilled its own requirement to subject the proposal to a cost benefit analysis anyway. They have bluntly refused to publish any information to that effect,[15] on the grounds that it is commercially sensitive. There are two instantly noteworthy points here.

Firstly, understanding the purpose(s) or benefit(s) of the proposed digital system and weighing that benefit against the system's cost is a sensible general approach to DDM, in my opinion.[16]

Secondly, the numbers matter even if they are difficult to quantify as is the case with something like terrorism. If we are spending money on information systems to achieve social ends, like fighting terrorism or protecting children, we need to understand something about how likely it is that the events the system is targeted at might occur; and how effective these systems might be.

The miners' canary was a simple, economical but effective early-warning information system. The *threat* or *hazard* of the build-up of noxious gases was clearly understood and the canary monitoring provided early detection and response to the danger.

A *hazard* or *threat* is something which is known to cause harm, like poisonous gases building up in a mine, a river flooding, a hurricane blowing through a city, a road traffic accident, a terrorist setting off a bomb on the London Underground or a bad decision about a large information system.

A *risk* is the likelihood or probability of the hazard occurring and the resulting damage should the hazard materialise.[17] The probability of a poisonous gas build-up in a well-ventilated mine might be relatively low but the seriousness of the consequences – dead or seriously ill miners – makes the risk important enough to require serious attention.

This presents us with a problem. We are pretty good at imagining threats and their consequences, such as terrorist bombings or murders. Even folks like me, lacking in imagination, get an abundant supply of such possible threats from the media, politicians and the vendors of security systems. We are not very good, however, at evaluating some kinds of risks, such as the risk of a terrorist attack or a child murder. Neither are most of us particularly good at handling the mathematics of probability theory.

The psychology of risk (perception v reality)

The psychology of risk is something of an addendum to the story I told in Chapter 2 about know-how. We brush our teeth to avoid painful visits to the dentist. The ship's engineer knows where to tap to get the engine working again. Babies learn to walk and talk and cope with the perils of growing older. Know-how in decision making essentially gets automatically programmed into our brains through our experience and interaction with the world around us. This know-how extends to an intuition about risk. We will avoid dark alleys at night, particularly those known to be frequented by street gangs. The public school boy in uniform may well cross the street to avoid a group of boys from the local comprehensive school in a poor area of town. We do not give sharp kitchen knives to young children. Evolution dictates that if we did not have a decent intuition about hazards and the risks of their occurring we would not have survived this long.[18]

So if we have a natural intuition about risk, why are we so bad at judging some risks? One reason is that the modern world pollutes our intuition about risk. Firstly, as technology changes rapidly and modern society becomes more complex, we cannot evaluate certain risks properly because we are so far removed from them. In the UK this includes the risk of terrorist acts, which thankfully are extremely rare. If we do not have direct contact with or past experience of particular types of situations, technologies or environments we cannot develop an intuition or know-how about the associated risks.

Secondly external factors such as media reporting of dramatic incidents lead us to overestimate the likelihood of certain risks and simultaneously underestimate the likelihood of others. After the train crash at Potters Bar in the UK in 2002 and the vast acreage of newsprint and TV coverage devoted to rail safety and how the lessons of the previous Hatfield crash were ignored, many rail passengers switched to commuting by road. Yet the chances of getting killed or seriously injured on the roads are far greater than on the railways. In the wake of the attacks of the 11th of September 2001 in the US, the 11th of March 2004 in Madrid and the 7th of July 2005 in London there was a massive increase in public fear of terrorist attacks and wild media, political and social speculation about everything from dirty bombs to chemical weapons attacks.

After the tragic Soham murders,[19] public fear focused on the dangers to children. When the Washington snipers were on the loose in 2002,[20] shooting at people at petrol stations, bus stops and school playgrounds, people understandably kept their children inside and drove out of town to get petrol. The snipers killed ten people. Yet the chances of getting caught up in a fatal road traffic accident, due to driving those extra miles, were far higher than the possibility of getting shot at by the snipers. Cass Sunstein says the risk did not justify the fear.[21] Mind you, if driving the children to and from school made them less fearful of getting shot, then the psychological benefits of having the children more relaxed probably justified the extra risk of taking the car. Though the long-term health effects on children largely ferried around in short journeys by car rather than walking or cycling is another hazard to factor into that particular equation.

Thirdly there are as many different perspectives about how risky a situation is as there are people thinking about it. Everyone has their own unique view. As people naturally talk to each other about prominent but rare cases with a high media profile, like plane crashes or earthquakes, Sunstein believes we get a kind of 'social cascade' where the size of the risk gets talked up out of all proportion to reality. This exaggeration of certain risks is therefore a function of our sociable nature, as well as what he calls a particular event's 'availability'. The more readily we can bring some event to mind, the more likely we are to believe it has a high probability of occurring. Hence terrorist incidents, brutal murders, natural disasters, brought to our attention by the media, have a disproportionate effect on our psyche and intuition about risk.

Group polarisation is a special case of these social cascades whereby a group of like-minded people can talk each other into believing a particular risk is even greater or less than any of them ever believed to begin with.

Group thinking of this nature is popularly thought to be behind President Kennedy's mistakes over the Bay of Pigs.[22]   Jacob Zuma, when Deputy President of South Africa, was also head of the council advising the South African President about AIDS. Zuma believes that having a shower after sex is an adequate means to prevent transmission of the HIV virus and that a 'healthy man' is unlikely to catch the virus from a woman.[23] Solid long-standing scientific and medical evidence demonstrates how wrong he is. That someone so influential should hold such demonstrably false beliefs should be of serious concern to all of us.

Teenagers are also typically branded as being unaware of the real dangers of unprotected sexual intercourse and boys, in particular, prone to egging each other on. It is unfair, however, to accuse all teenagers of being so ill-informed. My point is that some people, especially scientific and medical experts, may be expected to know more about the risks than others; and when particular experts have well-informed views backed by experience and solid scientific evidence, I believe those views should factor heavily in any decisions we make about assessing risk or other elements of DDM processes.

Unfortunately the scientific community are not good at communicating with the general public and often only come to wider public attention when the media reports spectacular failures or successes of the effects of scientific advice. This in turn can lead to a general mistrust of or alternatively a blind acceptance of what scientists say. Neither extreme is conducive to helping us as a society tap into science as a sound resource to aid decision making.

We tend to fear and exaggerate the risks of things we do not understand like complex new technologies. This engenders opposition to large-scale digital surveillance systems like ID cards or air passenger screening systems and science painted as 'scary' like nanotechnology, which some fear could turn the entire earth into lifeless grey goo.[24]   In Europe there is widespread opposition to genetically modified foods and gene therapy research. Interestingly, in the US where the technology is not widely discussed or publicised, people have been consuming large quantities of GM foods, seemingly without concern, for a generation.

At an Open University summer school at the height of the mad cow disease scare in the UK, the fire alarm went off one morning. A woman told me later she hadn't bothered to leave the building because she had just assumed it was a fire drill, yet on that occasion the alarm had been set off by a toaster catching fire in one of the kitchens. I asked her if she still ate beef and she forcefully told me that of course she did not because of the threat associated with mad cow disease. She was more inclined to take action against the risk of eating infected meat than the risk of staying in a burning building. In the wake of the mad cow disease episode many people were sceptical about advice, scientific or otherwise, coming from government on food safety.

One final point to make about risk psychology is that we readily bring to mind personal stories of victims and this has an effect on our assessment of a particular risk. Joseph Stalin said:

"A single death is a tragedy; a million deaths is a statistic."

Likewise it is a shocking fact that a quarter of all children die before they reach the age of five primarily due to water-borne diseases like cholera. That's a statistic of the Stalin variety. But if we see the story of Joe, a happy, smiling, cheeky, four-year-old, the life and soul of his family who, within months his photograph being taken for a press story, dies painfully of cholera and malnutrition, it personifies the tragedy in a way a pure statistic cannot do. It brings home the tragedy of the risks run by children like Joe in a much more concrete way than a number ever could.

So the psychology tells us that our intuition about risk will not always be reliable, perceptions of risk vary widely and the social aspects of risks are very important.

Formal risk assessment and uncertainty

There are a lot of people employed in the risk management business, in government, commerce and civil society.[25] Politicians, the police and security services, road traffic engineers, pressure vessel inspectors, health and safety professionals and child protection charity workers are a small fraction of the types of people involved in attempting to identify, manage and usually reduce risks within their realms of expertise.

They all use highly formalised, detailed, analytical, often quantitative risk assessment processes and procedures to assess the risks they are attempting to manage. These fall into the category of 'social technologies' mentioned in Chapter 2 – strict step-by-step processes, often involving calculations based on hard evidence, leading to an apparently clear answer about the level of risk.

Some of these formal techniques inevitability involve probability sums, since the definition of risk involves the probability of a hazard occurring as well as the damaging consequences if it does. 'Decision analysis' is a technique where 'decision trees' outlining possible options are drawn and the

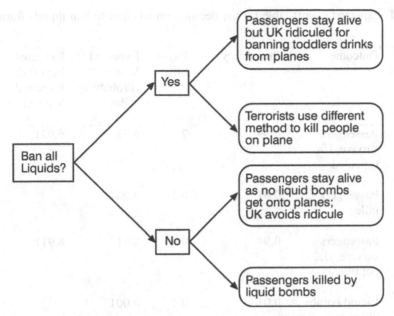

Fig. 5.1 A decision tree for aircraft security

'expected value' of each choice is calculated based on the probability of various outcomes.[26]

Suppose the security services detected and prevented a plot to smuggle bomb-making chemicals onto an aircraft. Suppose further that you are responsible for deciding whether to ban all passengers from carrying liquids onto aeroplanes.

A simplified decision-tree might look like that in Figure 5.1.[27] This is rather a contrived example and there are potentially an infinite number of other possible outcomes but suppose we could know with certainty that these were the only possible outcomes and we knew the probability of each, shown in Table 5.1.

Banning liquids leads to a probability of 0.99 that the passengers will survive and a 0.01 probability that the plane will be attacked with resulting fatalities. Not banning liquids has no effect on these probabilities as the measure is judged ineffective from a security perspective. Note that the probabilities of the two outcomes from each decision must add up to 1.

The payoff numbers in this case are assigned from a scale of 1 to 10. So though banning liquids, leading to the passenger survival outcome, could be considered to merit a 10 out of 10, it is assumed that the extra inconvenience associated with the ban, e.g. of not being able to bring drinks onto a

Table 5.1. Expected payoff table for the decision on whether to ban liquids from airliners

Action	Outcome	Probability	Pay-off	Expected Value (Probability × Payoff)	Expected Payoff (Σ Expected Values)
Ban liquids	Passengers survive, UK ridiculed	0.99	7	6.93	6.931
	Passengers killed	0.01	0.1	0.001	
Do not ban liquids	Passengers survive, UK not ridiculed	0.99	9	8.91	8.911
	Liquid bombs kill passengers	0.01	0.1	0.001	

plane (and the ridicule brought down on the UK for banning drinks from planes) reduces the value to 7. To assign a value to a situation where people actually get killed would be anathema to most people[28] but a security specialist will tell you that lessons learned from a fatal attack can help to defend against such an attack occurring in the future. Hence a small value of 0.1 is assigned to the outcomes where people get killed.

The payoff values multiplied by the probabilities give the expected value of each outcome. Then the expected payoff of each decision (i.e. to ban or not to ban liquids from planes) is the sum of the all the expected values for that decision. If the numbers are to be believed, the expected value of banning liquids is 6.931, whereas the expected value of not banning them is higher at 8.911. This would lead us to conclude that we should not ban liquids from carry-on luggage. If there was some uncertainty about the numbers, say we only knew the probabilities within a particular range, we could play around with the numbers calculating a range of expected outcomes for each decision. This kind of sensitivity analysis is widely used to test the robustness of a particular outcome.

It is easy enough to see then how similar calculations could possibly be made about whether to introduce ID cards to combat illegal immigration or air passenger profiling databases to fight terrorism. In his minority report to the presidential commission on the space shuttle Challenger disaster, Richard Feynman blamed NASA management for failing to take on board the safety warnings of engineers who understood the technology, assessed the risks and declared that the boosters were not safe to fly. In conclusion he said:

"For a successful technology, reality must take preference over public relations, for nature cannot be fooled."[29]

No matter how much we would like a particular technology to solve our problems, if it is not up to the job then we should not be relying on it.

The decision tree example also demonstrates the third key apex of the risk triangle, 'uncertainty'.

Uncertainty is a partial or complete lack of knowledge about a risk or a hazard e.g. the probability of it occurring or the extent the possible damage that might be caused. Thiokol engineers' presentation of the risks of launching the Challenger shuttle in below-freezing conditions carried sufficient uncertainty for the NASA management, given all the other pressures they were operating under, to dismiss the concerns.

Edward R. Tufte suggests that a considerable part of the problem contributing to the uncertainty was the lack of a clear presentation of the O-ring problems by the engineers.[30] He explains that in their anxiety to stop the launch they relied on presenting too much data, via thirteen complicated charts, rather than focusing on the key central problem of the performance of the O-rings at low temperatures. He believes that the seriousness of the problem, therefore, got buried in a mass of irrelevant detail contributing to NASA management uncertainty.

Tufte's work makes fascinating reading and explains a phenomenon I have observed in my own teaching about how technical presentation tools, like the charts drawn up by Thiokol engineers attempting to explain the dangers of launching in below-freezing temperatures, can inhibit rather than enable communication. It is remarkable, for example, how many students, when asked to draw a graph, get distracted by the number of colours their computer graphics tool can produce instead of focusing on the task at hand.[31]

Most formal risk analysis techniques are based on knowing the probabilities. We need to know the numbers before we can do any meaningful calculations with them but we cannot always know the numbers with any degree of certainty. A famous US economist, Frank Knight, put it like this:

"if you don't know for sure what will happen, but you know the odds, that's risk and

if you don't even know the odds, that's uncertainty"[32]

So whereas it is reasonable to assume that the professionals have developed sound risk assessment processes, know a lot about the numbers and are able to sift and analyse the evidence to present facts, it is also reasonable for ordinary people to question these numbers, analyses and facts. Often the level of uncertainty in relation to risk is the elephant in the room that no one wants to talk about. We cannot get away from uncertainty. Whereas it is sometimes possible to know the probabilities as assumed in the airline security example above, in practice the experts often guess the numbers rather than admit uncertainties; and the problem of doing these kinds of calculations can be completely overwhelmed by the level of uncertainty involved.

When the level of uncertainty is a dominant feature it is most frequently the values, beliefs, and agendas of the key decision makers which come to the fore in DDM, as explored in the next chapter. Even when the experts are making apparently rational assessments with hard figures it is worth bearing in mind that the situation may not be as clear cut as their figures might make it appear. Ignoring uncertainty or local know-how does not make them go away.

Does the road traffic expert with statistics demonstrating conclusively that a particular road is safe, because there has never been an accident on it, know better than the local resident who witnesses countless cars speeding down her street; and believes it is only a miracle and local people's sensitivity to the dangers that have avoided such an accident? The expert isolated from the environment he is making risk assessment judgements about does not have the know-how of the local resident. The resident does not have the detailed understanding of the expert's risk assessment processes but they can learn from each other in their efforts to reduce risk and improve local road safety.

It is interesting that the risk management industry's concern is most frequently with reducing risk. In the political arena this is particularly stark with leaders on both sides of the Atlantic regularly advocating the need, in the midst of their ongoing 'war on terror', to introduce measures like large-scale information surveillance systems in order to improve public safety. We are asked to give up a little bit of privacy to improve overall security. People with nothing to hide, we are told, have nothing to fear. The information systems proposed will help catch the baddies and protect the goodies. I will get onto political agendas and the validity of these claims a little later but for the moment I have a question. Is it true that people always want the level of risk they are facing in life to be reduced in accordance with the risk management business' efforts?[33]

Well, as I said above, evolution has effectively turned every single one of us into our own personal risk managers. We make decisions every day that involve taking risks. Some people eat, drink and smoke too much and do not take enough exercise, in spite of the health hazards associated with such a lifestyle. They may not always be consciously aware of it but they are balancing their interpretation of the long-term risks of damage to health against the short-term rewards[34] of enjoying their food, drink and smoking. Many actively seek out the thrill of risky pursuits or professions like mountain climbing or racing car driving. The motto of the Special Air Service (SAS) unit of the British Army[35] is "who dares wins". Just helping the kids to safely cross a busy road to get to the local park involves the balancing of risks and rewards. So perhaps a more legitimate pursuit for those professionally involved in risk management would be the *balancing* of risks against benefits rather than the reduction of risks. Which brings us back again to cost benefit analysis in DDM and the need to weigh the costs against the benefits when making decisions.

Schneier's five steps

Security expert, Bruce Schneier,[36] refers to the kind of cost benefit balancing of risks I've been dealing with here as "security trade-offs". Risk management in DDM is all about these kinds of trade-offs and it is important to understand clearly the trade-offs that are being made in DDM situations. Schneier uses a rational five-step risk management process which he believes applies universally to any decisions about risk management, including DDM, like the deployment of technology for security purposes. He basically asks a series of questions: [37]

- Step 1: What problem are you trying to solve?

- Step 2: What is your solution to the problem?

- Step 3: How well does your solution solve the problem?

- Step 4: What other problems does your solution create?

- Step 5: How much does it cost and is it worth it?

Step 1: What problem are you trying to solve?

Recall that in Chapter 4, when defining 'system', I noted that the question of purpose is incredibly important when dealing with information systems. Many information systems fail for the simple reason that the purpose of the system is never really identified or clarified. Is a database of airline passenger data like the US 'Secure Flight' system supposed to protect airports, passengers, airliners, the transportation system or the US nation from terrorists? These all represent different kinds of security problems. The question involves clarifying the problem and its scope.

It is common for those conceiving of large information systems to avoid this fundamental question by agreeing the system *could help* to solve lots of different problems, without ever identifying the nature of the individual problems clearly.[38] This list of possible problems that the new system could help to solve tends to grow exponentially as the project progresses. This is particularly the case with computer-based information systems because of the widespread belief that computers *should* be able to solve complicated problems.

It is worth noting that identifying the specific problems an information system is supposed to address in a DDM situation is not often easy. Terrorism, immigration, access to public services and social cohesion, to take the UK government's four most commonly cited reasons for introducing ID cards, cannot be categorised as simple 'difficulties'. Each of these is what Russell Ackoff [39] would have called a 'mess' i.e. a large, complex, dynamic, unstructured system of interacting problems and confusion. Nevertheless, extracting and clarifying specific problems from that mess is the function of Schneier's first question.

Step 2: What is your solution to the problem?

In the case of passenger security, for example, how do we defend against potential attacks e.g. against airline passengers, airports, planes, other buildings? One 'solution' might be 'know the history of all the passengers' (so that terrorists can be identified). This is the apparent solution offered by airline passenger databases like 'Secure Flight' in the US. Or it is 'ban liquids from planes, so that bombs cannot be made on board'? This is an apparent solution offered by the UK government in the wake of the foiled airliner terror attacks in the summer of 2006.

Step 3: How well does your solution solve the problem?

Will this solution genuinely protect us? This can be a tough question to answer and again is surprisingly frequently neglected. Basically if the information system does not address the original reason for building the system then it is no good. If it does solve the problem, how does it do so, how well does it do so and what impact does it have on the people and other systems which interact with it? In what ways can the system fail? How can it fail naturally e.g. power failures; and how can it be made to fail by an attacker with malign intent? What are the consequences should an attack succeed – death or serious injuries and damage to property – and how do we respond to such circumstances?

Step 4: What other problems does your solution create?

New information systems always have unanticipated, unintended and unpredictable (or emergent) effects.[40] What security problems might a new database have? What are the consequences of errors in the system? How likely is it that the system will contain errors? Will complexities in data processing procedures compound errors? A key problem is the creation of *dependency on the specific solution.* So people assume that 'the system' will notify them of hazards, and forget or neglect common sense checks.

Are the new problems more or less severe than the problems the system was built to solve? In 2006 the UK Criminal Records Bureau wrongly identified 2700 individuals as having criminal records, when they or an associated organisation applied for the standard check as part of a job application or undertaking a volunteer role.[41] Consequent loss of a job opportunity led to dire financial circumstances in some of those cases. In the wake of the publication of these cases the Home Office declared that the system was operating very effectively and that the people involved represented only a small proportion of the checks processed by the Bureau.

Step 5: How much does it cost and is it worth it?

How much does the system cost? If the new problems *are* less severe than the old problems, is the cost of reaching this new state justified both in terms of resources spent and other things? The cost of increased airport security, for example, in the wake of the terrorist attacks in the US on 11 September 2001[42] includes the inconvenience of passengers having to arrive at the airport much earlier for flights, provide extra personal information, remove shoes, be subjected to personal searches, prevented from carrying drinks on board and such like. These inconveniences don't always have easily measurable costs but some, like delays to flights, extra fuel use, additional crew requirements etc., do have simple, quantifiable costs.

Since it is a relatively straightforward, rational approach, I'd like to use Schneier's questions to help analyse a number of DDM situations that follow: ID cards and networked databases.

DDM: the database solution

The notion that if we collect enough data on everyone it will help solve a range of social, political and economic problems has gained a lot of traction in recent times. Now there is little doubt that databases are a useful commercial and administrative tool. Does this mean that large networked databases, such as that proposed for the UK identity card system, are the panacea that is sometimes claimed? The remainder of this chapter examines the robustness of the universal networked database solution.

Identity architecture – commerce and government

It is a fact of networked life that in order to do business reliably via the Internet, individuals, businesses and governments need some kind of identity system in order to generate confidence and trust that each party will follow through with their end of the bargain e.g. pay or send the goods. If I walk into a bookshop and choose a book, I can go directly to the counter, pay cash and leave with my book and receipt in the bookshop's carrier bag. The shop does not need to know anything about me. No further questions asked. If I buy a book from the Amazon bookshop online, I need to supply them with an email address and password, a mailing address and credit card or other payment method details. Actually Amazon do not really care who I am as long as they know where to send the book and they get paid.[43] If the government want to pay out social security benefits via the Net, however, they need to know that the person accessing the payment is the person entitled to it. So the identity system will have slightly different requirements.

The information age and the convenience of buying books via the Internet has changed the amount of information I have to release about myself, if I want to take advantage of these new services it facilitates. An extra identification process has been injected into the transaction. The new technology has created the need for an identification process and an identification policy which did not previously exist when buying a book.

People who use the Internet regularly may be familiar with two simple forms of identity systems:

1. Username and password e.g. increasingly media outlets like the *New York Times* provide full access to paying subscribers who use an account name and password to get onto the site.

2. Cookies are small files which get entered on our computers' memories when we visit some websites. That website and others,

depending on the type of cookie, uses that file to interact with the computer user by remembering where the user has gone before. They can be used to 'personalise information' and target advertisements for example. Some cookies are leakier than others in the amount of information they share and with which websites.

More generally government and commerce require systems of identity or 'identity metasystems' or 'identity architecture' which include the following features:

- authentication – you are who you say you are
- authorisation – you have the authority to spend £x or $y
- privacy – in communication
- non-repudiation – you cannot deny it was you who committed to the deal
- integrity – transmission not altered en route (someone receiving the message should be able to check whether it has been interfered with).

All of these together form what is called the system's 'identity architecture'.

We need to accept that if a government wants to deliver public services via the Internet some kind of identity or authentication system will be needed. For those who instantly recoil at the idea, though, this is not as bad as it might at first appear. It is possible to build an identity system that respects personal privacy and compartmentalises our dealings with government in a way that mirrors our real-world interactions.[44] It is also possible to build in safeguards in such a way that if ever a despotic regime came to control the system, they would find it difficult to exploit for oppressive or inhumane ends, as the Nazis did after invading Holland, in the case of the Dutch registration system created for relatively benign purposes before the war.[45] A system originally created for benign reasons came to be used for despotic ends by the Nazis because the Dutch failed to build in sufficient barriers against misuse.

Identity and identification policies are not well understood outside the small circle of bureaucrats, academics and professionals who work with identification systems and technologies or write about them. They are not things most people actively think about. They don't have to. How do I know a particular work colleague for instance? Well I know what they look like – male or female, skin and hair colour, how tall they are, general shape etc. – and perhaps their characteristic laugh. The Open University issues all employees with electronic ID cards with the employee's name, photo and a chip that acts as an electronic pass to allow entry to University buildings. I also might know them by their particular area of expertise, so for example if I need some technical advice on a computer problem I will contact a reliable colleague in our computer and network services department. All these things are identifying features and writers on identity generally categorise these under three distinct headings:

1. 'Something you are' which includes physical attributes such as whether you are male or female, how tall, what shape, voice, fingerprints, DNA, irises, signature, face and other biometrics. A feature of 'something you are' identifiers, including fingerprints and DNA (which we leave traces of when holding a mug or shedding a loose hair or piece of dead skin) is that they are public.

2. 'Something you have' such as your name, address, social security number, an ID card, a credit card, a key to a safety deposit box, a club membership card – just open your purse or wallet and see how many such tokens you have yourself. A feature of 'something you have' identifiers is that you have control of them, though some, like a name are given to you by others.

3. 'Something you know', for example a password to enable you to log onto your work's computer system or some element of personal or professional knowledge that few others know, like a mother's maiden name which financial institutions often use as a security check. A feature of 'something you know' identifiers is that they are secret to you and those you choose to share them with.

Everyone has multiple identities. For example, parent, partner, child, employee and/or employer, tenant or home owner, educator, sports fanatic, citizen, customer, traveller, driver, neighbour, coach and many more. We control and compartmentalise these identities to help manage our lives in a variety of roles. It is also possible to design an identity system whereby the user controls what information they share with the system.

If the notion of an ID card brings forth visions of Nazis or a police state that is because they are emotive and genuinely frightening visions of how ID papers have been misused in the past. We certainly need to actively avoid stumbling by default into such a state, just because the technology of mass surveillance is now more readily available and nominally more sophisticated. We also need to avoid deploying these technologies blindly in response to some perceived threat. Without sufficient reasoned analysis of the purpose and detailed requirements of the technical systems we propose to build to counter these threats, we could find ourselves building technological monsters.

Like it or not those of us who live in the privileged parts of the world that we can consider to be information societies, are constantly being tracked by our digital shadows: information we have disclosed to government and commerce, which thereafter is processed and aggregated, bought and sold in multiple transactions enabling digital profiles of our lives to be constructed.[46] Sometimes these profiles might be accurate. On other occasions they will be way off the mark. You only have to consider the children's game of Chinese whispers to see how things can get distorted. One child whispers a message to another and the message gets passed on in whispers, one at a time to every child in the group. Inevitably by the time it gets to the final person in the group the message has changed. Similarly electronic data released in the context of one commercial transaction, e.g. when buying a television, gets distorted and re-interpreted through multiple processes and aggregations. This can have serious consequences if the profile is being drawn to decide if you are a terrorist suspect or a poor prospect for insurance, rather than whether to send you another junk mail offer for a credit card.

I have a rough rule of thumb that, whilst they should not unreasonably constrain what we can and should do with new technologies, the real world and the past have a lot to teach us about how to do things on the Net in a whole range of areas from education to business. They also have a lot to teach us about *how not to* do things on the Net. This applies in the case of identity systems too. Microsoft's chief identity architect, Kim Cameron, puts it like this:

"the natural contextual specialization of everyday life is healthy and protective of the structure of our social systems, and this should be reflected in our technical systems. A technology proposal that aims to eliminate compartmentalization rejects one of the fundamental protective mechanisms society has evolved. The resulting central database, where everything is connected and visible to everything else, is as vulnerable as a steel ship with no compartments – one perforation, and the whole thing goes down."[47]

So, when building an identity system we should build in the compartmentalisation of identity that society has sensibly evolved to protect personal privacy. Cameron and others have developed a set of principles that should form the foundation of a technical identity system, which he calls the *Seven Laws of Identity.*[48] Briefly these laws mandate:

1. "User Control and Consent
Technical identity systems must only reveal information identifying a user with the user's consent.

2. Minimal Disclosure for a Constrained Use

The solution that discloses the least amount of identifying information and best limits its use is the most stable long-term solution.

3. Justifiable Parties

Digital identity systems must be designed so the disclosure of identifying information is limited to parties having a necessary and justifiable place in a given identity relationship.

4. Directed Identity

A universal identity system must support both 'omni-directional' identifiers for use by public entities and 'unidirectional' identifiers for use by private entities, thus facilitating discovery while preventing unnecessary release of correlation handles.[49]

5. Pluralism of Operators and Technologies

A universal identity system must channel and enable the inter-working of multiple identity technologies run by multiple identity providers.

6. Human Integration

The universal identity metasystem must define the human user to be a component of the distributed system integrated through unambiguous human–machine communication mechanisms offering protection against identity attacks.[50]

7. Consistent Experience Across Contexts

The unifying identity metasystem must guarantee its users a simple, consistent experience while enabling separation of contexts through multiple operators and technologies."

The essence of it is that just as we have multiple identities in real life – father, partner etc. – we need to be able to carry those identities into our online personas. And it is technically possible to facilitate this with a decentralised or 'distributed architecture' design. Basically Cameron's laws say that we need to compartmentalise our digital or online identities by using multiple user-friendly and privacy-enhancing identity systems. The informal social construction of identity has provided us with safeguards we have never really seriously considered or actively valued but which we should be careful not to lose in a rush to build systems quickly rather than thoughtfully. Otherwise we might only really appreciate it, like many things, when it is gone.

When the London School of Economics instigated a detailed study of the UK government's national identity card proposals, they started out by saying that an identity system to facilitate 'e-government' was a good idea in principle.[51] Incidentally I believe there is no such thing as e-government, e-speech, e-commerce, e-learning or e-anything else and in time most people will come to realise that just as the telephone, car, radio and all kinds of other technologies have been absorbed by society, the Internet will be too. It is just another communication medium.

In the wake of the attacks in the US of 11th of September 2001, the then Home Secretary in the UK, David Blunkett, proposed a national identity card system to combat terrorism and benefit fraud.[52] There have been multiple reasons citied by government spokespersons for needing an ID card system, most frequent amongst them being to reduce the risk of terrorism, benefit fraud and identity theft and to tackle the problems of immigration. With apologies to those who have done much more in-depth analyses, most notably the folks at the London School of Economics and their associated experts around the world, I would just like to take a quick look at the proposed UK ID system using Bruce Schneier's five questions.

The UK ID system and Schneier's five steps

Step 1: What problem is the UK ID card system attempting to solve?

Answer: From the UK Home Office website –

ID cards will:

- help protect people from identity fraud and theft
- ensure that people are who they say they are
- tackle illegal working and immigration abuse
- disrupt the use of false and multiple identities by criminals and those involved in terrorist activity
- ensure free public services are only used by those entitled to them
- enable easier access to public services.[53]

This list has evolved over the years since the original proposal and tends to be fairly fluid. The text of the Identity Cards Act 2006 is available online.[54] One of the more amusing reasons given by ministers for needing an ID card system was that it would help catch people who avoid speed camera fines.[55] Note that this is not related to any of the main reasons outlined on the Home Office site but is indicative of other planned multiple uses.

Immediately we run into a DDM problem. If the purpose of the system is not clear, if we are not organised in advance of designing the system and if the list of things the system is supposed to do changes frequently, it will certainly fail.

The government may be avoiding the fundamental question about what the purpose of the system really is by agreeing the system *could or should* (after all it is a computer system) help to solve these different problems. The problems listed are general and (Ackoff) messy. Immigration and terrorism are large, complex, dynamic, unstructured systems of interacting problems and confusion. Identity fraud is arguably less complex but is a different type of problem. Nevertheless, extracting and clarifying specific problems from that mess is the function of the decision maker and the decision making process. If the system is to aid the fight against terrorism the decision maker needs to specify how and what particular elements of the complex terrorism mess it will address. If you do not know what you want the system to do, computerising it will not fix your problem and it certainly will not sort out a mess.

Step 2: What is your solution to the problem?

Answer: The UK Identity Card System

The legislation mandating the introduction of the identity card system was passed in the spring of 2006. The system proposed by the government has four main technical subsystems

1. The identity card itself, embedded with personal details including biometrics such as fingerprints, iris scans and digital photographs
2. A collection of networked centres all round the country where people can go to get their details registered for the system (and updated as necessary)
3. A large networked central database which holds all the data on everyone
4. A large number of networked card readers held by government services, commerce and anyone else who is required to check the ID cards.

Given that three of the generic functions are to combat terrorism, immigration and benefit fraud this will mean that the central database will be connected to law enforcement, intelligence and immigration databases as well as social security and other government DDM systems. There are also proposals suggesting the system will enable a great number of government departments to link their data through the system to facilitate efficiency and economies of scale.

The proposed system, by using a large central database to hold all the data, immediately falls foul of the laws of identity since it breaches the compartmentalisation requirements. Arguably it breaches all seven laws.

Step 3: How well does your solution solve the problem?

Answer: It is not clear that the system addresses the messes it is being set up to tackle.

Step 4: What other problems does your solution create?

Answer: A large central database of the type that is envisaged is virtually impossible to secure, especially when the data it contains is so valuable. It suffers from the 'all the eggs in one basket' syndrome in being a large and very valuable data goldmine making it an attractive target for criminal gangs. When setting up a DDM system it is important to understand how it can fail. How can it fail naturally e.g. through errors in entering the data and how can it be made to fail by an attacker with malign intent e.g. an outsider or insider who wants to compromise the system for their own nefarious ends, such as engaging in fraud? Unfortunately at the time of writing the UK Home Office record on managing much, much smaller databases is not good. The chances of the database being compromised are very high and the impact on individuals who details are misused could be severe. People whose ID card gets damaged will run into difficulties getting a new one. People whose data is erroneously processed will have problems and the process of getting errors put right could prove complex. On top of all these is the solution dependency problem mentioned above. The lowly paid and bored check-in or security person will accept the stolen ID card used by a terrorist who does not even look like the real owner of the card 'because the card was OK'.[56]

Step 5: How much does it cost and is it worth it?

Answer: The government estimate the system will cost nearly £6 billion. The London School of Economics study estimates it could be more than three times as much. Other trade-offs, such as the inconvenience of having to attend a registration centre to get registered, problems arising from errors in the system, what happens when a card gets lost and lots of others are impossible to quantify at this stage. Is it worth it? That is a value judgement. The government have decided yes. You may agree or disagree. On balance if I was making the decision and had £6 billion to invest in tackling a complex mess like terrorism I would probably invest that money in better law enforcement and intelligence capacity and resources. An accountant would say that the 'opportunity cost' of investing in the ID card system is that the money is not available for the police and intelligence services.

Other networked database solutions[57]

Two other database related surveillance systems, which have received nothing like the publicity surrounding identity cards, are air passenger profiling and the proposed UK Children's Index.

Air passenger profiling

In addition to the ID card system, the UK government has set up a number of other databases to tackle perceived threats like terrorism, such as the £15 million 'air passenger profiling system' called 'Project Semaphore', developed by IBM. The general idea is to collect enough data about each passenger to build a profile of the kind of person they are and assess the level of threat they might pose. This was announced in 2004 as the first stage in the government's e-borders programme "which will use 21st century technology to strengthen border control".[58] The current system is fairly basic. Airlines record passenger details in advance of certain flights to the UK and provide these details to the UK Joint Border Operations Centre (JBOC), where it is checked against a suspicious persons list. Matching details are flagged to the immigration, law enforcement, intelligence and security services, theoretically in sufficient time to stop any nasty plots. All airlines operating into major UK airports are supposed to be wired up to the scheme by 2010.

The US has similar systems which it has been operating over a longer period of time, the US-VISIT[59] and Secure Flight systems. Secure Flight which has evolved from earlier Computer Assisted Passenger Pre-screening Systems (CAPPS and CAPPS II) set up in the 1990s, is the domestic version of the system and is used to screen US passengers against watch lists. This includes a no-fly list identifying individuals who should not be allowed on a plane because of the potential level of risk involved.[60] Notable people who have falsely appeared on the list and run into trouble as a result at airports include Senator Ted Kennedy, a four-year-old boy and quite a few high-ranking government employees with ultra high level security clearances.[61] The Electronic Privacy Information Center reported in December 2005 that at least 30,000 people had been wrongly matched to watch lists.[62] These 30,000 had written to the government asking to be taken of the watch lists and were sent letters to allow them to clear airport security without undue interference.

It is an attractive idea that if we collect enough information on enough people then a computer system will help identify those small numbers of individuals who pose a real threat to our security. It also turns out to be an unsound idea and leads to a potentially dangerous misappropriation of scarce resources for real security. Money that could be used to recruit and train more intelligence officers and provide the resource base for them to gather intelligence, investigate, engage in preventative measures and emergency response in the face of serious crime, is being invested in rather loosely specified computer systems like Secure Flight and Semaphore. Misplaced trust in the efficacy of these systems can also lead to security being compromised if security personnel rely too heavily on them and neglect other tried and tested security techniques. This is another example of the law of unintended consequences.

Think about the case of the 30,000. They were obliged to apply for a letter to declare they are not really terrorist suspects and most of them probably shouldn't really be on a no-fly list. How much effort is going into processing those claims alone? How does it help with airline security? What if someone getting an all-clear letter really is a serious security risk? At the time of writing neither Secure Flight nor Project Semaphore has lead to the apprehension of any terrorist suspects.

The Children Act 2004

The Children Act of 2004 committed the UK government to creating a Children's Index database. There are a whole series of databases relating to children in the UK run by public authorities with the aim of enhancing or protecting the welfare of children.[63] The Children's Index or 'Information Sharing and Assessment' (ISA) system is planned to provide comprehensive set of links to all public agency contacts with an individual child. The register should enable professionals who have had contact with a child to find and liaise with each other though not necessarily contain the case details.[64]

Lord Laming's investigations and report into the murder of Victoria Climbie identified serious failures in communications between agencies which had already identified the little girl as being at risk and recommended a clearer information-sharing process between police, social services, national health services, schools and other agencies with child welfare responsibilities. Similar failures in sharing information about Ian

Huntley, who had been identified by at least one police authority as a serious threat to young women and children, enabled him to get a job as a school caretaker. Huntley subsequently murdered two-ten-year old girls who attended the school in Soham, Holly Wells and Jessica Chapman. There are plans in government to link the Children's Index to the national identity card system, which is a neat example of both the blind dependency problem – i.e. assuming the system will work and ignoring all other alerts based on for example common sense – and the over-extension or 'mission creep' of the ID card 'solution' to an area it was not originally intended to address.

The networked database data mining fallacy

Tied up with all these database solutions is the idea that a computer can suck up vast swathes of roughly organised data and identify patterns, links and anomalies. So far, so good. Computers are very good at identifying patterns, links and anomalies, so-called 'data mining'. Computers are even good at mining for patterns without necessarily specifying the patterns in advance, since two UCLA professors, David Jefferson and Chuck Taylor, developed a program called 'Tracker' in the 1980s to simulate the behaviour of ants. It was based on the early theoretical work of John Holland on computer simulations and genetic algorithms in the 1960s and 70s.[65] Holland realised that natural selection might have something to teach us about computer programming. Evolution demonstrates that billions of tiny simple components, e.g. cells or genes, following simple rules could lead to complex emergent behaviour and life forms.[66] From simplicity and apparent chaos on a massive scale emerges life and the processing power of computers meant it could be simulated, at least with simpler life forms such as ants. Computers are brilliant at carrying out millions of simple instructions very quickly and generating patterns or useful results.

In order to be effective in dealing with specific and clearly identified problems related to terrorism, immigration, fraud or child welfare, though, these patterns have to be useful, reliable, precise and accurate. Just because computers can identify patterns does not mean they can sift through a mass of data about every member of the population and magically point at the bad guys, especially when the form of the data is rather vague. Simulating the emergent patterns of a large collective of simple organisms, which exhibit a limited number of simple individual actions or behaviours, is a completely different problem to simulating or predicting the emergent complex behaviours of one or a small group of members of a large population of complex organisms i.e. humans. And when that mass of data includes not just facts but value judgements very serious care is needed in interpreting any patterns or threats highlighted. Programming a computer to identify a threat is much more difficult than programming it to record the number of twos in a set of random data or to simulate the pattern of behaviour of a colony of ants. In its simplest form, for example, the ant program assumes that each and every ant acts in precisely the same way when faced with precisely the same set of circumstances. Yet different people act in different ways when faced with the same situation.

Another problem is the sheer quantity of data that has to be processed. In a database like the planned national identity register, which itself will hold three to four billion top level items of data, the numbers of links, patterns and anomalies it would be possible to identify are potentially infinite. And the kinds of patterns we need to flag in order to identify a potential threat are not obvious. Is the person who flies 100,000 miles a year a terrorist threat or a business traveller? Is the person who only takes five flying lessons the next 9/11 type attacker or someone who has decided not to pursue the flying hobby due to lack of funds or interest? Is someone called Ted Kennedy a risk because his name is on a terrorist watch list? When terrorists do use false identities they sometimes choose the names of famous people. Is someone who pays for all goods and services with cash rather than a credit card suspicious?

Suspicious and complex social behaviours have to be identified and specified in computing or mathematical algorithms *before* the computer can be programmed. Such behaviours are not easy to specify in computer code. Unlike evolution or Taylor and Jefferson's 'Tracker' programme, where they were trying to identify emergent patterns from simple instructions, we need to identify simple behaviour – e.g. 'an identifiable individual is going to attack' – from complex instructions which are extremely difficult to specify.

Identifying what specific data to collect, deciding how to sort and organise it, identifying specific types of analysis that can be stated as mathematical algorithms, which can be turned into computer programs to extract the patterns and useful information from your data, are all non-trivial tasks. Too often the approach in this kind of DDM is to say 'collect as much data as we can on everyone and let the tech experts sort out the details'.

The defence of the 'collect as much data as we can' line regularly used is the oft quoted 'If you have nothing to hide then you have nothing to fear.' I generally get irritated when someone says 'nothing to fear nothing to hide' because it is offered as a baseless, empty, rhetorical, debating trick, the like of which I will examine in more detail in the next chapter. I use the word 'debating' reluctantly there as it assumes a real engagement which does not exist in this case. Not only is it a lazy debating trick but it provides a ready-made excuse for decision makers not to address the hard questions, like those above and the fundamental question: 'what is the purpose of the system?'

There is an in-built assumption in all this pattern matching that if a pattern is found it is meaningful. To put it another way it assumes that *correlation* is the same as *causation*, always a lacuna of data mining. The standard example is that the number of Methodist church ministers and British grain imports in the 19th-century show a significant positive correlation.[67] Yet it is pretty unlikely that anyone would claim the number of ministers determined the amount of grain imported or vice versa. Correlation does not imply causation.

One of the algorithms for the air passenger profiling systems is that people with names similar to those on the watch lists should be subject to more intense scrutiny, since criminals sometimes travel under assumed names which are just slightly different to their real ones. This leads to one of the key problems of these kind of database profiling systems – innocent people being identified as suspicious – a 'false positive' identification. The other problem is the 'false negatives' – those who constitute a real threat given a clean bill of health by the system. The latter problem is arguably more serious, since the plotter with malign intent can carry on without any security worries. The false positive, on the other hand, 'only' inconveniences the person wrongly suspected of presenting a threat.

Now how do these kinds of errors – false negatives and false positives – affect the efficacy of our database data mining systems? Bruce Schneier has a sample calculation he uses regularly in his writings to assess this.

"assume the system has a one in 100 false-positive rate (99 percent accurate), and a one in 1,000 false-negative rate (99.9 percent accurate). Assume 1 trillion possible indicators to sift through: that's about 10 events – e-mails, phone calls, purchases, Web destinations, whatever – per person in the United States per day. Also assume that 10 of them actually indicate terrorists plotting.

This unrealistically accurate system will generate 1 billion false alarms for every real terrorist plot it uncovers. Every day, the police will have to investigate 27 million potential plots in order to find the one real terrorist plot per month"[68]

Now many readers go into glazed-eyes mode when faced with this kind of calculation but it is worth considering it closely. The numbers show that even assuming you could build an accurate terrorist-finding mass data mining system (no modern technology comes anywhere close yet), it leads to the police having to investigate tens of millions of potential terrorist plots every day to have a chance of finding one real plot every month. So the intuitively attractive notion that we can chuck a vast amount of data into the computer and expect it to pinpoint the bad guys turns out to be false.

If the numbers are confusing, you can look at it from the point of view of trying to find the few dangerous plotters in a population of honest law abiding people. The problem is a bit like the one of finding a needle in a haystack. You don't make it easier to find the needle by throwing more [data] hay on the stack or by creating more and bigger haystacks in other places.

The kind of blanket surveillance of all (mostly innocent) members of a population that underpins these kinds of DDM systems also has a number of general problems:

1. Cost – the systems can be costly to design, build and run.

2. Errors – they are prone to containing errors which have consequences for the subjects of the errors.[69]

3. Wild goose chases and limited resources – the false positive problem leads to excessive use of public authority resources for chasing dead ends. This has the related problem of desensitising those monitoring the systems for alarms. If the overwhelming proportion of alerts is false, the initial response to an alert will be to assume it is false. So the responses to real problems will be impeded.

4. Fishing and abuse – we know that the very existence of large stores of personal information means that there will be a certain amount of abuse. We know it because it has happened before and it doesn't necessarily have to be on the scale of Watergate.[70] Cardinal Richelieu once said that given six lines written by the most honest man, he would find the evidence to hang him.[71] And frankly if you watch someone for long enough you will find something to at least embarrass or even blackmail them with, simply by taking certain information out of context. Suppose a middle-aged businessman is caught on a hotel CCTV camera hugging a young lady in the lobby and then they both retire to his room, coming out a short time later laughing and joking. Many would jump to the wrong conclusion even if it was discovered later that it was just his daughter. Suspicious behaviour can always be found, especially when that is what you are looking for.[72] Limiting surveillance in accordance with thoughtfully constructed legal procedures helps to avoid this kind of abuse.[73]

5. Mission creep – an information store exists which is only supposed to be used for one purpose but it might be useful for another. Resisting

the pressure to extend that purpose can prove to be difficult. The notion of connecting the Children's Index to the National Identity system might be one example.[74] Allowing social services, or the tax authorities or the National Health Services to access the National Identity register in order to check someone out in a way that goes beyond their usual access rules is another example. The US National Security Agency's gathering of call data from the large telephone companies is another. The call data was collected by the companies for their own records and billing purposes. It was passed onto the NSA for spying purposes.[75] The risk that a large data store will be used for purposes other than the original reasons it was set up increases with time. Future authorities will not feel as duty bound as the originators of the system, to stick to its original purpose.

6. Modifying behaviour – people who know they are being watched, modify their behaviour.

7. Civil liberties groups argue that the whole ethos of these large DDM data mining systems undermines a fundamental right to privacy, necessary to maintain dignity. Jeffrey Rosen puts it very nicely "Privacy protects us from being misdefined and judged out of context in a world of short attention spans, a world in which information can easily be confused with knowledge."[76]

So, if we subject these data mining systems to Schneier's analysis what do we get?

Step 1: What problems are the air passenger profiling and children's databases trying to solve? (Or what is the purpose of the DDM system?)

Answer: Risks to the security and welfare of air travellers and children.

Step 2: What is your solution to the problem?

Answer: Building databases and responding to alerts generated algorithmically from these. There is no in-depth analysis of the information these systems will need to generate to fulfil their required purpose. The focus is on the data to be collected, in the hope that it will somehow prove useful, when processed through a computer.

Step 3: (Does it and if so) How well does your solution solve the problem?

Answer: Not at all in the case of the air passenger profiling systems. It all depends, in the case of the Children's Index, on how it gets built and whether it can improve communications between agencies. It essentially suffers from similar problems to the ID card system without the complications of the registration process and the biometric technologies. It is essential to note that computer systems or databases cannot and will not, on their own, solve serious existing social, cultural or political communications problems between different agencies.

Step 4: What other problems does your solution create?

Answer: A data fire-hose overwhelming practitioners with false positive alerts and false negatives leading to tragic outcomes. We need to think about how the systems can fail naturally through errors and how they can be made to fail by people with malign intent. All the data in a central store makes it potentially very insecure just like the old adage of having all your eggs in one basket.

Step 5: How much does it cost and is it worth it?

Answer: The technology hardware is probably the cheapest element of these systems. The cost of throwing more data hay on an already large haystack is arguably much more substantive. The air passenger profiling systems in their current stage of development do not represent a good investment. You do not even need to take my word on that. Four official government reports, including one by a US government task force specially set up to investigate the efficacy of the 'Secure Flight' system found it to be a complete mess.[77]

The jury's out on the Children's Index but a national linking database on its own is not going to solve systemic underlying communications problems between different agencies dealing with vulnerable children. Given that the system provides the master key to all the other children's databases it breaches the compartmentalisation principle of a sound identity system. Instinctively the idea of using technology to help prevent the kinds of tragedy that happened at Soham seems like a good idea but we know by now that instinct is not necessarily a reliable guide with complex information systems. The big concern must be that large numbers of false alarms will not only place unreasonable burdens on families so targeted but will also result in genuine cases of need getting completely missed in the ever-increasing data haystack and associated official activity.

In addition the increasing pressure on child support professionals and others coming into contact with children in a professional context not to miss signs that a child is at risk will encourage a defensive culture to fill in the boxes on official forms. In every organisation the pressure to fill in the form, just because the form exists and it might help the organisation to avoid getting sued in the future, evolves to a state where it becomes routine, even when the original purpose for the existence of the form is long since forgotten. The danger is that small or imagined concerns will get recorded just in case something terrible might happen in future and these concerns might just encourage another professional who had not noticed anything untoward to go back and think again. The pressure on public services to deliver to simple targets could also compound the problem by encouraging those services to concentrate on the easier cases, those that can be managed with resources they have available.

For example, as part of the government's 'Every Child Matters' agenda they have introduced a 'Common Assessment Framework' (CAF), which the government website describes as:

"a standardised approach to conducting an assessment of a child's additional needs and deciding how those needs should be met. It can be used by practitioners across children's services in England.

The CAF will promote more effective, earlier identification of additional needs, particularly in universal services. It is intended to provide a simple process for a holistic assessment of a child's needs and strengths, taking account of the role of parents, carers and environmental factors on their development. Practitioners will then be better placed to agree, with the child and family, about what support is appropriate. The CAF will also help to improve integrated working by promoting co-ordinated service provision." [78]

Any child who is thought not to be meeting government targets relating to lifestyle, health, and development[79] is supposed to be subject to a 'common assessment'. The form[80] can be filled in by anyone who works with children or families. It has well over a hundred data fields asking questions covering a range of issues from basic factual data e.g. name and address, to more subjective issues[81] e.g. relating to the family or home situation, family history, functioning and wellbeing, quality of parenting, physical development, diet, relaxation, emotional and social development, sexual behaviour, self-esteem, personal hygiene, educational development, ambition and quite a few more. The assessment is supposed to be carried out as an "informal non-threatening discussion". Once completed, access to the data will be potentially available to millions of individuals working with children and families, via the Children's Index. Civil rights activists have suggested that the system may breach both the principles of the Data Protection Act 1998,[82] which states that:

"Personal data shall be obtained only for one or more specified and lawful purposes, and shall not be further processed in any manner incompatible with that purpose or those purposes."

and Article 8.1 of the Human Rights Act 1998,[83] which says:

"Everyone has the right to respect for his private and family life, his home and his correspondence."

The government has the power under those acts, however, to sanction exemptions and have indeed said that:

"the Data Protection Act is not a barrier to sharing information".[84]

The government hope that this integrated system will help to provide more 'joined-up' child support and family services to those in need. It is a laudable aim but they need to be alert to the challenges associated with breaking the compartmentalisation principles of support and identity systems. Breaking the data separation between the various functions of government might seem like an attractive idea in the interests of delivering more joined-up government services. But it is itself a step over the line of an established principle which has generally served us well and we should be careful about dismantling i.e. that intimate personal data gathered for one purpose should not be used for a different purpose.

The frustrations of having to get the data subject's permission, before gaining access to or using the data in another context where it might be useful, pale into insignificance in comparison to the abuses that might be perpetrated should a malign influence come to control that data; or even gain illicit access, which may be much more likely. We have a long experience of the benefits of compartmentalisation even if we take them for granted. We have no experience in this country of the real effects of tearing down those functional walls and may not come to appreciate them until they are taken away.

In addition, the pressure to create records and generate patterns, even where they do not really exist, could get compounded exponentially in a large data mining context such as the linking of the multiple children's databases by the Children's Index. The subjective nature of much of the data which will be recorded on a 'common assessment framework' form, for example, sometimes by people not qualified to give a considered opinion in the area they might be assessing,[85] could result in higher numbers of 'false positive' alerts, with genuine cases of need being missed. Given that the object of the index is to provide an access route to patterns of behaviour or risk of every child in the country, in the hope of identifying those in need of support, the resulting fire hose of data could potentially prove overwhelming. The child protection problem is, as the Information Commissioner, Richard Thomas, has said a needle in a haystack problem. The challenge of finding the children in desperate need of the support of already over-stretched professionals is not made any easier by throwing more data hay on the stack.

Remember the basic rule of building information systems is that we need to get organised and decide what we want them to do *before* introducing the computers. Vaguely connecting computers in the hope that they will magically sort out a systemic mess will only add a problematic computer system to the list of existing problems. As I say to my own children, before you lean on something you should make sure it is going to support you.

Chapter 6 Facts, values and agendas

"He uses statistics as a drunken man uses lamp-posts – for support rather than illumination." Andrew Lang

Facts, values and beliefs[1]

Back in Chapter 2, when considering the factors that influence DDM, I said the personal values and relative power basis of key decision makers are fundamental. It is important to realise that we are all conditioned and predisposed to believe certain stories more than others. This is because of our individual prejudices and values. If someone doesn't like George Bush or Tony Blair, a song that makes fun of them will appeal. If we do like Bush and Blair, however, we might find the song offensive.[2]

The Royal Commission on Environmental Pollution,[3] defined values as follows:

"We understand values to be beliefs, either individual or social, about what is important in life, and thus about the ends or objectives which should govern and shape public policies. Once formed such beliefs may be durable."

So values are strongly held personal beliefs about what is important and about how the world *ought* to be.

Arguments about DDM can be very heated, as the public debate about ID cards and human rights has shown, for example. Those in favour and those against ID cards both argue passionately from the perspective that they are 'right' and the other side is 'wrong'.

In the interests of full disclosure here, it will be clear from the previous chapter that I believe the UK government's ID system is seriously flawed but that in principle an appropriately designed, privacy enhancing, identity system could facilitate the integration of Internet technologies into the delivery of government services. My personal values have had an important influence on my perspective.

Both the pro- and anti-ID card factions cite facts and statistics in their defence. To get to the bottom of some of the confusion, it is helpful to distinguish between facts and values.

A fact is something that we believe to be objectively true. A piece of steel weighs more than a similar-sized piece of aluminium. Water boils at 100 degrees centigrade (at standard atmospheric pressure). The price of *The Independent* newspaper in the UK was 70p on 12 June 2006. These are all things that can be observed and measured by processes that are not subjective. They can be agreed upon by all reasonable people.

A value, on the other hand, is a belief that something is good or bad. That the music of Cole Porter is better than that of Madonna; that ID cards are good; that corporal punishment is wrong; that children are born bad ('in sin') and have to be made good; that euthanasia is always morally wrong.

Facts are beliefs about what *is*, and values are beliefs about what *ought to be*. Our experience and aspirations often mean we cannot be convinced by rational argument to change our minds about something.

How is this distinction helpful? Well, because many public arguments involve a mix of facts and values. They are presented as if they are disputes only about facts, whereas they are really about conflicts in values. This is significant because disputes that are about facts can, in principle, be resolved by some objective process that can establish which assertions are factually correct. You can imagine a kind of impartial court that could adjudicate between the rival claims and reach a judgement acceptable to all.

But conflicts about values cannot be resolved in this way. There is no purely objective process by which the dispute can be resolved. There is no rational process by which someone who believes in euthanasia can convince someone who is opposed to it.

We usually settle conflict of values via politics or the legal system. In the UK, for example, capital punishment was abolished by a free vote in Parliament but this does not mean that those in favour of hanging are convinced that their values are wrong.

What does all this mean for us? Well, first of all, when we examine public controversies we should try to distinguish between their factual content and their value-laden contexts. The balance may determine whether or not they are resolvable by argument. Secondly, we should remember that the disputes between the protagonists in DDM situations often arise out of differences in values.

In defence of statistics: lies damned lies?

Both Mark Twain and Benjamin Disraeli are credited with saying:

"There are three kinds of lies: lies, damned lies and statistics"

and it has been much quoted ever since. There are a lot of statistics thrown around in DDM situations, particularly if we are dealing with government systems or regulations. Let us take a variation on Schneier's calculation in the previous chapter on finding terrorists through mass surveillance. This time Floyd Rudmin, Professor of Social & Community Psychology at the University of Tromsø in Norway, analyses President Bush's authorisation of the National Security Agency's (NSA) secret monitoring of the email messages and phone calls of all Americans:[4]

"The US Census shows that there are about 300 million people living in the USA.

Suppose that there are 1,000 terrorists there as well, which is probably a high estimate. The base-rate would be 1 terrorist per 300,000 people. In percentages, that is .00033%, which is way less than 1%. Suppose that NSA surveillance has an accuracy rate of .40, which means that 40% of real terrorists in the USA will be identified by NSA's monitoring of everyone's email and phone calls. This is probably a high estimate, considering that terrorists are doing their best to avoid detection. There is no evidence thus far that NSA has been so successful at finding terrorists. And suppose NSA's misidentification rate is .0001, which means that

.01% of innocent people will be misidentified as terrorists, at least until they are investigated, detained and interrogated. Note that .01% of the US population is 30,000 people. With these suppositions, then the probability that people are terrorists given that NSA's system of surveillance identifies them as terrorists is only p = 0.0132, which is near zero, very far from one. Ergo, NSA's surveillance system is useless for finding terrorists."[5]

Rudmin takes one basic statistic – 300 million people in the US – and takes a conservative guess at some others e.g. the proportion of terrorists in the population. He then does wonderfully simple analysis to prove mass surveillance is useless for finding terrorists.

Most people's eyes glaze over at these kinds of statistics and calculations. We either accept them without question or we resort to labelling them 'lies, damned lies and statistics' if they do not support our point of view. Both positions are based on a fundamental lack of understanding of statistics and probability theory, which are simply number crunching according to pre-determined, long-established rules. There are vast numbers of standard textbooks on this well-established area of mathematics, widely taught in schools and colleges. The kind of conditional probability calculation done here by Rudmin is based on Bayes' Theorem, taught in most introductory college statistics classes and is mathematically very sound.

The 'lies', as perceived, tend to come from:

- unreliable surveys producing unreliable data[6]
- numbers based on no evidence but plucked out of the air for effect
- interpretation or selective use of the results once the numbers have been crunched
- focus on style not content i.e. presentation of statistics in distorted or ambiguous, visually attractive graphical representations e.g. even the simple requirement that the number represented should be directly proportional to the size of the number is often neglected.

The lies follow from *abuse of*, rather than *use of*, statistics. Not all 'lies' arise from a deliberate manipulation of statistics. Sometimes it happens by accident as a result of a misunderstanding or even an error in calculation or even presentation.[7] Suppose that a Home Office spokeswoman says: "The number of terrorists caught each year by the UK has doubled since 1970."

Somebody else interprets that as: "Every year since 1970, the number of terrorists caught by the UK has doubled."

In the first case, if there was one terrorist caught in 1970, there would have been two caught in 2006. In the second case, if there was one caught in 1970, there would be two in 1971, four in 1972, eight in 1973 and so on, to 2^{36} or over 68 billion in 2006. The statistic has been distorted but people still accept it or glaze over it despite the fact that it claims the apprehension of more terrorists than there are people in the world.

The underlying mathematics of statistics and probability theory is eminently sound and very informative and effective when used by people who understand it like Professor Rudmin. Unfortunately it is not always understood or used with sufficient care and attention. The sad reality is that Rudmin-type analyses are all too rare and statistics tend to be wielded to support particular agendas rather than to truly inform, so we need to treat them with care.

Multiple perspectives

To understand a DDM situation we need to know who is involved in it. Different people look at the same situation in different ways.

Chernobyl

In the case of the Chernobyl nuclear power plant, the Soviet authorities, prior to the accident in 1986, knew of some serious design and operational problems with this kind of RBMK reactor[8] plant but refused to disclose them even to plant operators. The authorities had an overriding political interest in maintaining the fiction that Soviet nuclear installations were the safest in the world.[9] There had indeed been a series of incidents at Soviet nuclear power plants prior to the disaster at Chernobyl.[10] The details of these accidents were kept secret even from the operators of similar power stations, so no one could learn from previous mistakes. There was no accumulation of experience across the industry.

On the weekend of the disaster, in April 1986, operators of the Chernobyl plant were under pressure from company engineers in Moscow to carry out the series of tests that led them to breach safety protocols resulting in the reactor going out of control. They just wanted to get on with the job and when in the middle of winding the plant down towards a target of 25% capacity in order to do the tests, they were asked by grid engineers in Kiev to keep the plant on the grid due to an unexpected increase in demand for electricity. They agreed to do so. Then when they did come off the grid later in the day, the tests were behind schedule and given the nature of the dynamic system that a nuclear power plant is, they over-steered the wind-down to 1% of capacity.

Safety regulations dictated that the plant should not be brought below 20% as it would become unstable. The operators at Chernobyl, however, were highly experienced and considered amongst the best in the business, having won awards for their performance. So it is possible they felt they had a more intuitive feel for their operations than some remote safety specification writer. The safety inspector would have told them 1% was a dangerously unstable level of operation from her perspective.

The operators did manage to bring the plant up to 7% before starting the tests but the sequence of events that followed inevitably led to disaster. The control rods (which are like the reactor's brakes) were automatically and manually withdrawn as the tests, ironically undertaken in the interests of improving safety,[11] proceeded. When the operators noticed the reactor getting dangerously out of control and attempted to push the control rods back in rapidly, the rods got stuck.

When it became clear there was a major nuclear accident in progress, the authorities delayed the evacuation of the local communities in an attempt to hide the seriousness of the incident. Local people became aware there was a problem but were misled initially as to the seriousness of the situation. There were a range of reasons for this based on the variety of perspectives of the officials involved. Some officials were in denial, refusing to believe the situation could be so bad. Some were concerned to avoid mass panic and intent on playing down the seriousness of the accident in public. Others were concerned the damage the news of disaster would do to the Soviet nuclear industry and the Soviet political system more widely. Some were concerned with the impact on their own careers.[12] And in fairness many, many public officials fought to get the situation under control, attempting to secure the safety of the local population. Fire fighters, plant operators and others gave their lives in the effort. But it is hard to get away from high level neglect, incompetence and misunderstanding driven by the various perspectives of people in power.

A whole different range of perspectives drove actions in the Chernobyl power plant and official reactions to events on that fateful weekend and in the aftermath that inevitably led to tragedy.

The operators believed they 'knew' their machinery. They operated it to the best of their ability supplying the grid, even when they were supposed to be offline, doing safety tests. They wanted to get those irritating Moscow engineers out of their hair by the end of the weekend and breeched safety protocols, possibly as they had done without serious consequences on previous occasions.

The nuclear, political and scientific authorities knew of design and operation safety hazards but kept them secret in what they perceived to be the greater interests of the motherland and their own careers.

Safety engineers would not conceive of running an RBMK reactor down to 1% capacity, even unintentionally as the operators had done.

Local people including family members of the plant operators saw the plant as a source of income for the local economy and were kept in the dark about the unfolding disaster as it happened even when the radiation in the town reached highly dangerous levels.

Electricity users in the Soviet Union would barely have given this dot on a map a second thought but would want the grid that it supplied to produce a reliable source of power.

Most of us outside of the Soviet Union had hardly even heard of Chernobyl prior to April 1986.

Political and nuclear authorities and industries in a whole range of Western countries including the UK were quick to conclude their own investigations into the disaster with the comforting 'it could never happen here' mantra.

Our personal values influence our motivations and perspectives and those perspectives in turn influence our actions in complex DDM situations. The application of scientific theory to complex practical industrial contexts like nuclear power cannot survive the kind of closely controlled compartmentalisation of knowledge that happened in the former Soviet Union. This active inhibition of the evolution of the collective intelligence of the industry led eventually to the disaster at Chernobyl.

Growing mushrooms

As a thought experiment, imagine we had to attend an institution or a community in an isolated location which had 'strange' customs and practices. Suppose, for example, that this community was entirely devoted to growing mushrooms and had a number of odd social norms such as considering smiling to be offensive. We have to go along five days a week for eight hours a day.

We turn up on our first day and smile at the first group of people we meet in order to make a positive impression. Immediately we have insulted them but do not know why. Most people have a finely tuned social awareness aspect to their personalities so though initially puzzled we will soon figure it out ourselves, or be informed by a friendly native, that smiling is frowned upon. So we stop smiling. The atmosphere does not make us feel like smiling anymore anyway, so it is not too difficult.

We find out that the community grows mushrooms, looks after mushrooms or learns to grow and attend to mushrooms. That is its entire function. We do not try any mushroom jokes because laughing is even worse than smiling. We just get on with learning to grow mushrooms and by week 2, we feel confident enough to make some suggestions about the exciting possibilities of ecological diversification for the community. The community leaders take us to task for our outrageous behaviour and send us back to the classroom to learn what this community is all about.

Now this might seem like a ridiculous scenario and it is. Yet, as well as demonstrating the importance of perspective, in a way it also represents an exaggerated perspective of how we run our education system. The system is ultimately limited to training people for jobs, from the perspective of the government. This is a perspective which my values lead me to reject.

Education should be about facilitating the all round development of the individual,[13] not about job training, though the latter can be a convenient, though minor, emergent property of the process. A much more important emergent property should be an enlightened society. If I can paraphrase Richard Feynman, our responsibility is to learn what we can and do what we can to improve our world and pass it on to future generations. Education is at the heart of that process.

Children are taken into the education system in the UK at the age of five and expected to be at exactly the same stage of intellectual, emotional and social development as their class and age peers, at every stage of the system. A child who was reading at two is told to sit down and be quiet when they get bored in an over-worked teacher's classroom. By the same token a child who is not reading fluently until they are seven or eight can feel like a failure because the system doesn't have the time or resources to support them as an individual. The early and late readers might be equally bright but from their perspective the school community/system sees them as outliers or even outcasts, anomalies in a community obliged to focus on metaphorical mushrooms.

Perspective is important. It matters as much to the child who likes or dislikes school as to the minister making decisions about the education system as a whole. Unfortunately for the child, it is the minister's perspective that has significantly more influence on the system. Of course the perspective of the teachers, and to a much lesser extent the parents, has more influence in the local school context than either the child or the education minister. The perspectives of the children, those most affected by the education system, are the perspectives most neglected by that system.

Power and agenda

You can never fully understand how some decision making situations come about without understanding the power dynamics, the personal values and the interests or agendas of the people involved. DDM situations, as the Three Mile Island and Challenger disaster cases in Chapter 2 demonstrate, are always about more than the DDM system being designed, built, operated, controlled or regulated.

Government ministers have an interest in being seen to be *doing something* in the wake of a terrorist act, at the most cynical level because they want to keep their jobs and get re-elected.

We might criticise the amorality of such a mentality as we did in great numbers when a government spin doctor, Jo Moore, was caught sending an email on the 11th of September 2001 saying it was a 'very good day' to 'bury' bad news.[14] Unethical, insensitive and distasteful this behaviour may be but it is a standard public relations trick, widely used by government and commerce alike. Pretending or hoping it will not happen is not a sensible option when considering the agendas of the most powerful actors. The DDM situation needs to be evaluated from the positions of the various stakeholders involved, their separate agendas (where they can be deduced) and their relative power.

When a government minister visits the site of a disaster or makes an announcement in the aftermath of a terror attack that they will change the law[15] or speed up the introduction of ID cards, in the first instance they are engaging in political theatre[16] or acting in order to appear to be in control. This is not entirely cynical politics, as it does have the crucially important function of avoiding widespread panic.

In a security context it is also necessary to back this up with substantive and effective real security measures. Banning tweezers and nail clippers from aeroplanes is not an effective security measure, merely security theatre. Banning matches and cigarette lighters might have some small effect. Banning flying completely is the most effective way of preventing planes being used as missiles and protecting airline passengers from attack because there won't be any airline passengers.

This drastic measure, though implemented temporarily after September 11th 2001 when all aircraft were grounded, would not be an acceptable trade off for a society dependent on air travel. In the wake of the September 11th attacks tweezers and nail clippers were banned, matches and cigarette lighters were not. This was because the tobacco companies' lobbyists have some influence with the US Congress and worked according to their agenda to ensure these items would not be banned. The airlines, airports, government, regulators, airline staff like pilots and stewardesses do not care if passengers have to leave some small belongings behind when boarding a plane because it has no effect on them. Passengers might be bothered but it is largely a minor inconvenience and makes them feel safer. Everyone looks at the situation from their own perspective and with their own agenda.

If a government minister, or anyone else with a strong power base, believes some action is called for, it is difficult to get that person to question that belief. The most powerful actors also tend to have the means to act on their beliefs.

I mentioned in Chapter 2 the extra complication in the context of powerful actors, who tend to be surrounded by people whose jobs depend on keeping the boss happy. They therefore have an incentive to tell the prime minister, president or chief executive what they want to hear i.e. to reinforce their beliefs. Winston Churchill put it like this:

"The temptation to tell a Chief in a great position the things he most likes to hear is the commonest explanation of mistaken policy. Thus the outlook of the leader on whose decisions fateful events depend is usually far more sanguine than the brutal facts admit."[17]

One of the key reasons DDM is difficult is that it tends to be a complex mess often involving significant numbers of people, all with their own perspectives, values, biases and agendas. Individual agendas may or may not coincide with the stated purpose, if there is one, of the information system. Personal agendas are all about what the individual wants to get out of the DDM situation, including making sure someone else will be held responsible if it all goes wrong.

This becomes a problem or a mess of the Ackoff variety when no one, in particular those stakeholders with the strongest power base, takes an overall system perspective. Governments tend to work to time horizons of four or five years *at the very longest* because that is the interval between elections. Very often they are in the position of reacting to the latest news headlines. This means that information systems requiring a long-term perspective, stretching further than five years, may not have many influential stakeholders taking such a perspective.

The average term of office of the various Home Secretaries who have taken charge of the Home Office during the term of the current government, for example, is just a little over two years. The ID card system, the Semaphore air passenger monitoring system, the Criminal Records Bureau, the immigration databases, the Children's Index, the latest serious offenders' database,[18] the Probation Services systems and a huge range of other computer-based information systems all of which require very long-term organisation, design, planning, operation and regulation, are in the overall charge of someone who is likely to be in that post for no more than three years. Given the pressure to react to the latest media headlines, arguably the situation is getting worse.[19]

In the glasshouse of modern Western politics, ministers are constantly under pressure to cope with a political system that uses failures or apparent failures as ways of scoring points and that assumes that central 'command and control' is the most effective approach to government.[20] Also fear of failure or the next headline accusing the government of failing engenders a culture where full and frank feedback about the impact of policies and systems becomes impossible. We therefore get a variation on what David Luban[21] calls an asymmetrical assault on reality that goes something like this: [22]

Axiom 1: We are good people.

Axiom 2: Failure is bad.

Axiom 3: Anything that helps us, the good people, succeed, or more especially, *not fail*, is good.

Corollary 1: Whatever we do to avoid failure is good.

Corollary 2: Whatever hinders us from doing what we do to avoid failure is bad.

Theorem 1: Anything that makes us look bad is false. (Proof: If it makes us look bad, it must be false, because, according to Corollary 1, what we do to avoid failure is good, not bad.)

Corollary 3: Negative feedback on policies and our information systems cannot be true. (Proof: That would make us look bad. Whatever makes us look bad is false.)

Corollary 4: Facts that make us look bad are false. (This follows directly from Theorem 1.)

Theorem 2: People that bring us false facts are bad.

Axiom 4: Bad people are not welcome in government...

If all this seems rather harsh on the politicians, it is as much a criticism of the systems within which they operate as of their perpetuation of those systems. We the general citizenry also have to take our share of the responsibility for our lack of active participation in the political process.

When policymakers do have to think about the longer term, they do so through framing the DDM situation in a way that fits with an existing political agenda. So, for example, the airline industry desperately wants to increase airport capacity in the UK. Yet proposed airport expansions like Heathrow's terminal 5 face strong local opposition because of the associated increase in noise and pollution that would come with any such development. The industry therefore put pressure on the government to produce a national strategy for expanding air travel to and from the UK.

The government issued a public consultation document in 2000,[23] which asked three basic questions:

1. How much extra airport capacity will be needed in the next 30 years?
2. How will we deal with the environmental impact?

3. Where should we locate the new airport developments?

The White Paper, the policy framework that now influences future deci-sions on planning applications for airport expansion, that followed the con-sultation in 2003,[24] inevitably concluded extra runways should be built and suggested where these should be.[25] The three questions that framed the public consultation could hardly have led to any other conclusion. The aviation industry was pleased. Environmental groups were appalled. The process had avoided what they considered a fundamental question i.e. do we really need more airport capacity and more flights, given the impact these will have on the environment?[26]

Tactics of persuasion

As well as being aware of the agenda of the various stakeholders and their relative power base, it is important to be familiar with the kind of tactics people and organisations use to persuade us of the legitimacy of their point of view. The following is a list of some of the common tactics to look out for.[27]

Extrapolating opposition argument to the absurd and then refuting the absurd

This is also known as the 'straw man' approach – create a straw man, something which you can pretend represents your opponents' position, and knock that down. President Bush's declaration that anyone who opposed his actions in the wake of the attacks of 11th September 2001 was a sup-porter of terrorism is a classic example:

"Either you are for us or for the terrorists."

This has been one of the most important oratorical tricks in the president's armoury in his time in office. It has enabled him to take a range of actions including invading Iraq, legalising torture[28] and domestic surveillance that would arguably have been more difficult without the aid of painting his opponents as 'soft on terrorism'.

Appealing to emotion and prejudice

If someone tells us a story we want to hear, we are more likely to believe it. There are a huge number of ways of using this tactic. One example is appealing to nationalism, as in the following example from Jack Valenti, the President of the Motion Picture Association of America, in his testimony to a congressional sub-committee, on the 'Home recording of copy-righted works' (i.e. the use of video cassette recorders) in 1982.

"The US film and television production industry is a huge and valuable American asset. In 1981, it returned to this country almost $1 billion in surplus balance of trade. And I might add, Mr Chairman, it is the single one American-made product that the Japanese, skilled beyond all comparison in their conquest of world trade, are unable to duplicate or to displace or to compete with or to clone. And I might add that this important asset today is in jeopardy. Why?... Now, I have here the profits of Japanese companies, if you want to talk about greed. Here, Hitachi, Matsushita, Sanyo, Sony, TDK, Toshiba, Victor, all of whom make these VCRs. Do you know what their net profits were last year? $2.8 billion net profit."

Labelling or ghettoisation of interested groups

Group all opponents under one general heading. Once there, they can be labelled, on a spectrum from 'lunatics' to 'nice people who just do not understand'. Then conclude that their arguments are not worth taking into consideration because they are at best ill-informed. There is a whole range of ways of using this tactic. If scientists agree on an inconvenient truth like global warming or evolution they are intellectual snobs who think they know better than the rest of us. Conservative Christian advocates of the teaching of 'intelligent design' in science lessons in the US are very good at this.[29] One of the central themes of this book is the value to be gained from experts and ordinary people working together. The intelligent design debate is good example of ordinary people making what I believe is a bad judgement call, in defiance of contrary scientific evidence and advice. Their values and beliefs lead them to reject the scientific theory of evolution in an attempt to promote their own model, intelligent design, of how life came into existence.[30]

Balancing act

Modern journalistic practice of reporting that there are two sides to every story,[31] in an apparent effort to appear balanced, can result in all kinds of quacks getting a media platform. [Yes, I plead guilty here to using a denigrating label.] If someone says the moon is made of cheese on a slow news day, the headlines will say 'opinion divided on the composition of the moon'.

Deborah Lipstadt[32] provides an especially stark example in the media tendency to legitimise the views of people who deny the holocaust took place, in spite of the overwhelming mass of incontrovertible documented and eye-witness evidence of the Nazis' atrocities. Lipstadt refused all media offers to 'debate' the reality of the holocaust with holocaust deniers, since it would just present these people with a public platform in which their point of view would be considered to be of equal value.

Unfortunately an expert backed by solid evidence but with poor communication skills can fail to influence a DDM situation, when faced with someone who has a poor understanding of the evidence but a strong agenda and good communications skills.

Using jargon to confuse

With DDM being such a complex subject, any debate about the design, deployment or regulation of information systems is open to this tactic. For example: 'You will, of course, understand that the DRM or TPM anti-circumvention measures in the UK implementation of EU directive 2001/29/EC on copyrights and related rights in the information society, the EUCD, were a direct result of our international obligations, rather than something we would have chosen to write into UK law of our own volition.'

Making appeals to 'experts'

I refer to Bruce Schneier, James Boyle, Kim Cameron and others throughout this book as experts. A reader, who is unfamiliar with these individuals or their areas of expertise, may just be taking my word that they are indeed experts. Very often media reports quote named and un-named 'experts' in support of their assertions, though, and it can be well worth checking the credentials of these people.

Using sarcasm, innuendo, denigration and other forms of humour to belittle opponents

It is easier to get a low opinion of the opposing advocate if you are funny – the humour makes it easy for the audience to like you and diverts attention from the substance of your argument.

The dominant metaphor

George Lakoff [33] teaches that metaphors are the mental structures that shape the way we see the world. If someone tells us a story through appealing metaphors and language we are more likely to accept their point of view. By the same token, when Richard Nixon went on TV and said "I'm not a crook," immediately everyone believed he *was* a crook. It is also like telling someone not to think of an elephant. No matter how hard you try after someone has said this, the image of the elephant will come into your mind.

Using rhetorical questions

If you get your audience to subconsciously supply the answer invited by the question, they become more receptive to the views that follow as a consequence of the answer. To appreciate this, test the effect of taking the opposite answer to the one implied. The wonderful BBC comedy series *Yes Prime Minster* gave a classic illustration of this when Sir Humphrey Appleby[34] explained to Bernard Woolley[35] how to fix a survey:

Sir Humphrey: "Well Bernard you know what happens. Nice young lady comes up to you. Obviously you want to create a good impression. You don't want to look a fool, do you?"

Bernard: "No."

Sir Humphrey: "No. So she starts asking you some questions. Mr. Woolley, are you worried about the number of young people without jobs?"

Bernard: "Yes."

Sir Humphrey: "Are you worried about the rise in crime among teenagers?"

Bernard: "Yes."

Sir Humphrey: "Do you think there is a lack of discipline in our comprehensive schools?"

Bernard: "Yes."

Sir Humphrey: "Do you think young people welcome some authority and leadership in their lives?"

Bernard: "Yes."

Sir Humphrey: "Do you think they respond to a challenge?"

Bernard: "Yes."

Sir Humphrey: "Would you be in favour of re-introducing national service?"

Bernard: "Y... oh, well I suppose I might be."

Sir Humphrey: "Yes or no?"

Bernard: "Yes."

Sir Humphrey: "Of course you would, Bernard. After all you've told her you can't say no to that. So they don't mention the first five questions and they publish the last one." [36]

A variation on the rhetorical question is the use of words and phrases which suggest that the audience should accept without question, e.g. 'Obviously...' or 'It is clear that we all agree...'

The sound bite

It is very hard to find simple responses to counter established rhetoric. 'If you've got nothing to hide, you've got nothing to fear' for example.

You could try 'how much do you earn' or 'have you got curtains or a lock on your bathroom door' but they do not have the same effect. Likewise 'If I am not doing anything wrong, then you should not be watching me'; 'Everyone has something to hide because everyone is entitled to privacy'; 'Those engaged in the surveillance get to decide what's "wrong" and they keep changing the definition'; 'You might misuse my information'; 'I don't have anything to hide. But I don't have anything I want you to see, either'; 'The government is sticking its nose into my business without a reasonable excuse'; and so on. It is an uneven playing field, rhetorically speaking – the rhetoric is stacked against the nuanced but more complete argument or explanation. In a world of short attention spans, if you have to explain, you are losing the argument.

Presenting evidence or apparent evidence to make it appear to point to a particular conclusion

This includes using carefully selected evidence, while omitting contrary evidence. In the UK government consultation on the proposed 'entitlement card' in 2003, about 6000 people indicated opposition to the idea and about 2000 were in favour. The government at that time presented the results by saying that most people were in favour of the scheme by a ratio of 2 to 1. They later justified this by saying they had counted the 5000 or so who had expressed their opposition to the scheme via the Internet as *a single vote against* the scheme. David Blunkett, Home Secretary at the time, dismissed the people who used the Net to object as a vocal minority of civil liberties activists. The government then commissioned a survey, the results of which suggested 80% of the population were in favour of ID cards. They have been quoting this survey ever since, in spite of a lot of evidence showing a huge drop off in support for the system.

Taking what someone says out of context

People regularly take quotes from religious texts like the Koran or the Bible out of context to justify their behaviour. George Bush was vilified by critics for describing ten months of violence following the 2005 elections in Iraq as "just a comma" in history.[37]

Avoiding giving evidence whilst suggesting that evidence is being given

Put out a vague policy statement, saying the details will come later, then when asked about the details at a later date claim all the details were clearly included in the original policy statement and there is nothing further to add.

Non sequitur – 'It does not follow'

This involves drawing an illogical conclusion from sound data. Since the data are credible the conclusion which follows closely is also accepted. The subtle exponent of the art will embed the illogical conclusion between two logical ones. An example is the government's stance on the UK national identity system. It will be compulsory for everyone to have an ID card. Yet it is claimed that the card cannot be considered compulsory, since it will not be compulsory to carry it around all the time.

Repetition

Repetition of a claim, periodically and frequently, over a long period of time can often lead to general acceptance of the claim as fact, even though it may have been discredited on numerous occasions. This is a tactic used extensively by 'historical revisionists' like those who deny the existence of the holocaust.[38] In Chapter 8, I look briefly at the repeated efforts to introduce a software patent directive in the European Union. Those in favour of such a policy merely need to keep re-introducing it periodically over a sustained period. Those who oppose such a policy need to be alert and mobilise effective opposition to every attempt to implement such a policy. Those with the most stamina get their way in the end.

Corporate, civil society or politically funded think tanks

These institutions present an alternative to traditional academic and scientific peer review. Researchers publish the required results. Ordinary people find it hard to tell the difference between real research and advocacy research and the media rarely make the effort to distinguish or understand the difference between these when reporting on particular findings. Increasingly, research in universities is commercially sponsored.[39] A simple question which is always worth asking is: who paid for the research?

Astroturfing

This is the public relations trick of creating illusory grass-roots campaigns. Public relations companies acting, for example, on behalf of the energy, tobacco and pharmaceutical industries and political parties have been doing this for decades.[40] The idea is to send lots of letters or emails purporting to come from ordinary people to politicians or newspapers in order to make it appear that there is significant feeling about a particular issue. There is a huge industry engaged in buying and selling personal data for commercial and political exploitation of this sort. At the simplest level these details can be obtained from the voting register or the register of births and deaths.

Critical thinking

I hope it will be clear by now that when considering DDM situations (or messes), from nuclear power to intellectual property regulations, it is important to engage our critical thinking faculties.[41] Everyone in these situations has their own perspective and agenda. We need, therefore, to be careful about accepting arguments at face value, particularly given the range of persuasive tactics that are available to convince us of someone's point of view.

Try to consider the situation from each stakeholder's perspective and understand their agenda. Identify explicitly any underlying assumptions that they may be making and assess their credibility and that of the arguments derived from them. Aviation pioneer, Howard Hughes, made some of the most important commercial decisions of his life by instinct or gut reaction,[42] so this might not always be possible but it is important to try. Think about the *system's purpose* and whether any of the stakeholders are focused on it. Get behind the persuasive tactics. Analyse and evaluate the various claims, information and research. Even if we do not feel competent to evaluate research or models beyond our field of competence we can still ask the simple questions:

- What is the purpose of the system? It is ridiculously common for there to be no clear consensus on this, even amongst the key stakeholders.
- Who paid for the research and what are the underlying assumptions of any models used?
- What are our alternative courses of action?
- Are there other alternatives that have not been considered?
- How well does our proposed action address the purpose of the system and from whose perspective?
- What other problems is the system likely to create?
- What is the likelihood of these?
- Are the new problems/messes better or worse than those we have set out to address?

The DDM system will exhibit emergent positive and negative consequences – can we anticipate any of these and exploit or protect ourselves from them? How do Lessig's four constraints – law, architecture, market forces and social norms – affect our system? How can we monitor and improve the system iteratively, in response to what we learn?

Think about how the system might work in a 'best possible scenario' case and contrast this with a 'worst possible scenario' case. Round off with Schneier's final two questions:

- How much does it cost?
- Is it worth it?

And remember the response to the clinching 'this is what the public wants' argument is that just as in science, where truth is determined through the scientific method and rational and ethical peer review, the prevailing state of public opinion should not necessarily be the determining factor.[43] This system, with all its faults – scientists have values and agendas too – works fairly well for science (and university research generally). *Informed* and *critically aware* public opinion does, however, have a key role to play in DDM.

A note about Internet sources

Given the degree to which we, in the affluent West, are increasingly relying on the Internet as a primary source of news and information, it is particularly important to note that we should check our sources. Relying on websites, institutions and individuals with a track record of credibility is a sound (though not infallible) start. Do not neglect your own knowledge and experience – just because a normally credible source says that something is red doesn't mean that the source is right, especially when you've seen the thing and know it is blue. Here are some questions to ask when considering using information from a website:

- Does the person or organisation running the website have a track record of credibility?
- What are their credentials?
- Is the site well regarded by credible, reliable people and institutions?
- Do the people running the site have an agenda, e.g. who is the site aimed at?
- Where did the information on the site come from and is the source reliable?
- Is the site well documented and are the sources of information given?

- Is it a government (.gov or .gov.uk) or commercial (.com or co.uk) or educational (.edu or .ac.uk) or non-profit organisation (.org or org.uk) site?
- Are the claims on the site verifiable?
- Are any of the above unfair tactics in evidence?
- Can you verify the information on the site with other reliable sources?
- Are the links on the site up to date and do they link to other reliable sources?
- Is the page kept up to date?[44]

Chapter 7 Technology is just a tool

"What gets us into trouble is not what we don't know it's *what we know for sure that just ain't so.*" Mark Twain

Technology: a tool

There is a rather touching faith in the magical ability of technology to solve problems in a way which turns a mess into a mere difficulty. This belief is particularly widespread amongst decision makers who do not understand the technology.

It is also complicated by the false belief that expertise in one area enables that expert to offer informed advice across a whole range of domains where they do not have the necessary know-how. Modern technology induces a kind of techno-paralysis, whereby the victim suspends all sense of reason when dealing with it.

Yet technology, no matter how sophisticated, is just a tool. It is not magic and will not automatically evolve towards a state where it will comprehensively address an ill-defined mess. Policy makers, however, rarely seem to understand this. The computer on its own cannot rectify an ill-defined digital decision making (DDM) mess. Neither does computerising an existing process automatically make it more efficient or effective.

Being a technophile I never really noticed this seriously until I was in industry and wanted to commission software to do a structural analysis of some aircraft components I was working on. Vendors and consultants produced lovely colourful images on computer screens which highly impressed the management but they all singularly failed to apply their software successfully to even the simplest structural problems we were engaged with. An interesting parallel lesson from that episode was the importance of focus, boundaries and perspective. I wanted help with a difficult technical problem. None of the software that I saw addressed the problem. The senior management, on the other hand, had visions of demonstrating visually attractive modern technology to visiting customers, to impress upon them what a forward-thinking company we were. Management saw it as a promotional tool. I saw something that did not help solve a technical problem.[1]

One of the ways to get past techno-paralysis is to understand the difference between information technology (IT) and information systems (IS). This chapter covers two main case studies in an effort to illustrate that difference and point out the importance of experts cooperating with users in the development of complex systems. The first case study is on the information system which won the war and second on electronic voting.

Information systems, information technology, purpose, freedom, experts and system users

The 'information system which won the war' is the system which turned data from radar screens into instructions to the defending British fighter planes during the Battle of Britain in 1940. Those instructions guided the fighters to the location in the sky where they would find the enemy.

It was first pointed out by Checkland and Holwell in Chapter 5 of their book about the IS field[2] that these arrangements were in fact 'an information system', though that phrase did not exist in the 1940s. Moreover, the creation of the radar information system was a fine example – still relevant – of how to go about the provision of information for action; and it did not, of course, entail the use of computers. This air defence system in fact demonstrates very clearly the difference between information systems and information technology, and its story will be re-told here. It also illustrates the point made by Checkland and Holwell that:

"every information system, simply because it is a support to human action, will exist within a context of the never-ending political struggles which characterize all human situations".

Radar and the air defence information system that won the war

Radar technology in Britain at the outbreak of the war was fairly rudimentary. Radar operators would sit in a hut near tall transmitting and receiving towers monitoring a cathode ray tube screen. The outgoing signal would register as a blip on the screen and if it bounced off any incoming aircraft, the operator would see another, smaller blip further along the screen. The distance between these blips allowed the operator to estimate how far away the attackers might be. Tracking many planes in different formations simultaneously was more of a black art than an exact science with this equipment. As a result, radar operators' reports were sometimes difficult to interpret or even contradictory. In any case, a guesstimate of how far away the enemy aircraft might be tells us little about how to get the right defending squadrons to the right point in the sky to intercept at the earliest possible moment.

So before it became truly useful, that radar technology (the IT) had to be built into a fully integrated and operational air defence system (the IS) the kind of system Henry Tizard's 'Committee for the Scientific Survey of Air Defence' set out to commission in 1935. The terms 'information system' and 'information technology' were not part of the vocabulary of the time but that is exactly what the air defence system and radar were. The data collected by the radar stations would have been useless without the means to quickly filter, assess and act upon that data. The purpose of the system was to enable defensive action – getting the fighters to the enemy positions as soon as possible.

On 10 November 1932, the then Prime Minister of Britain, Stanley Baldwin, made what has often been described as a 'chilling' speech[3] in the House of Commons. Following advice from the Air Ministry, he said:

"I think it is as well for the man in the street to realise that there is no power on earth that can protect him from being bombed. Whatever people may tell him, the bomber will always get through."

The only suggestion the Air Ministry were able to offer in the realm of air defence in the early 1930s was the possibility of flying standing patrols in the hope that some of their planes would be in the air nearby when an attack came.

By 1934 the Nazis were in power in Germany and a civil servant in the air ministry, A.P. Rowe, who had originally trained as a physicist, decided to survey all the official documents available on air defence, of which there were 57. He was concerned that none seemed too promising. Some referred to the large and expensive sound location device built at Romney Marshes, which he himself had witnessed being rendered useless by the rattling noise of a passing milk cart. Rowe reported to his boss, Henry Wimperis, head of scientific research, that unless they came up with a decent air defence system they would be likely to 'lose the next war if it started within ten years'. Wimperis asked Henry Tizard, a respected government scientist,[4] to convene a 'Committee for the Scientific Survey of Air Defence'.

He also asked Robert Watson-Watt,[5] a physicist and radio expert at the National Physical Laboratory, if it would be possible to develop a death ray to blast enemy aircraft or pilots out of the sky. Watson-Watt reported to the first meeting of the Tizard committee[6] in February 1935 that the death ray idea was impractical but that 'radio-detection' might be a 'less unpromising problem' and that 'numerical consideration on the method of detection by reflected radio waves will be submitted if required'.[7]

Tizard and Air Vice-Marshall Hugh Dowding, who was soon to become Commander in Chief of RAF Fighter Command,[8] quickly realised that they had been presented with the technical basis of an early detection early response air defence system. Dowding asked for a demonstration of the detection ability of radio waves which Watson-Watt quickly arranged. Following a successful demo on 26 February 1935,[9] Tizard and Dowding set about arranging funding for the development of the technology and a chain of twenty radar stations to run round the coast from Southampton in the south to the Tyne in the north. This proved to be a relatively straightforward task, since by then the importance of developing some kind defence against attacks from the air was recognised at the highest levels of government, civil service and the military establishment. The process had support from the top right from the start.[10]

Watson-Watt got the job of organising the design and development of the technology and set up operations at Orfordness, moving to Bawdsey

Manor in 1936. In many ways he was the ideal leader for a group of clever, focused and enthusiastic young scientists and engineers. He believed in informality and the free exchange of ideas. He also understood that if you collect enough bright people together in one place, provide them with clear objectives, an understanding of the urgency of meeting those objectives, sufficient resources and the freedom to get on with the job, you get a remarkable degree of innovation and unbeatable productive capacity.[11] Watson-Watt only really had two basic rules for his young charges.

Firstly the radar and associated equipment had to be constructed from readily available existing components. There was no time to be wasted developing new basic components. Secondly, when the equipment being developed had evolved to the stage where it was good enough to do the job, it went into immediate production. Watson-Watt set development deadlines which were always met. He said he could deliver good enough machines today, second best tomorrow and if you wanted perfection then forget it. He was building the technology of the air defence system and it was more important that it be *available quickly and work in the system* than it be the best piece of technology of its kind. "Second best tomorrow" became a kind of a motto for the Bawdsey crew.

Within months significant progress had been made on one of the key problems, identifying the direction of any attack. The still embryonic team at Orfordness had set up four directional aerials facing towards the four main points of the compass and were able to get a rudimentary idea of the direction of an aircraft by comparing the relative signal strengths coming from each. The list of technical problems Watson-Watt's team had to solve grew and grew. The detection range of the initial chain of 20 radar stations, which became known as 'chain home', was 80 miles at 10,000 feet or 50 miles at 5000 feet. Enemy raiders flying below 5000 feet could escape detection completely, so radar sets were developed to detect lower flying aircraft and these made up the 'chain home low' line in the ether, capable of tracking planes at 500 feet, 25 miles away.[12] Compact sets, capable of being fitted to planes for detection in the air were also developed.

Contrast the 'just good enough' or 'satisficing' approach of Watson-Watt with a situation where the focus was on improving or perfecting the technology, as arguably was the case in Germany, Russia, Japan and the US In each of these countries development was led by technical experts and there was arguably no high level understanding of the importance of the technology or its potential as a component of a wider operations system. This resulted in Britain being the only country at the outbreak of war with an understanding of the real strategic and operational importance of radar as part of an air defence system.

Ironically the more primitive technology of the British resulted in an unexpected intelligence payoff too. When the Germans sent an airship up the east coast of Britain on an electronic reconnaissance mission in 1939 prior to the war, their relatively high tech equipment was unable to pick up any useful information. The Germans used centimetre radar equipment and did not conceive of anyone wasting time with longer wavelengths. They spotted the Chain Home stations but concluded that they had nothing to do with radar defence and thought the signals they picked up were from the electricity grid.[13] Also when the Germans captured a British radar set in 1940, a technical assessment declared it to be so primitive as to be useless. Recognition of the technology as merely a primitive component of a wider system might well have improved the scientific intelligence available to the Germans and influenced the conduct of the early part of the war. The technology was just one tool in the overall system.

In parallel with this technical development Tizard and Dowding were working on the wider system. They commissioned an army of Post Office technicians to install a dedicated network of phone and teleprinter cables linking all the radar stations, Fighter Command Headquarters, Groups, Sectors, airfields and the Observer Corps. The Observer Corps were a group of 30,000 volunteers who manned 1000 posts inland to visually monitor incoming aircraft once they had passed the coastal radar chains. Their tools consisted of little more than a pair of binoculars, a phone linking them to one of 32 Observer Corps Centres round the country and a book of aircraft shapes and markings which they memorised. The Observer Corps, with no high technology at their disposal, nonetheless constituted a critical part of the system.

By May 1936 the radar station at Bawdsey Manor became the first operational station. Tizard, Dowding and Watson-Watt now had the beginnings of their command and control air defence system. Dowding immediately instigated a series of air defence exercises, controlled initially from an experimental operations room at Bawdsey, later from Fighter Command Headquarters at Bentley Priory in North London. They used fighter planes operating out of the Biggin Hill airfield to the south of London and the radar station at Bawdsey.

Scientists, other technical specialists, RAF and WAAF[14] officers and civil servants were involved in these exercises from the start at the three centres, Bawdsey, Bentley Priory and Biggin Hill.

The fighters were scrambled to 'intercept' civilian planes. Right away the value of operational research[15] became apparent. Too much raw data from radar operators and observer corps, some of it just plain contradictory or wrong, swamped the controllers and pilots. So a 'Filter Room' was set up at Fighter Command to filter out inaccurate or misleading data. The job of the filter room operators became highly skilled and only experienced officers filled the post, judging and interpreting the data based on what they knew about the accuracy of previous reports or equipment or reported faults or inconsistencies.[16]

Dowding also set about educating his pilots to get used to taking directions from the ground, something they, as typical free-spirited adventurers, did not care for in the beginning. After all, what could people safe on the ground know about flying an airplane let alone the heat of battle? He made sure, for example, that the controllers in the operations rooms were experienced pilots who did understand the mindset and the problems of the men in the air. This created significant friction with the signals branch of the military who felt anything in the signals area was exclusively their domain. The airmen were also obliged to visit the operations rooms to get an understanding of the problems of the ground controllers as well as the vital jobs they were doing.[17] The skill, tenacity and insight of Tizard and another of his committee members, Patrick Blackett, proved crucial to convincing the pilots that they could not "run wars on gusts of emotion. You have to think scientifically about your own operations."[18]

If all the scientific and engineering development in the lead up to the war was to be of any use, then the pilots had to take notice of what the operations centres were telling them. The technology and the system could only be as good as the users allowed them to be.[19]

On a trip out in the car one Sunday I was explaining a bit about the development of radar when my younger son, who was then six years old, said "Dad, how did they tell the difference between the German and British planes?" Good question. By 1938 the air exercises had left the RAF pilots seriously worried about precisely that problem and the technology experts got to work on an IFF (identify friend or foe) device to be mounted on every RAF plane.[20] These would send out a signal identifying the plane as friendly. Later on signal bursts from the pilots radio telephones were also used to aid identification. In September 1939 just after the declaration of war, errors led to an incident where RAF Hurricanes and Spitfires engaged in a battle with each other, leading to two planes being shot down and one pilot killed. Before the end of the month 500 IFF sets were built and fitted to RAF planes.

Plotting the interception of a moving enemy in three dimensions, even with all the appropriately filtered radar and observer corps data, proved to be a very difficult 'four vector' (three-dimensional coordinates plus relative velocities) problem. So the scientists built specialist calculating machines and used books of trigonometric tables in an attempt to provide rapid answers. During one exercise, Wing Commander Grenfell at Biggin Hill got irritated with the scientists and their frenzied calculations and

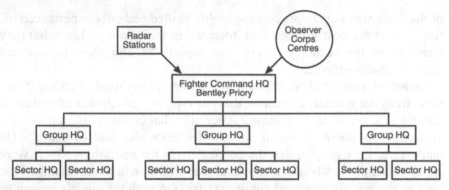

Fig. 7.1 Schematic representation of the structure of the British national air defence system

machines and said he could do a better job by eye. The disbelieving experts challenged him to do just that, whereupon he succeeded in coordinating a perfect interception with the aid of a pencil, ruler and some basic trigonometric calculations. This technique of calculating the "tizzy angle" became the standard method for operational controllers at 'sector' level to determine the interception course for the fighters in the air. The importance of involving the users of the information system in its development is summed up for me in that single story.[21]

By 1939 a fully functional, people and technology dependent, national air defence system was in operation. It was roughly set up as shown in Figure 7.1.[22] Fighter Command was the national command and control centre led by Dowding and responsible for strategic air defence for the whole country.

The country was divided into geographic groups, with four group headquarters by the outbreak of war. (The diagram is focused on the structure of the system and is not representative of the actual numbers of group or sector headquarters, radar or observer corps stations or centres.) These groups were further sub-divided into smaller sectors and sector headquarters would be located at the main sector airfield from which operational sorties would be flown. Each sector was also responsible for a number of additional satellite airfields.

The filter room at Fighter Command analysed and filtered the voluminous amounts of data flowing in from radar and observer corps and turned it into useful information. This was sent out to the operations rooms at Fighter Command and Group and Sector headquarters simultaneously to enable aircraft movements to be plotted on the large table maps that will be familiar to anyone who has seen the old war films depicting scenes from the Battle of Britain.

Each operations room at each level had their map tables, the controllers on a raised platform from which they could survey and assess the picture of the attack on the map below, a 'tote' board of lights showing the readiness of the various squadrons and a clock on the wall with each five minute section depicted in a different colour. Red moveable markers on the map showed the enemy positions and black markers the defending squadrons. The markers had reference numbers indicating height and strength and coloured arrows showing the direction. The arrows got changed every five minutes to coincide with the colours on the clock in order to track movement in time. Any counter with an inappropriately coloured arrow could be detected and the last time at which it had been tracked identified, in order to being it back into the picture again. The WAAF croupiers made all the adjustments to the markers on the maps in accordance with the information flowing from the Fighter Command filter room.

Fighter command controlled overall strategic defence and decided, for example, which pattern of air raid sirens should be sounded. Group commanders and controllers decided which sectors and how many squadrons should engage the incoming enemy raids. Sector commanders and controllers controlled the fighters directly until the enemy planes were sighted, at which point control passed to the squadron leader in the air. Once the battle was over, control passed back to the sector controller.

In addition, sector headquarters had an additional DF ('direction finding') room which contained a map table used to plot accurate RAF positions based on the information coming from high frequency direction finding (HF/DF) stations, of which there were three in each sector. The DF room was usually next door to the operations room and organised so that the controller could see both maps from his raised platform.

The Tizard Committee and Lindemann: how it could have failed

I have so far glossed over the politics of the situation but the politics at several levels could well have killed or significantly impeded the system's development. The Tizard committee succeeded in commissioning an ultimately effective air defence system because:

- They were clear about what they wanted to do

- They were able to articulate their aims and activities clearly

- Tizard had the inside track on the political establishment and was able to influence powerful people during the period leading up to the war[23]

- They inspired wholehearted commitment from an eclectic range of experts and users of the system and fully involved them in its operational development

- They took the initiative to act,[24] despite being considered a mere lowly departmental committee by some, rather than merely sit back and talk or advise.

There were a number of serious political rivalries which could have sent the development and operation of the system off the rails.[25] The most important of these was the relationship between Tizard and Winston Churchill's scientific adviser, Professor Frederick Lindemann. Lindemann and Tizard had known each other since they were students together in Berlin before the First World War. Both distinguished themselves during that war as expert fliers and Tizard was responsible for ensuring Lindemann was appointed to a professorial post at Oxford University in the early 1920s. They were close friends, therefore, for many years.[26]

The story of how their relationship initially became strained is a bit hazy but it reached breaking point during the four-year development of the air defence system overseen by Tizard's committee.[27]

Churchill met Lindemann for the first time after the First World War. The two men quickly developed a strong and lasting friendship based on mutual respect. In the wake of the Prime Minister's speech in 1932, declaring the "bomber will always get through", Lindemann wrote a letter to *The Times* newspaper accusing the authorities of a defeatist attitude. Churchill records that he and Lindemann became a lot closer from that time on:

> "We came much closer together from 1932 onwards… Lindemann, 'the Prof.', as he was called among his friends, became my chief adviser on the scientific aspects of modern war and particularly air defence, and also on questions involving statistics of all kinds."[28]

Churchill had been a lone voice in the political wilderness agitating for preparations for what he believed was the inevitable coming of a second global conflict. Churchill and Lindemann pushed for the formation of a high level committee on air defence, which then prime minister Ramsay MacDonald agreed to early in 1935. MacDonald then found out that the Air Ministry had just set up the Tizard committee. Things get a bit obscure at this stage politically with some accounts[29] suggesting Churchill convinced MacDonald to scrap the Tizard committee, since he and Lindemann so distrusted anything coming out of the Air Ministry. The Air Ministry, after all, had been the ones who had believed that "the bomber would always get through". That the committee did not get scrapped was probably down to Tizard getting the work off the ground so quickly and Churchill's strained relations with MacDonald.[30] Lindemann had apparently solicited Tizard's support for setting up a high level air defence committee late in 1934 and seems to have resented being kept in the dark about the fact that Tizard had already been approached by the Air Ministry.

An Air Defence Sub Committee of the Committee of Imperial Defence was, however, created by the Prime Minister and Churchill agreed to become a member as long as Lindemann would get to sit in on Tizard's committee. So began the battles between Tizard and Lindemann that could have proved fatal to the process of preparing for air defence. Right from the start Lindemann clashed with Tizard and the two other key scientific members of the committee, Blackett and Hill. You only have to read Lindemann's letter to *The Times* to see his passionate belief in the need to apply scientific methodology to the development of an effective air defence system. But whatever his motivation[31] – including his mistrust of Tizard and the Air Ministry – he became a thorn in their side. Whatever the three scientists agreed, Lindemann vehemently opposed and outside of the committee used his political connections to undermine. He insisted that aerial mines deployed by parachute would be more effective than anything Tizard and co. could come up with.[32] He encouraged Churchill to make life difficult for them and in 1936 facilitated a meeting between Watson-Watt and Churchill in an attempt to stoke up conflict. It is fair to say that Watson-Watt very much viewed Lindemann as an ally because of their shared sense of urgency about the looming war. At that point, however, Blackett and Hill had enough and resigned from the committee. Tizard promptly had the committee disbanded and reformed without Lindemann, who was replaced by world-renowned radio expert, Edward Appleton. The committee meetings, at least, went much smoother from then on.

Lindemann was a strong personality and a good, possibly even outstanding, scientist[33] who firmly believed in the absolute truth of his own perspective, even when he was wrong. He pursued with tenacity the aerial mines idea and many others including the notion that infra red technology research being undertaken by R.V. Jones, a scientist in his laboratory, would be more promising than the radio wave work instigated by Tizard.

Tizard's committee has been held up[34] as a hugely effective government decision making instrument – a small group of highly motivated experts and system users, with the clarity of purpose, influence and resources to get things done. It is impossible to know how or whether the air defence system work would have progressed as it did, had Lindemann rather than Tizard been in charge. Lindemann's efforts, pursued in what he believed to be the best interests of the country, however, made Tizard's job somewhat more difficult than it would otherwise have been. Whether they might ultimately have led to failure in the development of the system is something we can only speculate about. Both Lindemann and Tizard undoubtedly made mistakes, which only goes to show that smart people with impeccable motives can still get things wrong. But the air defence system did get built and it helped Britain to prevail in the Battle of Britain, though the margin of victory was extremely thin.

When Churchill became Prime Minister, Lindemann became his sole high level scientific adviser and the only scientist in the Cabinet.[35] Churchill admitted himself that he had a limited level of scientific literacy:

"Lindemann could decipher the signals from the experts on the far horizons and explain to me in lucid, homely terms what the issues were."[36]

Scientists, though, are not immune to the influence of personal bias and values, as the battles between Tizard and Lindemann demonstrate. The application of science and scientific intelligence to the prosecution of the war would have been different, if Lindemann's advice to the Prime Minister had been subject to regular critical review by a group of scientific peers.[37] The position of scientifically and technically illiterate politicians having to make decisions about things they do not understand in depth has not gone away. Lindemann and Churchill may well have argued that they did not have the luxury of time available to subject their decisions to the kind of scrutiny the scientific method requires. We have no such excuse, in a digital age, when deploying or regulating large-scale information systems likely to have wide-reaching and long-term effects.

Lessons of radar: boundaries and purpose

Tizard once said:

"The secret of science is to ask the right question, and it is the choice of problem more than anything else that marks the man of genius in the scientific world."[38]

Tizard knew a promising technology when he saw it – as when Watson-Watt dropped radar into his lap just at the moment he began to head up Britain's air defence initiative in 1935 – but more importantly he knew how to ask the right questions and set appropriate boundaries. A lesser group than the Tizard committee might well have got carried away by the technology and focused exclusively on that; or alternatively have planned grand schemes to use this technology to solve all kinds of problems, military and social, before the technology had even been tested.

Tizard's committee had a clear purpose with clear boundaries to build a system, with the aid of the information this technology could generate, to enable defending squadrons to intercept enemy raiding aircraft at the earliest possible moment. Being clear about purpose, as well as about the boundaries of the systems and the problems or messes we are setting out to tackle, is critical in DDM. 'Systems thinking' specialists[39] tell us the choice of system boundary has a profound influence on how effective we can be subsequently at tackling complex messes. If Tizard had got distracted by building a radar system rather than retaining his focus on an air defence system, the Battle of Britain might well have had a different outcome.

By 1939 Tizard and Dowding created an integrated information system to collect the raw data on approaching enemy aircraft, from their chain of radar stations (IT) and (visuals from) the Observer Corps (human IT). This raw data was passed on (via the radio telephone and teleprinter networks) to Fighter Command Headquarters' filter room and an integrated set of operations centres, where it was assessed, filtered, analysed and turned into useful information at varying levels.[40] This then facilitated the scrambling of the right fighter squadrons and even more specific instructions to be radioed to the RAF pilots once in the air, to enable them to intercept their enemy at the earliest opportunity.[41]

The Germans had better information technology (radar). The British had the better information system i.e. radar, human intelligence, signals intelligence, and an integrated, purpose-developed system, allowing the situation to be viewed holistically, as well as delivering the right information to the right users, at the right levels, in a useful format and in sufficient time to act on it. The better information system prevailed and it got built because Tizard, Dowding and co. had:

- a clear purpose
- clear boundaries
- the power and political influence to act
- and they engaged and enthused both the users and scientific and technical experts in the system's development.

Electronic voting

In May of 2004 after spending €60 million on a computer-based voting system,[42] the Irish government postponed its nationwide deployment. Following public concerns the government had set up a Commission on Electronic Voting in March of that year, which by April concluded that it was "not in a position to recommend with the requisite degree of confidence the use of the chosen system at elections in Ireland in June 2004".[43] A second report by the Commission in July 2006 concluded that though it could recommend the use of e-voting equipment in Irish elections subject to specific upgrades, it was "unable to recommend the election management software for such use".[44] So the machines recording the votes will be ok with some modifications[45] but the election management software used to set up the system for elections and count the votes once the polls close is not of the required standard.[46]

Computer, Internet and electronic voting (or e-voting) of various types has been in the news periodically in recent years. In the UK the government has been keen to consider e-voting as a way to improve voter turnout, reasoning that young people with an affinity for computers will be more inclined to vote if they can do so electronically. In the autumn of 2004 India held the largest entirely electronic general election ever, using over one million voting machines to record the votes of an electorate of nearly 700 million people.[47]

In the US after the problems in Florida in the 2000 presidential election,[48] the Help America Vote act was passed which essentially requires punch card or lever voting machines[49] to be replaced with computer voting technologies.[50] Most of the media accounts at the time focused on the problems with the lever and punch card voting machines, hence the move to legislation to get rid of these. Blaming the machines led to the erroneous belief that simply replacing them with more modern machinery would solve the problem. Yet the integrity of the voting process depends on the trust of the electorate, which it is not within the gift of any machine to provide.

Ironically the lever machines were originally introduced in an effort to curb the excesses of US election rigging with paper ballot systems in the late 19th century. The Florida situation arose, however, because of failures in the voting process, including poorly designed ballot papers, faulty machines and the political machinations of the Republican and Democratic parties in their efforts to ensure their respective candidates would win. Neither the Bush nor the Gore camp was interested in transparency, fairness or an accurate measure of the will of the Florida electorate. The kind of partisan (if expedient from the perspective of each camp) activities to stop the vote count whilst Bush was ahead or continue counting until Gore sneaked into the lead, that played out in public in the Bush v Gore case, is not something that we see very often in the wake of a democratic election, though. Conventional wisdom has it that Bush shaded it in the end because the Republicans controlled the State's political machinery and there was a conservative majority on the US Supreme Court, which also got dragged into the dispute, preferred to have a conservative president. The reality is that we will never really know who would have won, had the *intent of all those people who voted or attempted to vote been reflected in the final vote count* in Florida in 2000.[51]

The voting process, just like Britain's air defence system, is about more than the machines that are used. E-voting machines in addition to being individually fit for purpose can only be properly evaluated as an integrated part of the voting system as a whole under operational conditions. Just as Dowding and Tizard tested and developed their air defence system and the radar machines that formed part of it through operational research, so we must manage any large-scale transition from paper to electronic voting systems. In Ireland the Commission on Electronic Voting confirmed that one of its key concerns was that though all the components of the Irish e-voting system had been subject to extensive testing by the manufacturers and independent laboratories, *the system as a whole* had not been reviewed under operational conditions in the environment where it was supposed to be used.[52]

Computers are pretty good at counting. My first impressions were that computers should be pretty good at counting votes. In Holland they had been running elections with e-voting systems apparently without significant problems for many years. Then serious flaws in the system were brought to the attention of the Dutch electorate in the autumn of 2006.[53]

In Italy, an observer of an e-voting experiment in Rome, where the e-voting system was used in parallel with the standard paper ballots, raised some significant concerns.[54] The observer, Emmanuele Somma, a fellow of the Free Software Foundation Europe,[55] reported that the computer operator who was in charge of the system at the polling station did not have the official documentation certifying him as an approved e-voting supervisor. On the day of the election the operator noticed the machine had made some errors and attempted to re-program it to correct these. He gave up trying to fix the problem when Somma pointed out that the law prohibits any changes to the voting machines once they have been tested and certified.

Now it is very sensible to ban any tampering with a voting machine once it has been set up and certified but anyone who has ever used a computer will at some point have had problems with it. These systems will go wrong in operation and there needs to be some kind of back-up plan in place to deal with the situation when it happens. The operator probably quite reasonably felt that he was just trying to get the machine to do the job it was supposed to do – his version of a back-up plan. Yet unless the integrity of his changes could be tested, approved and certified on the spot e.g. by trusted and independent senior election officials who knew the technology intimately, the integrity of any voting subsequently carried out on the machine would be compromised. The computer, though nominally excellent at counting, introduces extra complications to the *voting process* that did not previously exist.

Somma also requested a copy of the software that ran the voting machine but was informed that it was a trade secret. Think about that for a minute. The instructions running the machines that count the votes are a trade secret. Joseph Stalin once said that:

"it's not the people who vote that count but the people who count the votes."

Even if the voting machine manufacturers and all their employees are the most upstanding and honest individuals in the world, the integrity of the voting process is compromised if *the very instructions which tell the machines how to register and count votes are secret.*[56] Strangely enough he says he later found a copy of the CD with the software in a bin outside the polling station, along with details of the access codes for the system.[57]

I am all for using technology to tackle problems and improve processes like voting, if appropriate. However, the Italian experience and more broadly the radar story demonstrate that to be useful it has to be used in a purposeful way. There needs to be a clear focus. The technology has to be used as a reliable and properly integrated component of the overall system and with a clear understanding of the other problems it generates, as well as ways of managing these effectively. Computers are complex, prone to programming errors, crashing and mischievous or malicious interference. They do what they are programmed to do, *not what we would like them to do* and any software that has over two hundred thousand lines of programming instructions, as the Irish e-voting system has for example, will contain errors. So the electronic voting scenario is not as simple as it first appears.

In the UK we use a paper-based system first introduced in Australia in 1856.[58] The big change in Australia at the time was to introduce a standardised ballot listing all candidates and parties, the printing of which was funded by the government. Previously each political party had printed and distributed their own ballots with their own distinctive shapes and colours.[59] Under the new system the ballots were provided to voters at the polling stations, where they were required to vote in secret in curtained-off booths and then immediately deposit the ballot with their vote into a sealed ballot box. Compare that with the system in Ireland at the time when voting was done in public and tenants who failed to vote in accordance with their landlord's wishes were subject to immediate eviction from their homes and the small patches of land on which they etched out a meagre living for their families. The security against voting fraud provided by the

Australian ballot is fairly obvious by comparison. As Professor Douglas Jones of the University of Iowa said in the wake of the Florida 2000 episode:

"A properly administered Australian paper ballot sets a very high standard, assuring voter privacy, preventing voters from revealing how they voted, and assuring an accurate and impartial count. It sets such a high standard that voters from many parts of the world find it remarkable that we in the United States are willing to trust our votes to anything else. This is particularly true of the British Commonwealth, where paper ballots remain the rule."[60]

The paper ballot system is a classic example of the social technologies introduced in Chapter 2 – a set of tried and tested, tightly coupled rules and procedures to regulate the voting process, which when honestly, fairly and effectively administered has consistently delivered election results describing the preferred choice of the majority of electorate in each constituency.[61] The system is labour intensive, relying on many volunteers staffing the polling stations and the vote counts but each step of the process is simple and transparent. This simplicity and transparency, monitored by many eyes, makes it extremely robust. It also has the security of compartmentalisation, since no one person or small group can engage in highly damaging levels of electoral fraud without compromising significant numbers of individual polling stations or ballot boxes. What is really impressive, though, given the nature of complexity whereby apparently remote components of a system can interact in unforeseeable or unexpected ways, is that the voting systems in places like the UK, Canada and Ireland work as well as they do. Yet when his attempts to replace this system with new electronic voting machines began to raise concerns Taoiseach Bertie Ahern (the Irish Prime Minister) was dismissive of calls to build an auditable paper trail into the system. He said "We are not going to go back to pushing pieces of paper around the place" and accused critics[62] of wanting "to keep old ways, old things, the old nonsensical past".[63] Within a couple of months, however, he had the sense to agree to have the Voting Commission examine the issues.

The paper system was introduced in Britain in 1872 and in Canada in 1874 and basically remains the same today. We go to the polling station, identify ourselves,[64] collect our paper ballot, mark our vote in secret on the ballot paper with a pencil and deposit it in the sealed ballot box. The ballot boxes remain sealed until the polls close and the count begins under public scrutiny. All the votes get counted and the winners are elected. The process sets a high standard but can it be improved or made more efficient by using computers? It does not seem too complicated. Surely it is no more complicated than the bank's cash machine counting the amount of cash I take out with the help of my trusty bank card? Well the story of electronic voting turns out to have more in common with the story of radar than of banking (though the expertise of bookkeepers and accountants would be highly relevant to ensuring the integrity of the process). Except that in this case it concerns the failure rather than the success of the development of an information system.

The electronic banking situation is actually significantly different to electronic voting because the bank customer gets a monthly statement, providing *a paper-based customer-verifiable audit trail* relating to the electronic transactions done via a cash machine. Most electronic voting systems currently in existence have no equivalent.[65] When a voter presses the buttons on an electronic voting machine, they have no way of knowing that the vote they cast is recorded or counted accurately by the computer; or that the processing it gets subjected to by the electronic innards of the machine (and those machines it is connected to) does not corrupt that vote in some way.[66]

It is a trivial exercise for a computer programmer who knows what they are doing to get the computer to display one message on the screen e.g. saying a vote has been recorded for candidate 1, whilst recording a vote for candidate 2 in a memory card or disk. Alternatively a computer could be programmed to secretly transfer a percentage of candidate 1's votes to candidate 2 and then delete the code making these changes when voting closes.[67] This problem is exacerbated by the fact that most voting machine manufacturers use proprietary software meaning the instructions that run the machines are secret. There is no way for the voter to know if something goes wrong. Often voting officials with little or no understanding of the inner workings of the technology let the computer experts tell them the results. There was a wonderful illustration of the difficulty in monitoring electronic elections in the 2002 Governorship election in Nebraska. The law in Nebraska states that the candidates are entitled to watch the count when the votes have been cast. One of the candidates, eager to see democracy in action asked if he could be allowed to monitor the count. He was shown an optical scanning machine and then a computer in another room with a blank screen.[68]

A voting system could be considered to require all of the following components (though this is not an exclusive list):

- voter registration and register
- system for registering and identifying candidates for election
- system for creating ballots (e.g. designing and printing paper ballots or programming or setting machines)

- voter identification at polling booth (or absentee e.g. via post or Net)[69]
- system for recording votes, privately, secretly, anonymously and securely[70]
- a way for voters to know their vote has been recorded accurately and securely without providing them with takeaway proof they voted in a particular way to collect a bribe or satisfy someone engaging in voter intimidation
- systems for counting votes precisely, accurately and with integrity
- systems for testing systems that record and count votes i.e. advance certification of integrity of the computers and the process
- systems for auditing the integrity of elections.

The system fundamentally has to ensure that the vote as intended by the voter must be recorded and counted with integrity and the final certified result must identify the will of the majority of those who have voted at the time they cast their vote. The final vote count must clearly represent the intent of the voters. The paper ballot systems in use in the UK, Ireland and other parts of the European Union, have a proven record of operating to the high standards required to ensure public trust in the mechanics of electoral process. We should be careful, therefore, in introducing computing machinery to replace parts of that process, that we understand clearly what we might be giving up, as well as what challenges the use of the new technologies provide.[71] Just as failure of any of the components of a tightly coupled complex system can have all kinds of unintended knock on effects, replacing some of those components with different technologies – e.g. computers instead of paper – can also have unintended consequences.

Computer scientists[72] and civil rights activists in the US have been explaining some of the security problems with the e-voting systems deployed there for some years.[73] There are four main suppliers of evoting systems in the US: Election Systems and Software (ES&S), Diebold Election Systems, Sequoia Voting Systems and Hart InterCivic. There are hundreds of documented cases of these systems failing in some way.[74] The most famous example comes again from Florida and the Bush v Gore presidential election in November 2000. In the 216th precinct of Volusia County, Florida, a Diebold machine recorded that 412 people had voted out of 585 registered voters in the area. That would seem pretty reasonable. Unfortunately the machine translated those 412 votes in the vote count into 2813 votes for Bush and also subtracted 16,022 votes from Gore's total.[75] In a race finally decided by 537 votes that is a significant error. Fortunately the error was noticed. In the end they found out that 22 people in the precinct had actually voted for Bush and 193 for Gore.[76]

Since the e-voting machines are based largely on ordinary personal computers adapted for this new purpose of recording and counting votes, the computer scientists have been able to identify standard computer security problems well known from other contexts. It means that since they have been able to fix these problems[77] on ordinary computers it should be possible to fix them on the voting machines too. But introducing these computers into tightly coupled complex voting systems without taking steps to address even their standard known failure modes can put the entire system at risk. Also, unlike a soundly administered paper system, small numbers of attackers, with the right kind of access, can compromise large parts of the system, especially when the machines are networked. Even when not networked the equivalent of the paper system's large sealed metal ballot box is a small memory card the size of a credit card or a CD.[78] Securing the chain of custody of small items like memory cards between the voting machine and the counting centre is slightly more difficult than larger items like big sealed boxes. It remains a mystery to this day how the faulty memory card got plugged into the system in the early hours of the morning in Florida's Volusia County, in the Bush v Gore 2000 election, temporarily favouring one candidate to the tune of over 18,000 votes.

In June 2006, New York University's Brennan Center for Justice published a report[79] by a team of international experts assessing the main e-voting systems used in the US. It concluded that the systems were vulnerable to attack but that the threat of interference with the voting process could be reduced by taking some simple steps, including randomly auditing paper records. They said:

- The systems had significant security and reliability problems, "which pose a real danger to the integrity of national, state, and local elections".
- The worst problems could be "substantially remedied if proper countermeasures are implemented at the state and local level".
- Few of these remedies have been implemented anywhere

So, as in the Irish case, the e-voting systems could work but at the moment are not to be recommended, at least in the ways that they are currently being used. One of the key remedies most serious computer scientists have been recommending is the use of a voter-verified paper audit trail with these systems. Known as the Mercuri method,[80] it involves the voting machines printing out a paper version of the recorded vote, as well as displaying it on the screen. The voter can then be confident that the computer is not displaying the required vote for candidate 1 on the screen whilst secretly allocating the vote to candidate 2. The paper print-outs stand as ordinary paper ballots which are counted in addition to the machine counts. If the paper and machine counts then tally we can say with a high degree of confidence that the system worked securely and reliably.

It is a sound idea but again, in itself, not a panacea to the problems thrown up by e-voting systems. Adding printers to these machines adds more technical complexity and therefore more potential technical problems. One very simple problem with a printer that is used for a few days every couple of years is that the ink cartridge will dry out. Another typical problem is that printers occasionally chew up the paper.[81] In addition the voter-verified paper audit can only help to shore up the integrity of the system if the other system components and the system as a whole merit the trust of the electorate.

In a story on the state of the US electoral system, Robert F. Kennedy Jr., writing in *Rolling Stone* magazine in June 2006, wondered whether George W. Bush really won the 2004 election.[82] It is a long story, filled with statistics, analysis and accusations, focused on anomalies in the key swing state of Ohio.

The gist of the allegations was that the Republican Party orchestrated a campaign to:

- purge thousands of Democrat-leaning eligible voters from the electoral rolls
- block the processing of registrations generated by Democratic voter drives
- provide too few voting machines to Democrat-leaning districts and more than enough to Republican areas, leading to longer waiting times for mainly Democratic voters
- illegally fix a recount that could have given Kerry the presidency
- illegally alter paper and electronic ballots, switching votes for Kerry to favour Bush
- intimidate and aggressively challenge the right of Democratic voters to vote, at the polling stations on election day
- illegally destroy 'provisional ballots' of Democratic voters.

In the article, Kennedy says:

"In what may be the single most astounding fact from the election, one in every four Ohio citizens who registered to vote in 2004 showed up at the polls only to discover that they were not listed on the rolls, thanks to GOP efforts to stem the unprecedented flood of Democrats eager to cast ballots.[83] And that doesn't even take into account the troubling evidence of outright fraud, which indicates that upwards of 80,000 votes for Kerry were counted instead for Bush. That alone is a swing of more than 160,000 votes – enough to have put John Kerry in the White House."

The sheer scale of the alleged fraud, the numbers of people supposedly involved in achieving it and the hundreds of thousands of Ohio voters apparently affected make it pretty unlikely that it could be covered up. Indeed Rep. John Conyers of Michigan and Democratic Members and Staff of the House Judiciary Committee published a report[84] on some of the anomalies in Ohio in January 2005, but I am not aware that it led to any further action, legal or otherwise, in pursuit of alleged perpetrators of fraud. Kennedy and Conyers raise some important questions but Kennedy's allegations relating to fraud in electronic vote counts would be difficult to investigate without a Mercuri-type voter-verifiable paper audit trail.

The key figure behind all this was supposedly Kenneth Blackwell, the co-chair of President Bush's re-election committee and also, as Ohio Secretary of State, the man in charge of counting the votes in Ohio. Even if Mr Blackwell,[85] as a decent, honest and upstanding citizen, did not break any rules[86] he would not be considered by his own party to be doing his job as the top official in Bush's election campaign if he did not exploit the rules to their limits in order to favour his own candidate. It just does not make any sense for someone[87] with formal duties giving rise to a conflict of interest – ensuring the voting is fair and ensuring their boy wins – to be in charge of the voting process. That is a problem a voter-verified paper audit trail alone cannot put right.

The Australian paper ballot system can of course be compromised before voters get anywhere near a polling station. Ireland in particular should be sensitive to this and to any substantive changes they might make in the machinery of the electoral process. A treaty with Britain in 1921 granted independence to the Irish Free State[88] and introduced the border whereby the British parliament retained sovereignty over the six counties that became Northern Ireland. The treaty also contained a provision for the setting up of an independent boundary commission to review the wishes of the people of Northern Ireland with the intent of re-drawing the border should a majority of the people be in favour of such a move.[89] In an early indication of how the voting process was to pan out in Northern Ireland for most of the rest of the 20th-century, the British government failed to follow through with the commitment to the boundary commission and dropped the proposal by 1925, largely as a result of pressure from Unionists in Northern Ireland.[90]

Had the commission expedited the required duties, the chances are that it would have recommended re-drawing the border with the counties of Fermanagh, Tyrone and probably most of Derry being ceded to the Free State. Most of the residents of these areas were Catholics and nationalists anxious to move under the jurisdiction of the Free State.[91] This systematic undermining of the rights of a certain section of the population – largely poor, nationalist and Catholic – was a feature of Northern Irish politics for the greater part of the 20th-century.

Blatant manipulation of the electoral process formed the keystone of this discrimination. There was rampant gerrymandering whereby constituency borders were regularly redrawn to ensure even the unionist minority populations in certain areas always controlled elected bodies.[92] By the 1960s the 'Campaign for Social Justice' set up by Conn and Patricia McCluskey began to document all the cases of discrimination and electoral manipulation in detail. Unlike the rest of Britain, whereby people become entitled to vote on reaching a certain age, there was no such right in Northern Ireland. Only the owner of a house and their spouse, or the tenant of a council house and their spouse, was entitled to vote.[93] No one else who lived in the house had a vote, even children of voting age. Austin Currie in 1964 the youngest MP ever elected to the Northern Ireland parliament did not have a vote in local elections because he lived with his parents and their large family. Currie said:

"Housing was the key to the vote. The vote at local government elections was restricted to property owners and their spouses. Or to tenants of public authority houses and their spouses... The purpose of the exercise was to ensure that Unionists had supremacy in the areas where in fact they were in the minority... This was the only way in which Unionists could remain in control. That's why housing was such a fundamental matter. The allocation of a public authority house was not just the allocation of a house. It was the allocation of two votes. Therefore, in marginal areas he who controlled the allocation of public authority housing effectively controlled the voting in that area."[94]

80,000 people of voting age in Belfast alone were denied a vote in local council elections, whereas about 12,000 mostly protestant Queen's University Belfast graduates controlled four out of fifty two seats in the national parliament at Stormont. In Derry city, the population was about two-thirds Catholic and one-third Protestant but gerrymandering and the property vote system ensured that the Unionists always retained majority control of the city council. The city was divided into three constituencies or 'wards'. Two of these wards controlled twelve seats on the council between them. The third controlled eight seats. The first two wards together had about 12,000 voters, with Protestants outnumbering Catholics by about two to one. They returned Unionist representatives to all twelve seats. The third ward also had about 12,000 voters with Catholics outnumbering Protestants by ten to one and returning Catholics to all eight seats.

Tim Pat Coogan questions how such a situation could arise in any part of Britain whereby the "housing system and much else besides embodied such marked departures from British practice".[95] It seems that there was a ruling by the Speaker of the British Parliament at Westminster in 1922 that

Northern Ireland matters could not be raised in the House of Commons. But Coogan concludes the real reason was the unwritten and unspoken agreement amongst Westminster politicians that Ireland was a thorny issue best stayed clear of for the sake of political expediency.[96]

Technology will not and cannot cure an electoral process that is broken and distorted to that extent, whether the mechanics of voting are done through paper or computers. The paper ballot system, properly administered, can indeed be more robust than e-voting systems currently deployed but there is no voting process that has ever been devised that is immune from the possibility of manipulation. The trustworthy implementation of e-voting systems will come down to issues beyond the control of computers.

Though I endorse the current call, of most computer scientists with an understanding of these systems, for a voter-verifiable paper audit trail, this will not in itself rectify the problem of deploying these systems safely and securely. As for voting via the Internet or post, that takes the control of the voting outside the polling stations. This makes these votes too easy to manipulate, so in my opinion is not to be recommended at the moment. A simple illustration of the problem is that a family or gang matriarch could dictate which way family members would vote or even cast all the family votes herself.

I had a chat about computers and voting with my two children, Jack who was eight years old at the time and Nicholas who was seven. Jack loves computers and ever since he was a toddler has taken an interest in coming along with me to the polling station whenever there is an election. He quickly decided that evoting machines could be compromised – someone could program them to vote for dad while pretending on the screen that they recorded a vote for Jack. He had two solutions:

1. You have to be able to examine the software that runs the systems and all the detailed instructions they include.

2. The machines should print out the vote as well as showing it on screen and the voter should check the print out and put it in a ballot box like an ordinary paper ballot. Then these can be checked in the vote counting to ensure no one messed with the computer.[97]

He had a couple of other ideas too. He thought that the machines should be programmable once only and "un-re-programmable" after being set up and security checked for an election. Then he decided that might be difficult to achieve, so he thought maybe they should be physically locked away and if possible electronically locked too once they have been set up for an election. Finally he thought some more and said:

"You should stick to the paper system dad. It's much better and not so complicated."

For a boy who is pretty obsessed with computers that is quite a statement. Nicholas took a much more straightforward line, believing that the computers would be much quicker at actually counting the votes. He figured that all that paper would just take "ages and ages".

What if someone programmed the machine to secretly give a vote to dad instead of Nicholas?

"That would be unfair, dad!"

How do you stop it?

"That's easy. Only let the good people programme the computers."

What if they made a mistake?

"Hmm. You mean like I make mistakes with computer games sometimes?"

Yes a bit like that.

"Or it might get a virus too dad! So you need to be able to look and see what it's telling Ella and Ernie to do, especially if you have to get rid of the virus."

[At this point I need to explain that in order to answer my children's questions about electronic devices, a few years ago I made up some stories about families of electrons running around inside the machines and making them work. 'Ella' and 'Ernie' are the two main characters. But like Jack he has got the idea that the instructions cannot be secret.]

What if the machine broke down?

"Fix it. Computers are always going wrong."

You're not allowed to fix it once it's been set up for the election.

"That's stupid dad."

What if the person fixing the machine secretly set it up to give Nicholas' votes to dad?

"Would the fixing person do something like that?" [Nicholas was both worried and annoyed at such a prospect.]

Well luckily most people are honest, so probably not.

The conversations went on and I learned a lot more from the boys than they did from me. The moral of the story is that if two young children can quickly understand that voting is a complicated process and that introducing computers can present more questions than answers, then those in charge of managing the system should also be capable of asking and getting informed answers to those questions. They also need:

- a clear purpose
- clear boundaries
- the engagement through thorough operational research of both the users[98] and scientific and technical experts[99] in the system's development
- an absolutely clear understanding that the technology is just a potentially useful tool – the information system is not limited to the technology and the technology alone will not fix major systemic or structural problems when it comes to the electoral process.

Above all, whether in Ireland, the UK or other places considering replacing paper with computers, or the US where various forms of voting machinery have been used for over a hundred years and now they are migrating to computers, the utmost care should be taken in 'improving' a highly integrated, tightly coupled complex system, which has consistently delivered what has been required of it for generations,[100] even if, on this side of the Atlantic, paper is beginning to seem somewhat old fashioned.[101] Simple systems which fulfill their required purpose are better than complex systems which do not.

Chapter 8 DDM in intellectual property

"Only one thing is impossible for God: to find any sense in any copyright law on the planet." Mark Twain

Introduction

In this chapter I want to return to the areas of intellectual property and access to knowledge covered explicitly in the context of James Boyle's ideas outlined in Chapter 2. As I suggested earlier in the book, the default rules of the road in digital decision making (DDM) are the laws governing information flows and technologies. The rules of intellectual property constitute a significant chunk of those laws and no book on DDM would be complete without at least some cursory consideration of how those laws get made.

In Chapter 4 I explained that US intellectual property laws very often get drafted by the interested industries.[1] Here I will look in a bit more detail at how decisions about intellectual property policies are made, how the most important influences are national and international and what that might mean for the 'including the stakeholders and experts' model of DDM this book has been advocating. Over the course of the last fifteen years, since the World Wide Web made an impact on the public consciousness, the knowledge economy and the rules which govern it have been going through something of an upheaval. Larry Lessig describes the situation as revolution in innovation, put down by a counter-revolution by established commercial interests.[2]

For the greater part of 150 years prior to this, information production had been an industrial-scale operation open to those with the resources to invest in printing presses, broadcasting technologies and the workforces needed to keep these running. Now the printing press and a potential worldwide audience are in the hands of anyone with a computer connected to the Internet. Of course, even today printing presses are smashed and their owners abused by those who fear the message they spread e.g. Zimbabwean newspapers opposing President Mugabe or civil rights bloggers in China. Having access to a printing press is no guarantee of access to an audience. The focus of this chapter, however, is the story of how the intellectual property system has developed in the late 20th and early 21st-centuries, through growing extra barnacles rather than through coherent systemic development.

Before getting into this process though, I would like to outline some general concerns I have about the sustainability of our current communications architectures and what that might mean for access to knowledge, if Boyle is right about an impending second enclosure movement. The underlying theme of this book is that information gathering, storage and sharing is key to decision making, and good DDM needs these processes to be available to the widest possible set of participants. None of these processes can be carried out without the use of energy, and energy currently comes almost entirely from fossil fuels like oil and coal. Fossil fuels are scarce, becoming scarcer, and there are competing demands for them. Therefore, access to information is likely to be curtailed by energy shortages.[3]

Sustainable infodiversity

We have burned through a large proportion of the earth's fossil fuel resources in the blink of an eye on evolutionary timescales. Over the course of the past two hundred years or so, through our increasing consumption of the earth's coal, oil and gas, not only have we depleted those resources but we have slowly poisoned and over-heated the earth.[4]

A – so far I believe – largely neglected effect of this pattern of consumption is the impact it will have on digital information in the knowledge economy, through the energy, material and environmental costs of current information and communications technologies (ICTs).[5] In the UK alone we throw away tens of millions of computers, mobile phones, printers, and other ICT items every year. Since information is what economists call 'non-rivalrous' – so if I tell you my idea, I still have the idea[6] – there is a widespread belief that, once information is digitised, it can be copied and distributed at zero marginal cost, i.e. 'for free'. Yet digital information fundamentally depends on access to a source of energy; and our main sources of energy like oil, coal and gas are a depleting resource. Before moving on, ask yourself a few questions about this assumption that digital information is free:

- Have you got a broadband internet connection at home?
- Is it free?
- Do you have free access to the Internet somewhere else?
- Did you get your PC for free?
- How about your printer?
- Free scanner?
- Free digital camera?
- Mobile phone?
- Perhaps you have free electricity?
- Or maybe these devices run on free everlasting batteries, without the need for re-charging?[7]
- Did you ever get a virus through downloading a song 'freely' from the Internet?

So we need a whole pile of moderately costly hardware and software, which rapidly becomes slow, obsolete and in need of replacing, as well as access to energy and communications utilities *before* we can get access to all this 'free' information. Thomas Jefferson said:

"If nature has made any one thing less susceptible than all others of exclusive property, it is the action of the thinking power called an Idea, which an individual may exclusively possess as long as he keeps it to himself; but the moment it is divulged, it forces itself into the possession of everyone, and the receiver cannot dispossess himself of it. Its peculiar character, too, is that no one possesses the less, because every other possesses the whole of it. He who receives an idea from me receives instruction himself without lessening mine; as he who lights his taper at mine, receives light without darkening me. That ideas should freely spread from one to another over the globe, for the moral and mutual instruction of man, and improvement of his condition, seems to have been peculiarly and benevolently designed by nature"

As someone interested in facilitating access to knowledge and ideas, this is one of my favorite quotations but just as wine needs bottles, digital information needs electronic container vessels like computers. So even if it was free, in the sense of 'free beer as opposed to free speech',[8] digital information will always have an energy cost and our current ICT architectures are energy intensive.[9] The big technology companies' energy bills can run into hundreds of millions of dollars. Up to half of that energy can be taken up with the cooling needed by large computer server farms run by companies like Google, AOL or Microsoft. We use a lot of energy to run the computers, which because the equipment generates so much waste heat, needs as much energy again just to cool them down. In a world possibly facing an energy crisis this means digital information is a little more rivalrous than we originally thought.[10] We cannot just put some digital information on a computer connected to the Internet and assume that it then automatically constitutes an infinitely deep well from which we can forevermore draw that information freely.

I did a little experiment with my relatively old, low specification home computer one day, when my wife took the kids to visit their grandparents. I shut off all the other electrical devices in the house and checked the electricity meter to see how much energy my home PC and associated peripherals used. It turned out that they use about a unit of electricity every nine hours, when not doing any heavy processing, or 1/9th of a unit an hour. That is just my one home PC. Multiply this by 20 million, assuming there is that number of household PCs in the UK. That is about 2.2 million units of electricity per hour if the PCs are just switched on and running on idle. UK domestic PCs, just ticking over, rate over 2 megawatts. Now factor in the commercial sector and are you are suddenly faced with very high energy costs, simply to keep the high tech network that is the Internet, with its energy guzzling PCs at the ends, merely ticking over. Sun's chief technology officer, Greg Papadopoulos,[11] estimates that large technology companies' data centres alone need about 25 gigawatts. This is the energy output of dozens of power plants before even thinking about the hundreds of millions of networked user PCs.

Current ICTs are energy intensive and could be greatly improved. In an energy-rich economy these costs might not get a lot of attention but a global economy, in which we may see rationing of dwindling energy resources like oil, has implications for digital information and who gets access to it. That concerns me at a time when we are increasing our level of dependence on digital information especially since, if scholars like Boyle and Lessig are right, developments in intellectual property and other information laws are moving in the direction of restricting access to information. The combination of energy rationing and Boyle's second enclosure movement[12] could threaten our ability to make informed decisions about complex information systems and our access to the basic raw materials of education. Critics will rightly point out that access to information has been a problem in the developing world for generations, a situation which the affluent West has been complicit in creating. Now such access issues might come to the middle classes in the West, ironically in an age where so much information is allegedly free.

Deciding intellectual property policy

Since the intellectual property system has a big impact in the regulation of access to information, it is important that the system is balanced in the interests of all the relevant stakeholders, including those who produce intellectual property such as authors and those who value access to it, like readers. I am pessimistic about the impact an impending global energy crisis will have on access to information, so it seems even more important that the system should be well balanced. There are numerous arguments suggesting the system is too skewed in favour of big industry and others saying it is not tough enough on those who infringe intellectual property. For now, though, let us look at the decision making processes through which those laws get made and evolve.

Uphoff's levels of decision making

In 1992 Norman Uphoff wrote a paper for the International Institute for Environment and Development[13] outlining his belief in the importance of local institutions and local participation in decision making to facilitate sustainable agriculture. He said:

"Sustainable development involves many things… One contributing factor that deserves more attention is local institutions and their concomitant, local participation. However, it must be recognised that local institutions can produce practices that do not favour sustainability. If factionalism prevails, some groups may use them to exploit local resources to their short-run advantage and others' loss."

Uphoff suggested that thinking of decisions in terms of different levels and activity can provide some helpful insights into decision making processes. He outlined ten levels as follows:

1. International level
2. National level
3. Regional/provincial level
4. District level
5. Sub-district level
6. Locality level
7. Community level
8. Group level
9. Household level
10. Individual level.

DDM in intellectual property firmly resides in Uphoff's top two levels, national and international, where the most influential decision making forums are the World Trade Organisation (WTO), the World Intellectual Property Organization (WIPO),[14] the US Congress and the European Union's Commission and Council of Ministers. Yet the kind of factionalism that concerns Uphoff at local level is just as likely to infect the national or international arenas, as small groups, usually representing large institutions or governments, tend to have a disproportionate degree of influence. The key to getting the kinds of intellectual property laws you want is to exert influence in the decision making bodies listed above. In his examples of institutional channels and roles for decision-making and action, Uphoff lists: bilateral and multilateral donor agencies, the Society for International Development, multinational corporations, international NGOs, national ministries, central government ministries, parastatal corporations, national cooperative federations, national corporations and national NGOs.

He omits to mention influential individuals and small groups with connections. There has been no place at the table for ordinary users of intellectual property, simply because ordinary people very rarely have direct access to the forums involved in national and international negotiations. But in spite of the difficulties involved, every DDM process so far explored in this book, from radar to the management of biodiversity, has benefited from the involvement of informed and sensible system users and ongoing operational research. Nevertheless intellectual property DDM does not work like that.

A short history of intellectual property

The first copyright law is reputed to be the Statute of Anne enacted in England in 1710.[15] The continental tradition of copyright, including a strong recognition of the moral rights of authors, arguably began during the French revolution. In the US, the first federal copyright act was passed in

1790 and was based on the English experience. Internationally, through most of the 18th and 19th-centuries copyright in foreign works was largely ignored and publishers all round the world engaged in mass piracy of popular or important foreign works. Interestingly, these publishers saw themselves as honourable men engaged in a public service of making cheap books widely available[16] whereas today, at least in the West, they would be accused of masterminding criminal enterprises. Gradually, bilateral agreements between states led to reciprocal recognition of copyrights in those countries.

Eventually, due to trade pressure and prominent advocates for change like the author Victor Hugo, the multilateral Berne Convention for the Protection of Literary and Artistic Works was agreed in 1886. The agreement gave international protection to books, music, art, architecture and the moral rights of creators, protections which had developed in signature countries. The Berne Convention has seen a number of significant revisions since its inception, the most recent being in 1971, and it remains one of the most important international copyright treaties to this day (with 159 nations subscribed).[17]

Patents, like copyrights, began life as crown-granted monopoly trade privileges over a whole range of basic goods such as iron, textiles and oil. The first intellectual property rights were, therefore, tools of monopoly and censorship and as such became the focus of severe criticism amongst advocates for free trade.

Information feudalism?[18]

The making of modern intellectual property laws is a complicated process dominated by the World Trade Organization (WTO),[19] the United Nations' World Intellectual Property Organization (WIPO), the United States and the European Union. The WTO and WIPO are very complex bureaucracies and the US and EU are not exactly models of simplicity when it comes to making laws either. So in the interests of attempting to make this section readable I am going to skip over some of the detailed mechanics of the decision making committees and processes in these organisations. The danger in doing this is that I will fail to present a sufficiently comprehensive picture of DDM in intellectual property to enable the reader to appreciate it in all its glory. Nevertheless, in the interests of achieving accessibility it is sometimes necessary to sacrifice complexity. Hopefully a reader who can get a feel for the process here will subsequently be able to tackle richer accounts[20] of the same story with greater confidence.

My father once said to me that if you like black pudding or beef burgers, you should never watch them being made.[21] Having looked at some of the processes involved I have come to the conclusion that intellectual property laws are a bit like that. The most important international agreement on intellectual property over the past thirty years (and arguably the most important of the entire 20th-century) is 'TRIPS,' the 'Agreement on Trade Related Aspects of Intellectual Property Rights' of 1994.[22] It sets an international minimum standard for intellectual property protection for any country wanting to be a member of the WTO and here I would like to outline the story of how TRIPS came about.

Anyone who has spent any time working in government services will testify to the complex maze of interrelated committees and procedures that take care of the day-to-day business of those institutions. Very often it can lead to the kind of gridlock whereby very little can seem to get done over a long period of time[23] and the World Intellectual Property Organization (WIPO) was felt to be suffering from precisely this kind of seizure through much of the 1970s and 1980s.[24] Often the way to get things moving in this kind of situation is to place the right people in the most influential committees or to bypass the committees and sometimes even the institutions completely. The US industries dependent on intellectual property for their income, such as the pharmaceutical, entertainment and high tech sectors, set about doing both. Pfizer and IBM led the efforts to bypass WIPO, much to the disgust of WIPO officials,[25] by successfully arranging for intellectual property to become the centre of the US strategy in the international trade negotiations at the General Agreement on Tariffs and Trade (GATT).[26]

Pfizer systematically, through the 1970s, populated the committees of US trade associations and business networks with their executives. They very effectively gathered support within the business community for their message that intellectual property protection was the key to the future health of the US economy. Towards the end of the 1970s and into the early 1980s they also found a receptive audience amongst the lawmakers in Washington DC, who were concerned about the loss of jobs and decline in the US manufacturing sector. The inhabitants of Capitol Hill were in the market for a solution to the country's perceived economic woes and were happy to jump on the intellectual property bandwagon, even though most of them had little understanding of the system.[27]

So the domestic politicians were being educated about intellectual property but that was only one more step towards getting it on the international trade agenda. Another critical route to that goal was through the 'Advisory Committee on Trade Negotiations'[28] which was considered the US business community's voice of wisdom on US economic interests. Its job was to advise the US President, through the 'Office of the US Trade Representative,' on trade policy. Pfizer, IBM, the entertainment and semiconductor sectors and other like minded commercial interests decided they need to control that committee. Pfizer's chairman and chief executive, Edmund Pratt became a member of the committee in 1979 and was its chairman between 1981 and 1987. John Opel, chairman of IBM, led the committee's special task force on intellectual property. In addition to influencing the major US business networks they ensured that respected independent public policy think tanks, such as the Heritage Foundation[29] and the Brookings Institution,[30] received financial support for projects which would highlight the importance of intellectual property to the US economy.

In addition to this domestic activity, Pratt and Opel oversaw, through the Advisory Committee on Trade Negotiations, a huge international lobbying effort, particularly focused on the European business community. If the Europeans could be brought on board the developing nations' long-time opposition to including intellectual property in the GATT international trade talks might be overcome. Developing countries understandably saw WIPO as the forum for negotiating intellectual property policy, as the United Nations agency set up for just that purpose.[31]

In 1981 the US trade representative set up the 'Quad', an informal group of trade negotiators from the US, Canada, Europe and Japan, an inner circle which could reach a consensus in advance of GATT negotiations on key issues. By 1986, the US trade representative told Pfizer's Pratt and his committee that there was no deep commitment from the other Quad members for a strong stance on intellectual property at the imminent Uruguay round of GATT talks: "I'm convinced on intellectual property but when I go to Quad meetings, they are under no pressure from their industry. Can you get it?"[32]

Pratt and Opel then created the 'Intellectual Property Committee' (IPC) made up of senior executives from thirteen US multinational companies. Working the boardrooms of Europe and Japan, within the available six months they succeeded in convincing their counterparts to apply the requisite pressure to European governments and trade regulators. The result was that the Quad's trade representatives showed up at the initial meeting of the Uruguay round of trade talks all singing from the same hymn sheet on intellectual property. They presented a coordinated draft *Statement of Views of the European, Japanese and United States Business Communities'*. The message was that unless substantive negotiations on intellectual property were to be included in the talks there would be no deal on anything including, crucially, agriculture.

The international lobbying and networking had done its job. Intellectual property was on the table at GATT, despite developing nations' efforts to resist it at the first Ministerial Conference in Punta del Este in Uruguay in

1986. And in a situation that was to become a feature of the eight-year negotiations of the 'Uruguay round' of trade talks, US trade representatives
were accompanied by advisers from the Pratt and Opel Intellectual Property Committee (IPC).

Whilst Pratt and Opel had been hard at work, the copyright industries
had not been idle. In 1984 they had formed the International Intellectual
Property Alliance (IIPA) made up of eight trade associations representing
the various branches of the publishing, entertainment and software industries, covering about 1500 companies altogether. In addition, the IIPA and
Pratt's and Opel's lobbying succeeded in obtaining a change in US trade
law in 1984 to Section 301 of the 1974 Trade Act. From the overview of
the statute:

> "Section 301 of the Trade Act of 1974, as amended (19 U.S.C. § 2411), is the
> principal statutory authority under which the United States may impose trade
> sanctions against foreign countries that maintain acts, policies and practices that
> violate, or deny U.S. rights or benefits under, trade agreements, or are unjustifi-
> able, unreasonable or discriminatory and burden or restrict U.S. commerce."

The 1984 change meant that for the first time the US could take Section
301 action against countries where they considered US patents, copyrights
or trademarks were not respected. Europe also implemented its own version of these regulations in 1984 to allow action against perceived transgressors of European intellectual property rights.[33]

In order to get public officials in other countries to take accusations of
large-scale piracy seriously, US officials needed some evidence. Also,
contrary to the belief that Section 301 actions could be initiated when
some industrial lobby demanded it, the regulations did require the application of due process of law. Following the required legal procedures in
gathering sufficiently convincing evidence from all over the world is a labour intensive activity and not one the Office of the US Trade Representative had the resources to pursue. So the International Intellectual Property
Alliance (IIPA) stepped in with its ready-made intelligence network made
up of 1500 companies with branches all over the world.

Real data on the cost of intellectual property infringement is notoriously
difficult to find. Even if you could say for certain that a factory in China
or the Philippines made and sold 10,000 copies of the latest US block-
buster film, would that really amount to 10,000 lost sales for the film company? Given that citizens of developing countries could not afford to pay
Western prices, it seems highly unlikely. Nevertheless IIPA member
company employees were happy to present estimates of how big they felt
the piracy problem to be in their corner of the world.

Incentives to inflate the figures are fairly obvious. Unless piracy could be shown to be costing the US vast sums of money, the IIPA's message that US copyrights must be protected at all costs would not hold much weight. Even those collecting the local data could, for example, excuse low sales levels by suggesting rampant piracy was undermining their efforts in that country.

If you have read anything in the media about the music industry in the past few years, you can hardly fail to have seen the repeated claims about how music sales are being destroyed by song swapping on the Internet, for example. Larry Lessig has suggested[34] there are four generic categories of those who swap songs on the Internet:

1. those who download instead of buying
2. those who use the Internet to sample before buying
3. those who get songs that are otherwise difficult to buy
4. those who get content that is released under a less restrictive licence like creative commons.[35]

You can extend and/or refine Lessig's categories or choose your own but the key point is that the claim that the *number of songs downloaded = number of lost sales* is demonstrably false.

So it might be a slight exaggeration, though not too much, to say that estimates and reports of the level of 'piracy' around the world are made up of unsubstantiated guesses of big numbers, multiplied by other big numbers, which are then all added together. And this is all done by people attempting to sell the message that because the problem of intellectual property infringement is so huge, only draconian protectionist and enforcement policies will constitute an adequate response.

This is not to deny that there is a big black market in counterfeit, patent and copyright infringing goods. The black market in these goods is huge. It is just to note that any claims about how much it all costs US or European business should be taken with a pinch of salt. The real size of the problem is almost impossible to quantify and the real impact of these black markets on the Western economies is a lot more complex than it would appear at first glance, as Lessig's four categories help to illustrate.[36] All the deal making, manipulation and arm twisting that is done in the name of improving intellectual property laws is not based on solid empirical evidence or scientific measurement of how big the problems are or what effects proposed changes might be likely to have.[37] Rather it is based on subterfuge and the ability of interested parties to drive their agenda through the key decision making bodies and decision makers.

The IIPA's first report in 1985,[38] in response to the US government's request for comments on barriers to US trade, encouraged the government to take action against developing countries listed that were believed to be violating US copyrights, leading to US industry losses of $1.3 billion. This estimate had a predictable impact on the media and the politicians, leading to a blizzard of condemnations and calls for action against the ten countries and others listed in the report as presenting substantial problems.[39]   The numbers and the outcry gave the US trade negotiator an apparently solid grounding to approach public officials in these countries, encouraging them to upgrade their intellectual property laws and enforcement policies or else come under threat of trade sanctions.

This has pretty much remained the pattern ever since, as the Office of the US Trade Representative and the International Intellectual Property Alliance (IIPA) have developed a mutually beneficial close working relationship. The bureaucrats are obliged to produce a Special 301 report every year identifying the intellectual property situation in countries giving rise for concern. Every year the IIPA funds the 'evidence' gathering and supplies the figures.[40]

So intellectual property was on the negotiating table at GATT and the US had section 301 trade sanction procedures to lean on problem states. The generally accepted line on why the developing nations eventually agreed to the TRIPS provisions at GATT was that there was a quid pro quo – the US, Europe and Japan got their intellectual property line and the developing nations got a deal on agriculture.[41] In reality once the US and Europe had intellectual property on the table they used every power lever at their disposal, every negotiating trick in the book to ensure that TRIPS became a reality. Uphoff's factionalism was given full reign. For a full account of these shenanigans you really need to read *Information Feudalism* by Peter Drahos and John Braithwaite[42] but a few of the tactics merit attention here.

Firstly a small point struck me, since I have seen it done so often throughout my working life. The highly skilled chairman of the TRIPS group, Lars Anell, said right at the start that the incompatibility of national laws with TRIPS proposals could not be used as an excuse for objecting to such proposals. Given that there were over 40 countries represented in the TRIPS negotiations it seems remarkable that this ruling was accepted and never thereafter challenged. It still never ceases to amaze me how, so often, in business or even social contexts, someone who assumes authority can declare an arbitrary rule, which subsequently becomes the unquestionable equivalent of a rule of law in that context.

Secondly, by 1988 the Intellectual Property Committee (IPC) set up by Pfizer and IBM bosses, Pratt and Opel, was responsible for a report called the *"Basic Framework of GATT Provisions on Intellectual Property: Statement of Views of European, Japanese and United States Business*

Communities". This document, essentially the wish list of the thirteen US multinationals that the IPC ultimately represented, became the basis of four of the five drafts of TRIPS that came to be considered from 1990 onwards. The fifth draft was coordinated by developing nations, led by Brazil and India, who were attempting to resist what they felt to be the worst excesses of the US protectionist lobby. US tactics, however, led to a large part of the *"Basic Framework..."* making it into the final draft of TRIPS signed in 1994.

Thirdly, when the developing nations, particularly Brazil and India, formed the basis of a strong coalition against TRIPS, the US decided that they would pick them off one by one outside the talks. In 1987 they started Section 301 action and by 1988 had implemented trade sanctions against Brazil for failing to protect US pharmaceutical interests. Brazil had a thriving generic drug manufacturing sector and was not interested in protecting US pharmaceutical patents, since access to cheap drugs was also such a hot political issue in the country. The problem was that a quarter of Brazil's exports went to the US, so that the US sanctions hit them very hard.

The US sanctions were illegal under GATT[43] and Brazil did make a complaint but the dispute resolution process at GATT is long and cumbersome and could easily have been drawn out for years by a powerful US delegation. By 1990 Brazil folded and agreed to implement the domestic patent legislation that the US wanted. Now they had agreed to drug patents at home, they could not object to them in the multinational negotiations at GATT. India, the most powerful remaining developing nation at the talks, remained resolute even in the face of US section 301 action in 1991. The US action in this case had little effect, since India's trade with the US was not nearly as critical to their economy as was the case with Brazil. India even had some last minute success by aligning themselves with the European negotiators and watering down the wording which would have led to TRIPS encouraging the patenting of "anything under the sun".[44]

It was a long road to success with TRIPS, but a handful of US business executives had managed to transform the global landscape on the regulation of intellectual property. In doing so they had managed to hold together a disparate coalition of competing national and commercial interests throughout Europe, the US and Japan over a period of 15 years. That in itself has to be recognised as a monumental achievement, when you consider merely the constant battle that goes on between the entertainment and the technology industries. Pfizer's Edmund Pratt considered it one of the highlights of his career.[45] The development of every technology from the player piano to the Internet has raised concerns in the prevailing entertainment industry, which ultimately learns to live with the new gadgets, control, exploit or kill them.[46] Yet Pratt, Opel and a small number of like-minded executives and trade officials managed to coordinate and manipulate those interests for long enough to get TRIPS signed. One former US trade negotiator reckons less than 50 individuals in total were truly responsible for TRIPS.[47] And though the pharmaceutical and entertainment industries especially complained that the final text of the agreement had not provided everything they wanted, it did not take them too long after the ink had dried on the agreement to begin demanding action under TRIPS against targeted 'pirate' states.[48]

Digital fences and the making of the WIPO copyright treaty

In Chapter 2, I complained about the abuse of laws protecting digital rights management (DRM) technologies – digital fences built into CDs or DVDs in an attempt to stop them being copied. The short version of the complaint, just to remind you, is that it is ridiculous that the companies that sell the music or the films get to decide which music or video player you can use and what you are allowed to do with that player.[49]

You want to play Apple iTunes music on a Microsoft music player? Forget it. iTunes files come with a digital fence that prevents that. You want to fast forward past those irritating adverts and copyright warnings at the beginning of a DVD? Not allowed and the digital strait-jacket prevents it. You have been to the US on holiday and want to play a DVD you purchased legitimately from there on your UK DVD player? No. You see your DVD player is region coded and will only play DVDs which come with a digital strait-jacket that proves to your player they have been bought in your own part of the world.[50]

Bypassing these digital fences, making tools that can bypass them or telling someone how to bypass them is now illegal, under the European Union's copyright directive of 2001[51] and the US Digital Millennium Copyright Act (DMCA) of 1998. In Chapter 2, I outlined stories of researchers getting threatened and jailed under the DMCA. Both the DMCA and the copyright directive are based on the World Intellectual Property (WIPO) Copyright Treaty of 1996, though arguably much more protectionist in their provisions.[52] The story of how the Copyright Treaty was passed is again one of US and European influence.

Flush with their success with TRIPS and the disgruntlement of senior WIPO officials at being effectively sidelined, US and European negotiators felt they now had the influence to make an impact at WIPO. The thinking was that if WIPO wanted to re-assert its authority over international intellectual property policy, it would have to be much more accommodating to US and European wishes than it had been hitherto. Again the agenda was to be set by US officials, most notably US Commissioner of Patents, Bruce Lehman.

Lehman, who prior to taking on his public service role had been a lobbyist for the software industry, led the working group on President Clinton's 'Information Infrastructure Task Force' which produced a radical White Paper, in September 1995, on the future of copyright in the digital age.[53] Amongst the eight key provisions was the outlawing of circumvention of digital locks nominally intended to protect copyright. Lehman, in what you will recognise as the 'getting things done' model of decision making, largely ignored most of his committee and drafted the proposals with his senior staff.[54] The White Paper was hugely welcomed by the entertainment and software industries and condemned with equal vigour by the telecommunications companies, internet service providers, consumer electronics industries, writers, scholars, library, civil rights and consumer groups. The result of the widespread opposition was that the proposals never made it out of committee in Congress.

Far from being downcast, though, Commissioner Lehman, who was the leading US delegation at the World Intellectual Property Organisation (WIPO), intensified his efforts to get his blueprint built into the drafts of treaty proposals to be discussed imminently on the international stage. He reasoned that if he could get his radical plan incorporated in the WIPO treaties, he could return to Congress claiming there was an international treaty obligation to build the provisions into US law. This ratcheting up of intellectual property laws – their law is tougher than ours, so we have to catch up by making our law just as tough, if not bigger, better, stronger and longer – is a very common lobbying tactic. Lehman found an ally in the chairman of the negotiations at WIPO, Jukka Liedes, who incorporated the US proposals into early treaty drafts. They had been heavily watered down by the intervention of European, African, Latin American and Asian country delegations, however, by the time the final text of the Copyright Treaty was signed in 1996.

One of the really interesting things about this process of watering down the more radical elements of the Lehman blueprint was that the national delegations that forced through the changes included government officials who *were not copyright specialists*. Ordinary officials were prepared to ask the kinds of questions that perhaps copyright experts would have left unsaid.

On the 'thou shalt not bypass a digital fence' front though, the treaty did include these words in article 11:

"Contracting Parties shall provide adequate legal protection and effective legal remedies against the circumvention of effective technological measures that are used by authors in connection with the exercise of their rights under this Treaty or the Berne Convention and that restrict acts, in respect of their works, which are not authorized by the authors concerned or permitted by law."[55]

Arguably the requirement to "provide adequate legal protection and effective legal remedies against the circumvention" was already part of UK and US law, for example. But the inclusion of these fairly weak words more than adequately served the purpose of a political lever. Arguments for anti-circumvention provisions in Europe and the US became 'WIPO plus' arguments i.e. 'at a minimum we need to include the WIPO provision but really we need something stronger'. Something much stronger is what the US got in the Digital Millennium Copyright Act of 1998, the law which later landed the young visiting Russian researcher, Dimitry Sklyarov in jail.[56] The Section 1201 – don't bypass a digital fence – provisions of the act run to five pages of print, compared with the short paragraph in the 1996 WIPO Copyright Treaty.[57]

With the 2001 copyright directive, EU member states came under an obligation to introduce anti-circumvention measures.[58] Since 2001 just such measures with various degrees of potency have been filtering their way down into the national laws of EU member states.[59] The provisions became part of UK law in the autumn of 2003 and the French introduced their version in the summer of 2006, for example.[60]

Since TRIPS and the 1996 WIPO treaties, US and European multilateral and bilateral trade negotiations have all heavily factored intellectual property into the deal-making process.[61] The US in particular start with a 'WIPO and TRIPS plus' stance, demanding compliance with minimum standards of intellectual property protection for US goods before a deal will even be considered. The net effect tends to be the gradual ratcheting up of intellectual property protections for US industries worldwide. The strong-arm tactics are not limited to less-developed countries either. The US–Australia free trade agreement which came into force in 2005 is likely to lead to an increase in the cost of pharmaceutical products for Australian citizens.[62]

Software patents and the IPR enforcement directive in the EU

Decision making processes in the European Union can, like GATT, WIPO and the US Congress, be quite awe inspiring in their ability to facilitate poor decisions. The EU has three main decision making institutions:[63]

- the Council of Ministers

- the European Parliament and
- the European Commission.

The Council of Ministers is the most powerful of the three and involves a minister from each member state, the minister who attends depending on the subject of the meeting. Each country gets to be president for a six-month period. Since the EU has expanded to twenty seven states that means the presidency now rolls round on a thirteen and a half year cycle.[64] Unfortunately this means that the opportunity for national political leaders to be seen to make an impact on the European agenda can possibly only happen once in a political lifetime. The pressure to get things done, close deals and get regulations passed, preferably deals in your country's own best interest (and, some have suggested, in the interests of the sponsors of your presidency), is now that much more than was the case when there were fewer states. The result is that states can come to support certain measures which the presiding minister may know little about, just because the timetable ensures the issue comes up and has a chance of getting passed within the timescale of that country's presidency.

This leads to silly seasons where for example you get the Dutch presidency, in December 2004, trying to slip through a software patent directive without discussion in the midst of a Council meeting on agriculture and fisheries.[65] Poland's science minister, however, insisted it be taken off the fisheries meeting list of items to be nodded through without discussion. This directive had previously been repeatedly rejected by the EU parliament. Regardless of whether someone supports, opposes or has no interest in the issue of software patents, agriculture and fisheries is hardly the forum you would choose to be making decisions about it.

Less than a week earlier, the Dutch presidency tried to sneak the directive through an environment ministers' Council meeting without discussion. In the face of being accused of misleading their own national parliament, however, they withdrew the item from the meeting. In May that year, the Dutch parliament for the first time in history revoked their previous support for an EU directive after they decided that they had been misled about the level of support for the directive at European level.[66] A minister had suggested in a letter to the Dutch parliament that the European Parliament and the European Council were in agreement on the directive when basically the two were are loggerheads.

To make a very long story short here, the parliament repeatedly added numerous amendments to the directive reversing its meaning every time they considered it. This was repeatedly followed by the Council completely ignoring those amendments and pushing ahead with the original draft. The theory is that if you put forward proposals often enough over a long period of time eventually opposition will shrink, get worn out with the fighting or distracted with other things for long enough not to notice what you are doing.[67]

Earlier in the year the Irish presidency had used various administrative manoeuvres to get a qualified majority of votes in favour of the directive in a Council meeting where it *was* actually a discussion item on the agenda. The transcript of the discussions in that meeting makes fascinating reading.[68] It presents a wonderful example of the person chairing the meeting assertively bringing the business to a close. I particularly enjoyed this extract:

> Danish delegate: We're not happy
> Irish chair: But you are 80% happy?
> Danish delegate: But... I think...
> Irish chair: We don't need you to be totally happy. None of us are totally happy.
> Danish delegate: I know that. I know that.
> Irish chair: If we were we wouldn't be here.
> Danish delegate: I think we're not very happy but I think we would, we would...
> Irish chair: Thank you very much.
> Danish delegate: ...we would like to see a solution today.
> Irish chair: Thank you very much Denmark.

So the Danish delegate got persuaded into going along with a proposal reluctantly just so the business of the meeting could be pushed along.

The intellectual property rights enforcement directive,[69] rather ironically given the Dutch presidency's woes later that year with the software proposals, was adopted at an EU Council agriculture and fisheries meeting in April 2004, two days before ten more countries expanded the membership of the EU to twenty five states. The timing is significant because the supporters of this directive had serious concerns that it might be defeated if it were to be considered following the expansion.

Largely through the efforts of Janelly Fourtou, a French member of the EU parliament, supported by another MEP Arlene McCarthy, from the UK, the directive was fast-tracked through the 'codecision procedure'. Briefly, the codecision procedure allows the EU Council and the EU parliament to adopt a law after a single reading, if they can both agree on an identical text. The process is supposed to be applied only to economic, social and environmental policies.[70] That in itself was controversial since the directive essentially covers issues related to search and seizure and it originally included provisions for strong criminal sanctions [against people infringing patents or copyrights], which do not qualify for consideration under the codecision procedure.[71]

The directive facilitates the issuing of secret court orders authorising private raids[72] on premises to look for evidence of intellectual property infringement. It also allows for the freezing of assets before a court hearing,[73] the admissibility of anonymous accusations as evidence in court and power to demand the revelation of commercially or privately sensitive information, on suspicion that someone is engaging in intellectual property infringement.

In addition to being closely involved with its drafting, Janelly Fourtou was the EU parliament's rapporteur on the directive, which meant that she was responsible for steering the legislation though the various processes (like the codecision procedure) and committees it needed to negotiate, including the parliament's powerful JURI Committee on Legal Affairs. Fourtou came in for some significant criticism whilst working on the progression of the directive and was accused by opponents of having a conflict of interests because she was married to the CEO of the entertainment giant, Vivendi Universal,[74] one of the biggest intellectual property based companies in the world. In addition, she ran the *Janelly and Jean-René Fourtou Foundation*, with her husband, a charitable institution which derives significant funds from intellectual property interests.[75] In parallel with the case in the US electoral system in the previous chapter, even though it is clear she does some wonderful charitable work through her family foundation, it does not matter if Mrs Fourtou is the most honest, decent, upstanding individual in the world. If she is in charge of managing a foundation, the financial health of which could be dependent on a law being considered by the EU, it is at the very least questionable whether she should be in charge of shepherding that law through the EU's decision making institutions.[76]

SLIM on stakeholders

In Chapters 5 and 6, I suggested that we should use evidence-based decision making processes when making decisions about the regulation and deployment of complex DDM systems. In Chapter 7, I suggested that complex DDM systems can only be effectively deployed through the involvement of the whole range of necessary users and experts, working together through a collaborative program of operational research and the skillful application of the levers of power by key, influential and well-informed decision makers.

In this chapter I have outlined the story of the making of international intellectual property policy. The reality of decision making in the EU, the

WTO, WIPO and other international forums is the kind of browbeating the Danish delegate got from the Irish chair in the meeting considering whether to introduce a software directive. In one classic case of the kinds of tactics that can sometimes be deployed in these forums, a group of civil society observers of discussions on a new broadcasting treaty at the World Intellectual Property Organization in November 2004, found that papers they had tabled for the meeting were stolen by political opponents of their position.[77] Some of the papers were later found dumped in a rubbish bin in the men's toilets and others were found hidden behind a desk somewhere in the same building.

Intellectual property has been going through a process of upheaval which is having a big impact on a range of Uphoff's levels from the individual through to the international. The power dynamics underlying this are complex and not necessarily benign to the wider public or less powerful nations. In Chapters 3 and 4, I pointed out that the system may have changed in ways which undermine its original purpose, to promote progress.

The decision making process which has brought these changes has more in common with Uphoff's factionalism, infighting and leveraging of power advantages in the local community context than we might like to believe. So the default legal rules of the road for the knowledge economy are being set in international forums by people and institutions with a vested interest in ensuring these rules are biased in their favour and the pharmaceutical, large software and entertainment industries, in particular, have been very effective players of the game.

These institutions are big stakeholders and should certainly be involved in the process but it seems that, when it comes to intellectual property, the users of the system have little or no say. It is very easy to buy into the cynical perspective that it is big business' money and power, acting with unethical self-interest that sets policy but very often these top executives and trade negotiators genuinely believe that the way to protect and enhance the global economy (and not just their part of it) is to enforce more and stronger property rights.[78] Yet the radar story tells us we must involve users, as does electronic voting and nearly every big information technology system failure that has ever occurred.[79] If we want the system to succeed we need to involve the users in its operational design, deployment and development.

Many intellectual property experts would be horrified at the notion of involving ordinary users of the products of the entertainment or pharmaceutical industries in the process of setting intellectual property policy. How on earth can anyone without the appropriate expertise be expected to get their head around complex intellectual property rules, when even the experts often struggle to keep up?[80] Perhaps they could be persuaded to include economists in the process. Economists are, at least, experts in dealing with complex economic models and perhaps it is getting to the stage where some empirical economic evidence might be considered useful to demonstrate the need and the value of all these new intellectual property rules? After all, the standard argument for the rules is that they are good for the economy, though it is a theory that has never really been subject to any degree of serious scientific or economic evaluation. In a possible indicator of the slight movement in this direction, the EU Commission recently did an empirical evaluation of the effect of their Directive 96/9/EC of 11 March 1996 on the legal protection of databases. They concluded that the economic impact of the directive is "unproven."[81]

Now considering the opinion of peer experts from the economics field is one thing but what about involving ordinary people in this intellectual property DDM process? Would they not just be out of their depth? In the mechanics and the details of the rules there is little doubt that a lay person would, in the first instance, be out of their depth. In relation to the basic principles of what the intellectual property system is supposed to deliver, however, I have no doubt that ordinary people have the capacity to understand and defend those principles in the development of policies.

I would draw your attention to two examples of the importance of ordinary people used in complex decision making situations. Firstly the jury system, where ordinary men and women are expected to engage in a reasoned debate about a situation involving the guilt or innocence of someone accused of a crime. Jeffrey Abramson puts it like this:

"The deliberative ideal...seeking to inspire jurors to put aside narrow group allegiances in favor of spying common ground... believes that face-to-face meetings matter, that voting is secondary to debate and discussion, that power should ultimately go to the persuasive, that collective wisdom results from gathering people in conversation from different walks of life, that unanimity is desirable, and that there is a justice shared across the demographic divides of race, religion, gender, and national origin." [82]

Now juries are subject to bias or personal values or interests, just as international trade negotiators are, and there have been energetic attempts to compensate for this by taking demographic profiles into account when selecting juries. Yet sometimes these efforts, in trying to administer possible bias out of the system, vastly underestimate the ability of informed individuals to make the right decision. As Abramson says:

"...we should seek to inspire jurors not to represent their own kind but to use their different starting perspectives to educate one another, to defeat prejudiced arguments, and to elevate deliberations to a level where power goes to the most persuasive."[83]

This deliberative ideal, Abramson admits, is rarely achieved in practice but it is an ideal we are capable of approaching given a widening of the other educational ideal of universal access to knowledge.

The second example is from the field of environmental decision making and a European Commission research project which some of my colleagues at the Open University have been leading. The 'SLIM' project[84] examined the management of a whole range of water catchment areas all over Europe, particularly in relation to the socio-economic aspects of the sustainable use of water. Amongst other things they concluded that the EU's Water Framework Directive[85] assumes that science can measure good ecological status with hard numbers, yet the scientific knowledge is not complete and experts disagree about the value of the models being used to generate the numbers.

"The systems of interest in any situation chosen for study by scientists, or recognised by other stakeholders, are personal constructs, not objective descriptions of an agreed reality. While scientific knowledge is essential for effective management, it needs to be complemented by the views of other stakeholders on the nature of the system of interest"[86]

Basically they are saying that people should work together – farmers, environmentalists, hunters, anglers (i.e. the users) and the scientists – to evolve a real operational understanding of how to manage the water catchment area. The expert scientists can learn from these other stakeholders in the catchment area, just as these stakeholders can learn from the experts.[87] In a similar manner, trade negotiators and intellectual property experts, immersed in the deal making and mechanics of detailed rules, need to look up from their busy activity and engage with the people that activity ultimately affects when it comes to gaining access to the fruits of the modern knowledge economy.[88]

Chapter 9 Experts and ordinary people

"It takes thirty leaves to make the apple." Thich Nhat Hanh

Feynman's school books

In 1964 Richard Feynman was asked to join the California Board of Education's Curriculum Commission to help them choose the mathematics textbooks for state schools.[1] When he agreed he was inundated with letters and telephone calls from publishers offering to help him assess their books. Feynman politely insisted he did not need help, gifts, or seminars explaining the books, he just would read them and assess them in the old-fashioned way.

This turned out to be a big task as there were a lot of books and strangely enough his approach was a radical departure from the practice of other committee members. The other members of the commission acquired lots of copies of each book and sent them out to school teachers and administrators to assess. They also attended the publishers' presentations about their books. They would then make their evaluation of each book based on the information from the publishers and the gradings of these readers, who though they were education professionals, were not necessarily experts in the subject area of the books being considered. Then at the commission's meetings, the individual members would discuss their ratings and try to choose the best books.

Feynman meanwhile had been getting himself worked up as he read through the collection of books taking up 17 feet of shelf space in his home because he found them to be "useless", "lousy", "false" and loaded with sloppy and confusing definitions. The books covering the 'new math' that had been introduced in US schools around about that time in an effort to make the subject more interesting were particularly bad. He reckoned they were written by people who did not understand mathematics.[2] So when the discussions at the commission came round to rating each book, Feynman quickly earned the respect of the others. He was the only maths expert on the committee and the only person who could speak with direct first-hand knowledge of the content of the books.

The value of his opinion became starkly clear on one occasion, when he had not rated a particular book, the third in a series of three from that publisher. The other committee members had rated the book highly. Feynman explained he had not rated it because it had not been sent to him, so he had not read it yet. Someone from the book depository which handled the warehousing and dispatch of the books then explained that the publisher had not managed to get it printed in time but hoped that their series could still be considered by the commission. In the meantime they had sent a version with blank pages. The decision making processes of the committee, if Feynman had not been involved, would have given one of the highest accolades to a book with nothing in it. That caused a lot of embarrassment all round.

The committee did eventually manage to agree on a balanced portfolio of textbooks that satisfied Feynman and made their recommendations to the California education board, only to be told that budget cuts meant they could not afford these books. The politics surrounding the process left Feynman frustrated and angry and he resigned from the commission but he retained a lot of respect for the dedicated, caring individuals he had worked with.[3]

The evaluation of a mathematics textbook should not be a difficult process. You need some mathematics experts to review it to ensure it is mathematically sound. You need experienced, preferably gifted, maths teachers to ensure it is pedagogically sound. You can then, in the case of a universally highly rated book, employ it on trials in the classroom to see whether it really does engage children and help them to learn mathematics, i.e. to ensure it is operationally sound.

There will inevitably be emergent issues, positive and negative, in the use of the book in the classroom that the experts might not have considered. But as long as the experts are appropriately qualified, have the requisite know-how, have been thorough and have had a free hand to review the books as they see fit,[4] this kind of evaluation process should guarantee high quality texts in schools. It is nothing like as complicated as building an air defence system or an ID card system. It is also a tried and tested process and it works.[5] It is also a nice illustration, for my purposes, of the importance of using experts in decision making processes.

Information technology in education

In the 1980s a widespread belief developed that every school should have computers in the classroom because... well because... er... children needed to know about computers, since they would be important in the future. So a lot of money was spent acquiring computers for schools. But 30 or more children per computer was not a practical situation, so sometimes schools put aside special rooms with suites of computers. The education revolution that these machines were supposed to bring to schools, though, never happened. Nobody really knew what the computers were for and very few schools had the know-how, training or experience to use these new machines effectively to complement existing teaching processes. Indeed it was often the children, the computing natives who were growing up with the technology, rather than the teaching staff, the computing immigrants who had to absorb the new social context visited upon them by the technologies, who were better able to understand and use the machines.

The Open University

The Open University (OU) was partly born out of a similar idea in the 1960s that radio and television could revolutionise education. Well the OU did revolutionise university education but not because it was the 'university of the airwaves'. Rather, the University made serious open and distance learning a viable prospect for millions of people for the first time, by producing high quality, fully integrated, self-contained and pedagogically sound educational materials,[6] supported by a system of personalised tuition that was unmatched even by conventional universities.

Today, as back then, course materials are produced collectively by course teams. Typically, each section of the course went through at least three rounds of drafting and subsequent intensive peer review and revision by academic and teaching subject experts before it got anywhere near a student.

The University also had an extensive regional support infrastructure through which the personal tuition system was supported and administered. And the key to the University's success turned out to be putting people in touch with people, both the students' tutors and educational counsellors and, almost more importantly, fellow students. In addition to the system of face-to-face tutorials, and support from tutors via the telephone and a variety of multi-media and online approaches, students were encouraged to form self-help groups and keep in regular contact with each other as they worked through their courses. They were also encouraged to attend summer schools, where they spent a week at a conventional university,[7] with fellow students from around the country, working through OU course-related activities.[8] The result was a vibrant, energetic, university community, albeit one that was significantly more geographically dispersed than in a conventional university.

The University stood on an enormous foundation of goodwill born out of the simple idea of putting people in touch with people. It now uses a vast range of modern technologies in its operations, including the airwaves of TV and radio. The efficacy of almost all of these relies firstly on the ability to deploy them in such a way as to complement the sound open and distance educational practices already in place, as well as the new activities they facilitate; and secondly to improve that process of putting people in touch with people.

TV and radio productions were only a small part of what the OU did even in the early 1970s but the commitment to be open to people, places, methods and ideas has meant that the potential for using modern technologies in the University's work has always been taken seriously. It has also led to some spectacular internal battles as the commitment to using innovative technologies in teaching is sometimes thought to be incompatible with the commitment to universal access to the university's services. The theory was that poorer sections of the community would not be able to afford new technology in its earliest incarnations. The technophiles believe that as the technology evolves it becomes more affordable and universally accessible but the cutting edge research on its potential utility in education should start when the technology first appears.

The OU has been using computers in its courses for the best part of a generation and initially required students to have access to the Internet on a large scale on a first year foundation course in 1995.[9] As I recall, that involved about six thousand people. By 2006, there were about a quarter of a million users of the University's email and online conferencing system, OpenText's FirstClass®.

With the learning about the reality of these technologies at the educational coalface that has gone on in the slightly more than a decade, nowadays the OU probably contains the most concentrated group of distance learning educational technology, craft-aware experts in any single institution anywhere in the Western world. That craft awareness is by no means exclusive to the OU, though, and the beauty of the Internet is that experienced educational technologists all over the world can more readily share their experiences, to a degree that would not have been possible before the advent of the Net. Several shelves full of books that could be written[10] about the OU experience alone but I am just going to outline one small story arising from the first course that we delivered entirely online, *T171 You, Your Computer and the Net.* The course was written by my colleagues, Martin Weller, John Naughton and Gary Alexander, who were positively evangelical about the possibilities for using the Internet in our teaching.

One of the things we decided to try with T171, given that all the course material was going to be delivered online, was a 'reveal' publishing model. The idea was that the material would be published in small self-contained chunks on a regular basis, say like a fortnightly magazine rather than publishing the whole course right at the start. We had for several years by then been using computers for computer mediated communications (CMC). This enabled students to email each other, their tutors or other university staff such as members of the course team, and post contributions to open 'conferences' or bulletin boards that could be read by every member of a group with designated access to that conference area.

The conferencing and email had to some extent strengthened the crucial process of putting people in touch with people. The skills involved in managing the conferencing environment were significantly different to those for managing the traditional forms of communication, however, and socio-psychological factors were critical. To take a simple example, a few confident, articulate, apparently 'way ahead' individuals in a conference could exert a disproportionate degree of intimidation over the rest of the group, often entirely unintentionally.

The confidence of first year OU students is one of the most important things to nurture in the early days, as many of these people will not have done any formal studying for many years and may be concerned at their ability to cope with the academic demands of university. Merely posting a message to a public conference for the first time can be a big deal, as you wonder if it is going to be dissected and analysed to size you up and decide whether you will be a worthy participant in this forum. Sometimes people are just worried about their basic writing skills or ability to spell. If someone has already posted ten long messages to a conference, littered with words you need a dictionary to understand, by the time you get there, then the nerves will not be helped.

Most OU students thought that their peers were way ahead of them with the course material. One of the nice things about summer school was that they tended to find that most of them were in the same boat. Electronic conferencing, in some ways, had the opposite effect. There were always some students who were ahead of the study schedule and the difficulty with conferences was that these particular students were now more visible than they had ever been in the distance learning context. FirstClass® has a system of placing a little red flag against an unread message and even those of us who have been using the system for over ten years still open a conference, see 30 or 40 red flags and think "oh no, it's only been a day since I checked this!" It does not matter that most of the contributions have been from a few individuals and we have now developed skills at filtering out the messages we do not need to read. To a student who had only just learned to switch their computer on[11] and successfully make contact with the OU system, it could be devastatingly off-putting.

One of the ways that this intimidation factor could be tempered was with a more controlled scheduling of conferencing activities.[12] A mechanism for doing this was revealing the course materials in stages at regular intervals, rather than making the whole course available right at the start. It is probably fair to say that there was a significant amount of metaphorical blood split in the intense course team debates about the reveal publishing model but a second important reason probably tipped the balance for me in its favour at the time. Given the dynamic medium we were using to deliver the course material we could, theoretically at least, incorporate all the latest developments in the subject area and almost operate the course like a scholarly news site. In the end we only pushed this as far, in T171, as doing annual reports on the stage of development of the Microsoft anti-trust case that was then making its way through the US courts and about to hit the European Union too. In many ways we have still only started to explore this possibility, a potentially revolutionary pedagogic paradigm.[13] This had to be balanced by some stability for a first year university course, as it is not hard to imagine the reaction if the website was to be changed the day after the students had 'learned' it.

One of the other key ways we tried to manage the socio-psychological environment was to impose a set of basic rules of etiquette or 'netiquette', basically requiring that contributors to conferences be nice to each other.

This micromanaging of the scheduling did make it appear to some as if this, first all Internet course, was less flexible than conventional OU courses delivered through printed materials. Many students come to the OU because of the flexible learning system the University offers, whereby students can study the courses at their own rate, as long as they can get the assignments in on time. Even then the University has various processes to accommodate students' special circumstances if they are unable to submit assignments to the required schedule. But now a course delivered entirely via the Internet was apparently being tied down in ways we would not have considered on a 'normal' course. In actual fact, conventional OU courses in their first year of presentation often had a delivery schedule [via the post] equivalent to the schedule under which the various sections of T171 were published in its first year.

Later generations of the course incorporated online group activities that required students to be on the system during specified weeks, for up to a third of the time scheduled for the entire course. It could almost be considered equivalent to being required to attend lectures at a conventional university.

In addition, the heavy emphasis on netiquette sometimes drew a virtual veil of niceness over the conferences that sometimes limited the likelihood of full and frank discussion and debate. Given the barriers that are inherent in attempting to communicate via the written word alone,[14] this can inhibit the learning process. We do also have to deal with the range of conflict that you might see in many online forums and this exposes the inherent brittleness of conferencing whereby one or a small number of individuals can, at worst, turn a conference into a no-go area for students.

Looking back, I think this 'expert' micromanagement of the student experience had a disproportionately negative effect on the OU students' valued flexibility. It also reduced the possibility of the emergence of learning patterns and opportunities facilitated by the technologies that the academics had not conceived of in advance. I now believe that the hierarchical instinct to control the student experience really needs to be curtailed if we are to get the best out of these technologies in the educational context. Whereas much of this was discussed in the debates we had whilst producing the course, the reality of the impact of our decisions only came through during the presentation of the course. The 'experts' had to learn through operational research from the ordinary users of the course materials – tutors, students, administrators and the course team ourselves. Since no one had ever done an online university course on the scale of T171, which had a thousand students on a pilot presentation in 1999, and opened with twelve thousand in 2000, we could not really be called 'experts'. In delivering a course that proved to be a big success, however, we learned a hell of a lot from our students and tutors, primarily again the value of putting people in touch with people, regardless of the communications medium.

There was another inflexible feature of the course that came built into the technology, the computer and Internet connection that people needed to get access to the course materials. That big ugly contraption in the corner of the room was not as portable as a conventional printed book or course booklet, so it was not as easy to read on the train. Now we have smaller, portable devices, broadband and wireless networking but you still cannot beat the readability of the printed page. Reading off a computer screen can be up to 25% slower than from the printed page and worse on smaller devices. The course team was determined that students were going to learn about the Internet by using the Internet. We tried to micromanage this idea, by deliberately refusing to provide a single printer-friendly version of the whole course, but students still printed it off in droves and still read it on the bus. Despite our wish to enforce learning through using the computing equipment, the physical limitations of the technologies themselves provided a strong incentive for students to find what they felt was a better way.

I just have one final note about the use of the Internet at the OU before moving on. It had what I think is a really interesting side effect on the organisation. Prior to the integration of the Internet into our teaching, members of course teams, based in the main campus at Milton Keynes, had very little contact with students directly except for the face-to-face teaching at summer schools every year. The day-to-day routine student and tutor services were and are managed by the large regional support infrastructure. The people in regional centres and a large body of personal tutors and educational counsellors managed the huge number of processes in place to support these students.

Suddenly that vast range of daily student and tutor needs became visible to those at the central campus who had never had to think about them before. The course team was also visible to students on the FirstClass® conferencing system and the temptation to go straight to them if the student wanted something done was difficult to resist. Headquarters will always be assumed to have more power and influence than decentralised units. But emails like 'what is the date of my next tutorial', or 'the postman delivered my course materials to my neighbour's house and her dog chewed them up', or 'my wife is seriously ill so I won't be able to get my assignment in on time' started arriving on the virtual doorsteps of members of the central campus course teams.

The regional infrastructure, which routinely and efficiently expedited such queries, was getting bypassed and course teams were faced with problems they did not know what to do with. Fortunately they were able to turn to a 'staff tutor', who is a kind of combined academic and director of studies, based in the regional centre providing the academic link between the regions and the academic units at the headquarters in Milton Keynes. Routine queries could then be processed through the appropriate channels and dealt with as efficiently as before. But the technology had facilitated 'point-of-contact' confusion, giving students an easy option to contact parts of the organisation not best placed to deal with their specific problems. Since OU staff in the regions and the student services administration at the central campus use a completely different email system[15] to that used by the course teams and the [two hundred thousand or so] students and tutors that they support, the problem is even more complicated than I have outlined. But that is a discussion for another day. This improved central visibility of routine decentralised processes, however, has been a terrific, and possibly unique in the annals of large organisations, institutional learning experience.

We have learned a lot through operational research in the past ten years about the value of digital technologies in university education i.e. designing, deploying, regulating and learning with the users of our systems.[16] We have also learnt a lot about the power of these technologies to complement rather than replace the core elements of supported open and distance learning provision the OU had already been providing for over a quarter of a century. In addition we have had more than a few hard lessons about how the technologies can complicate, inhibit or undermine the process, when they are neither robust nor deployed appropriately.

Digital technologies continue to raise challenges for educational institutions, as does the legal context and potential commercial impact of patents and some of the fundamental access issues raised throughout this book. But hopefully these institutions will continue to be shaped by their 'experts' (academic, technical and administrative) and users (students and academics), the latter increasingly being those who are growing up with the technologies, technology natives. In the end it is the ordinary users of the system who become the experts.

Experts and ordinary people

It has been my contention throughout this book that experts and ordinary people (or ordinary stakeholders) have got a lot to learn from each other in dealing with DDM situations. I would like to explore that idea a bit further here starting with two stories of where the experts got it wrong.

Shirley McKie and the fingerprints experts

In January 1997, Shirley McKie was one of a team of police officers investigating the brutal murder of Marion Ross in her home in Kilmarnock in Scotland. David Asbury was soon arrested as a suspect in the murder based on fingerprint evidence found at the scene.

Fingerprints were first seriously considered as a means of personal identification by Dr Henry Faulds, a surgeon superintendent working at the time in a Tokyo hospital.[17] He had a letter published in *Nature* on the 28th of October 1880 outlining his ideas.[18] By the turn of the century police forces had begun to use the technique in their investigations and over a hundred years later fingerprints are widely accepted as an infallible means of personal identification. The fingerprint identification process can go wrong though and it did in the Ross murder case.

In addition to the fingerprints at the scene implicating David Asbury in the murder, another print was found there, which four fingerprint experts at the Scottish Criminal Records Office identified as belonging to officer McKie. Since McKie had never been in the house she suggested there must have been a mistake. Since a large part of the case against the murder suspect, Asbury, amounted to the fingerprint evidence, senior officers believed that it must have been McKie who had made the mistake and forgotten about entering the house. After all, not just one but *four* experts had confirmed the identification of the print. Whereas it might have been possible for one examination to be in error, it was highly unlikely that four experts using this long-established scientifically reliable identification technique could be wrong. Or was it?

Officer McKie then came under pressure to change her story since all the fingerprint evidence would come into question if the experts were seen to have made a mistake with the print identified as hers. McKie refused to yield to the pressure as she knew she had never entered the house and that the print could not have been hers. What she did not know at this stage was that four other fingerprint experts at the Scottish Criminal Records Office had also examined the disputed fingerprint and had *refused to confirm* it belonged to her.

During the murder trial of David Asbury, McKie denied under oath on the witness stand that the fingerprint belonged to her. Asbury was convicted of murder and McKie was subsequently prosecuted for perjury. In her defence she employed two overseas fingerprint experts who confirmed the disputed print could not belong to McKie and explained in some detail why this was the case. Their clear explanation, accessible to ordinary people, has since been shown in several BBC TV programmes on the case. In May 1999, McKie was unanimously acquitted of perjury and the judge, unusually, commended her for

"...the obvious courage and dignity which you have shown throughout this nightmare... I very much hope you can put it behind you. I wish you all the best."

Three years later David Asbury's murder conviction was quashed by the Appeal Court, which agreed that the fingerprint evidence against him was unreliable.

In 2000, after a lot of campaigning and a couple of BBC programmes, an investigation by Her Majesty's Inspectorate of Constabulary concluded that the fingerprint mark could not have been made by McKie.[19] Hundreds of fingerprint experts from all over the world have now examined the evidence and come to the same conclusion. There have been numerous investigations and reports, TV programmes and in 2006 a parliamentary inquiry in the Scottish parliament.

I am not going to speculate on any of the motivations of any of the actors involved. What is clear is that the process surrounding the fingerprint science in the Scottish Criminal Records Office went seriously wrong in the McKie case and the investigation of the Ross murder.[20] By the autumn of 2006 the four fingerprint experts at the centre of the case were coming under pressure to resign or retire but that is like blaming the workers in the engine room of the Titanic for running the ship into an iceberg.[21] There was a complete failure of the social technologies – the processes, procedures and management – in the Scottish Criminal Records Office, the police and the Crown Office and Procurator Fiscal Service (COPFS)[22] which brought the McKie prosecution. The system surrounding the science and the scientific experts failed and failed badly, when those experts made a mistake.[23]

The McKie case is a clear indication that the application of scientific expertise to decision making processes should never be accepted with blind faith, especially if there is clear evidence of a professional difference of opinion between the experts, which subsequently gets hidden from public view.[24] The reliability of the expert opinion crucially depends not just on the science but the integrity of the organisational, social, legal and technical systems supporting and surrounding it.

Bret McDanel and the legal experts

The Bret McDanel case is an example of where an unfortunate mixture of two areas of expertise – law and computer system security – led to a computer scientist wrongly going to jail for 16 months. McDanel was a computer expert who worked for Tornado Development Inc., when he found a security flaw in a web-based email service the company provided.[25] He informed the management but became frustrated when the company was slow about fixing the problem.

He then resigned and emailed 5600 Tornado customers through the Tornado servers, which he was still authorised to use. The email pointed out the security hole and directed the customers to a website set up by McDanel to learn more about the problem.

The customers were angry that they had been kept in the dark about the security problems. The Tornado management was angry with McDanel for publicly disclosing the problem and convinced federal prosecutors to bring criminal charges against him. Under the US Computer Fraud and Abuse Act, Section 1030(a)(5)(A),[26] it is a crime to knowingly, without authorisation, transmit information or programs (like computer viruses) with intent to damage a computer system. The statute also says that if the action results in the loss to one or more persons of $5000 in the course of a year, then it is a crime.

In court the company and the prosecutors admitted the truth of the contents of McDanel's email and website but claimed he had damaged the company's reputation, thereby costing them $5000. Yet the law is primarily supposed to apply to damage to a computer system, not reputation.[27]

The second claim made by the prosecutor was that McDanel's 5600 emails had slowed down the company's servers, thereby damaging their system. This was almost laughable to computer experts but it is easy to see how 5600 would seem to be a lot from the perspective of the legal experts – including the trial judge, sitting without a jury – or ordinary members of the public. In an earlier case in the California Supreme Court, Intel v Hamidi, an ex-employee, who used Intel servers without authorisation to send six separate emails to over thirty thousand people, was found not to have impaired the working of the Intel systems.

In addition the prosecutor argued in court that by making the security flaw public, McDanel had disclosed information which could be useful to any attacker who cared to use it. Mark D. Rasch, former head of the US Justice Department's computer crime unit, described this expansion of the definition of 'impairing the integrity' of a computer system as "a dangerously slippery slope".[28]

McDanel spent 16 months in jail and the short explanation for it was that legal experts, convinced that they were dealing with a malicious hacker, applied their legal expertise to ensure they gained a conviction. Their lack of real understanding of the computer systems, however, led to someone getting jailed when at worst he could have been accused of irresponsible rather than criminal behaviour. The state prosecutors later accepted this when, in an extremely unusual move, they supported McDanel's appeal against his conviction. The appeals court subsequently quashed the conviction in February 2004.

Again I am not going to comment on the motives of the people involved in the McDanel case but it is yet another example of the way in which the experts can get it wrong.   In addition it is a warning that expertise in one area should not be accepted, by the general public, as evidence of an expert's competence to make informed decisions in a completely different area of expertise.[29]

Experts make mistakes

Experts can and do make mistakes, all the time. They are only human after all and, hard as it is for most people, in some ways it can be even more difficult for an expert to admit a mistake. Their professional reputation, and that of the system that they operate within, is vested in that opinion and the admission of a mistake might well put a dent in the reputation of both the expert and the system. In addition it can put a dent in the public's confidence in that whole field of expertise and any associated systems of which it forms a part.

In the Shirley McKie case, the experts' mistakes were backed up by the full weight of the Scottish criminal justice system. Even when clear evidence of the existence of the mistaken expert judgments was provided, the entire system found it nigh on impossible to admit the errors.

Yet an expert's mistake does not necessarily mean the science is wrong. It just means that the expert made a mistake. The general public should, therefore, be alert to the possibility of such mistakes, through critical questioning of expert opinions and understanding of the mistakes when they happen, to help ensure they can be accepted and corrected. The systems which require those expert opinions as part of their ongoing operations should be equally ready to understand and rectify such mistakes when they occur. To the extent that such mistakes expose serious systemic, management or structural problems in a system, the people involved should be prepared to take the necessary steps to ensure those systems and structures are put right accordingly.

In that sense at least the US Department of Justice, or at least that branch that dealt with the McDanel case, is way ahead of the parts of the Scottish system Shirley McKie had the misfortune to cross. McDanel's prosecutors actually accepted they got it wrong and actively worked towards having his conviction quashed, even after he had served his jail sentence. McKie continues her fight for justice and we should not forget the murder victim, Marion Ross, whose killer, presumably, still remains at large.

Experts and models

Though you may not have considered them as such, you have already come across many models in everyday life and in reading earlier parts of this book. Maps are models of the layout of roads, towns and villages. The decision tree and expected payoff table in Chapter 5 are models considering the decision to ban liquids from passenger airlines. When many of us hear the word 'model' we think of model trains, various toys or engineer's models of proposed construction projects or even computer models of weather forecasts. In other words, scaled down or simplified representations of some aspect of reality. That is a pretty good definition of the term for the purposes of this book:

A model is a simplified representation of some aspect of reality, constructed for a particular purpose e.g. to help with a DDM situation.

Models used by experts tend to be used with a particular purpose and we need to be clear on that purpose when assessing the value of a particular model. We also need to be very careful about using models constructed for one purpose in a different context.

Despite the ability to cope with the thousands of stimuli that compete for the attention of our five senses in an average day, people have a limit to their information processing capacity. The operational research on radar before the war quickly noted that the huge quantities of raw data from radar operators and observer corps, some of it contradictory or wrong, swamped the controllers and pilots. Though we are very good at recognising patterns,[30] we are just not able to process large amounts of that kind of data or multiple complex calculations quickly and easily. We have to find ways to simplify those situations when we need this kind of data to help with decisions and we often turn to experts to construct and run these models to help with the process.

Often in DDM this means computer models but it does not matter whether the models are physical, computer based, mathematical or graphical, it leads to these models having a crucial role in framing any subsequent decisions we make. Very often, early and careful framing of particular aspects of a DDM situation, by those in positions of power, completely closes off alternative decision routes which they would rather not consider; so it is important we understand the perspectives of the experts, how the models are constructed and the defining underlying assumptions that might be built into them, as well as what their limitations might be.

Uses of models

We use models for

- prediction
- communication and
- optimisation.

If we want to predict how much a large new computer system is going to cost, we work out a project planning schedule, estimate the cost of the equipment and the work in building the system, when those costs are likely to become due and when the new system is going to start generating revenues to pay for itself. We then plug all the estimates into a cost benefit analysis spreadsheet and see what the computer tells us.

A nice example of a communication model is the simulation program that the BBC now uses when televising the Wimbledon tennis tournament. Once a point is completed, if there has been a close call or a dispute about whether the ball landed in or out, the TV viewers are shown the animated computer simulation. This shows the flight of the ball and precisely where it is supposed to have landed. I could have sworn on a couple of occasions that the simulator showed the ball landing on the line when I was sure my eyes had told me, when watching the real version of the point, that the ball was clearly out. Now was that my eyes deceiving me or did the computer simulation have a glitch in it? Most people, no doubt, would believe the computer and not my ageing eyes.

When it comes to optimisation, we often have to take lots of factors into account when making decisions. Mathematical and computer models make it possible to plug a whole range of possible values for each of the influential factors into the machine and quickly get a picture of the range of outcomes. We can then theoretically pick the combination of factors that produces the best outcome. Maths or computer models are suitable for all three purposes listed above, i.e. communication, optimisation and prediction. Physical and graphical models tend to be suitable for communication and prediction. Mathematical models also tend to produce good results but, if we are working on them without the aid of a computer, can be laborious.

The advantage of computer models is that they are fast and as a result can give us access to the kinds of information that would otherwise take a long time or be practically impossible to generate. They can, however, induce constraints in thinking, whereby the people using them are only inclined to try the options made available by the computer.[31] Physical models can take time and significant skill to build. They allow us to run operational tests to assess how a full-scale version might perform in practice, at a fraction of the cost, for example, of building a real bridge and then finding out it vibrates and collapses in high winds.[32]

Economic models for DDM – cost benefit analysis

Most big organisational or government decision making situations are dominated by one factor – money. How much is it going to cost and how much is it going to earn or save us? We calculate the costs and the benefits of the various options and choose the one with the highest net benefits. It is the kind of rational cost benefit analysis I referred to in Chapter 5, though there I also suggested that factors other than the money were important in considering the costs and benefits, even when those factors are difficult to quantify.

The commitment to this kind of economic rationality comes from the ingrained belief [at least in the US and EU] in Adam Smith's economics. Smith theorised that as long as everyone worked hard at pursuing their own interests in free markets then the dominant emergent property of the economic system would be the maximising of everyone's welfare or profits. The approach apparently produced unrivalled growth in Western economies through the course of the 20th-century.[33]

The modelling of this is derived partly from the simple and compound interest calculations we all learned in primary school. If you invest £500 for two years at 10% simple interest per annum, you will earn £50 in interest after the first year and a further £50 after the second year, or £100 in total. Most financial institutions use a compound interest formula on borrowings or investments. So the interest earned each year is added to the original investment, for example and interest for the following year is based on this accumulated sum. So in the case of the example above, the interest would be £50 after the first year. Then you would start the second year with a total investment of £550, earning you further interest at the end of the year of £55. So the total interest earned under the compound interest system is £105. You will be £5 better off than if the bank were using a simple interest formula.[34]

This leads to the concept of the time value of money. £100 today is worth more than the same £100 a year from now because of the interest that could be earned from investing it in the meantime. On big projects money flows happen over a period of years. One way to get an assessment of these costs and benefits is to reduce all future flows to their present values, using what is called discounted cash flow analysis. This is a kind of inverted compound interest calculation. So standard, usually computerised, cost benefit analysis calculations for big projects have to use estimates of how much money is coming in and out at various times. In addition they need assumptions of the likely prevailing interest rates over the course of the development and operation of the system.

The kinds of assumptions that underlie all these estimates can be of epic proportions, which is why we should not be surprised to read regular media condemnations of cost overruns of major government information systems projects. We should actually be more appreciative of the vast numbers of big projects [though there are not many of these in the IT sector] that run to budget and planned timescales, but which do not come to our attention because people doing a good job is not a newsworthy story.

The benefit of the computer model is that it can quickly provide estimated outcomes for best-case and worst-case scenario estimates to help with our decision making. Use of cost benefit analysis computer models is an almost compulsory part of the planning process for government projects. I have already said in Chapter 5 that I think it is important to weigh the costs against the benefits when making decisions. But we always need to be aware that the output of the computer models is only as sound as the data fed into them and the validity of the assumptions underlying the construction of the model.

Discounted cash flow modelling can give us a surprisingly powerful insight into the value of intellectual property. If you do the calculations, assuming a discount rate of 10% per annum and a constant income each year, the 20-year typical patent term gives the owner of the patent 85%, in present value terms, of what she and subsequent owners of the patent would earn if the patent lasted forever. Owning a patent for just 20 years is very nearly as good as owning it forever. Who would have thought it? Copyright typically now lasts for the life of the author plus 70 years. So if a copyright lasted 110 years, for example, again assuming a discount rate of 10% per annum and a constant income, the copyright holder earns 99.997% of what she would earn if the copyright term lasted forever. Reduce the discount rate to 5% and these figures drop to 62% for patents and 95% for copyrights.

So clearly we need to be extremely sceptical of arguments declaring that the only way intellectual property owners are going to derive an appropriate income from their creative assets is by further extending the term, as has happened eleven times in the case of copyright in the US between 1960 and 1998. As I write, the British Phonographic Industry, using Cliff Richard as a leading figurehead, are requesting the term of copyright for sound recordings be increased by at least 20 years, in order to help poor artists with their retirement. In real terms, this would make a difference in the income of a fraction of a percentage point, on recordings made with the extended term of copyright. In the case of recordings made in the 1950s on which the copyright is about to expire, however, it would instantly provide an extra 20 year monopoly to companies or individuals holding those rights, rather than releasing them into the public domain.[35]

Limitations of models

Models have inherent limitations because they are *simplified representations* of some aspect of reality, *constructed* for a particular *purpose,* usually by an expert with a particular *perspective* of the situation. The models therefore have the modeller's assumptions built into them. Sometimes the simplification and assumptions do not make a big difference to the value of the model but in many cases they can be critical.

A computer programmer building a computer version of a mathematical model, not being a mathematician, may assume that certain difficult-to-program elements of the maths can be simplified or skipped without significant consequences. The mixing up of the expertise as in the McDanel case then leads to problems as we end up with an invalid model that gets used as if it were valid.

Ensuring that the simplifications, modeller's world view, assumptions and the underlying purpose of the model do not undermine your DDM process is an important job and not always easy.

When I was in school I believed that you could do anything with mathematics. I even had a secret ambition to disprove Heisenberg's uncertainty principle using mathematics and thereby opening the way to predicting the future.[36] I first realised with a shock that mathematics had its limitations one day on the farm on which I spent a lot of my childhood, since it was the place where my best friend from school days, John, grew up.

One of the big trailers had been overloaded and got a twisted chassis so they decided to strap it to the support girders of one of the barns and pull it back into shape with a tractor. I wondered if the girders would be strong enough and realised I understood the mathematics to work it out, so I ran inside got some paper and a pencil, drew up a model of the trailer strapped to the barn and worked out all the various equations. Very pleased with myself I then suddenly realised I did not have the specific properties of the barn or trailer materials. I had a nice mathematical model and no numbers to run through it.

By the time I had trudged outside dejectedly John and his dad had straightened out the trailer and it was back in operation. Whilst I was playing with mathematics they got the job done. I tell this story mainly in order to note that some experts and modellers have never yet reached the stage of having their models brought up short by the real world. Sometimes they are so immersed in their models and theories that they seem more real than the real world itself, so those assumptions are always worth testing.[37]

I still believe, by the way, that mathematics is a very powerful tool. I just do not have the blind, idealistic faith in it that I did when I was younger. Likewise other forms of modelling can be very powerful tools when built and used appropriately and with integrity. But they are just tools. Ultimately the decision making is done by people and those people need to understand the limitations of their tools.

Multi-criteria decision analysis modelling and targets

I have suggested that money can be the main driving force when dealing with big projects or systems. But big DDM situations, such as building a high tech ID card system to tackle terrorism, incorporate a whole range of complex issues. Each of these issues holds different degrees of importance from the perspective of different people. How many terrorist suspects is the system going to help to detain? How much time is it going to take to register on the system? How long is it going to take to get everyone on the system? How reliable will it be? How many people will not be able to register because their biometrics are incompatible with the technology? How many people are going to be wrongly detained or fined or inconvenienced in some way because of system errors? Will it improve access to public services and to what degree?

Different people will want to measure all these things [and more] using different indicators and in different ways. The government will set a target for example for everyone to be on the system by a certain date. Inevitably this target will not be met simply because of the technical complexity of the whole system and so it will have to be revised. Critics will then claim it is a disaster because the government failed to meet its target and yet this is only one tiny, and in the scheme of things, insignificant partial indicator of whether the system is serving its stated purpose [or in the case of the ID scheme dynamic, ever-changing purposes].

This tends to be one of the key problems with target setting. The target is only a partial measure of how well a complex system is meeting its required purpose. Those managing the systems are then forced to concentrate on one of a small number of indicators. The result is that other equally or more important issues, often to which it is difficult or impossible to assign a numeric value, get ignored or neglected with serious resulting consequences for the whole system.

The simplest way to illustrate is with an example. Ambulance crews quite often get emergency calls to non-emergency situations. John Robertson, an Emergency Medical Technician in the West Midlands tells the story, on his blog,[38] of a late night call out to an eight-year-old with a sore wrist. They discovered the boy had been bowling earlier in the day and was just suffering some later stiffness from the activity. Robertson goes on to say they could not have refused to bring the boy to the hospital if that is what his mother wanted because the government's 'Patients Charter' sets the target that everyone who wants an ambulance gets one and everyone that wants a ride in an ambulance to hospital is likewise entitled to have that wish fulfilled. Ambulance crews, according to their targets, have no choice but to attend to non-emergency situations. Yet despite having to use a significant proportion of their time dealing with these kinds of situations they still get criticised when they take too long to attend a real emergency. In addition, if by the time the ambulance reaches, say, a choking patient, the cause of the problem has been dealt with, the ambulance crew is obliged to fill out a form. They then need the potential patient or their carer to sign this indicating they are refusing the kind offer of an ambulance ride to the hospital. The form is essentially for insurance against later claims of negligence.

A second example is completely hypothetical. Suppose an organisation sets a target to train all their employees in diversity awareness. Everyone is obliged to undergo the training or be subject to disciplinary procedures. All employees get sent a thick booklet outlining demographic statistics, relating to ethnicity, gender, sexuality, religion, age and disability. Suppose, for example, that it covers things like the percentage of women or ethnic minority groups employed in particular jobs or sectors.

Employees have to read the booklet and then take a computer-controlled multiple-choice test over the telephone before some target date. They call the computer via the telephone, punch in a pin number identifying them and answer twenty questions, via the touch pad on their phones. The questions relate to the statistics in the booklet. If the individual gets 14 or more correct (i.e. 70%) they pass. Less than 70% means they have to take the test again. They get three chances to pass, after which they get issued a new pin number to try again. The computer naturally keeps track of who has passed and who has failed, so that the organisation can monitor the target of all employees becoming sensitive to diversity.

No one would doubt the good intentions of anyone who created such a training initiative. A well-written and informative booklet will clearly make some individuals aware of their lack of knowledge of or respect for people in their workplace or community. We might, however, reasonably doubt the ability of computer-controlled multiple-choice tests, based on the need to memorise some statistics, to have any impact on the organisation's capacity to engage sensitively with the variability of the human condition.[39]

Given that focusing on a single factor can distort incentives to pursue valuable system goals, another approach is to develop aggregate indicators. In this case the values of lots of different indicators are determined, plugged into some mathematical formula which takes account of the relative importance of each, and then an overall performance indicator is calculated. Gross National Product (GNP), for example, is one aggregated indicator used to measure performance of the UK economy. There are a lot of these kinds of aggregated factors used in many different contexts today and an equally large number of different multi-criteria decision analysis models used to calculate, them.

One simple model we teach students at the Open University is the Kepner–Tregoe method. In brief this works as follows:

- Decide the purpose of your decision situation e.g. to choose between five options when commissioning an information system
- Decide the 'musts' i.e. the things your system *must* do. Any system failing to meet any of these 'musts' can immediately be eliminated
- Decide the 'wants' i.e. the things you would like the system to do
- Allocate each of these 'wants' a weighting (between 0 and 1) based on their relative importance. Clearly this is a fairly subjective exercise
  Rate each of the systems you are considering on a scale of say 1 to 10 according to how well it meets each of your 'wants' i.e. determine on a scale of 1 to 10 how well each system meets each 'want'
- Multiply the ratings for each 'want' (a number between 1 and 10) against the weighting of each 'want' (a number between 0 and 1) for each option
- Add all the weighted scores for each system being considered

- Choose the one with the best score.[40]

All of these aggregate indicators and the models used to generate them have been heavily criticised – for excluding important indicators, measuring the indicators that are used in an inappropriate way, failing to take account of the perspective of different stakeholders and generally failing to account for the true complexity of the things they purport to measure.

Ordinary people and models: critical questions

Ordinary people have a crucial role to play in questioning the simplifications and assumptions that go into all these decision making models. I am going to try and demonstrate that with a somewhat complicated example involving an aggregated indicator of the type just discussed above, which hopefully the ordinary reader will be able to follow.

A lack of understanding of the make up of these composite or aggregated indicators can lead to them being used inappropriately. In May 2006, for example, the EU Commission published a memo declaring intellectual property rights were "at the heart of the Commission's job and growth initiative".[41]

The memo made a number of strong statements about patents. For example:

"The European Innovation Scoreboard 2005 provides empirical evidence that a lower level of patenting to a large extent accounts for the difference in innovation performance between EU countries and to the innovation gap between Europe, the US and Japan... The available data clearly shows that *patent indicators are highly correlated to countries' global innovation performance*. Countries doing well in terms of innovation performance also score high in patenting."

So the evidence from the 'European Innovation Scoreboard 2005' appears to indicate that more patents mean more innovation. This would suggest that we need to start registering patents as fast as we can if we want to improve innovation. Before we do that, however, let us look at what the 'European Innovation Scoreboard 2005' actually means by 'innovation'. Well, you guessed it, the scoreboard measures 'innovation' as an aggregated indicator.[42] 'Innovation' is made of up an average of ten indicators, five of which are related to intellectual property (and three of those to patents). So it is a bit circular to argue that 'innovation' depends on the 'numbers of patents', when a big part of the composite indicator you use to measure 'innovation' is 'numbers of patents'.

It is a bit like saying you have discovered empirical proof that the overall health and welfare of the country is improved when more people take regular exercise, whilst neglecting to point out that you measure 'health and welfare' by counting the number of people who exercise regularly.

Models and the experts that build and use them need to be scrutinised closely. We all have the critical thinking faculties to do that, even if the models or language of the experts or institutions like the EU Commission might appear, at first glance, to be beyond us.

You will be aware from the foregoing discussion of some of the strengths and weaknesses of models as tools for DDM and no matter how complicated or intimidating they appear we can still ask the simple questions:

- What exactly do you mean by that?
- How was it measured?
- Does that include things I would consider important such as...?
- This is a simplified model, so what have you left out that might be important?
- What is the purpose of the model?
- What assumptions did you make?
- Can we just explore those assumptions a bit further?

Ordinary people are also much more capable of understanding complex models than they think and hopefully this chapter has indicated the importance of studying these models in detail, particularly when they are likely to have a big impact on a DDM situation which will affect you. Even if you cannot instantly attain high levels of expertise, it is possible to quickly grasp the key essence of many of these models, or enough detail to challenge the experts to robustly defend and prove their value.

I have a few final points to make before moving on to Chapter 10. Firstly, this chapter is not intended to imply experts and the models they use are useless, merely that they have their limitations and it is worth challenging them with a composite degree of common sense and scientific rigour. The really valuable models and expert opinions will stand up well to such testing.

Secondly it is important to realise not only when the experts might be providing us with bad advice but also when they have good advice. When the experts on weapons of mass destruction were saying that Saddam Hussein had no such weapons, the advice was ignored largely for political reasons.[43] That brings us sharply back to the focus on DDM. If a government, for example in the UK, decides that it is going to introduce a large children's index database to be seen to be doing something about child welfare, then no amount of expert advice, cost benefit analysis or other modeling is likely to dissuade them. Even if the experts are advising a sound, rationally defensive approach, decisions makers do not always behave rationally, particularly when trying to manage a messy DDM situation.[44]

And finally I would like to round off the chapter where I started, with Richard Feynman and the need for awareness when using collected second hand ratings to make important decisions. He used the example of trying to determine the length of the Emperor's nose, when no one was allowed to see the Emperor. You could go all over the country asking people to estimate the size of his nose and then take an average of all the guesses. You would have a lot of data and could process it through a mathematical model but as Feynman said:

"It's no way to find anything out; when you have a very wide range of people who contribute without looking carefully at it, you don't improve your knowledge of the situation by averaging."[45]

Chapter 10 A modest proposal

Access to knowledge is like oxygen. We may only appreciate it when it is gone.

A DDM framework

In the first part of this final chapter, I offer a theoretical digital decision making (DDM) framework. It is based on some of the Open University work I have been involved in over the past ten years, producing and delivering masters degree courses in the area of environmental decision making.[1]

The frameworks developed in the Open University make the assumption that many environmental decision making situations are unstructured messes – complex systems of problems all mixed up together – rather than easily identifiable simple difficulties.[2] Before you can outline solutions to perceived problems, you need to make an effort to understand these messes and the multiple perspectives different people have on them. Through understanding you can begin to identify the real problems in the situation and then start thinking about how to deal with them. Decision making is also seen as an ongoing learning process involving interested or affected parties, often called 'stakeholders'.

DDM situations all too often begin with imagined technological solutions to complex messes instead of attempts to understand those messes. ID cards and passenger database computer profiling systems are the solution to terrorism, a computer in every classroom the solution to the problems of education, the children's index database the solution to the welfare of vulnerable children, changes to intellectual property laws the solution to the mass copying capacity of the Internet. If we ask how well these solutions address the problems they are apparently targeted at, the answer is, inevitably, 'not very well if at all'.

My proposed DDM framework is shown in Figure 10.1. Like the Open University's, it starts with the need to understand and to some degree provides a 'how to' guide for decision makers. The framework, however, is a modest proposal and should in no way be considered to be an ivory tower academic's one-true-guide to digital decision making.

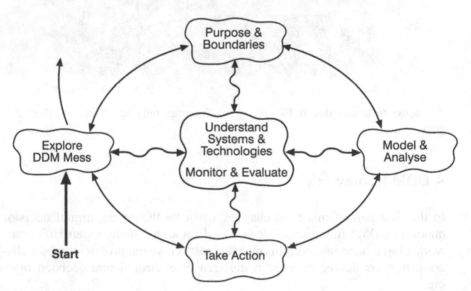

Fig. 10.1 Digital decision making framework

The idea behind the framework is that it provides a structure to think about DDM. The cyclic shape is a deliberate attempt to generate the picture of DDM as an ongoing learning process. Although there are sometimes clear and specific decisions to be made at the 'take action' stage, this is not the end of the process. Frequently, even when information technology projects are well planned, the whole thing falls apart in the implementation of the system, because the decision to go ahead with the project is the cut-off point. Actually building or deploying the system becomes someone else's problem and the demanding reality of deployment and operation is not taken into account in the resources set aside for implementation.

In the summer of 2006 correspondence from senior UK government officials responsible for the ID cards system was leaked to the press.[3] It had become very clear during the commissioning process for the scheme that it had a lot more problems than government ministers were prepared to admit publicly and that it could not be delivered to the required timescales. In addition to the widespread political opposition to the scheme, nearly every serious identity systems professional in the Western world had been saying as much ever since the scheme was conceived. The government's response to the internal reports about problems was to propose a cut down, 'early variant', cheaper version of the system,[4] to gain some breathing space on building the full-scale system. By September 2006, government ministers were publicly talking about building a cheaper system by combining existing government databases rather than building an entirely new system from scratch.[5]

Rather than understanding and learning from expert and senior official advice, the focus was on the need to be seen to deliver something. With so much political capital invested in promises about ID cards, it is difficult to step back from the scheme. Yet sunk costs, monetary or political, should not be the determining factors in DDM processes, when our evolving understanding is telling us that the scheme, as proposed, will not work. If a car has recently cost thousands of pounds in repairs, the money already spent has no relevance to the decision on whether to replace the car now, to avoid continuing unreasonably high maintenance costs in the future. The costs were created by a past decision to repair rather than replace the car and cannot be changed by any future decision on whether or not to replace the car. We can only learn from the past, we cannot change it.

Of course the government finds it hard to treat political capital as a sunk cost because of the absolute guarantee of being accused of an embarrassing U-turn, should they abandon a big scheme like the ID cards system. The question of the raising of the barriers to introducing a sound, privacy-enhancing and service-improving identity architecture at some point in the future also get vaguely mixed up in the mess. Ultimately, though, an ability to demonstrate a capacity to understand complex DDM messes and learn from mistakes would enhance the government's ability to deliver DDM projects. An emergent long-term bonus would be the acquisition of public confidence in the ability of government to manage these kinds of systems professionally and with integrity.

Hence the suggested framework includes the decisions, at the 'take action' stage, as one element in a continuous learning process. The decisions are crucial but the cycle does not suddenly stop at that point if the systems are to be successfully deployed or regulated, as should be clear from the story of the development of the British air defence system prior to World War II.

Take a look at the various stages of my suggested DDM framework:

- Explore the DDM mess
- Be clear about your purpose and your boundaries
- Use models, where appropriate, to help analyse, understand and frame the situation and the feasible and desirable options
- Take action
- Understand the systems and technologies; and continually monitor and evaluate proceedings at each stage of the process.

Not surprisingly the need to understand the systems and the technologies is at the centre of my framework, since I have suggested right from the start of the book that this is the key to improving DDM processes. Every other stage of the framework is linked to that centre by double-headed arrows indicating a two-way flow of information. Tizard and Dowding could never have built a successful air defence system without understanding what radar and its associated technologies could and could not do. That understanding was derived from the operational research that took place between 1935 and the outbreak of war.

Tizard and co. recognised the growing geo-political mess developing in Europe with Hitler's consolidation of power in Germany. Out of the mess they extracted the possibility of war with Germany within the decade, and decided that a critical survival factor for Britain would be the development of an air defence system.

They set themselves a clear purpose to build that air defence system. Wimperis' enquiry to Watson-Watt about a possible 'death ray' to kill enemy pilots led to the realisation that radar would be the key technology in the air defence system. Blue-skies research[6] with the technologies would have been interesting but that was not within the boundaries they set. Where possible, only existing components and technologies were used and they were deployed on a 'just good enough' basis.

They built models, did trials,[7] tested and developed the technologies, discovered the need for the filter room and operations centres at Fighter Command, Group and Sector levels and generally the decision makers, the experts and the users acquired a sound operational understanding of the system.

Tizard, Dowding, Watson-Watt and co. took the initiative to act and plunder the necessary resources from government coffers to make sure the system got built. Landmark action points, such as the decision to disband the Tizard committee and reform it without Professor Lindemann and the challenges he posed, are easy to pick out but they are clearly actions in the context of a much wider and ongoing DDM process.

This process between 1935 and the outbreak of war in 1939, and continuing on through the war years, could be viewed as going through repeated cycles of my DDM framework. The various activities did not necessary always happen in the neat sequence that a two-dimensional framework is restricted to portraying. The very nature of a messy DDM situation means it is rarely neat or sequential, though it may be possible to identify emergent patterns in the mess. It is possible to identify each of the stages of the framework in the radar story, however.

The various stages of the framework are represented by blobs rather than neat, sharp shapes like ellipses or rectangles, in order to emphasise the dynamic nature of the process. The stages are not simply neat, fixed and sequential. Each can change shape like an amoebic micro-organism and be active in parallel with all the others, as the developing of understanding and the operational learning process proceeds.

At this point if I was presenting the DDM framework to students in a classroom I might ask them to think about whether they had come across similar models in other contexts, whether and how these were helpful and perhaps how the framework matches up to the kind of personal approach they have taken to complex decisions they have faced in their lives. That is not possible with a book but we can look briefly at how the framework compares with approaches discussed earlier, such as the rational decision making in Chapters 2, 5 and 7 or Schneier's five-step system in Chapter 5.

The clearest visual distinction between the framework and all the other systems in the book is its continuous cyclic or iterative nature, emphasising the importance of the learning process. Other approaches have distinctive starting and end points, though Schneier too stresses the importance of appreciating complexity and thinking about security decisions as part of a continuous learning process. Some people find it helpful to think of this cyclic continuous process as a cascading series of cycles round the framework, as shown in Figure 10.2.

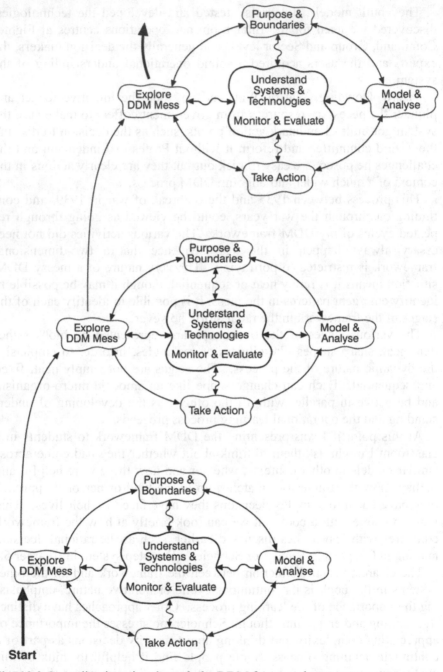

Fig. 10.2 Cascading iteration through the DDM framework

The idea is to portray the feeling of moving upwards and onwards as the DDM stakeholder progressively works through cycles of the framework. Of course real-world messy DDM situations will never be as neat and sequential as a two-dimensional diagram might imply.

In Chapter 7, I noted that after the debacle of the Florida vote count in the 2000 presidential election, Congress was under pressure to do something to 'ensure it could never happen again'. They decided to blame the machines and settled on the technological quick fix, with the Help America Vote Act requiring the use of electronic voting machines. Yet the scale of the electoral process mess in the US is beyond the capacity of technology to fix. Spending a lot of money on technology which does not work will merely introduce further problems into an already messy DDM situation. Could the DDM framework have helped? Let us take each of the stages in turn.

1. Did Congress explore the electoral system mess and identify a selection of key problems and opportunities such as:
- The voter registration process
- Gerrymandering
- The possibility for the same people to be simultaneously in charge of one candidate's election campaign and the process of ensuring the election is fair
- The stretching of existing electoral rules by both main political parties
- Fraud
- Disenfranchisement of various sectors of the electorate
- Problems with voting technologies like punch card machines?

Not really.

2. Did they, based on a deeper understanding of the mess including the perspectives of multiple stakeholders, undertake a clear purpose to tackle one or more of these problems specifically and did they set a clear boundary on the elements of the mess they were going to focus on?

Arguably the answer to both questions is yes since they focused on the voting technologies and decided specifically to upgrade them. In reality they homed in on a single technological difficulty and, without any real understanding of the mess, within which the malfunctions in the machines merely were a single contributory factor, decided that replacing those kinds of machines with modern computers would solve the problem. The decision about whether to allow votes where the machines had failed to completely punch out the chad[8] in the end was more important than the faulty machines. There was no attempt to understand the perspectives of different stakeholders including, crucially, that of the computer scientists who truly understood the technologies and their associated problems.

3. Did they use models and empirical evidence to analyse their chosen problems, frame the potential feasible and desirable options to the situation and identify a clear way forward?

Not really. They chose a solution – computer voting technologies – to an imagined big problem – mechanical voting machines – and decided to pass a law to require a lot of money to be spent on that 'solution'.

4. Did they take action?

Yes they did. Then again, there is a distinction to be made between action that progresses the DDM situation and mass frenzied activity which is often used to disguise the lack of purposeful action. The classic simile that the reader will be familiar with here is 'it's like rearranging the deck chairs on the Titanic'. It is the illusion of progress through activity which can hide the need for effective action until it is too late.

5. Did they base their activities on a deep understanding of the election technologies and system and did they monitor and evaluate the ongoing process?

No, there was little understanding and yes, the spending of federal and state funds does require some oversight and evaluation.

6. Did they then go round the DDM learning cycle again?

No, though the work of a small number of computer scientists like professors Avi Rubin of John Hopkins University and Edward Felten at Princeton is continuing to highlight the technical and security problems with currently deployed electronic voting machines in the US. This has led to a number of state governors taking actions such as requiring the use of parallel voter verifiable paper voting trails. Six weeks prior to the November 2006 elections, following big problems in the September primaries, the Governor of Maryland even declared a desire to scrap e-voting machines and run with an all-paper ballot.[9]

Could the DDM framework have helped the decision making surrounding the US electoral process mess, a mess already over-burdened with complex systemic problems and merely compounded further by bolting an extra layer of complex technological problems on top? I believe it probably could have but then it is very easy to say this with 20:20 hindsight. As an old college friend of mine used to say,

"It's a clever man who has his afterthoughts beforehand."

Congress is hardly short of rules and regulations, processes and committees and other social technologies designed to theoretically enforce the integrity and rationality of the legislative process that churned out the Help America Vote Act. Yet reality politics, commercial lobbying and other pressures still combine to ensure the outcomes of the democratic processes in the US or elsewhere are, shall we say, less than perfect. Even without subscribing to conspiracy theories of the corruption of the political process, an appreciation of complexity leads to the realisation that, even when the parts of the system and the people therein are working as intended, things can still go wrong.

Ireland and the UK are at a much earlier stage of the electronic voting revolution than the US. Both have already shown an inclination to take a different approach to considering these systems than was the case in the US. It could be argued, I guess, that Ireland initially started down a similar road to the US. The Irish government spent €60 million on an electronic voting system before being forced to set up an electoral commission to consider its viability.[10]

The Electoral Commission in the UK[11] published a report in 2003 stating:

"In relation to electronic voting, we are clearly some way from an e-enabled general election... We said in our report on the 2002 pilots programme that a clearer strategic direction was needed to demonstrate the key milestones in moving towards 'an e-enabled general election sometime after 2006.' We remain convinced that there is a need for more detailed planning towards this goal." [12]

In other words if we are going to go down this route we need a much better understanding of the systems, the technologies and the challenges they present. The Electoral Commission has also published several reports on pilot e-voting schemes run in 2002, 2003 and 2006.[13] Clearly the Electoral Commission are doing a lot of work but the government are under no direct obligation to take their findings into account when deciding on changes to the complex, messy system that constitutes the UK electoral process.[14]

We can see with hindsight, and if we choose to use it with the help of the DDM framework, the things that went wrong and continue to go wrong in the US electoral process. Similar or related DDM processes are ongoing in jurisdictions all over the world right now, however. I would suggest that they should be tackled in a different way. If a modest DDM framework like mine might help then I would be delighted. Whatever the approach, it should be based, in the first instance, on the acquisition of greater understanding by decision makers, experts and users of systems, technologies and the environment in which these are to be used, to enable the possibility of more successful outcomes.

I have not covered the enormous range of data gathering, systems diagramming and modelling techniques that are available for making detailed sense of a complex system mess at each stage of my suggested framework.[15] Perhaps if I had set out to write a decision making manual, I would have started out with my DDM framework and then taken readers through each stage in detail, with an in-depth exploration of some of the techniques available for doing so.[16] All of this would have to pay attention to scientific rigour and the scientific method. Instead the focus of this book has been on what the reader ought to know about modern digital technologies, how they are used and regulated and why you need to know it.[17]

Access to knowledge: education from Colmcille the knowledge society

A significant part of this book has been devoted to the complex and messy regulatory system known as intellectual property because of its ever increasing impact on the global knowledge economy. It is an area dominated by the needs of large companies smart enough to gather large intellectual property portfolios and exert influence in the important forums where policy is set.[18]

Trying to interest an ordinary person in this abstract, fuzzy, confusing regulatory mess is about as easy and as welcome as extracting teeth. In addition the intellectual property regulatory landscape – a really complicated, messy and unbalanced system – has been undergoing an upheaval of earthquake proportions in the past three decades.[19] This rapid change makes it difficult to keep up with. Why should ordinary people take notice of an abstract and complicated regulatory area, which has little immediate apparent connection to their daily lives and concerns?

Well, it is an area that affects the food we eat, our entertainment, the medical treatment we get, the books we read, the other technologies we use, the schools, libraries and universities that make up the frontline infrastructure of our education systems and the kind of employment, lifestyles and basic information we have access to. It is having a profound impact on the knowledge economy and is probably the most important area of public policy to which the general public remains largely oblivious.

In arguably the most important DDM arena, the cost of getting the policy wrong in medicare, gene or agricultural patents can be the destruction of livelihoods or even make the difference between life and death. Myriad

Genetics' tests for the cancer-causing mutations of the BRCA1 and BRCA2 genes, on which they retain patents in many jurisdictions all over the world,[20] cost thousands of dollars. Given all the work they did on these genes there is no reason why Myriad should be prevented from making money on these tests. Scientists complain, however, that the company's test for BRCA2 does not detect all the cancer-causing mutations of the gene and their excessively litigious policing of their patents mean that other scientists are effectively barred from attempting to develop a more comprehensive test until the patents run out.[21] This could take twenty years or longer, depending on how good Myriad's lawyers are at tweaking the rules of the patent system to gain extensions to the patent terms.

As I write the *Guardian* have published a front page story implying the large pharmaceutical companies have been unethically lobbying government ministers to facilitate fast-track approval of their drugs for clinical practice in the UK.[22] My purpose here is not to criticise the drugs or biotech industries. This has been widely done elsewhere, particularly in relation to the lack of available and affordable life-saving medicines, such as AIDS drugs, in the developing world.[23] If these companies are to continue supply their important drugs anywhere in the world, they have to remain viable commercial entities i.e. they have to be able to make money. How much money they should be able to make, under what conditions and what kinds of drugs they have incentives to produce[24] are other empirical questions, ultimately determined by the balance of national and international trade rules and the intellectual property landscape.

There is no easy way out of this one. The economists' dream world is one of perfect price discrimination where everybody pays what the market will bear. Drug companies use their patent monopolies to generate revenues for profits and recover their research and development costs. They cannot sell at high prices and huge profit margins in the developing world because the market will not bear it – people just cannot afford it. So they sell the drugs at a premium in the developed world. With today's global markets, though, people in one area ask why they should pay more than those in another area of the world.[25] Economists will answer – because they can afford to. That is a completely unsatisfactory answer to most of us. But, but, but, we ask, why should I pay a premium when someone else can get them cheaper. I can just fly to Africa, India or Canada, buy a large batch and take them home with me and still have it work out cheaper – what the economists call arbitrage.[26] What is more I can probably get a decent holiday thrown into the bargain.

Free market absolutionists' answer would be: leave it to the free market to sort out. The question then is: which free market? The producer-loaded one with perfect price discrimination or the perfect information, customer loaded one, with perfectly informed global consumer discrimination? A similar question goes to the anti-capitalist perspective – how can drug companies supply the need for medicines fairly across the globe and still generate respectable (or even optimum) revenues?

Information economics and intellectual property's place in it is a complex business.[27] I do not have an answer and though there are models which help work out optimising theories, we live in an imperfect world.

My focus in this final part of this final chapter, however, is the impact of DDM in the intellectual property arena and otherwise on education. In a sense it brings me right back to the story of Colmcille in Chapter 1 and the sad fallout in the dispute over a book. Colmcille was passionate about education or at least access to information. Some might suggest that he was passionate about Christianity rather than education or access to information but in addition to his religious beliefs he had a deep devotion to the Celtic culture, people and the natural world.[28] He also understood that the road to success was through engagement with ordinary people, the very people that experts, decision makers and scholars all too often become disconnected from.

Incidentally, if Colmcille had stopped long enough to consider the socio-political, tribal, economic, religious and cultural DDM mess he was stepping into the middle of, in the high court arbitration hearing over the book, he might have thought twice about agreeing to it. There is no doubt he was streetwise enough to see this bigger picture yet he still walked into it, probably blinded by the righteousness of his cause. What he initially saw as a simple difficulty – the disagreement about who owned the copy of the book – became part of a much bigger mess. Maybe he could have found the DDM framework useful too, if only to run through the early stages and explore the context, possible perspectives and agendas of those likely to be involved in the hearing and the range of possible outcomes. The simple realisation that there was a wider context and that his preferred result was not guaranteed would have been sufficient to get his astute political mind working on the problem in a different way.

Colmcille wanted to facilitate wider access to contents of what he believed to be a very important book, the definitive Latin translation of the Bible. He wanted to do it by copying the book and spreading those copies around. That is pretty much what education is all about – spreading access to knowledge around – and pretty much what universities do, through books, other technologies and people.

An education wish list

It is my belief that access to knowledge is essential to enable every individual to fulfill their potential. This is especially true in the knowledge economy and Eben Moglen[29] even casts it as a moral issue:

"If *all* knowledge, all culture, all art, all useful information can be costlessly given to *everyone* at the same price that it is given to anyone; if *everyone* can have *everything, everywhere, all* the time, why is it *ever* moral to exclude *anyone* from *anything*? If you could make lamb chops in *endless* numbers by the mere pressing of a button, there would be *no moral argument for hunger ever, anywhere.*"[30]

To the degree that DDM in intellectual property or elsewhere opens up access to knowledge and education, I welcome it. To the degree that it shuts off or encloses access to knowledge, in the way that Larry Lessig and James Boyle have articulated far better than I can, it gives me some significant concerns. There is nothing new in this. DuPont tightened its position on scientific publications after one of its scientists published a paper related to nylon in 1931, leading to their competitor, IG Farben developing nylon 6 by 1938. Everything thereafter had to pass through the lawyers and tough internal procedures.[31] The scientific community began to see DuPont as a parasite and free rider but all the other large chemical companies quickly went down the same path. You might recall a quote I used from Edward O. Wilson[32] in Chapter 4:

"The wise procedure is to use the law to delay, science to evaluate and familiarity to preserve. There is an implicit principle of human behaviour important to conservation: *the better an ecosystem is known, the less likely it will be destroyed.*"[33] [My emphasis]

I suggested then that the better our important knowledge ecology is known, the less likely it will be to be destroyed by limited understanding or development of the intellectual property landscape or other DDM processes. If you spread knowledge around, through books, people or the Internet, it becomes difficult to subsequently to take it back. It also becomes difficult to exert control over the distribution of that knowledge in a way that subsequently limits access, since people will notice and object. If books were widely and cheaply available in every corner of the world, then the withdrawal of books from poorer countries on the basis of inability of distributors to generate high enough revenues would be noticed and sufficiently important to energise political action.

The trouble with intellectual property and most other complex DDM is that people do not notice or object (or applaud) because the decisions, good or bad, do not have an immediately visible impact in ordinary people's lives. Yet it is only the ordinary people in conjunction with people who have a deep understanding of the systems at the outset who are going to ensure that these DDM systems work. In 2006 a report for the Trade Law Centre for Southern Africa stated:

"There can be little doubt that education is a cornerstone of social and economic development, or that access to learning materials is a crucial factor in the success of any educational system."[34]

I could not agree more and in that spirit I would like to close this book with my wish list in the area of DDM and education.[35] I should say that this wish list is as much about what we have and where we are, plus making these work through e.g. better targeted services, as it is about exploring the real and exciting potential of what we could be doing with information and communications technologies in education. It also expresses some of the concerns I have about the impact of DDM in education, yet it still only scratches the surface of the complexity of this messy[36] subject area.

Understanding, understanding, understanding...

Top of my wish list (though the rest are in no particular order) is the requirement that policy makers, in government, international forums *and* other relevant organisations, understand the technologies, the systems and the context (in this case educational environment) they are dealing with. This is central to my book, my suggested DDM framework and my wish list. We will not improve education without understanding.

Technology infrastructure, like the Internet, is to information as bottles are to wine.[37] The Internet is a useful tool for making certain kinds of information more accessible and valuable. The Net does not 'do' education better. It moves electronic bits of information from one connected computer to another on the network very quickly.[38] The computers are just machines that process these bits. So the Net can and does complement, spectacularly in some notable instances, what we already do in education and gives us the capacity to store, manipulate, access and distribute the information in a way that adds significant educational value.

In Chapter 7, I noted, through the story of the development of radar, that technology is just a tool.[39]

The British created an integrated system to collect the raw data on approaching enemy aircraft, from their chain of radar stations (information technology) and (visuals from) the Observer Corps (human information technology). This raw data was passed on (via radio telephone and teleprinters) to headquarters and an integrated set of operations centres, where it was assessed, filtered, analysed and turned into useful information at varying levels. This then facilitated the scrambling of the right fighter squadrons and even more specific instructions to be radioed to the RAF pilots once in the air, to enable them to intercept their enemy at the earliest opportunity.

The Germans had better information technology (radar). The British had the better information system (radar, human intelligence, signals intelligence, and an integrated, purpose-developed system, allowing the situation to be viewed holistically, as well as delivering the right information to the right users, at the right levels, in a useful format and in sufficient time to act on it). The better information system prevailed. Adolf Galland, one of Germany's best-known fighter pilots, credited with shooting down over a hundred allied planes during the war, said:

> "The British had an extraordinary advantage, which we could never overcome throughout the entire war: radar and fighter control."[40]

Purpose, purpose, purpose...

Throwing money at technology will not solve your DDM systems problems, especially if you do not know what your problems are or what you want that technology to do. Worse still, whilst you are distracted with the resource-intensive and frustrating job of trying to get inappropriately deployed technologies to work, it blinds you to some of the great things you could be doing with such technologies. For example, in the context of education, we could be using multimedia and communications technologies creatively to improve the lot of people with dyslexia.

Open educational archives

Open educational archives are being set up all over the world.[41] The most well known is MIT's OpenCourseWare, the mission of which is to:

- Provide free access to virtually all MIT course materials for educators and learners around the world.
- Extend the reach and impact of MIT OCW and the "opencourseware" concept.

In the autumn of 2006, the Open University launched its own open content initiative, OpenLearn.[42] The second item on my wish list is the smooth facilitation of the creation, growth and global networking of these open educational archives, in order to make the whole spectrum of high quality educational materials as widely and easily available as possible.

There are enormous problems with basic access to educational materials all over the world, even in affluent societies like the UK or the US. We now have the technical capacity to make all recorded human knowledge and culture available in an accessible form at an affordable cost. So why don't we do it?[43]

There are not-insignificant technical, cultural, political and legal challenges and serious questions of policy and principle on things like the technical architecture. The publishing industry is already working through many of the legal issues, as a result of Google's 'Google Book Search' project. Google's initial intention was to digitise all the world's books and make their contents searchable but not downloadable online. Publishers naturally had concerns and have been working these out through negotiations and the courts. The project actually offers benefits to readers, authors and publishers, in the latter case as a way of bringing particular books to the attention of potential customers who might not otherwise consider buying or even know about those books. Heated debates about the technical architecture leave even more metaphorical blood on the floor between the technical experts who understand these systems. But it is seriously economically and technically possible to make a much wider range of educational materials available to a much wider range of people – the electronic equivalent of the Great Library of Alexandria of our time.

It would also be seriously possible, with sufficient imagination, to transform teaching in the higher education sector. At the moment academic status depends on research and publications. There is a siphoning of funding towards 'world class' research institutions and departments and little in the way of credit for teaching in universities. Open archive repositories could pave the way for academics to gain kudos not just on research publications but on the quality of their peer reviewed contributions to teaching materials in high quality education repositories. Giving gifted university teachers an incentive to spend time developing those teaching gifts could have incalculable benefits for the university sector.

There is a fear that such open content initiatives could do away with the need for universities altogether. Yet such schemes would never survive in the wild without a viable and indeed thriving university and publishing sectors to support them. In their current incarnations there is some wonderful material available in open content schemes but it does not substitute for a university education.

Just as the pharmaceutical companies need to be commercially viable to facilitate the supply of desperately needed medicines to all areas of the world, open content needs universities which will be viable and preferably thriving organisational entities with sustainable incomes.[44] Indeed just as the Internet does not do away with the services that publishers provide,[45] open content does not negate the services that universities provide. There are some complex business models to be developed that will make open content sustainable but such initiatives cannot afford to cannibalise the very institutions they will largely be relying on in order to remain viable.

Supported open learning

The Internet and related communications technologies have tremendous potential to facilitate and improve what the Open University calls 'supported open learning at a distance'. Let us focus on and work with that potential.

This, incidentally, is not just about putting lecture notes or electronic copies of books or paintings on the Web as many perceive 'e-learning' to be. Neither is it about insisting that every course have some kind of Internet or computing activity associated with it.[46] MIT's OpenCourseWare is a fantastic initiative but even though this material is available freely on the Web, you still need to attend MIT to get an MIT education. Supported open learning at a distance is where the student:

- Has a tutor(/s) to support their studies face to face, via the phone, online, via correspondence or any other communication medium
- Has control over the pace of learning
- Is geographically separated from their tutor, their learning institution (e.g. university) and, sometimes, even their original course/learning materials.

When you break it down like this we can start asking questions about how we can:

- use the available technologies to improve/complement the tutor's existing capacity to facilitate the student's learning
- use the (e.g. multi-media) technologies to make the materials more accessible
- use the technologies to help students help each other
- tap into the students' experience and skills and get them to actively use technologies in ways which build on their own preferred learning styles
- put people in touch with people.

It turns out that there are loads of ways to do all of these things. As long as we do not get distracted by the tedium and ridiculous requirements to do things with the technology that it is not suited to (common problem), we can start help people. We can help people with dyslexia or those who have not had a shot at a decent education (e.g. disadvantaged groups in inner cities or poorer parts of the world) to start to learn to communicate through e.g. multimedia technologies. We then build from there. The sky's the limit on this kind of thing if we only focus on the utility and the *purpose* – there is that word 'purpose' again. We need to focus on the utility and the purpose behind the use of the technologies, not just using these tools for their own sake.

Focus on the educational function of what you want to do with the technologies, not the technological tools themselves. Focus on what the network is supposed to do not the network for its own sake. Focus on what the educational literature and the Higher Education Funding Council are currently labelling 'blended' approaches to teaching and learning, where technologies are used in ways that complement and integrate into what we already do well. At the same time we should not let our current methods constrain our thinking in a way that ignores the novel opportunities that new technologies might present.

Not that playing with the tools in different educational contexts is a bad thing. On the contrary that is a fundamental part of finding out what the technologies can do but deploying them inappropriately towards serious ends without realising what they can and cannot do is a good way to guarantee failure. Incidentally the same thing goes for pedagogy. It is just a tool. It is in vogue in 'e-learning' circles at the moment to say pedagogy comes first and that we should not get blinded by the technology. It is one of those statements that it is hard to disagree with but is basically empty of meaning, regardless of how many wise nodding heads you trigger when saying it. Excessive blinkered focus on technology or pedagogy (or 'learning objectives' which are often used as a surrogate for pedagogy) leads ultimately to content-free courses. My view is that people come first and we should play with the tools to find out what they can do and then use them purposefully. Martin Weller did propose a wonderfully attractive idea, though, to test the robustness of the 'pedagogy should come first' meme:

> "Just to be contrary – Instead of creating a course by starting with learning objectives, or pedagogy, I wonder what it would be like to ask 'what are the ten coolest technologies?' and then construct a course around them. My guess is that it would be as pedagogically sound as the more worthy approaches and maybe a bit more fun."[47]

Publicly funded research publicly available

Next on my wish list is that publicly funded research should ultimately be made available openly to the public. This notion is supported by the Organisation for Economic Co-operation and Development,[48] numerous Nobel Prize winners,[49] the Research Councils UK,[50] and a report commissioned by the EU Commission in 2006,[51] amongst many others. The UK's John Sulston, himself a recent Nobel Prize winner for medicine, for his work on the Genome project, is also a big advocate of research as a collaborative enterprise in which "discoverers are acknowledged but their results freely showed".[52]

E-learning panacea

Can we please get away from this notion of 'e-learning' as an autonomous pedagogic entity?[53] In the Open University, we have done a lot of work with computers, the Net and other multi-media technologies.[54] Hopefully that has, on balance, enhanced the educational experience of many of our students. But 'e-learning' has most definitely been complementary, and not a stand-alone alternative, to the kinds of things we have always done well, as a supported distance learning institution.

The degree, however, to which the education sector and policy makers still get distracted by the bells and whistles of the technologies, rather than their real utilities in an education context, is lamentable. As discussed in other contexts earlier in the book, there is a naive Boys' Own belief in the ability of computers to automatically make things better.[55] Yet at the same time there exist significant pockets of hard-earned craft knowledge and experience on what things work (on an industrial scale, in some cases) in this environment and, almost more importantly, what things do not work.

Never underestimate the constraints imposed by computer or other technological architecture in any context, let alone education. You only have to think about the portability and readability of a book compared with a standard desktop computer to realise this. We have got to work hard to ensure the architecture and educational materials we use to support/deliver/facilitate learning is enabling rather than restrictive. Too often we are dealing with restrictions of inappropriate technologies deployed in inappropriate ways.

Interoperability, standards and open code

This is a huge issue about which I could bore for my native Ireland, but I am only going to mention a few things.

An example of the tools driving the users is the increasingly widespread adoption by educational institutions of closed, so-called 'virtual learning environments' (VLEs), a market dominated by a very small number of players. Despite their positive features and given that this is something of a wish list, I wish that these systems were open, interoperable, extensible, adjustable and any number of other '...ables' – i.e. that they basically allowed users the technical and legal capacity to tinker with and improve them. The existing architectural constraints of these systems make it impossible to develop the technologies in ways that we should and could be doing to improve the education environment.

One of these companies, Blackboard,[56] has recently been granted a broad patent[57] in the US on technology used for "internet-based education support systems and methods" causing concern in universities and the educational technology community. Though I am not a lawyer, my understanding of the legalese is that it says Blackboard have a patent on:

Any system of online courses which can be accessed via different computers by different users. Those people can be students, instructors or system administrators. The courses sit on a computer server and the kind of access a user gets to one or more courses depends on whether they are a student, teacher or administrator.[58]

The patent also covers the mechanics of the systems administration required to set up the different levels of access, put up the course materials etc. The company assured the Association for Learning Technology in August 2006 that they:

"have a stated business policy of not going after individual universities, nor are we focusing on Open Source initiatives".[59]

Universities, including the Open University since we have adopted the open source 'Moodle' system, can take some comfort from this, though business policies can change over time. Blackboard's patent and their quick lawsuit against competitor, Desire2Learn,[60] for infringing the said patent, has sent significant ripples through the educational technology community, a community not best known for an interest in obscure intellectual property regulations. Well, if it takes this kind of patent litigation to wake the education sector (I emphatically reject the notion that universities constitute 'an industry') up to the damage that can be done by an imbalance in the intellectual property system then maybe it will serve some useful purpose.[61]

I do not really wish to do any more, here, than flag the patent and the follow-on case. The relevant point is that instead of innovating, educators will get told by risk averse university managements that 'we have spent lots of money on this system, now use it; but do not mess about or tinker with it because we do not want to be hearing from Blackboard's lawyers'.[62] Given that the University sector is fundamentally about facilitating access to knowledge, the concern arises that the very platforms on which they deliver that knowledge in electronic form could potentially be subject to external control of an unwelcome nature.

The patent and my hypothetical on university managements' response to it are arguably contrary to the historical trend of open cooperation in e-learning and the current trend in Internet technology, particularly the Web

2.0 developments[63] which are all about openness (open application program interfaces (APIs), open licences, open source, etc.) and democratisation (user-created content and tools). With open systems we could and should be releasing the capacity of creative educators and others to innovate. The patent may prove costly for the company in the long term if it really does alienate the very people in universities who have been using their systems for so many years.

The history of the economics of information and communications is littered with lessons of the problems of compatibility, interoperability and interconnectedness ranging through such diverse areas as railways, telephony, airlines and computers. In the latter case, Netscape, dominant in the initial browser market, was always vulnerable to the monopoly Microsoft Windows operating system, that it needed to operate with, in order to exist. Allowing a small number of incumbent companies to dominate the educational technology market, locking in educational institutions and locking out competition with patents, does not augur well for innovation or creativity in this area. Facilitating open, component-based educational technologies, however, based on open standards – and that can be regulated or facilitated by the government – leads to systems competition, whereby component manufacturers/producers' only requirement is that their products or services are compatible/interoperable with the rest of the [open standard] system. Follow the open standard and your component will work. Just as on the Internet, where your innovation/creation only had to 'speak' the technical language of the Internet,[64] the potential for innovation explodes and barriers to entry are minimal.

In the case of a limited number of players, however, dominating a market on the basis of closed, proprietary systems, this leads to lock-in of educational institutions, high switching costs and high barriers to entry for competitors. Hence innovation gets controlled by the incumbent suppliers, not the end users or external players.

Economics also teaches us about what economists call 'network externalities' or 'network effects'. This is where you get long lead times for the penetration of the product/service followed by explosive growth once the market reaches 'critical mass' i.e. the value of the network increases with the number of users, as was the case with telephones and email. But with educational technologies the incumbent players are the only ones who will benefit from the network effects.

Fear of the effects of the Blackboard patent and lack of understanding of intellectual property may well cause more universities to seriously consider going down the open source route. If open systems like Moodle were to make inroads into Blackboard's market share then the company would have to find some means to protect their revenues. It will be interesting to see how the patent stands up to being tested in court in the meantime.

The people who build virtual learning environment systems (including dominant players) and other information and communication technologies systems for the education sector, should work more closely with those of us who use the systems, on their design, implementation, maintenance and evolution. The danger of shutting out the users is that your systems will eventually fail.

The ripples and litigation from the Blackboard patent show it is important for regulators to make a serious effort, now, to address some of the predicted and other emergent negative constraints on education arising from developments in intellectual property laws in recent years. These have worrying long-term implications for the entire education sector and especially in relation to our exploitation and deployment of information and communications technologies. This is another incredibly complex issue in itself and again I am merely superficially flagging it here.

I have one final basic plea to policymakers (institutional and government) on interoperability. Where we do have non-compatible systems, do *not* try to 'solve' the problem by buying in a new system you hope (or a vendor promises) will magically make the incompatibles communicate. It will not. It is quite typical in, but not exclusive to, the education sector to have the administrative staff using one email/communications system, whilst the teaching staff and students use another which at best can communicate poorly with the former and at worst is totally incompatible. I know of a number of institutions who have bought in new systems to bridge this communications gap only to be disappointed.

Share the craft, be creative, and build the networks

Find a way – both government and institutional policymakers – to free up the really experienced coalface practitioners, who hold the deep craft knowledge of what you can, cannot, could and should do with these technologies in education, to share their experience more widely. The use of modern technologies in education, like the IT industry generally, is still in its infancy. There is a growing, if still relatively small body of skilled practitioners, who have a deep level of understanding of both the technologies and education. Their individual craft knowledge needs to be translated into institutional learning in universities, commercial companies and government policy making institutions.

One way to do this would be to stick lots of these smart, energetic people together in one place and give them the resources and the freedom to be creative. The US Congress is considering something along these lines in the 'Digital Opportunity Investment Trust' (DO IT) bill.[65] The idea is to use the billions of dollars which will be generated from the sale of the analogue television spectrum to set up a trust for to develop educational technologies and materials. The committee that reported to Congress on the recommended structure of the trust actually focuses on some of the key central issues if we are going to exploit the potential in this area: instructional design, learner modelling and assessment systems, simulation and environmental exploration systems for authors, teachers and learners, open integration standards. The list goes on and sounds amazing, if only it gets through the Congressional legislative minefield unscathed and then the money can be used with sufficient intelligence, energy and creativity. We need to be looking at the possibility for similar schemes in Europe and the rest of the world.

So far we have been doing a fair job, sometimes, in getting the technologies to complement what we already do in education. But we have not really even scratched the surface of the things the technology could help us do better, or tapped into the new environments these technologies are creating or could create if we applied sufficient imagination, even just to harness some the emerging properties of these technological systems.

The places where technology complements or parallels what has gone before are interesting but even more interesting are the gaps – the places where our metaphors for the technology do not quite work. Where are the differences, the discontinuities, the latent ambiguities, the puzzles and opportunities and how can we exploit them for positive ends in the educational context?

Let us work with the possibilities of multimedia as a mass writing/creating tool, especially with those whose particular talents may be released through these media, when the written word may be difficult e.g. due to dyslexia or dyspraxia.[66] We can mostly consume the output of these technologies (generated by experts) as students or consumers. Or we can be active users of and writers/creators with these technologies in ways that open up huge educational possibilities.

There has been lots of talk over the years of the 'information superhighway'. This is wishful thinking but given the initiative in the US at least worth raising – I would like governments to put vast funds into the construction of an open physical broadband infrastructure, such that we facilitate access for everyone; in the same way as it funded the road and rail networks.[67] Open content projects like MIT's or the Open University's remain inaccessible to those who cannot afford the technologies. Broadband networks could well be construed as public goods, like the road and rail networks and therefore requiring public investment.

Then we can build it on an open platform with an 'end to end' architecture. Commercial companies funding this construction quite naturally want control over their networks, otherwise there is no incentive to invest in them in the first place. But the lesson of the history of the Internet is that innovation explodes when central control is minimised.

Drowning in electronic data

Can we work intelligent filters into the deployment of these systems please? We have had fantastic organisational filters in place for centuries, like secretarial and clerical staff, who do a terrific job of ensuring the organisational information system works well, with paper and telephone based information getting sifted, assessed, processed and directed to the people who need it. A bit like the principles of the information system that won the Battle of Britain, in fact. And the technologies now give us the facility to refine that filtering, to degrees that would have been unimaginable only ten years ago. So why am I drowning in electronic 'information', having to deal with tens of thousands of emails and other electronic messages every year, direct to my various university electronic mailboxes?

A couple of final education-related wishes

I would like to see a networked computer on every desk in every educational institution and experienced teachers with the capacity and enthusiasm to exploit these machines in that context in appropriate ways.

That could be very expensive but it does not have to be if we get serious about using different, more sustainable kinds of technological architecture.[68]

Finally could we please keep the current generation of 'digital rights management' or 'DRM' technologies out of education and out of libraries? As director of the British Library, Dr Clive Field, told the BBC in commenting on his written submission to the All Party Internet Group enquiry into DRM:

"We have genuinely tried to maintain that balance between the public interest and respecting rights holders.

We are genuinely concerned that technology inadvertently may be disturbing that balance, and that would be unhelpful ultimately to the national interest."[69]

Conclusion

Having detoured into the specifics of DDM in education, I would like to round off now by returning to the general themes of the book. The central claims in this book are that:

1. The far-reaching implications for commerce and society, of decisions in invisible or opaque specialist fields regarding the regulation and deployment of large information systems, mean they should be matters of concern for all of us.

2. Ordinary citizens working together with experts and regulators will prove more effective than each group acting in isolation. In the application of science and technology to social problems, technologies, systems and policies must be developed together by users and experts.

3. The default rules of the road in DDM are the laws governing the flow of information and the restrictions built into the architecture of technology; Lessig and Boyle have it right when they say we need to be much more active in ensuring these regulators are operating in the best interests of the societies they are supposed to serve

I started with the story of Colmcille and his quest for widespread access to a book. Some of the decisions we have to make about DDM systems might involve tough new personal, political, regulatory, technical and socio-economic choices, challenges and opportunities. Yet the experience of a 6th-century monk, Colmcille, that of a 19th-century parliamentarian, Thomas Babbington Macaulay, and stories of the past ranging from the development of radar to electronic voting remind us that, though the context and the tools might change, many of our important guiding principles do not. What I found really striking in Colmcille's closing argument to the Irish high court all those centuries ago was that it could have come straight out of one of the modern digital copyright disputes, from the Rio through to the Google book search or Grokster cases. In creating, deploying, regulating and operating modern digital communications technologies we really do have a lot to learn from going back to the future. In that spirit I would like to end with three of my favourite quotes, the first from reporter, John Lawton, speaking to the American Association of Broadcast Journalists in 1995:

"The irony of the information age is that it gives new respectability to uninformed opinion."

The second is from civil rights icon, Martin Luther King Jr.:

"Cowardice asks the question: is it safe? Expediency asks the question: is it political? Vanity asks the question: is it popular? But conscience asks the question: is it right? And there comes a time when one must take a position that is neither safe, nor political, nor popular – but one must take it simply because it is right."

Finally from satirist, Henry Louis Mencken:

"I believe that liberty is the only genuinely valuable thing that men have invented, at least in the field of government, in a thousand years."

Notes

Chapter 1

[1] Colmcille (pronounced 'Col-um-kill') was brought to the attention of the popularly labelled 'copyfighting' community on the Internet by Seán McGrath, http://seanmcgrath.blogspot.com/2003_03_23_seanmcgrath_archive.html#200053874, who wrote of a small story in *Ingenious Ireland: A County-By-County Exploration of the Mysteries and Marvels of the Ingenious Irish* by Mary Mulville (Simon & Schuster UK, 2003), referring to the monk's part in the Battle of the Book at Cooldrumman. To get at the detailed story, however, you cannot beat a few days digging in a good library and there are 189 tomes on the saint in Oxford's Bodleian library. There is a vast amount of myth and legend surrounding our knowledge of the saint's life, as there is very little surviving *direct* evidence or records of his activities. The definitive account repeatedly referred to by scholars is Adomnán's biography, translated by various scholars, the versions I referred to being, *Adomnan's Life of Columba (Oxford Medieval Texts)* Edited by Alan Orr Anderson & Marjorie Ogilvie Anderson (Clarendon Press, 1991) and *Adomnán of Iona: Life of St Columba* Translated by Richard Sharpe *(Penguin Classics)*, (Penguin Books, 1995). Adomnán, born 27 years after the death of his hero, nevertheless came to Colmcille's monastery at Iona at a young age, so probably knew some of the Saint's contemporaries. Mediaeval biographers tended to idolatrise their subjects and it is no accident that a lot of the miracles associated with Colmcille are similar to those connected with Jesus Christ in the bible. (Adomnán would be more accurately described as a hagiographer, rather than a biographer and many of the stories are hagiolatry and folklore rather than historical accounts.) He is alleged in various accounts, for example, to have raised people from the dead (including his foster father, Cruithnechan), turned water into wine and multiplied loaves and fishes. And when he was a baby Cruithnechan came home from church one night to find his house bathed in bright light, the source of which he found was a spectacular fireball hovering over Colmcille's cot. The more parallels the biographer could draw between Colmcille's life and that of the founder of the church, the more important they could make him out to be. Having said all that, however, it must be noted that the provenance of Adomnán's text is impressive. A manuscript at the Stadtbibliothek at Schaffhausen in Switzerland was transcribed by Dorbenne from Adomnán's original. Dorbenne succeeded Adomnán as

Abbot of Iona 9 years after the latter's death. Dorbenne himself died within 5 months of ascending to that office. An earlier abbot, Cummene, who actually knew Colmcille, had also written a life of the saint and it is thought that Dorbenne added extracts from Cummene's Life of Columba in his transcription.

[2] Also in the literature called Culdreimhne, Culdreimhe, Cul Dreimhne, Cul Dreimne, Cul Drevny, Cul Dremne, Culdreibhne.

[3] Google (http://www.google.co.uk), in July 2006, produces more than 94 000 links to webpages on Colmcille (81 000 if you use the Columcille spelling). Using his given name, Columba, that goes up to over 4 300 000. He also, in common with many saints, has an entry in the online encyclopaedia, Wikipedia, http://en.wikipedia.org/wiki/Columba.

[4] Colmcille's kinsfolk were the northern O'Neills. Ian Bradley, *Columba: Pilgrim and Penitent* (Wild Goose Publications, 1996). His father headed the Donegal branch of the family. Donegal is situated in the north-western corner of Ireland and geographically contains the northernmost territory of the country. It is, however, still part of the Republic of Ireland, rather than Northern Ireland which constitutes 6 northern counties that are politically part of the United Kingdom. Up until 1998, when they were amended through a referendum as part of the peace process, articles 2 and 3 of the Irish Constitution laid claim politically to the territory of Northern Ireland. The current text is available online at http://www.taoiseach.gov.ie/upload/static/256.pdf.

[5] The people surrounding the young royal personage nurtured the boy's considerable talents and also encouraged him and others to believe in and live up to his own legend.

[6] Hurling is an ancient Gaelic game, still played widely today not only in Ireland but all over the world amongst the Irish diaspora. 15 players on each team carry wooden hurley sticks, roughly the length of a golf club but with a wider shaft, which they use to collect, carry and strike the sliotar (a small tough leathery ball, similar to a cricket or baseball ball). The object of the game is to score more points than the opposing team by putting the sliotar in their net (which earns three points) or over the opponents' bar, between the tall goalposts (which gives you one point). It is one of the fastest and most skilful field sports in the world, when played properly.

[7] There are some stories to suggest he delighted in a good scrap, though occasionally lost control of his temper to a degree which led him to seriously injure his opponent and on one occasion to bite his mother's hand. See *St. Columba* by M.V. Woodgate (St Paul Publications, 1969). It is possible he took part directly in some of the serious battles between tribes when he was a young lad, as it was the duty of a prince and a churchman to 'smite any foe' that threatened but there are no records of this.

[8] An assistant priest http://en.wikipedia.org/wiki/Deacon.

[9] *The Story of Saint Columba (Columcille) Iona* (M.H. Hill & Son, Dublin, 1928), p19 and *Saint Columba of Iona* by Lucy Menzies (Llanerch Press, 1992, originally published in 1920 by J.F.M. Books). This included one at Kells on land donated by the High King, Diarmaid, who would later rule against him in the dispute over the book; and one at Durrow, which, next to Iona, was to become his most fa-

mous. In fact the monks at Durrow always considered their monastery to hold a higher standing in the church than Iona. *Betha Colaim Chille* by Manus O'Donnell (1532) (A. O'Kelleher, G. Schoepperle published an edited translation in Chicago in 1918, which the Dublin Institute for Advanced Studies published a version of in 1994) claims he set up as many as 300 churches during this time, though this account of the saint's life needs to be enjoyed purely as a fireside folk tale rather a factual account. Nearly every page tells of some spectacular triumph for Colmcille and anyone that provides him with any difficulties is painted in the darkest light.

[10] By the 6th-century the church had become increasingly enlightened as to the power of books and sophisticated in the use of the written word to organise and control its institutions and followers.

[11] Which ran from the middle of the fifth century AD to the end of the tenth century AD. See http://en.wikipedia.org/wiki/Dark_Ages

[12] The Vulgate was the definitive Latin translation of the bible done by St Jerome about a century earlier.

[13] An address which echoes through intellectual property disputes in our modern digital age.

[14] He would have been referring here to the book's physical integrity, as well as its spiritual, economic, social and philosophical value.

[15] Mine is something of a clumsy translation of the original argument recorded in *Betha Colaim Chille* by Manus O'Donnell (1532) and it relies on *Manus O'Donnell, Betha Colaim Chille* (1532) edited and translated by A. O' Kelleher and G. Schoepperle as *Betha Colaim Chille/ Life of Columcille* (University of Illinois Press, 1918), pp178–179, *Saint Columba of Iona* by Lucy Menzies (Llanerch Press, 1992, originally published in 1920), p.25 and *The Legend of Saint Columba* by Padraic Colum (Sheed and Ward, London, 1936), pp76–81. But its meaning remains fairly clear. Colmcille was an accomplished and impressive public speaker, much more so than my efforts at getting his meaning across would make it appear.

[16] A pagan druid and none too fond of Colmcille, though legend has it that the saint converted him to Christianity on the day MacDe died. Colum, op.cit, pp31–35.

[17] Ibid.

[18] This basically covers computing machinery and networks and their associated environments but you can think of 'technology', for the purposes of this book, as the application of knowledge to practical tasks and 'digital decision making' as decisions about digital technologies. Academics will immediately say that these definitions are very loose, which I accept, but sometimes with broad definitions we can begin to see links between things we would not otherwise intuitively connect together: the 6th-century manuscript and cryptography, identity card systems and electronic voting, radar and computer facilitated education, biotechnology patents and digital libraries. Colmcille and Dan Bernstein might be separated by 14 centuries but they showed a shared interest in testing and spreading what they felt to be important ideas. The authentication issues thrown up by an identity card system share a number of features with those required for electronic voting. Radar

alone did not help to solve air defence problems in the war without being integrated into a comprehensive, fit-for-purpose air defence system; any more than sticking a computer in the corner of every classroom will automatically improve education in our schools. The restrictions imposed on research due to the patenting of BRCA1 and BRCA2 genes (http://www.genome.gov/10000940) which demonstrate a potential susceptibility to breast cancer, contrast with the potential for learning and development that could be facilitated by the universally accessible, digital equivalent of the library of Alexandria.

[19] Or 'systemic overview'.

[20] An 'expert', for the purposes of this book can be considered to be someone with professional experience and training in a particular field such as a scientist, engineer, information systems specialist, academic, lawyer etc. Experts are much maligned in our anti-intellectual culture but it really is not a crime to actually know something about the subject area at the centre of a particular decision.

[21] Or 'information age' if you prefer.

[22] Whilst, perversely attempting to make the technology do tasks it is not suited to.

[23] Such as the current consideration been given to abolishing jury trials in complex fraud cases in the UK.

[24] The users, as well subjects and objects of information systems.

[25] *Shamans, Software and Spleens: Law and the Construction of the Information Society* by James Boyle (Harvard University Press, 1997).
The Future of Ideas: the fate of the commons in a connected world by Lawrence Lessig (Random House, 2001)
Free Culture: the nature and future of creativity by Lawrence Lessig (Penguin Books, 2004)
Boyle and Lessig have blazed a trail in explaining the potential impact of changes in intellectual property law and technology to an extent that I would say that their works should be compulsory reading for anyone with a serious interest or involvement in information systems policymaking.

[26] The Library of Alexandria in ancient Egypt was the world's largest library. See Wikipedia for a brief history at
http://en.wikipedia.org/wiki/Library_of_Alexandria#The_Collection.

[27] James Boyle, *The Second Enclosure Movement and the Construction of the Public Domain*, (2003) http://www.law.duke.edu/pd/papers/boyle.pdf. See http://www.law.duke.edu/journals/lcp/indexpd.htm for a full set of related papers from the Duke conference on the public domain of November 2001, in Duke Journals *Law and Contemporary Problems* Vol 66 Nos. 1&2. Special edition edited by James Boyle.

[28] The Consumers International, Asia Pacific Office, Kuala Lumpur, Report, *Copyright and Access to Knowledge: Policy Recommendations on Flexibilities in Copyright Laws*, February, 2006. Available at:
http://www.consumersinternational.org/Shared_ASP_Files/UploadedFiles/23775A
AE-3EE7-4AE2-A730-281DCE859AD4_COPYRIGHTFinal16.02.06.pdf.

[29] I have run a course at the Open University along these lines, *Law the Internet and Society: Technology and the Future of Ideas,* based on Lawrence Lessig's

book, *The Future of Ideas,* op. cit. which it is planned to make available freely as part of the Open University's 'OpenLearn' initiative.

[30] Intellectual property is a complicated area of law covering patents, copyrights, trademarks, industrial designs and trade secrets.

Chapter 2

[1] Entitled the US International Traffic in Arms Regulations (ITAR) http://www.pmdtc.org/itar_index.htm and the Export Administration Regulations (EAR) http://www.access.gpo.gov/bis/index.html. Wikipedia has some information on the ITAR regulations at http://en.wikipedia.org/wiki/ITAR.

[2] The Office of Defense Trade Controls.

[3] There are a vast number of articles, papers and web pages where you can find out more about the wide range of issues covered in the Bernstein dispute, if you're interested. Daniel Bernstein maintains a website on the case at http://cr.yp.to/export.html and the Electronic Frontier Foundation (EFF) which supported Bernstein's legal fight also have a web page devoted to the case at http://www.eff.org/Privacy/Crypto_export/Bernstein_case/.

There are also a large number of resources on the fascinating story of the political disputes (of which the Bernstein case forms a part) over cryptography, which as one researcher described it, is where security engineering meets mathematics. For a decent introduction I highly recommend *The Code Book: The Secret History of Codes and Code-breaking* by Simon Singh (Fourth Estate, 2000) and *Crypto: Secrecy and Privacy in the New Code War* by Stephen Levy (Penguin Books 2000). Levy includes a succinct 5-page description of the Bernstein case.

[4] *Method of Deciding Doubtful Matters* Benjamin Franklin letter to Joseph Priestley, 6 June 1753.

[5] *Beyond Fear: Thinking Sensibly About Security in an Uncertain World* (Copernicus Books 2003, pp 14–15). I will look at Schneier's approach in more detail in Chapter 5.

[6] Stanford University's Jack Steele Parker Professor of International Management, Emeritus and a widely cited decision making theorist.

[7] *A Primer on Decision Making: how decisions happen* by James March (The Free Press, 1994) pp198–206.

[8] Ibid.

[9] *Models of Man* by Herbert A. Simon. (John Wiley & Sons, 1957).

[10] Both the Germans and the British were adversely myopic about each others' technical capabilities during the War (often to the point of damaging their own war effort).

[11] The UK's Minister of the Interior

[12] *Freedom in Rocking a Boat: Changing Values in an Unstable Society* by Geoffrey Vickers (Penguin Books, 1970) p15.

[13] *Advocates* by David Pannick (Oxford University Press, 1992) is particularly compelling and lucid on this point.

[14] Again in the interests of full disclosure, I have never really lost this belief!

[15] *Normal Accidents: Living with High Risk Technologies* by Charles Perrow (Princeton University Press, 1999), p304.

[16] The interface between people and machines was a critical factor at Three Mile Island. The control room was large and complex, with a huge number of instruments, controls and indicators but in spite of this would only be staffed by a single operator during normal operations.

[17] One indicator light was covered with a tag label and the indicator relating to the valve was indirect in that it only showed the solenoid (electrically controlled switch) connected to the valve had worked. So although the valve got the signal to close, it stuck open and there was no way for the operators in the control room to know immediately that this had occurred. The label under this indicator light read 'Light On RC RV 2 Open' which would suggest light off meant the valve was closed *not* 'an electrical signal has been sent to the valve telling it to close'.

[18] Though the presidential commission said there were gaps in the operators' training in dealing with emergencies, all four operators in the control room at the start of the accident had at least five years experience of nuclear reactors in the US Navy before joining the nuclear power generation industry. The US Nuclear Navy created by Admiral Hyman G. Rickover has never had an accident and is renowned for producing top class technical operatives. See *Rickover: The Struggle for Excellence* by Francis Duncan (Naval Institute Press, 2001), *Rickover and the Nuclear Navy: The Discipline of Technology* by Francis Duncan (Naval Institute Press,1990) and *The Rickover Effect: How One Man Made a Difference* by Theodore Rockwell (Naval Institute Press, 1992).

[19] The plant was still a long way from being safe and indeed there was a big release of radioactive gas into the atmosphere two days later. The rest of the story makes fascinating reading, and is told wonderfully well in Chapter 2 of *Understanding Systems Failures* by Victor Bignell and Joyce Fortune (Manchester University Press, 1984) and many other scholarly tomes. Bignell and Fortune also do a superb analysis of the person–machine interface problems created by the set-up in the control room.

[20] *The Report of the President's Commission on the Accident at Three Mile Island. The Need for Change: The Legacy of TMI* by The President's Commission on the Accident at Three Mile Island (U.S. Government Printing Office, Washington, DC, 1979).

[21] Accident investigators reconstructed the sequence of events from the launch pad to the destruction of the Challenger.

A small plume of black smoke was seen emerging from the right-hand booster rocket just as the Challenger began to take off.

Hot combustion gases were starting to blow by the first O-ring.

By 56 seconds into the flight a large section of the first O-ring had burnt away and the hot gases poured out past the displaced second O-ring.

Flames could be seen at 58 seconds coming out of the booster.

The flames burnt a hole in the side of the booster and the side the main fuel tank. This lower section of the main fuel tank contained liquid hydrogen. The upper section contained oxygen.

By 64 seconds into the flight, hydrogen was escaping and getting ignited.

The hydrogen tank then ruptured six seconds later and at 72.3 seconds the fire finally burned through the support strut securing the booster rocket to the main fuel tank, causing the lower end of the booster to swing away.

The rocket nozzle on the booster adjusted itself sharply to try and compensate for the swinging rocket.

The bottom of the hydrogen tank fell away and the igniting gas, acting like a rocket engine, rammed the hydrogen tank into the bottom of the oxygen tank above. At the same time the nose of the swinging booster rocket crashed into the top of the main fuel tank.

The oxygen tank was destroyed. The mix of oxygen, hydrogen and flames resulted in a massive fireball.

The Challenger, subject to huge, unbalanced, vibratory, thermal and supersonic aerodynamic forces, broke apart with the front section containing the astronauts coming away in one piece. The crew compartment hit the sea about two minutes later at terminal velocity, over 200mph.

The final data radioed from Challenger to earth came 73.2 seconds into the flight.

[22] *The Challenger Launch Decision: Risky Technology, Culture and Deviance at NASA* by Diane Vaughan (University of Chicago Press, 1997).

[23] According to Lawrence Mulloy, NASA's Manager of the Solid Rocket Booster project, in his testimony to the Presidential Commission, there were over a thousand "Criticality 1 waivers" on the launch. The failure of any one of these components would have been enough to lead to the loss of the shuttle and the death of the crew.

[24] President Reagan's 'State of the Union' speech on the evening of the 28th of January may have been set to include a mention of Ms McAuliffe. So there was some speculation that the White House put pressure on NASA officials to launch but subsequent detailed investigations failed to come up with any evidence for this. It's pretty unlikely that such pressure came from the White House, as they did not even have an official at the launch site on the day, though Vice President Bush would have been there if it had flown as originally scheduled two days earlier.

[25] This section on Lessig's four forces is loosely adapted from Open University course, *T182, Law, the Internet and Society: Technology and the Future of Ideas.*

[26] *Code: And Other Laws of Cyberspace* by Lawrence Lessig (Basic Books, 1999)

[27] He died in 1981.

[28] According to Moses' biographer, Robert A. Caro, Moses often said about the neighbourhoods he demolished: "When you operate in an overbuilt metropolis, you have to hack your way with a meat axe." See *The Power Broker: Robert Moses and the Fall of New York* by Robert A. Caro (Knopf, 1974). This Pulitzer Prize winning biography is still considered the definitive account, especially by Moses' critics. For an alternative approach to urban planning, see *The Death and Life of Great American Cities* by Jane Jacobs (Modern Library, 1961).

[29] Larry Lessig tells this story in *Code and Other Laws of Cyberspace* (Basic Books, 1999).

[30] http://www.bridgeandtunnelclub.com/detritus/moses/ Moses said of Caro's book: "The biography is... full of mistakes, unsupported charges, nasty baseless

personalities, and random haymakers thrown at just about everybody in public life." He also says "Under fair libel laws [some of the claims in the book] would be actionable."

[31] Intellectual property covers things like copyrights, trademarks and patents and is a large part of the subject of the next two chapters and Chapter 8.

[32] See Chapter 6 on 'Facts, Values and Beliefs' for more on this. Also *Don't Think of an Elephant: Know Your Values and Frame the Debate* by George Lakoff (Chelsea Green Publishing Company, 2004).

[33] MP3 basically compresses digital audio files by a sufficiently high factor to make it easy to transport them via the Internet.

[34] The US Supreme Court, in ruling that Grokster could be held liable for the illegal trading of songs by users of the software, accepted without question that nearly 90% of the traffic on peer-to-peer networks on the Internet involved files infringing copyright (27 June 2005). In reality there is very little empirical evidence as to how much of the material is actually copyrighted and it is virtually impossible to quantify. The best that can be said at the time of writing is that it is probably a substantial proportion. As for Grokster and Morpheus, they may well be consigned to the annals of history by the time this book is published. The Supreme Court decision is likely to lead to them getting sued to the edge of extinction if not beyond it. Indeed in September 2006, the US District Court for Central California issued a summary judgement holding Streamcast Networks Inc., the owners of Morpheus, liable for inducement of widespread copyright infringement. See http://b2fxxx.blogspot.com/2006/09/summary-judgement-v-streamcast-in.html for a summary of the judgement. The full judgement is available at http://www.eff.org/IP/P2P/MGM_v_Grokster/motion_summary_judgement.pdf.

[35] The Audio Home Recording Act of 1992 made it illegal to sell a digital recording device, without a 'Serial Copy Management System' or 'any other system certified by the Secretary of Commerce as prohibiting unauthorized serial copying' that prohibited the making of copies from copies. (Unlike analogue recordings where there is a progressive degradation of the quality when serial copies are made, digital recording produces almost no degradation of sound quality through successive generations of copies.) It also required the payment of a levy to a collection agency which would then distribute the proceeds amongst the artists. The Act is widely believed to have killed off the embryonic consumer digital audio tape market.

[36] Onto which the songs had to be copied before uploading them to the Rio.

[37] Judge O'Scannlain described the issues extremely articulately in his judgement written on behalf of the court and concluded that allowing the sale of the Rio was consistent with US copyright law. His judgement is available at http://www.edwardsamuels.com/copyright/beyond/cases/rio.html

[38] Try telling someone at a social gathering that you are interested in intellectual property and watch for the 'party-bore-alert' body language, leading rapidly to a range of actions from polite excuses plus swift exit to a settling into the resigned miserable belief that the 'victim' has been cornered for the evening.

Chapter 3

[1] This chapter is adapted from a keynote presentation I gave to the IEEE International Symposium on Consumer Electronics in September 2004.

[2] I use the term generically here to also encompass grey markets. Black markets generally refer to illegal transactions, whereas grey markets are those where legitimate goods are moved through distribution channels not authorised by the producer.

[3] In a reprise of the efforts of the Venezuelan street trader in the summer of 2005, thousands of German Harry Potter fans, who could not wait the planned three months to get the official German translation of the sixth novel, *Harry Potter and the Half Blood Prince*, collaborated via the Internet to translate the book into German within two days (or to be more precise 45 hours) of its release. According to the *Guardian* the German publisher threatened legal action though the translators pledged not to distribute their efforts outside the group of people who participated.
http://books.guardian.co.uk/news/articles/0,6109,1540225,00.html?gusrc=rss.

[4] *Harry Potter and the Half Blood Prince* by J.K. Rowling (Bloomsbury, 2005).

[5] *The Sun* reported that they had agreed to buy the manuscript to enable them to return it to the publishers and tip off the police. Two years earlier the publishers had obtained an injunction against News Group Newspapers Ltd. (which owns *The Sun*), after they had obtained unauthorised copies of *Harry Potter and the Order of the Phoenix* in advance of publication. The court ordered the return of the book to the publishers and banned the newspaper group from revealing the plot in advance of publication.

[6] A nine-year-old from New York bought the book legitimately and read two pages before agreeing to return it to the bookshop. Two men in Indiana bought it from a local bookshop and 14 people in Coquitlam got it in a supermarket. See, for example, http://www.hpana.com/news.18674.html,
http://www.usatoday.com/life/books/news/2005-07-14-potter-leak_x.htm,
http://www.cnn.com/2005/WORLD/americas/07/11/canada.potter.reut/index.html
and http://www.timesonline.co.uk/article/0,,2-1691805,00.html. *The Times* article quotes Neil Blair, a legal expert for Christopher Little, J.K. Rowling's agent, as saying: "The fact is that this is property that should not have been in their possession. Copyright holders are entitled to protect their work. If the content of the book is confidential until July 16, which it is, why shouldn't someone who has the physical book be prevented from reading it and thereby obtaining the confidential information? How they came to have access to the book is immaterial."

[7] At the time of writing a copy of the injunction can be seen on the Canadian publisher's website at http://raincoast.com/harrypotter/injunction.html.
Wikipedia have a hand-marked copy of the actual injunction at
http://upload.wikimedia.org/wikipedia/en/8/86/Harry_Potter_Injunction.pdf.

[8] Most notably, Canadian law professor, Michael Geist
(http://www.michaelgeist.ca/index.php?option=content&task=view&id=896)
and founder of the Free Software Movement, Richard Stallman, who called for a boycott (http://www.stallman.org/harry-potter.html).

[9] Extract from Raincoast Marketing Director Jamie Broadhurst's Letter to the Editor of *Quill & Quire* in response to an article by Professor Michael Geist on the Raincoast legal action. The full original letter is well worth reading and is available at Raincoast Books website at http://raincoast.com/harrypotter/injunction-commentary.html. See also *Understanding The Harry Potter Injunction: Protecting Copyright and Confidential Information* by Barbara Grossman, Aaron Milrad and Annie Na (the lawyers who represented the publishers in the British Columbia action) for an explanation of the legal basis of the injunction at http://raincoast.com/harrypotter/understanding-injunction.html.

[10] The version of the book *Larry Potter and His Best Friend Lilly* submitted in evidence contained only one reference to 'Larry Potter'. The character is referred to only as 'Larry' in the rest of the book. Scholastic's lawyers provided undisputed evidence to the district court indicating that a key paragraph "was printed using fonts that were not available until 1993". Yet it was claimed that the books had been written in the 1980s. Larry Potter author, Nancy Stouffer, was sanctioned for falsifying evidence and ordered to pay the legal costs of the case. The judge said: "In conclusion, the Court finds, by clear and convincing evidence, that Stouffer has perpetrated a fraud on the Court through her submission of fraudulent documents as well as through her untruthful testimony." The judgement (Scholastic v. Stouffer, 2002 U.S. Dist. LEXIS 17531, Sept. 17, 2002) is available online at http://www.eyrie.org/~robotech/stouffer.htm and http://www.authorslawyer.com/case/02USDL17531.html. The latter site, run by Charles E. Petit of *Scrivener's Error* (http://scrivenerserror.blogspot.com/) fame is slightly more browser friendly. The judgement is surprisingly readable and is worth reading in full to get the complete details of the case. The appeal judgement is available at http://www.entlawdigest.com/story.cfm?storyID=3094 on a subscription basis. Ms Stouffer filed another appeal in April 2006.

[11] Claire Field, who was 15 years old at the time, ran a fan site at www.harrypotterguide.co.uk. See, for example, http://news.zdnet.com/2100-9595_22-503255.html and http://www.theregister.co.uk/2000/12/08/warner_brothers_bullies_girl_over/.

[12] North Foreland Lodge School in Hampshire in the UK, in the year 2000. See *Potter school play ban* BBC Wednesday, 25 October 2000, at http://news.bbc.co.uk/1/hi/education/990673.stm.

[13] Rowling visited the school by way of compensation.

[14] http://www.watleyreview.com/2005/072605-3.html.

[15] For example *The Sugar Quill* (http://www.sugarquill.net/). See also *Harry Potter and the Copyright Lawyer* by Ariana Eunjung Cha in the *Washington Post*, Wednesday, 18 June 2003 at http://www.washingtonpost.com/ac2/wp-dyn/A7412-2003Jun17?language=printer.

[16] There was a fake fifth book released in China before the real one was published in June 2003, called *Harry Potter and Leopard Walk Up to the Dragon*. A series of books about a character called Tanya Grotter have been published in Russia. See http://en.wikipedia.org/wiki/Harry_Potter_and_Leopard-Walk-Up-to-Dragon and *Harry Potter and the International Order of Copyright* by Tim Wu Friday, 27 June 2003 at http://www.slate.com/id/2084960/. Wu is a professor at Columbia

Law School and co-author with Jack Goldsmith of a terrific book, *Who Controls the Internet?: Illusions of a Borderless World* (Oxford University Press, 2006).

[17] The work came to Manches via a merger with another firm of solicitors, Morrell Peel and Gamlen, who acted for Tolkien during his lifetime and took on the management of his estate, along with Tolkien's son, Christopher, when the author died. I understand that Cathleen Blackburn was the head of a small team of lawyers looking after the Tolkien affairs at Morrell Peel and Gamlen at the time of the merger with Manches. Following the merger, Steven Maier joined the team and now he and other litigators in his team deal with all contentious cases for the estate.

[18] *Wrong About Almost Everything: Editing J. R. R. Tolkien* by Michael Drout at the Medieval Academy, http://www.medievalacademy.org/medacnews/news_drout.htm.

[19] In the 1960s Ace Books published paperback versions of the *Lord of the Rings* books in the US without paying royalties. Tolkien fans and the Science Fiction Writers of America group campaigned on behalf of the author and Ace eventually agreed to pay him royalties. Some two decades later, after a six-year legal battle, the Tolkien estate won its case in the US Court of Appeals against a book packaging company called Ariel Books, which had sought a declaration that *The Lord of the Rings* was in the public domain.

[20] For example, Houghton Mifflin is licensed to publish the books in the US.

[21] The story of how TRIPS came about is told brilliantly in *Information Feudalism: Who Owns the Knowledge Economy* by Peter Drahos with John Braithwaite, published by Earthscan, 2002. I provide an outline of the story in Chapter 8. In addition to TRIPS, Cathleen Blackburn pointed out that much more important to the matter of international protection of copyright are the two major copyright conventions, the Berne Copyright Convention and the Universal Copyright Convention, to one or both of which most countries of the word are now parties. These provide a procedural framework for enforcement of copyright rights in foreign jurisdictions.

[22] Combining the stories of the first two books *The Fellowship of the Ring* and *The Two Towers*. A planned sequel based on the third book, *The Return of the King,* was never produced.

[23] Zaentz had won the Oscar for the best picture with *One Flew Over the Cuckoo's Nest* three years earlier in 1975.

[24] Christopher Tolkien, the author's son and director of the Tolkien company which administers Tolkien's estate, is particularly keen to maintain the integrity of the works and was not in favour of the Peter Jackson films, as he has always genuinely believed that *The Lord of the Rings* was not suited to be made into films. However, since the film rights are owned by New Line Cinema, neither Christopher Tolkien nor the Tolkien Estate had any control or influence over the production of the films. http://www.everything2.com/index.pl?node=Christopher%20Tolkien.

[25] Though I know of at least one abridged graphic novel version of *The Hobbit* licensed by the estate's publisher, *The Hobbit: Graphic Novel* by JRR Tolkien, Charles Dixon (editor), Sean Deming (editor), David Wenzel (illustrator), pub-

lished by Grafton Books (HarperCollins) 1991. This was first published as a single volume by Unwin books in 1990 and originally published in 3 volumes by Eclipse Books in 1989 and 1990.

[26] The online bookstore, Amazon, sells over 1200 books alone either written by or about Tolkien and his work. I know some of the details of about a couple of dozen Tolkien cases, so in relative terms it is a very limited perspective.

[27] I nearly said he 'hadn't an inkling of a problem' but decided the phrase would be inappropriate here. His publisher is called "Inkling Books."

[28] In his review, for example, of David Bollier's *Brand Name Bullies* (John Wiley & Sons, 2005) at the Amazon.com website, http://www.amazon.com/gp/product/0471679275/103-0342707-1878208?v=glance&n=283155.

[29] Puffin Books published *The Magical Worlds of the "Lord of the Rings": An Unauthorised Guide – A Treasury of Myths, Legends and Fascinating Facts* in 2002, *The Magical Worlds of Harry Potter: A Treasury of Myths, Legends and Fascinating Facts in 2003, The Magical Worlds of Narnia: A Treasury of Myths and Legends* in 2004 and is planning to publish *The Magical Worlds of Philip Pullman: A Treasury of Myths, Legends and Fascinating Facts* in 2007.

[30] *Bored of the Rings* by Henry N. Beard and Douglas C. Kenney for The Harvard Lampoon (Signet, 1969)

[31] *The Soddit, or Let's Cash in Again* by A.R.R.R. Roberts (Gollancz, 2004).

[32] The first of which was *Barry Trotter and the Shameless Parody* by Michael Gerber (Gollancz, 2003)

[33] Aside from the obvious effort to use the stories as a hook to interest the reader in copyright.

[34] Also manufacturers and distributors.

[35] In the interests of full disclosure I should note that I am an engineer employed in academia.

[36] Unlike most of us, I would think.

[37] Though I understand the movements can vary in length as long as the total is 4 minutes 33 seconds.

[38] The original score was handwritten and signed by Cage. I believe the retail price of a printed copy of the score was about £5 in 2005.

[39] *Classical Graffiti* The Planets, EMI Classics 2002.

[40] For a fulsome appreciation of Cage's piece see *The Sounds of Silence* by Peter Gutmann at http://www.classicalnotes.net/columns/silence.html.

[41] *Chance Operation: The John Cage Tribute* Koch International Classics, 1993. Zappa was just one of many performers on the album.

[42] Though, as Bernard Coen pointed out to me, composers and playwrights have had periods of silence or indeterminate pauses in their works for thousands of years. Some of these are still protected by copyright. I wonder how long a silence in a play or a film might have to be before lawyers representing the Cage estate or any other copyright owners with periods of silence embedded in their works might decide to get involved?

[43] Ironically, if you play the 'A One Minute of Silence' track on the Batt CD, it runs to one minute and two seconds.

[44] *Shamans, Software and Spleens: Law and the Construction of the Information Society* by James Boyle (Harvard University Press, 1997).

[45] *The Future of Ideas* by Lawrence Lessig (Random House, 2001).

[46] http://cryptome.sabotage.org/hrcw-hear.htm

[47] The Author, Consumer, and Computer Owner Protection and Security (ACCOPS) Act of 2003 targeting people engaged in peer-to-peer song swapping over the Internet http://www.eff.org/IP/P2P/CONYER_069.txt.

[48] California Democrat, Howard Berman, in an interview with CNN on 8 August 2003 said "The penalty would range from...eh up to eh five years in jail. Notice, no death penalty but eh it i..it's part of our effort to send a message that that which is already illegal and that which is criminal should be avoided..." http://www.lisarein.com/videos/tvclips/cnn/8-9-03-wendy-eff-cnn-1of2.mov

[49] Democrat Fritz Hollings.

[50] The Consumer Broadband Digital Television Protection Act.

[51] See Princeton Professor Edward Felten's *Fritz's Hit List* at http://www.freedom-to-tinker.com/?cat=13 for a long list of other innocuous electronic devices that would have been caught by this act.

[52] Also known as 'technological prevention measures' (TPMs), 'copy protection' technologies or 'digital restrictions management'.

[53] The UK Statute of Anne, enacted in 1709/10, protected works for 14 years renewable once for another 14 years by authors only. Most European Union (EU) countries extended the term of copyright – how long the copyright in a work lasts – in the 1990s following an EU directive in 1993. In the US the term of copyright was increased 11 times between 1960 and 1998.

[54] Plus the European Intellectual Property Rights Enforcement directive in 2004. Another European Intellectual Property Rights Enforcement Directive is planned for 2006/07. The World Trade Organisation are also pressurising a variety of jurisdictions throughout Asia, particularly large countries such as China, to introduce similar regulations based on the 1996 World Intellectual Property Organisation (WIPO) treaties.

[55] Both the EUCD and the DMCA are based on a 1996 World Intellectual Property Organisation (WIPO) Copyright Treaty (http://www.wipo.int/treaties/en/ip/wct/trtdocs_wo033.html) the development of which is discussed in Chapter 8.

[56] Like the 'Messiah 2' mod chip for the Sony Playstation 2.

[57] In fairness to the judge in that case, his technical reasoning was very clever and the judgement, believe it or not, makes very entertaining reading – not something you can say about most legal documents. What I found most amusing was how he saw clean through the publicity-seeking tactics of both sides in the case. The judgement can be read at http://www.tomwbell.com/NetLaw/Ch07/Universal.html. It was appealed but the decision was affirmed by the appeal court.

[58] Called the CSS (Content Scramble System).

[59] Who was nicknamed 'DVD Jon'.

[60] Popularly labelled 'DeCSS'.

[61] Jon Johansen now lives and works in the US and continues to develop and circulate DRM circumvention methods. His weblog entitled 'So Sue Me' is at http://nanocrew.net/.

[62] This positive enabling of backing up electronic files is a requirement of Russian law.

[63] The SDMI (Secure Digital Music Initiative).

[64] Digital Millennium Copyright Act, Section 1201.

[65] Jennifer Jenkins of Duke University has a terrific write-up of the case at the Chilling Effects Clearinghouse,
http://www.chillingeffects.org/weather.cgi?WeatherID=383.

[66] The Open University has never used Blackboard though we have considered it and WebCT, a prominent Blackboard competitor, since taken over by Blackboard. My colleagues who have had dealings with the people at Blackboard and WebCT hold those folks in high regard. The Open University has recently adopted the open source 'Moodle' VLE system.

[67] A US patent (no. 6,988,138) awarded in the summer of 2006 to Blackboard for "internet-based education support systems and methods" did send shockwaves through the educational technology community, though. See, for example, Stephen Downes at http://www.downes.ca/cgi-bin/page.cgi?topic=135, Alex Reid at http://alexreid.typepad.com/digital_digs/2006/08/blackboards_pat.html and Michael Feldstein at
http://mfeldstein.com/index.php/weblog/permalink/quick_blackboard_updates/.

[68] By Lewis Carroll. The author died in 1898 which means the copyright in the book expired in 1948.

[69] They 'discontinued' them early in 2006.

[70] See Chapter 4, plus Boyle's *Shamans, Software and Spleens* (Harvard University Press, 1996) and Lessig's *The Future of Ideas* (Random House, 2001) and *Free Culture* (Penguin Books, 2004).

[71] Of course the publishers published, rather than 'created' but industry rhetoric tended to gloss over the distinction.

[72] See *Free Culture* (Penguin Books, 2004) by Lawrence Lessig, Chapter 4, p56.

[73] Jack Valenti, Head of the Motion Picture Association of America, called cable TV a "huge parasite".

[74] Killed at birth by a 1992 law (the US Audio Home Recording Act) that required producers to incorporate a 'serial content management system' (SCMS) and levies on the sale of the tapes and the machines.

[75] http://www.freedom-to-tinker.com/index.php?p=214.

[76] If the experiences of my tech-savvy colleague, Martin Weller, are anything to go by it will not be just average users that get annoyed either. Martin is Professor of Educational Technology at the Open University. See his iTunes DRM woes at http://nogoodreason.typepad.co.uk/no_good_reason/2006/08/yes_itunes_is_u.html and
http://nogoodreason.typepad.co.uk/no_good_reason/2006/08/is_itunes_becom.html.

[77] The Nobel prize winning economist (in 1976) agreed to sign up to an amicus brief in the Eldred case, which Larry Lessig brought to the US Supreme Court in

2003, on the condition that it said that the negative effect of excessive terms of copyright was a 'no brainer'.

[78] Interestingly making a commercial comeback with sales of vinyl singles in the UK in 2006 passing the 100,000 mark for the first time in a generation.

[79] And uploading. Generally the music industry tend to be more concerned with those making thousands or tens of thousands of copyrighted songs available on peer to peer (P2P) networks. The mechanics of how P2P systems work vary depending on the network and the software being used but users tend to be both uploaders and downloaders. See my Open University course *T182 Law, the Internet and Society: Technology and the Future of Ideas* for a simple animated simulation of how P2P works.

[80] In the summer of 2005, the US Supreme Court ruled that Grokster could be held liable for 'inducing' copyright infringement. The text of the decision is available at http://caselaw.lp.findlaw.com/scripts/getcase.pl?court=US&vol=000&invol=04-480 and there are numerous commentaries on the case available online. Grokster and Sharman Networks, owners of Kazaa, subsequently settled out of court rather than having a lower court rule formally that they were liable and decide the level of damages to be paid. The remaining defendants, Streamcast Networks, owners of Morpheus, fought out the legal process and the district court for the central district of California awarded a summary judgement on liability against them in September 2006. A useful source on the case is the EFF at http://www.eff.org/IP/P2P/MGM_v_Grokster/.

[81] With its centralised indexing system it was not a true peer to peer system of the Gnutella variety but it did facilitate sharing of content from PCs at the edges of the network.

[82] Though the industry had worried about the possibility of large-scale copyright infringing song swapping over the Net for a few years prior to Napster, it had done nothing to actively channel the Net as a new distribution medium.

[83] The current content-at-the-centre model, Clay Shirky says, "has one significant flaw: most Internet content is created on the PCs at the edges, but for it to become universally accessible, it must be pushed to the center, to always-on, always-up Web servers. As anyone who has ever spent time trying to upload material to a Web site knows, the Web has made downloading trivially easy, but uploading is still needlessly hard." http://www.shirky.com/writings/content.html.

[84] It was later resurrected as a legitimate licenced commercial music sales service by its new owners Bertelsmann. These bullet points on Napster are loosely adapted from one of several sections originally drafted for my Open University course *T182 Law, the Internet and Society: Technology and the Future of Ideas* by my colleague John Naughton. In addition I highly recommend John's wonderful book on the history of the Internet, *A Brief History of the Future: The Origins of the Internet* by John Naughton (Weidenfeld & Nicolson, 1999).

[85] Ronald D. Coleman and Matthew W. Carlin. http://www.gibney.com/LegalNews/Record/hacker.cfm.

[86] In the field of children's literature there have been some fascinating cases related to Winnie the Pooh, Peter Pan and Beatrix Potter stories, which sadly I do not have the space to outline here. See *Peter Pan's Rights: "To Die Will Be an*

Awfully Big Adventure" by Catherine Seville in the *Journal of the Copyright Society of the USA* (2003) Vol. 51 pp1–77.
[87] Have you noticed, by the way, that the Ministry for Magic (in the Harry Potter books) has an Office of Ludicrous Patents? Rowling has a lot of interesting social and political commentary in the Potter books. See *Defence against the Dark Arts: How the British Response to the Terrorist Threat Is Parodied in J K Rowling's "Harry Potter and the Half Blood Prince* by Judith Rauhofer at the GikII Workshop of VI Computer Law World Conference, Edinburgh University September 2006. http://www.law.ed.ac.uk/ahrb/complaw/docs/rauhofer.pdf.

Chapter 4

[1] *Shamans, Software and Spleens: Law and the Construction of the Information Society* by James Boyle (Harvard University Press, 1997); James Boyle, *The Second Enclosure Movement and the Construction of the Public Domain*, 66 Law & Contemp. Probls. 33 (2003), available at:
http://www.law.duke.edu/journals/lcp/articles/lcp66dWinterSpring2003p33.htm.
[2] Boyle goes on to advocate the need for the articulation of a shared interest in the public domain in the context of modern developments in intellectual property law.
[3] This purpose is even written into the US Constitution, Article 1, Section 8 which states "The Congress shall have the power to promote the progress of science and useful arts, by securing for limited times to authors and inventors the exclusive right to their respective writings and discoveries". See
http://www.law.cornell.edu/constitution/constitution.articlei.html.
[4] Before coming to the Open University and having it explained to me in everyday language by brilliant colleagues like John Naughton and Dick Morris, systems' thinking was one of those subject areas I had endured through various computing and information systems courses which formed part of my formal studies over the years.
[5] *The Fifth Discipline: Art and Practice of the Learning Organization* by Peter Senge (Random House, 1992).
[6] As stated, for example, in Article 1, Section 8 of the US Constitution.
[7] John Godfrey Saxe (1816–87). The whole poem, *The Blind Men and the Elephant*. is available at
http://en.wikisource.org/wiki/The_Blindmen_and_the_Elephant.
[8] Ibid.
[9] Or more than one purpose in the case of some systems.
[10] This four-part definition was developed and has been used for many years by my colleagues at the Open University Systems Department. I first came across a version of it in the Introduction to a widely respected, though now discontinued, Open University level 1 course called *Living with Technology*.
[11] *Redesigning the Future: A Systems Approach to Societal Problems* by Russell L. Ackoff (John Wiley & Sons, 1974). See also *Ackoff's Best: His Classic Writings on Management* by Russell L. Ackoff (John Wiley & Sons, 1999) and *The*

Art of Problem Solving: Accompanied by Ackoff's Fables by Russell L. Ackoff (John Wiley & Sons, 1978).

[12] He was building on John Dewey's idea that problems are extracted from unstructured states of confusion. See for example *Managing Crises in the Twenty-First Century* by Bruce W. Dayton, International Studies Review (2004) Vol.6, pp165–194 and http://www.open2.net/systems/.

[13] See Chapter 2. Sklyarov is not the only person wrongly jailed for allegedly breaching intellectual property laws. Petr Taborsky went to jail for taking out three patents on his own ideas. They related to a corporately funded project at the University of South Florida where he was a student and a laboratory assistant. The project was abandoned but he continued to think about the problems involved as part of his master's thesis. He was convicted of stealing trade secrets (in the form of his own notebooks) in 1990 and the patents violated the terms of his suspended jail sentence. When the media became involved the Governor of Florida offered Taborsky a full pardon. He declined the pardon on principle saying it would have involved him accepting he had been guilty of some criminal wrongdoing. See, for example, *Intellectual Chain Gang* by Leon Jaroff in the February 10, 1997 issue of *Time* magazine at http://www.time.com/time/magazine/article/0,9171,985892,00.html.

[14] This was the second patent at the heart of the dispute.

[15] Many elements of the journal such as a selection of research articles remained freely available at bmj.com.

[16] *Importance of free access to research articles on decision to submit to the BMJ: survey of authors* by Sara Schroter BMJ 2006 332: 394–396 (18 February). http://bmj.bmjjournals.com/cgi/content/full/332/7538/394.

[17] *The Future of Ideas* by Lawrence Lessig (Random House, 2001) pp5–16.

[18] From their website at http://www.ndiyo.org/, "Ndiyo! is a project set up to foster an approach to networked computing that is *simple, affordable, open*, less environmentally damaging and less dependent on intensive technical support than current networking technology."

[19] However, care is required in the use and dissemination of this information. From the Bulletin of the World Health Organization (BLT), Volume 84, Number 5, May 2006, 337–424, *The impact of open access upon public health* by Virginia Barbour, Paul Chinnock , Barbara Cohen & Gavin Yamey. http://www.who.int/bulletin/volumes/84/5/editorial20506html/en/index.html.

"Arthur Amman, President of Global Strategies for HIV Prevention (www.globalstrategies.org), tells the following story:

'I recently met a physician from southern Africa, engaged in perinatal HIV prevention, whose primary access to information was abstracts posted on the Internet. Based on a single abstract, they had altered their perinatal HIV prevention program from an effective therapy to one with lesser efficacy. Had they read the full text article they would have undoubtedly realized that the study results were based on short-term follow-up, a small pivotal group, incomplete data, and were unlikely to be applicable to their country situation. Their decision to alter treatment based solely on the abstract's conclusions may have resulted in increased perinatal HIV transmission.'

Amman's story shows the potentially deadly gap between the information-rich and the information-poor. This gap is not the result of lack of technology or of money, but of a failure of imagination. We live in the most information-rich era of history, when the Internet allows immediate global dissemination of crucial health information, and the inter-linking of online information creates an integrated, living body of information – the ultimate vision of which is the semantic web.

What is preventing such a living web? For scientific and medical information, two obstacles are vested interests and traditions."

[20] *Shamans, Software and Spleens: Law and the Construction of the Information* Society by James Boyle (Harvard University Press, 1997); James Boyle, *The Second Enclosure Movement and the Construction of the Public Domain*, 66 Law & Contemp. Probls. 33 (2003), available at:

http://www.law.duke.edu/journals/lcp/articles/lcp66dWinterSpring2003p33.htm.

I would emphasise again this is not about banning the system because it is 'bad' but about reforming it and how it is used to better serve its original purpose.

[21] If we take the birth of intellectual property as being the Statute of Anne in 1709/10, then the system has been around for about 300 years.

[22] See in particular *The Long Tail: How Endless Choice Is Creating Unlimited Demand* by Chris Anderson (Random House Business Books, 2006) for a comprehensive analysis of this potential and already visible trend.

[23] Council Directive 93/98/EEC of 29 October 1993 harmonising the term of protection of copyright and certain related rights.

[24] Jessica Litman, *Digital Copyright* (Prometheus Books, 2001), pp23, 25.

[25] Council Directive 93/98/EEC of 29 October 1993 harmonising the term of protection of copyright and certain related rights.

[26] Sometimes known as Serjeant Talfourd since he had been made a serjeant-at-law not long before becoming an MP. See

http://en.wikipedia.org/wiki/Serjeant_Talfourd and
http://en.wikipedia.org/wiki/Serjeant-at-law.

[27] Copies of Macaulay's speech are widely available on the Internet and I highly recommend reading it in its entirety. A couple of sources are Baen Books at

http://www.baen.com/library/palaver4.htm and Kuro5hin at
http://www.kuro5hin.org/story/2002/4/25/1345/03329.

[28] Council Directive 91/250/EEC of 14 May 1991 on the legal protection of computer programs.

Council Directive 92/100/EEC of 19 November 1992 on rental right and lending right and on certain rights related to copyright in the field of intellectual property.

Council Directive 93/83/EEC of 27 September 1993 on the coordination of certain rules concerning copyright and rights related to copyright applicable to satellite broadcasting and cable retransmission.

Council Directive 93/98/EEC of 29 October 1993 harmonising the term of protection of copyright and certain related rights.

Directive 96/9/EC of the European Parliament and of the Council of 11 March 1996 on the legal protection of databases.

Directive 2001/29/EC of the European Parliament and of the Council of 22 May 2001 on the harmonisation of certain aspects of copyright and related rights in the information society.

Directive 2004/48/EC of the European Parliament and of the Council of 29 April 2004 on the enforcement of intellectual property rights.

[29] Mark Twain once said "I never let my schooling interfere with my education".

[30] *The Wealth of Networks* by Yochai Benkler (Yale University Press, 2006) is the definitive work on this process.

[31] I use the word 'knowledge' here not just in the sense of long-living structures of meaningful information but also to incorporate creative endeavours like inventions.

[32] Interestingly, Thailand's Supreme Court ruled in the summer of 2006 that whole works can be copied for free for educational purposes.
http://b2fxxx.blogspot.com/2006/07/free-copying-for-education-in-thailand.html.

[33] Campaigning group, Downhill Battle, organised a series of screenings of the film in 2005 to raise awareness of the problem.

[34] The documentary was *Sing Faster*. Matt Groening, creator of the Simpsons, had told Else it would be ok but that he should just double check it with the Fox lawyers. Another documentary producer, making a film about education, noticed that in a classroom scene there was a TV running in the background and he had captured 2 seconds of the Simpsons. When he reached the Fox lawyers they wanted $25,000 for permission to use the clip.

[35] In two main episodes, as I understand the story, one starting about 150 million years ago and the second about 90 million years ago.

[36] The Royal Dutch/Shell group's embarrassing admission at the beginning of 2004 that they had been knowingly publicly inflating their oil and gas reserves estimates was thought by some to be a significant indication that the oil industry recognises the reality of looming shortages. We just do not know precisely yet whether they are coming in 10, 50 or 100 years though the excellent *Hubbert's Peak: The Impending World Oil Shortage* (Princeton University Press, 2001) by Kenneth S. Deffeyes suggests that oil *production* will peak within the next ten years.

[37] These figures come from a presentation *Joining the dots* given at the Energy Institute's *Oil Depletion: No Problem, Concern or Crisis* conference, on 10 November 2004 by Chris Skrebowski, editor of the UK journal, *Petroleum Review*.

[38] The expression "the man on the Clapham Omnibus" was coined by Lord Justice Bowen in the case of *McQuire v. Western Morning News* [1903] 2 KB 100, and is often used to refer to the hypothetical "reasonable man" in law.

[39] I use the made-up term 'infodiversity' here purely as a rough vehicle for further exploring the parallels with sustainability in the management of biodiversity.

[40] *The Diversity of Life* by Edward O. Wilson (Penguin Books, 2001).

[41] Wilson estimates it at about 25,000 professional lifetimes over a likely period of about 50 years.

[42] This definition was offered in the UN Brundtland Commission Report on Sustainable Development: *World Commission on Environment and Development Report: Our Common Future*, 1987.

[43] The RSA's Adelphi Charter, drawn up by an international commission of artists, scientists, lawyers, politicians, economists, academics and business experts, led by James Boyle, outlines a core set of nine principles to achieve this end. It is available online at http://www.adelphicharter.org/adelphi_charter_document.asp.

[44] *The Diversity of Life* by Edward O. Wilson (Penguin Books, 2001, p306).

Chapter 5

[1] Both from the media and internal to the government. The National Audit Office, for example, produced a critical report in the summer of 2006, on the government's National Programme for IT in the NHS, which can be found at http://www.nao.org.uk/publications/nao_reports/05-06/05061173es.pdf.

[2] Which in November 2004 suffered what was described at the time as the largest computer crash in government history.

[3] A £10 million project eventually went live in 2005, and has had various problems since.

[4] http://www.connectingforhealth.nhs.uk/.

[5] http://www.hpa.org.uk/.

[6] According to a spokesman speaking to the BBC, http://news.bbc.co.uk/1/hi/health/5154556.stm.

[7] Tim Berners-Lee created the Web protocols and released them free to the world in 1991.

[8] And retains an overview as a top official in the government's Cabinet Office.

[9] A number of people I know recently renewed their passports and were full of praise for the efficient service they received though the Passport Agency, recently re-named the 'Identity and Passport Service' with the looming introduction of the new identity card system. However, the government has plans to include multiple biometrics like iris scans and fingerprints in passports and the agency will almost certainly experience technical problems with these.

[10] See, for example: http://www.idealgovernment.com/index.php/weblog/transformational_government_and_what_it_was_like_for_me/.

[11] One minister who took on an e-government portfolio in 2006 cheerfully explained she had little or no idea what e-government was about until she was given responsibility for it and then she decided it was a good idea. http://society.guardian.co.uk/e-public/story/0,,1786041,00.html. In May 2006 Angela Smith, the new junior government minister in charge of 'local e-government' said "People don't know what e-government is – I didn't know myself until I got this job."

[12] Schneier is the author of one of the most readable books on security available, *Beyond Fear: thinking sensibly about security in an uncertain world* (Copernicus Books, 2003). If this chapter were to have no other effect than to encourage a policymaker who comes across it to read and inwardly digest Schneier's book then it will have been successful.

[13] The nature of traditional cost benefit analysis, however, is such that there is a lot of uncertainty involved in determining costs and benefits, as well as projecting these into the future, and establishing their time value by estimating possible future money market interest rates. This leads many critics to suggest it is anything but a rational approach, especially when we examine how it actually gets used in practice.

[14] Though a report done by the London School of Economics has estimated the cost at between £10 billion and £19 billion. See http://is2.lse.ac.uk/idcard/.

[15] Though sensitive emails criticising the proposals, written by senior officials involved with the scheme, were leaked to the press in the summer of 2006. http://www.timesonline.co.uk/article/0,,2087-2261631,00.html. One explicit concern in these emails was "the lack of clear benefits from which to demonstrate a return on investment".

[16] In practice it can be a very messy business – in the Ackoff sense – establishing the real costs and benefits and their evolution over time.

[17] Note that there is a prevailing debate over the definition of risk with some authors defining *risk* solely as the probability that the hazard will occur, with the seriousness, consequences or detrimental after-effects of an event being considered a property of the *hazard*. This is the approach we have taken in the various courses at the Open University I have been associated with which consider the issue. Other authors still separate risk, hazard and detrimental effects of an event into three separate categories. Bruce Schneier links consequences of a hazard coming to pass to his definition of risk, so that is the definition I have used here.

[18] Richard Dawkins *The Selfish Gene* (Oxford University Press, 1976) is particularly enlightening on the subject; the Darwin Awards website http://www.darwinawards.com/ and series of books celebrates those whose lack of sensitivity to risk took them out of the gene-pool.

[19] http://www.soham.org.uk/hollyandjessica.htm Ian Huntley, a caretaker at the girls' school, murdered two ten-year-old girls, Holly Wells and Jessica Chapman.

[20] And similarly the Phoenix sniper(/s) in 2006.

[21] *The Laws of Fear* by Cass R. Sunstein (Cambridge University Press, 2005). Sunstein is the Karl N. Llewellyn Distinguished Service Professor of Jurisprudence at the Law School and Department of Political Science at the University of Chicago and a fairly prolific author, often publishing two or more books every year.

[22] The Kennedy administration (and the previous Eisenhower administration) had trained and financed a group of anti-Castro rebels who invaded the Bay of Pigs in 1961. Castro's forces killed about a hundred and captured over a thousand of the invaders. The captives were dispatched to the US on payment of a large ransom over a year later.

[23] BBC news report 'S Africa's Zuma cleared of rape', May 2006. http://news.bbc.co.uk/1/hi/world/africa/4750731.stm

[24] http://en.wikipedia.org/wiki/Grey_goo Eric Drexler, a nanotechnology pioneer, suggested in his book *Engines of Creation: The Forthcoming Era of Nanotechnology* (Anchor, 1987) that this was a possibility and the popular press have been

happy ever since to periodically sensationalise the idea. The book is available
online at http://www.foresight.org/EOC/.

[25] The London School of Economics Centre for Civil Society defines civil society
as follows:

"Civil society refers to the arena of uncoerced collective action around shared interests, purposes and values. In theory, its institutional forms are distinct from
those of the state, family and market, though in practice, the boundaries between
state, civil society, family and market are often complex, blurred and negotiated.
Civil society commonly embraces a diversity of spaces, actors and institutional
forms, varying in their degree of formality, autonomy and power. Civil societies
are often populated by organisations such as registered charities, development
non-governmental organisations, community groups, women's organisations,
faith-based organisations, professional associations, trade unions, self-help groups,
social movements, business associations, coalitions and advocacy groups."

[26] There is a whole interesting area of statistics and probability theory devoted to
aiding decision making under conditions of uncertainty, of which decision trees is
just one of the simpler techniques.

[27] Note this is strictly for illustrative purposes and does not include the conventions of a technically accurate decision tree, whereby particular meanings are at-
tributed to the shape of the nodes for example.

[28] Though widespread public support for public executions in places like the US
might suggest I am wrong on that score? In addition airlines and insurance companies are making these kinds of calculations all the time. At the time of writing
RyanAir are considering suing the UK government for the cost to them of extra
security measures introduced at UK airports in the wake of a foiled plot to blow
up nine airplanes flying from the UK in the summer of 2006. The measures include a ban on all liquids in carry-on luggage.

[29] *The Pleasure of Finding Things Out* by Richard Feynman (Penguin Books,
2001, p169).

[30] *Visual Explanations: Images and Quantities, Evidence and Narrative* by Edward R. Tufte (Graphics Press, 1997). I would also recommend Tufte's *Envisioning Information* (Graphics Press, 1990), *The Visual Display of Quantitative
Information* (Graphics Press, 1992) and his essay on *The Cognitive Style of
PowerPoint*, which graphically indicates, if you will excuse the pun, the student
cognitive constraints with computer graph work.

[31] See also *Making Newspaper Graphs Fit to Print* by Howard Wainer in *Processing of Visible Language 2* by Paul A. Kohlers et al (editors) (Plenum Publishing Corporation, 1980) p139. Wainer says "Evidence gathered by the committee
on graphics of the American Statistical Association indicates that formal training
in graphic presentation has had a marked decline at all levels of education over the
last few decades."

[32] *Risk* by John Adams (Routledge, 1995, p25) refers to this quote in *Risk, Uncertainty and Profit* by Frank Hyneman Knight (Houghton Mifflin Company, 1921).
Knight was one of the founders of the 'Chicago School' of economic thinking.
http://en.wikipedia.org/wiki/Frank_Knight

[33] I use the term 'risk management business' here to encompass all those in commerce, government or civil society engaged in risk management.

[34] That the risks are long term and the rewards short term in this instance provides part of the explanation as to why uncertainty means some people don't attempt to avoid these risks – the time delay is too great.

[35] Formed in 1941 to conduct raids behind German lines in North Africa. http://en.wikipedia.org/wiki/Special_Air_Service.

[36] Chief Technology Officer of Counterpane Internet Security, Inc. and author of several books on security, computers and cryptography including *Beyond Fear: Thinking Sensibly about Security in an Uncertain World* (Copernicus Books, 2003), *Secrets and Lies: Digital Security in a Networked World* (John Wiley & Sons, 2000), *Applied Cryptography: Protocols, Algorithms, and Source Code in C* (John Wiley & Sons, 1995) and *Practical Cryptography* with Niels Ferguson (John Wiley & Sons, 2003).

[37] See *Beyond Fear: Thinking Sensibly about Security in an Uncertain World* by Bruce Schneier (Copernicus Books 2003), pages 14–15. Schneier uses a slightly different version of these questions in the book to the one I have outlined –

Step 1: What assets are you trying to protect?

Step 2: What are the risks to these assets?

Step 3: How well does the security solution mitigate those risks?

Step 4: What other risks does the security solution cause?

Step 5: What costs and trade-offs does the security solution impose?

[38] Editor-in-Chief of *Digital ID World*, Phil Becker, calls this Identity Fallacy #1: "We'll Add It In Later". http://blogs.zdnet.com/digitalID/?p=32.

[39] *Redesigning the Future: Systems Approach to Societal Problems* by Russell L. Ackoff (John Wiley & Sons, 1974).

[40] Unanticipated effects can be both unintended and unpredictable, though something unintended is not necessarily unpredictable.

[41] See BBC report *Criminal records mix-up uncovered*, Sunday, 21 May 2006. http://news.bbc.co.uk/1/hi/uk/5001624.stm.

[42] And the foiled attacks on airliners flying from the UK in August 2006.

[43] Amazon do, however, gather data about a customer's history of purchases and use it to build a profile of that customer in the hope of identifying other products that might be of interest.

[44] *Rethinking Public Key Infrastructures and Digital Certificates: Building in Privacy* by Stefan Brands (The MIT Press, 2000). In the book and other writings Brands specifies, in great technical detail, how part of this might be achieved. Brands has a weblog at http://www.idcorner.org/ which provides lots of useful pointers to his and others' writings in the area.

[45] Most Dutch citizens, including Jews and other peoples considered ethnically inferior by the Nazis had routinely registered because the system facilitated the efficient allocation of government services. The Dutch people never really considered that the system might come to be controlled and misused as it was by the Nazis. Though Holland later introduced a national identity card it was initially considered just before World War II. At the time it was felt that it would undermine Dutch tradition, which felt that the role of the state was to serve the people

and requiring people to hold an ID card would be tantamount to requesting individuals to justify themselves to the state. The other much-quoted example of the abuse of identity registration systems for brutal repression is Stalin's Soviet Union. More recently, though we regularly here the mantras "We must ensure it never happens again" and "It could never happen here", the Rwandan genocide of 1994 was partly facilitated by the country's ID card system.

[46] *The Digital Person: Technology and Privacy in the Information Age* by Daniel Solove (New York University Press, 2004) and *No Place to Hide* by Robert O'Harrow, Jr. (Free Press, 2005) are recommended reading.

[47] http://www.identityblog.com/?p=453   Kim Cameron's weblog should be compulsory reading for anyone involved with identity systems.

[48] http://www.identityblog.com/?page_id=352/#lawsofiden_topic3.
If you wanted a gentle introduction to Cameron's "7 Laws of Identity" you could do a lot worse than listen to a radio programme (http://channel9.msdn.com/ShowPost.aspx?PostID=151819) where he is interviewed by Ron Jacobs.
There are some real gems from Cameron in this.
"Privacy concerns ultimately end up being security concerns." So an appropriately designed identity layer of the Internet would be equivalent to a privacy enhancing layer. He talks about Toby Stevens' notion of data rejection being the highest form of data management. He mentions his signature is in thousands of scanned databases, so what now is the value of his signature?
And when it comes to building an identity layer for the Net he notes that as architects and technologists we have to assume our system will be breached, so that we are ready to react appropriately when they are. If a decent identity layer is not built into the Net then people will rapidly get fed up with the negative consequences to the extent that all trust in the infrastructure will be lost. We also have to build the system in such a way as to avoid locking out the possibility of innovative developments in identity architecture in the future. We're just at the beginning of what identity systems can be technologically and there are some amazing developments in universities, so we have to be able to build these into the system when they are developed.

[49] The technical jargon gets a bit difficult to follow here but by omni-directional identities he means identities that are widely available to the public like a company's website address. A customer can then choose to set up a uni-directional identity like the information I have to give to Amazon to buy books from them. By *"preventing unnecessary release of correlation handles"* he means the systems should not leak data enabling third parties to join the dots and find out more about an individual than they are entitled to.

[50] What he is getting at here is the need to achieve *very high levels of reliability* in the communication between the system and its users. Are we really ever going to get away from the real-world situation whereby people borrow each others' access codes, passwords, system ID cards or other identifiers?

[51] The LSE Identity Project http://is2.lse.ac.uk/idcard/, coordinated by the LSE's Department of Information Systems and an advisory committee of 16 LSE professors and sixty experts from all round the world, the LSE report, *The Identity Pro-*

ject: An Assessment of the UK Identity Cards Bill and its Implications, available at
http://is2.lse.ac.uk/idcard/identityreport.pdf, constitutes one of the most comprehensive studies of a government proposal, still in the process of going through parliament, ever produced. It runs to over 300 pages but is very readable and anyone
wanting a detailed understanding of the multiple issues in the UK ID cards debate
will not find a better single source.

There has been a lot of media reporting on the ID cards system, Henry Porter in
the *Guardian* and John Lettice in the *Register* being amongst the most informative
UK reporters on the subject. William Heath's *Ideal Government* blog at
http://www.idealgovernment.com/ is consistently one of the most informed online
sources. And the campaign group, NO2ID, also tend to be well informed and can
be found at http://www.no2id.net/.

Niels J Bjergstrom, editor of the *Information Security Bulletin* is another good
source of information.

[52] In the late 1990s the then Home Secretary, Jack Straw, talked about the possibility of introducing identity cards and got a lot of bad press, so when his turn came
David Blunkett decided to call it an 'entitlement card'. However, people did not
generally like the label according to government polls and focus groups, so they
changed it to 'identity card' in the end which allegedly proved more popular in the
polls.

[53] At the time of writing available the Home Office website at
http://www.homeoffice.gov.uk/passports-and-immigration/id-cards/why-we-need-
id-cards/.

[54] http://www.opsi.gov.uk/ACTS/acts2006/20060015.htm.

[55] See *Observer* report *Drivers use address scam to cheat speed cameras* by Gaby
Hinsliff, Sunday 9 April 2006 at:
http://observer.guardian.co.uk/uk_news/story/0,,1750138,00.html.

[56] See the LSE *The Identity Project: An assessment of the UK Identity Cards Bill
and its implications* report, Chapter 13 on *Biometrics*.
http://is2.lse.ac.uk/IDcard/identityreport.pdf.

[57] The Markle Foundation Task Force on National Security in the Information Age
Third Report, "*Mobilizing Information to Prevent Terrorism: Accelerating Development of a Trusted Information Sharing Environment*" is also recommended
reading here. It is available at
http://www.markle.org/downloadable_assets/2006_nstf_report3.pdf with the associated press release and summary at
http://www.markle.org/resources/press_center/press_releases/2006/press_release_
07132006.php.

[58] See Home Office press release *Cutting Edge Technology to Secure UK Borders
for 21st Century* at
http://www.gnn.gov.uk/content/detail.asp?NewsAreaID=2&ReleaseID=130801.

[59] See US Department for Homeland Security website at
http://www.dhs.gov/dhspublic/interapp/content_multi_image/content_multi_imag
e_0006.xml.

[60] The no-fly list according to Bruce Schneier has 30,000 to 40,000 names and another 'Selectee list' has a further 30,000 to 40,000.

[61] The US also has a 'no buy' or 'Specially Designated Nationals and Blocked Persons List' that American businesses are supposed to check before selling anything to anybody according to the *Washington Post* in *Hit-and-Miss List* 9 April 2006 .
http://www.washingtonpost.com/wp-dyn/content/article/2006/04/08/AR2006040800157.html.

[62] http://www.epic.org/alert/EPIC_Alert_12.25.html EPIC (the Electronic Privacy Information Center) obtained the information from Jim Kennedy, head of the Transportation Security Administration redress office, under a Freedom of Information Act request.

[63] *Action on Rights for Children* have an excellent summary online of what these databases are for and what information they contain at http://databasemasterclass.blogspot.com/.
National Pupil Database – mainly used for research
Connexions – careers and advice service for teenagers to ensure they are employed or in education
Numerous localised databases associated with predicting, monitoring and correcting potential young offenders
RYOGENS (Reducing Youth Offending Generic National Solution) national database
Different police authorities run their own systems for sharing information about children they have reason to be concerned about.
The Common Assessment Framework (CAF) is a standardised assessment tool to be used by agencies in contact with children to facilitate easier information sharing between the various agencies.
Integrated Children's System (ICS) is a national standardised system for sharing information about children who come into contact with social services.
The Children's Index or 'Information Sharing and Assessment' (ISA) is the proposed unifying national database on all children under 18. It is initially being piloted by twelve local authorities.

[64] The regulations outlining the specific details to be recorded are available online at http://www.opsi.gov.uk/si/si2006/20060983.htm. Scroll down to 'The Schedule'.

[65] See *Adaptation in Natural and Artificial Systems: An Introductory Analysis with Applications to Biology, Control, and Artificial Intelligence* by John Holland (MIT reprint edition, 1998. 1st edition University of Michigan 1975) and *Emergence: From Chaos to Order* by John Holland (Perseus Books, 1998).

[66] See *Emergence* by Steven Johnson (Penguin Books, 2001) for a fascinating, succinct and accessible account of Holland's, Jefferson's and Taylor's work. See also *Out of Control: The New Biology of Machines, Social Systems, and the Economic World* by Kevin Kelly (Perseus Books, 1995) and *The Origin of Wealth* by Eric Beinhocker (Random House Business Books, 2006) pp167, 168, 323–333.

[67] Thanks to Dick Morris for pointing out this example. There is another unusual correlation in the US, where every Presidential election year since 1936, the incumbent president has lost the election whenever the Washington Redskins American football team have lost their final home game prior to the election.

[68] This version was printed in the *Star Tribune* on May 31, 2006 and is available on Schneier's website at http://www.schneier.com/blog/archives/2006/03/data_mining_for.html.

[69] Paul Rosenzweig and Jeff Jonas *Correcting False Positives: Redress and the Watch List Conundrum*, June 2005, at http://www.heritage.org/Research/HomelandDefense/lm17.cfm is an excellent paper on the issues and processes associated with getting false positive errors on watch lists corrected, whilst attempting to avoid giving real threats the all-clear. They believe the key is transparency.

[70] See for example Kim Cameron's comments on the Centrelink scandal in Australia at http://www.identityblog.com/?p=545 noting that the big centralised databases worry him more than any other aspect of identity technology.

[71] Playwright Friedrich Durrenmatt also said if you examine someone's life in enough detail "a crime can always be found".

[72] http://archrights.blogspot.com/2006/06/curious-incident-of-children-who-stood.html 'The curious incident of the children who stood still' is another nice example, where CCTV operators called out the police because they saw a group of four children standing around in a town centre *doing nothing*.

[73] So for example the 4th-Amendment to the American Constitution limits "unreasonable searches and seizures" and formed the basis of Federal Judge Anna Diggs Taylor's decision in August 2006 to call a halt to National Security Agency wiretapping authorised by President Bush.

[74] It is probably also an example of Phil Becker's 'we'll add it in later' identity fallacy. http://blogs.zdnet.com/digitalID/?p=32 Becker is Editor-in-Chief of *Digital ID World*.

[75] At the time of writing there is some significant controversy in the US over the National Security Agency's domestic wiretapping programme and the telecommunication companies' cooperation with it. The NSA at the direction of President Bush, bypassed all the judicial processes that would usually be required to sanction this kind of wiretapping and a federal judge declared the action unconstitutional (decision at http://www.aclu.org/pdfs/safefree/nsamemo.opinion.judge.taylor.081706.pdf). She said "The President of the United States, a creature of the same Constitution which gave us these Amendments, has undisputedly violated the Fourth [Amendment] in failing to procure judicial orders as required by FISA, and accordingly has violated the First Amendment Rights of these Plaintiffs as well... We must first note that the Office of the Chief Executive has itself been created, with its powers, by the Constitution. There are no hereditary Kings in America and no power not created by the Constitution. So all 'inherent power' must derive from that Constitution." There is an excellent commentary on the situation in the Balkanization blog archives for 2006, http://balkin.blogspot.com/balkin_archive.html, written by some high profile US legal scholars.

[76] *The Unwanted Gaze: The Destruction of Privacy in America* by Jeffrey Rosen (Random House, 2000).

[77] Called the 'Secure Flight Working Group on Privacy and Security', the group found the system to have poorly designed targets, inadequate testing and not clear

system architecture. There were two other reports by the Government Account-
ability Office and one by the Department for Homeland Security Inspector General, which came to the same conclusions. (Note: Take a look at Bruce Schneier's
Cryptogram of December 15, 2005 for some more thoughts on this.)
In December 2005, the US Department for Homeland security said the US_VISIT
program had processed 44 million visitors in the two years since January 2004 and
caught nearly 1000 people with 'criminal or immigration' violations. The system
is estimated to have cost $15 billion, which works out at $15 million per 'criminal
or immigration' violator. At the time of writing no suspected terrorists have been
caught by the system.

[78] http://www.everychildmatters.gov.uk/deliveringservices/caf/.

[79] More specifically, the 'five outcomes' to:
- Be healthy
- Stay safe
- Enjoy and achieve
- Make a positive contribution
- Achieve economic well-being
which the government green paper described as "universal ambitions for every
child and young person, whatever their background or circumstances".

[80] The computerised form, the blank version of which runs to 8 pages of A4 print
can be seen at
http://www.everychildmatters.gov.uk/_files/3C64C3ADEBAB7CBA9248B43683
CDDD9B.doc.

[81] But the 'Practitioners Guide' does make clear that: "Wherever possible, you
should base the discussion and your comments on *evidence*, not just opinion. Evidence would be what you have seen, what the child has said and what the family
members have said. Opinions should be recorded and marked accordingly (for example 'Michael said he thinks his dad is an alcoholic')"
http://www.everychildmatters.gov.uk/_files/A19154AA073AF2F7216B25A69391
6CF6.pdf.

[82] http://www.opsi.gov.uk/ACTS/acts1998/80029--l.htm#sch1.

[83] http://www.opsi.gov.uk/ACTS/acts1998/80042--d.htm#sch1.

[84] More generally government plans to improve the sharing of information between departments, which would previously have been in breach of the Data Protection Act, were revealed in August 2006.
http://www.guardian.co.uk/guardianpolitics/story/0,,1856760,00.html.

[85] Government guidelines say "You do not have to be an expert" in order to fill in
the form.

Chapter 6

[1] This chapter is based on Sections 4.1 to 4.3 of my Open University course *T182
Law, the Internet and Society: technology and the future of ideas*. Section 4.2 of
the course, *Facts, values and beliefs, or why some issues are controversial*, was
originally drafted by my colleague, John Naughton.

[2] There is a great example where video clips of the two men are synchronised to make it appear as if they are singing the *Endless Love* duet at http://politicalhumor.about.com/library/multimedia/bushblair_endlesslove.mov.

[3] *Royal Commission on Environmental Pollution 21st report: Setting Environmental Standards* 1998, Chapter 7. The report can be downloaded from http://www.rcep.org.uk/standards.htm.

[4] Washington Post *Bush Authorized Domestic Spying: Post-9/11 Order Bypassed Special Court* 16 December 2005.

[5] *The Politics of Paranoia and Intimidation Why does the NSA engage in mass surveillance of Americans when it's statistically impossible for such spying to detect terrorists?* Posted May 24, 2006 by Floyd Rudmin http://www.counterpunch.org/rudmin05242006.html   Rudmin goes on to do a sensitivity analysis adjusting the estimated probabilities for best and worst possible cases and proves that mass surveillance of the NSA domestic spying variety is useless for catching terrorists. It may, of course, be useful for other things. Because, as Rudmin says, the folks at the NSA know this already because they certainly know Bayes Theorem, they are presumably using the information for other things.

[6] See *Information, Systems and Information Systems: Making Sense of the Field* by Peter Checkland and Sue Holwell (John Wiley & Sons, 1998) pp86–92 for an articulation of the different natures of data, information and knowledge.

[7] See *The Visual Display of Quantitative Information, Second Edition* by Edward R. Tufte (Graphics Press, 2001) Chapters 2 and 3.

[8] The RBMK (Reactor Bolshoy Moshchnosty Kanalny) is a pressurised water reactor which uses water as its coolant and graphite as its moderator. The design makes it unstable at low power levels.

[9] *The Truth About Chernobyl* by Grigori Medvedev, translated by Evelyn Rossiter (Basic Books, 1991). Medvedev outlines a damning catalogue of Soviet officials' and public institutions' systematic misleading of the general public for decades, as well as in the immediate aftermath of the Chernobyl tragedy, on the subject of nuclear power. His main conclusion about the disaster was that "Above all else, it is that this horrible tragedy summons us forcefully to the Truth – to tell the truth, the whole truth and nothing but the truth… Chernobyl calls on us to use our reason and our analytical powers, so that we will not forget what happened, and will look clearly at our misfortune and avoid glossing over it." P259.

[10] There had over the 35-year history of the Soviet deployment of Nuclear power been a series of breakdowns, incidents and serious accidents which, Medvedev alleges, were systematically covered up by the Soviet Union State Committee on the Use of Nuclear Energy and the other relevant parts of the Soviet political establishment. (Medvedev lists 11 specific examples in the Soviet Union, including one at Chernobyl in 1982, and 12 in the US.) The chairman of that committee, A.M. Petrosyants showed something of his perspective when he declared at a press conference about 10 days after the Chernobyl disaster that "Science requires victims." Not long before the Chernobyl disaster the entire directorate of design and research in the Energy ministry was abolished. Some senior officials seem to have

viewed the engineers and scientists as people who used scientific and technical restrictions as excuses for not getting the job done.

[11] The operators of several other Soviet nuclear power plants had come under pressure to carry out these tests but refused to do so on the grounds that the risks were too great.

[12] *Chernobyl: The Forbidden Truth* by Alla Yaroshinskaya (University of Nebraska Press, 1995) tells the detailed story of the official cover up in the wake of the disaster. The "Testament" of Valery Legasov, the First Deputy Director of the Kurchatov Institute of Atomic Energy in Moscow at the time is also very illuminating on this part of the story. It was published posthumously by Pravda and an English translation was published for the first time in Chapter 19 of *Chernobyl: The Definitive History of the Chernobyl Catastrophe* by R.F. Mould (Institute of Physics Publishing, 2000).

[13] Article 29 of the UN Convention on the Rights of the Child says as much: "States Parties agree that the education of the child shall be directed to (a) The development of the child's personality, talents and mental and physical abilities to their fullest potential." http://www.unicef.org/crc/.

[14] BBC reports *The nature of the beast* by Nick Assinder, 9 October 2001 at http://news.bbc.co.uk/1/hi/uk_politics/1589164.stm and *Aide apologises for 'attacks memo'* 10 October 2001 at http://news.bbc.co.uk/1/hi/uk_politics/1588323.stm.

[15] The UK government, for instance, introduced over forty Acts of Parliament relating to crime between 1997 and 2006.

[16] Bruce Schneier calls this "security theatre" i.e. creating the illusion of security without real security.

[17] See *Most Secret War* by R.V. Jones (Wordsworth Editions, 1998) p161.

[18] The latest £10 million system introduced in 2005, not the £100 million system scrapped in 2000.

[19] Professor Ian Loader of Oxford University makes precisely this point in a searing submission to the Prime Minister, *Rebalancing the Criminal Justice System?* in June 2006. http://www.pm.gov.uk/output/Page9701.asp.

[20] For a much more detailed look at this I recommend the Open University's ten-week course, T188 *Making Policies Work: systems thinking in government and management,* http://tscp.open.ac.uk/t188.htm.

[21] Frederick Haas Professor of Law and Philosophy at Georgetown University's Law Center and Department of Philosophy.

[22] Luban's mathematical logic at the Balkanization blog is absolutely masterful. http://balkin.blogspot.com/2006/06/asymmetrical-assault-on-reality.html.

[23] *The Future of Aviation – Consultation on air transport policy* Department for Transport (2000). http://www.dft.gov.uk/stellent/groups/dft_aviation/documents/page/dft_aviation_5 03446.hcsp

[24] *The Future of Air Transport* Department for Transport (2003). http://www.dft.gov.uk/stellent/groups/dft_aviation/documents/divisionhomepage/ 029650.hcsp.

[25] The first at Stansted to be delivered by 2012. Heathrow, Gatwick and Birmingham International airport were also earmarked for further development.

[26] For a full exploration of the development of the aviation white paper and the decision making process surrounding it, see Open University course, *T863 Environmental Decision Making: A Systems Approach*

[27] This list is adapted, with the kind permission of the Open University, from my Open University course, *T182 Law, the Internet and Society: technology and the future of ideas*, which is fairly heavily focused on intellectual property and digital technologies. The course is based on Larry Lessig's book *The Future of Ideas* (Random House, 2001). Both Jessica Litman in Chapter 5 of *Digital Copyright* and Peter Drahos and John Braithwaite in Chapter 3 of *Information Feudalism: Who Owns the Knowledge Economy* do a terrific job of outlining the long term process of changing public perception of what intellectual property is about.

[28] See *The Torture Debate in America* Edited by Karen Greenberg (Cambridge University Press, 2005) and the Balkanization blog at http://balkin.blogspot.com/2005/09/anti-torture-memos-balkinization-posts.html.

[29] For a particularly good collection of essays dissecting their position see *Intelligent Thought : Science versus the Intelligent Design Movement* Edited by John Brockman (Vintage, 2006).

[30] Incidentally, whether or not you believe in God, is it seriously beyond the bounds of possibility that He might understand enough science to work with evolutionary processes?

[31] And usually *only* two sides.

[32] See *Denying the Holocaust: The Growing Assault on Truth and Memory* by Deborah Lipstadt (Penguin, 1994).

[33] *Don't Think of an Elephant: Progressive Values and the Framing Wars a Progressive Guide to Action* by George Lakoff (Chelsea Green Publishing Company, 2004); *Metaphors We Live By* by George Lakoff & Mark Johnson (University of Chicago Press, 1989).

[34] Played by Nigel Hawthorne.

[35] Played by Derek Fowlds.

[36] The episode in question was *The Grand Design*, which first aired on the BBC on 9 January 1986.

[37] *'Just a Comma' Becomes Part of the Iraq Debate* by Peter Baker *Washington Post* 5 October, 2006 at http://www.washingtonpost.com/wp-dyn/content/article/2006/10/04/AR2006100401707.html.

[38] David Irving, for example, went to prison in Austria for this.

[39] See, for example, *Deterring Democracy* by Noam Chomsky (Vintage, 1992) p.303. Chomsky says: "One fundamental goal of any well-crafted indoctrination program is to direct attention elsewhere, away from effective power, its roots, and the disguises it assumes."

[40] *Toxic Sludge is Good For You: Lies, Damn Lies and the Public Relations Industry* by John Stauber, Sheldon Rampton (Common Courage Press, September 1995) has some excellent examples.

[41] There are some excellent books available on the subject of critical thinking, such as *Critical Thinking: An Introduction* by Alec Fisher (Cambridge University

Press, 2001) and *Thinking for Yourself: Developing Critical Thinking Skills Through Reading and Writing, 7th Edition* by Marlys Mayfield (Thomson Heinle & Heinle, 2006).

[42] See *Howard Hughes: The Secret Life* by Charles Higham (St. Martin's Griffin & Virgin Books, 2004); and the 2004 Leonard Di Caprio film *The Aviator*, made by Miramax Pictures; the screenplay was written by John Logan.

[43] A wonderful *This Modern World* cartoon by Tom Tomorrow illustrating a hypothetical scenario whereby the US decides to blow up the moon illustrates the point so much better than I can.
http://dir.salon.com/story/comics/tomo/2003/01/13/tomo/index.html.

[44] This final section of the chapter, 'A note about Internet sources', is taken from my Open University course, *T182 Law, the Internet and Society: technology and the future of ideas*, with the kind permission of the Open University.

Chapter 7

[1] My close friend and colleague, Bernard Coen, on reading this story commented "So you are saying that once enchanted by what the technology could do the management forgot what they actually wanted – a modern fairy story!" It tickled me so much I nearly used it in the main text but the very least I could do was to credit the author, so Bernard gets his own footnote, though he is responsible for many more improvements to this entire book than I can ever properly thank him for.

[2] *Information, Systems and Information Systems: making sense of the field* by Peter Checkland and Sue Holwell (John Wiley & Sons, 1998), Chapter 5, pp127–154.

[3] *The Invention that Changed the World: the story of radar from war to peace* by Robert Buderi (Simon & Schuster, 1996), p.53.

[4] Who had also appointed Wimperis to his position when Tizard was secretary to the Department of Scientific and Industrial Research. Tizard had left government service to become Rector of Imperial College in 1929 but had taken on the role of Chairman of the government's Aeronautical Research Committee in 1933 and continued to move in official circles.

[5] Rather than another world-renowned radio expert, Professor Edward Appleton at the University of London, who later joined the Tizard committee. Appleton, who was something of a hero to Tizard, did not become aware of the radar work until 1936 and thereafter, Louis Brown reports, there was a 'fierce animosity' between Appleton and Watson-Watt. Watson-Watt formally changed his name to include the hyphen when he was later knighted in 1942. I have used the hyphenated version throughout this book.

[6] The key members of the committee were Tizard, Wimperis, Rowe as administrator, Archibald V. Hill, a physiologist who had won the Nobel prize in Physiology or Medicine in 1922, Patrick M.S. Blackett, who would go on to win the Nobel prize for physics in 1948 and Air Vice Marshall Hugh Dowding.

[7] Having consulted with one of his key Scientific Officers at the Radio Research Station near Slough, Arnold 'Skip' Wilkins. Wilkins carried out the calculations

and the later experimental demonstration at Daventry to demonstrate that radar could be an effective detection device. See *The Birth of British Radar: The Memoirs of Arnold 'Skip' Wilkins* edited by Colin Latham & Anne Stobbs (Speedwell for the Defence Electronics History Society, 2006).

[8] Dowding was Wimperis' boss and also at the time in charge of research and development at the Air Council. Fighter Command was formed in 1936 with the express purpose of controlling the country's air defence operations and Dowding was its first commander.

[9] Skip Wilkins used a rudimentary apparatus he made himself to bounce radio waves off a passing Heyford bomber at Daventry. His account in his memoirs of how he tuned the equipment in the dark the night before the experiment with the aid of a succession of lighted matches is well worth reading.

[10] I am over-simplifying here a bit as both Tizard and Dowding did come up against significant opposition and obstacles in some quarters e.g. Professor Lindemann, as we'll see in the next section, 'The Tizard Committee and Churchill's man: how it could have failed'.

[11] This kind of informal set up can have its drawbacks too, particularly when in place over long periods of time, as it attracts lazy free riders (or what the Americans call freeloaders) who contribute nothing to the enterprise.

[12] Later in the war, as an offshoot of the development of a cavity magnetron at Birmingham university, described in detail in *The Invention that Changed the World: the story of radar from war to peace* by Robert Buderi (Simon & Schuster, 1996), Chain Home Extra Low stations tracked planes as low as 20 feet off the ground. Buderi also describes in some depth how the magnetron proved a key element of the Tizard mission to share scientific intelligence with the US later in the war.

[13] See Walter Blanchard's letter to the editor, Defence Electronics History Society Newsletter, *Transmission Lines*, Vol. 11 No. 2, June 2006 and *LZ 130 "Graf Zeppelin" and the End of Commercial Airship Travel* by Manfred Bauer and John Duggan (Zeppelin Museum Friedrichshafen Press, 1996).

[14] Royal Air Force and Women's Auxiliary Air Force.

[15] Which Watson-Watt defined as "investigation by scientific method on actual operations – current, recent or impending – and explicitly directed to the better, more effective and more economical conduct of similar operations in the future".

[16] Another low tech activity but a crucial part of the system.

[17] The presence of pretty WAAF croupiers who moved the markers on the map table proved a not insignificant incentive for the young pilots to do just that.

[18] *Science and Government* by C.P. Snow (Oxford University Press, 1960) p29; *The Professor and the Prime Minister* by The Earl of Birkenhead (The Riverside Press Cambridge, Houghton Mifflin Company Boston, 1962), p201. Birkenhead (Frederick Winston Furneaux Smith, 2nd Earl of Birkenhead) goes so far as to say that it was Tizard's influence with the RAF which proved to be his most important contribution to the development of the system.

[19] Indeed pilots cursed operations centres and controllers on more than one occasion when upon reaching a designated point in the sky, there appeared to be no en-

emy aircraft to engage with but the system worked to deliver successful intercepts on many more occasions and came to be trusted by the people relying on it.

[20] See the *Birth of British Radar: The Memoirs of Arnold 'Skip' Wilkins* (Speedwell, 2006) Chapter 9.

[21] It rates right up there with NASA spending hundreds of thousands of dollars developing a pen that would work upside-down in space, compared with the Soviet space programme which simply used pencils.

[22] This is a simplified schematic. The observer corps centre data for example actually got routed through Group HQ before going to the Filter Room at Fighter Command.

[23] This changed when Churchill became Prime Minister.

[24] *Science and Government* by C.P. Snow (Oxford University Press, 1960) p75.

[25] Amongst them Edward Appleton (a later member of the Tizard committee) v Watson-Watt, Number 11 Group Commander Park v Number 12 Group Commander Leigh-Mallory (and his charismatic Squadron Leader Douglas Bader), Dowding v Deputy Chief of Staff at the Air Ministry Sholto Douglas (according to Dowding's biographer, Robert Wright, the Commander in Chief of Fighter Command was not a political animal and did not suffer fools gladly, so made a number of powerful political enemies); A.P. Rowe's introduction of bureaucratic formalities at Bawdsey Manor after taking over from Watson-Watt in 1938 were not appreciated by the residents used to being given a free rein but he earned their grudging respect in time by demonstrating his commitment to the cause and his belief, like Watson-Watt, in the frank and free exchange of ideas. Watson-Watt did not always see eye to eye with Tizard either and on the Lindemann–Tizard battles, later described Lindemann as having provided "indispensable" support at the highest levels to the radar team.

[26] Lindemann was also godfather to one of Tizard's children.

[27] *Friends and Rivals*, Chapter 2 of *Most Secret War* by R.V. Jones (Hamish Hamilton Ltd, 1978, Wordsworth Editions Ltd. 1998), has an excellent account of the Lindemann–Tizard and Lindemann–Churchill relationships at the crucial time, as does *The Professor and the Prime Minister* by The Earl of Birkenhead (The Riverside Press, 1962), Chapter 6, *Air Defence*.

[28] *The Second World War Volume I: The Gathering Storm* by Winston S. Churchill (Penguin Books, 1985 edition), p72.

[29] See for example R.V. Jones op. cit. pp16–17

[30] Churchill had once called the Labour Prime Minister "the boneless wonder" in a speech in the House of Commons, 28 January 1931.

[31] Birkenhead, in particular, in *The Professor and the Prime Minister,* is very informative about his frustrations and positive motivations to get things done urgently.

[32] Lindemann got his wish to test these aerial mines in 1940 and they proved useless.

[33] Tizard considered him one of the smartest people he ever knew and on a par with Ernest Rutherford. This is widely disputed though. The rift between Tizard and Lindemann divided the scientific establishment and many, though admitting

Lindemann had a decent intellect, felt he was not a great scientist. C.P. Snow once even joked about Lindemann's "non-quantitative statistics".

[34] By C.P. Snow op.cit. amongst many.

[35] The highest level decision making committee in the government, led by the Prime Minister and attended by senior ministers.

[36] Chapter 19 *Wizard War* in *The Second World War Volume II: Their Finest hour* by Winston S. Churchill (Penguin Books, 1985 edition), p338.

[37] It is unlikely, for example, that Lindemann's advocacy for the "strategic bombing" of working class German homes between 1942 and 1943 would have succeeded if Tizard or Blackett's analysis of his statistical calculations outlining the impact of such action had been taken seriously.

[38] See *Research in Theory and Practice* by Sir George Thomson, the *Inaugural Sir Henry Tizard Memorial Lecture* at Westminster School, 21 February 1963

[39] Like West Churchman, Russell Ackoff, Peter Checkland, Geoffrey Vickers. See *Systems Practice: Managing Complexity* at Open2.net. http://www.open2.net/systems/.

[40] There are a lot of books which provide absorbing accounts of the radar story, though unfortunately some of these are no longer widely available. In addition to those already cited I highly recommend: *Duel of Eagles: The Struggle for the Skies from the First World War to the Battle of Britain* by Peter Townsend (Phoenix Press, 2000; first published in the UK in 1970 by Cassell Publishers); *Instruments of Darkness: The History of Electronic Warfare 1939–1945* by Alfred Price (Greenhill Books, 2005); *A Radar History of World War II: Technical and Military Imperatives* by Louis Brown (Institute of Physics Publishing, 1999); *Fighter: The True Story of the Battle of Britain* by Len Deighton (Alfred A. Knopf, 1977); *Tizard* by Ronald W. Clark (Methuen & Co., 1965); *Dowding and the Battle of Britain* by Robert Wright (MacDonald, 1969); Winston Churchill's six volumes on *The Second World War,* most notably *Volume 1 The Gathering Storm* and *Volume II Their Finest Hour* (Penguin Books version, 1985); *The Battle of Britain* by R.T. Bickers (Salamander Books, 1990); *The Battle of Britain* by Basil Collier (Batsford, 1962); *The Battle of Britain: Dowding and the First Victory, 1940* by John Ray (Cassell Military Paperbacks Series, 2000); *Battle of Britain* by Leonard Mosley (Time Life Books UK, 1977); *The Hardest Day: Battle of Britain, 18 August 1940* by Alfred Price (Cassell Military Classics Series, 1998; originally published by Jane's Publishing Co. in 1979); *The Battle of Britain, July–October 1940* by Matthew Parker (Headline Book Publishing, 2001); *The Last Enemy* by Richard Hillary (Pimlico, 1997; originally published by Macmillan, 1942); *The Most Dangerous Enemy: A History of the Battle of Britain* by Stephen Bungay (Aurum Press, 2001); *The Narrow Margin: The Battle of Britain and the Rise of Air Power, 1930–1940* by Derek Wood (Pen and Sword Books, 2003); *A Summer Bright and Terrible: Winston Churchill, Lord Dowding, Radar and the Impossible Triumph of the Battle of Britain* by David E. Fisher (Shoemaker & Hoard, 2006).

[41] There is one final point worth noting about many of these sources on the radar story. Peter Butcher, the editor of the Defence Electronics History Society's *Transmission Lines,* pointed out to me in conversation that many of the accounts written in the aftermath of the war were filtered through the security services, in

the interests of national security. Peter suggests that information recently released by the Public Records Office, under the 50-year rule, is beginning to shed even more light on the fascinating history of the time.

[42] *NEDAP/Powervote* electronic voting systems, also used in Holland and Germany and sold under the brand *Liberty Voting Systems* in the US. It is also being considered for use in a number of other European countries.

[43] Interim Report of the Commission on Electronic Voting, April 2004, available at: http://www.cev.ie/htm/report/view_report.htm.
This quote is from the first paragraph of the 'Conclusion' in 'Executive Summary' of the report.

[44] Noted on page 14 of the second Report of the Commission on Electronic Voting, June 2006, available at: http://www.cev.ie/htm/report/download_second.htm.

[45] The machines also seem to be very user friendly and easy to use. Indeed the first report by the voting commission, before going on to note serious concerns, had many positive things to say about the system:
  - It is easy to use
  - It eliminates many inadvertent voter errors
  - It has been piloted in an election and a referendum
  - The system suppliers also supply e-voting machines to Germany and Holland
  - It has been tested and can accurately and consistently record and count votes in most situations including "unusual or difficult electoral situations"
  - End-to-end testing suggests it can accurately record and count votes in multiple simultaneous elections
  - It can produce results quickly
  - It may save costs in the future.
The official website for electronic voting in Ireland provides a lovely animated demo of how the machines actually operate at
http://www.electronicvoting.ie/english/demo.html.

[46] Part 7 Summary and Conclusions of the report, which is well worth reading in full, states:
"The election management (Delphi code) software installed on the hardened PC and used to prepare elections and to aggregate and count the votes …is thus unlikely to be capable of meeting the high standards … required in a mission critical system. Design weaknesses, including an error in the implementation of the count rules … could compromise the accuracy of an election…
This finding is significant in view of the critical role of the election management (Delphi code) software in configuring all of the other hardware devices and peripherals within the system at elections and its role in handling all election data, including votes...
Given the Commission's findings about the inadequacies of the development process for the election management (Delphi code) software, and the functional errors and other weaknesses that continue to emerge it is unlikely that this software could be feasibly amended to enable its reliability to be confirmed. Accordingly, the Commission does not recommend the use of the election management (Delphi code) software at elections in Ireland but notes that it is likely that alterna-

tive election management software, compatible with the hardware and embedded C code software of the system, could be developed at a reasonable relative cost." In its original report in May 2004, the Commission had also raised concerns about the lack of access to the source code of the software and the frequency with which the software was changed without being subject to further testing: "as changes are made to the system, each new software version needs to be reviewed and tested in full before it can be relied upon for use in real elections" (First Report of the Commission on Electronic Voting, Part 6, p74).

[47] For an excellent description of the Indian system see http://amit.chakradeo.net/2004/05/14/indias-electronic-voting-machines-compared-to-diebold/. The Election Commission of India have a description and pictures of the system at http://www.eci.gov.in/EVM/index.htm.

[48] There were multiple problems with voting in Florida in 2000, the State which eventually decided the election for George W. Bush by 537 votes. For a polemic account of the problems with butterfly ballots, hanging chads, disenfranchised African American and Jewish voters, see *The Best Democracy Money Can Buy* by Greg Palast (Constable and Robinson, 2003). Another account can be found in *Steal this Vote: Dirty Elections and Rotten History of Democracy in America* by Andrew Gumbel (Nation Books, 2005).

[49] Section 102 of the Help America Vote Act 2002.

[50] Section 301 of the Help America Vote Act 2002.

[51] Two media organisations, entitled to access to voting data under Florida state law, who did their own recount after the election concluded that Gore would have won but we can never really know. See Gumbel op.cit. pp 208, 209.

[52] The Irish Commission on Electronic Voting put it like this: "While analysis and testing of the chosen system were clearly carried out by the Manufacturers, the Department and others during the development and adaptation of the chosen system for use in Ireland prior to the appointment of the Commission, different parts of the system were reviewed by different independent bodies, both within Ireland and internationally. None of these bodies was asked to take a view of the chosen system as a whole, incorporating all relevant aspects of its hardware and software components, its physical environment and the operational arrangements for its use. This led the Commission to take a broad view of the system within the particular scope of its terms of reference. In taking this broad view, the Commission has had regard to the key principles that any system is 'more than the sum of its component parts' and is 'only as strong as its weakest link'." (Second Report of the Commission on Electronic Voting, Part 7, p185, 186) My systems colleagues at the Open University would be delighted at an official government commission taking such a systems perspective.

[53] See Nedap/*Groenendaal ES3B voting computer, a security analysis* by Rop Gonggrijp, Willem-Jan Hengeveld et al published by the "We do not trust voting computers" foundation, October 2006, available at: http://www.wijvertrouwenstemcomputersniet.nl/Nedap-en. See also the Organization for Security and Co-operation in Europe (OSCE) report on the Dutch elections of November 2006, *The Netherlands Parliamentary Elections 22 November 2006 OSCE/ODIHR Election Assessment Mission Report*, pub-

lished by the OSCE Office for Democratic Institutions and Human Rights (ODIHR), March 2007 and available at http://www.osce.org/documents/odihr/2007/03/23602_en.pdf.
[54] *Alarming results from Italian experimental e-voting* European Digital Rights EDRI-gram report by Andrea Glorioso, 10 May 2006 available at http://www.edri.org/edrigram/number4.9/evoting.
[55] http://www.fsfeurope.org/.
[56] Professors of Computer Science at Princeton and John Hopkins Universities respectively, Edward Felten and Aviel Ruben have said "We believe that the question of whether DREs based on commodity hardware and operating systems should ever be used in elections needs serious consideration by government and election officials. As computer security experts, we believe that the known dangers and potentially unknown vulnerabilities are too great. We should not put ourselves in a position where, in the middle of primary season, the security of our voting systems comes into credible and legitimate question." 'DRE' stands for direct-recording electronic voting machines and the wider background to the comments can be found at http://www.freedom-to-tinker.com/?p=1014. Felten also released a paper with Ariel J. Feldman and J. Alex Halderman, in September 2006, *Security Analysis of the Diebold AccuVote-TS Voting Machine*, demonstrating that this particular voting machine is "vulnerable to extremely serious attacks". The paper and a video of how the machine can be compromised in under a minute is available at http://itpolicy.princeton.edu/voting/.
[57] These access codes could potentially provide him with control of any voting machine of this type used anywhere in Italy.
[58] Gumbel op.cit. pp113–118.
[59] Which Gumbel, op.cit. p113, suggests "were an invitation to coercion, bribery, and outright theft".
[60] Douglas W. Jones *Problems with Voting Systems and the Applicable Standards* Testimony before the US House of Representatives' Committee on Science, Washington, DC, May 22, 2001. At the time, as well as being an associate professor (now a full professor) at the University of Iowa, Professor Jones was Chairman of the Iowa Board of Examiners for Voting Machines and Electronic Voting Systems and a Member of the Iowa Election Reform Task Force.
[61] At least within the constraints of the type of voting process being operated. The first past the post system in the UK has been widely criticised, particularly by the Liberal Democrats, for not reflecting the will of the electorate. They have long called for a proportional representation system like that used in Ireland. Under the single transferable vote proportional representation system the Liberal Democrats would have significantly more MPs in the UK parliament. They would also probably hold the balance of power, given the unlikely scenario of Labour and Conservatives agreeing to operate together in a coalition government.
[62] Including the Labour party which had issued a report in December 2003 suggesting the e-voting machines might be a "threat to democracy".
[63] This was in February 2004. I have to admit to being pretty scathing about his attitude at the time on my blog http://b2fxxx.blogspot.com/2004/02/according-to-independent-general-angst.html.

[64] In the UK by handing over a polling card we will have received by post prior to the election (if the card arrives in time which it doesn't always) and providing our name and address to the presiding official at the polling station.

[65] And the integrity of most voting systems requires, in the interests of avoiding voter fraud that voters do not receive and retain documented proof that they have voted for a particular candidate. Voting is supposed to be secret and anonymous.

[66] See Avi Rubin's website at http://avirubin.com/vote/. See also Rubin's terrific book on e-voting, *Brave New Ballot: The Battle to Safeguard Democracy in the Age of Electronic Voting* by Aviel D. Rubin (Morgan Road Books, 2006).

[67] See 2006 *Security Analysis of the Diebold AccuVote-TS Voting Machine* by Edward Felten, Ariel J. Feldman, J. Alex Halderman (September 2006) http://www.freedom-to-tinker.com/?p=1014.

[68] *Black Box Voting: Ballot Tampering in the 21st-Century* by Bev Harris with David Allen (Pan Nine Publishing, 2003). It is not easy to see democracy in action when the work is being done by electrons running around inside electronic machines.

[69] Absentee voting introduces huge security issues, as police investigations into postal vote fraud in the Midlands in the UK has shown in recent years.

[70] A journalist campaigning to raise awareness of problems with e-voting, Lynn Landes, now wants open voting. See *Scrap the "Secret" Ballot – Return to Open Voting*, 4 November, 2006 at http://www.ecotalk.org/VotingSecurity.htm and *Elections In America - Assume Crooks Are In Control*, 16 September 2002 at http://www.commondreams.org/views02/0916-04.htm.

[71] Cambridge Professor Roger Needham, who died in 2003, once described automation as "replacing what works with something that almost works, but is faster and cheaper". Many of the electronic voting systems in use today almost work, are arguably faster but are much more expensive than earlier systems.

[72] In particular Aviel Rubin of John Hopkins University, Rebecca Mercuri of Notable Software (http://www.notablesoftware.com/evote.html), David Dill of Stanford University, Peter Neumann of the SRI Computer Science Laboratory at Menlo Park and Ed Felten of Princeton.

[73] Mark Fiore created an amusing, if caustic, animation outlining his view of these systems in February 2004: http://www.markfiore.com/animation/voting.html The Daily Show likewise produced an amusing sequence on e-voting in April 2004: http://avirubin.com/vote/dailyshow.mov.

[74] Harris, op.cit, covers about a hundred of these cases. A report by Harri Hursti, a computer graphics databases and security expert from Finland, considered by computer experts to have revealed the most serious security flaws with Diebold or similar machines was released in May 2006. Available at http://www.blackboxvoting.org/BBVtsxstudy.pdf. Aviel Rubin, Adam Stubblefield, Tadayoshi Kohno had Dan Wallach previously published a paper on what were considered serious security flaws with the Diebold system in July 2003. The John Hopkins University Information Security Institute Technical Report TR-2003-19, July 23, 2003 is available at http://avirubin.com/vote.pdf and was subsequently published in *IEEE Symposium on Security and Privacy* (IEEE Computer Security Press, May 2004).

[75] http://en.wikipedia.org/wiki/Volusia_error. The machine also subtracted even more votes from the Green Party candidate, Ralph Nader.

[76] The accepted explanation for the error was a faulty memory card though internal Diebold memos relating to an investigation of what went wrong with the machine suggested the remote possibility that "the 'second memory card' or 'second upload' came from an un-authorized source". These and other leaked Diebold memos led to a fascinating saga all of its own involving a number of legal cases as the company tried to recover the documents and prevent them from being publicised.

[77] 'Patch' is the word more frequently used than 'fix' when it comes to computer security. Just because some known security holes get patched up does not mean that the computer is necessarily then safe or secure.

[78] CDs were used by many testers in the Irish trials.

[79] The Brennan Center Task Force on Voting System Security *The Machinery of Democracy: Protecting Elections in an Electronic World* http://www.brennancenter.org/programs/downloads/Full%20Report.pdf. Executive summary available at http://www.brennancenter.org/programs/downloads/Executive%20Summary.pdf. The list of people involved in compiling the report included Douglas Jones, David Dill, Harri Hursti and Bruce Schneier and is available at http://www.brennancenter.org/presscenter/About%20the%20Taskforce.pdf.

[80] Since it was first suggested by Rebecca Mercuri in *Physical Verifiability of Computer Systems* presented at the 5th International Computer Virus and Security Conference in March 1992. See also Mercuri's website on electronic voting at http://www.notablesoftware.com/evote.html.

[81] The Election Science Institute released a report in August 2006 on real experience with e-voting machines in a May 2006 primary election in Ohio. The report, in one of the still rare examples of real operational research in this area, is based on observations of how the technology was actually used in practice. The officials in the county involved deserve massive credit for allowing the election to be monitored in this way, as it is only by seeing how these systems are used in practice and learning from the experience when things going wrong that we will really begin to improve them. All too often very busy election officials, who in the US after all have a legal obligation to use electronic voting now, tend to avoid finding problems with e-voting systems because they already have more than enough problems and insufficient capacity to deal with them. Sure enough the printers in Ohio went wrong during the day on about 10% of the machines. Paper rolls came out blank or chewed up or smeared or torn. Printers can go wrong. That is not big news but it is important to take into account when insisting on voter-verified paper audit trails. The report is available at http://www.electionscience.org/Members/ccro/report.2006-08-22.1967932557/report_contents_file/. Ed Felten has his usual insightful comments on the report at http://www.freedom-to-tinker.com/?p=1061.

[82] Robert F. Kennedy, Jr. *Was the 2004 Election Stolen?* Rolling Stone 1 June, 2006.
http://www.rollingstone.com/news/story/10432334/was_the_2004_election_stolen
[83] Democratic National Committee Voting Rights Institute report, *Democracy at Risk: The 2004 Election in Ohio,* 22 June, 2005, p5. The report is available at:
http://a9.g.akamai.net/7/9/8082/v001/www.democrats.org/pdfs/ohvrireport/fullrep ort.pdf.
This was reference number 14 in the original article. The exact quote from page 5 of the report is "New registrants were much more likely to be required to cast ballots provisionally: 26.5 percent of voters who first registered to vote in 2004 were required to cast a provisional ballot versus 2.5 percent of voters who registered before 2004."
[84] Status Report of the House Judiciary Committee Democratic Staff *Preserving Democracy: What Went Wrong in Ohio,* 5 January 2005, available at
http://www.house.gov/judiciary_democrats/ohiostatusrept1505.pdf.
The report was also edited and released as a book *What Went Wrong In Ohio: The Conyers Report on the 2004 Presidential Election* by Congressman John Conyers, Anita Miller (Editor), Gore Vidal (Introduction), (Academy Chicago Publishers, May 2005). See also *Stealing Democracy: The New Politics of Voter Suppression* by Spencer Overton (W.W. Norton & Company, 2006), pp42–48.
[85] Or his counterpart in Florida in 2000, Katharine Harris. Secretary of State in Florida Harris was in charge of the electoral process as well as being head of the 2000 Bush campaign in the state.
[86] And there is no evidence that he did so. Farhad Manjoo at Salon, who has been writing about the problems with electronic voting machines for a few years, says Kennedy's article is flawed and that no, Bush didn't steal the 2004 election. Manjoo and Kennedy had a follow-up discussion online at Salon. They both agree that the voting system is in urgent need of reform but disagree about the extent of the real problems in Ohio in 2004 and therefore what the starting point of the reform should be.
http://www.salon.com/news/feature/2006/06/03/kennedy/index_np.html.
[87] Republican or Democrat, Conservative or Labour, Fiánna Fáil or Fine Gael.
[88] The treaty, signed by Michael Collins on behalf of the Irish delegation, required Irish parliamentarians to take and oath of allegiance to the British Crown. This oath became the source of a dispute between Collins and Eamonn DeValera which led to a short-lived but bitter civil war, the effects of which were to be felt in Ireland for generations. The country later became a republic in 1937, with Douglas Hyde becoming the first president.
[89] For a full account of the treaty negotiations and associated economic, cultural, environmental and political background see Tim Pat Coogan's wonderful biography of Collins, *Michael Collins* by Tim Pat Coogan (Arrow, 1991).
[90] There were attempts to set up the commission but the Unionists in Northern Ireland refused to nominate a representative and the British government nominated a South African rather than a Britain as the terms of the treaty required. The charismatic Collins, who would have been most likely to ensure the treaty commitments were adhered to had been killed in the civil war and the Irish government had

many other concerns including coping with the aftermath of the war to pay too much attention to following up the small print of the treaty.

[91] The situation is much fuzzier than the implied suggestion here that the divisions were on religious grounds. Not all Catholics were nationalists and not all Protestants were Unionists but for simplicity's sake and given that this book is not an in-depth treatise on the politics of Northern Ireland it is fair to assume that most of the Catholic population had nationalist sympathies and most of the Protestant population leaned towards favouring unionists.

[92] In the US, in another angle on the electronic aids for voting, there is a piece of software which is popular with state legislatures. Caliper Corporation's 'Maptitude' is a GIS (geographic information system) mapping program with built-in demographic profiles, which can help urban planning and redistricting. Caliper's website helpfully points out: The Profile of General Demographic Characteristics contains 69 population and 25 housing variables. The Profile of Selected Housing Characteristics contains 97 housing variables. The Profile of Selected Economic Characteristics contains 107 population variables. The Profile of Selected Social Characteristics contains 99 population variables. These are all based on the 2000 Census data. The software allows you to do quite a lot with a redistricting plan, when planning to change voting districts. You can plan districts balanced by race, by gender, by likely voting patterns in the space of anything from a few minutes to a couple of hours. I have no evidence to suggest the software is abused in the interests of gerrymandering but it is fairly easy to see how it might have been abused if it was available in Northern Ireland in the 1960s. This kind of GIS software, of course, has all kinds of wonderfully useful applications in business, environmental decision making and public health, to name but three.

[93] There was also a 'business second vote' and a 'company vote' in the case of local elections and a 'university vote' in the case of general elections to the Stormont parliament.

[94] *The Troubles* by Tim Pat Coogan (Arrow Books, 1996) pp34–35. Chapter 2, *Bicycling to Busby,* of Coogan's masterful work provides as comprehensive and interesting an account of the politics of Northern Ireland in the 1960s as you are likely to find.

[95] Coogan op. cit. p38.

[96] Coogan quotes Peter Rose, author of *How the Troubles Came to Northern Ireland* (Palgrave MacMillan, 1999) as saying "during the 1960s the amount of time spent on Ulster at Westminster averaged less than two hours a year" Coogan op. cit. p39.

[97] Rebecca Mercuri would have been proud of him!

[98] Including voters, administrators, politicians, campaign managers, political parties and other users of the electoral system.

[99] Including computer scientists, forensic accountants and auditors, book keepers, registrars, voting administrators, voting historians, legal and constitutional experts.

[100] At least in the Ireland and UK, the merits of proportional representation versus first past the post aside.

[101] The Irish government announced in October 2006 that they would be going ahead with full-scale deployment of their e-voting system after 2007.

Chapter 8

[1] See also chapter 4 of *Digital Copyright* by Jessica Litman (Prometheus Books, 2001), pp23, 25 and *Information Feudalism: Who Owns the Knowledge Economy?* by Peter Drahos with John Braithwaite (Earthscan, 2002).

[2] Lessig has told this story in hundreds of talks around the world and in two books *The Future of Ideas* (Random House, 2001) and *Free Culture* (Penguin Books, 2004). The latter is probably more accessible to the lay reader.

[3] Thanks to Dick Morris for framing this section in a much more coherent way than the original draft.

[4] There is no serious scientific evidence disputing the fact that the levels of greenhouse gases now pervading our atmosphere are leading to global warming. What that actually means for different parts of the world is a different question. As far back as 1971 economist Nicholas Georgescu-Roegen was pointing out that there were limits to growth based on the combined finite nature of the earth's resources and a little-known law of nature, the second law of thermodynamics. The second law says that when you use energy you always waste some. It is nature's version of the old adage 'there is no such thing as a free lunch'. See *The Entropy Law and the Economic Process* by Nicholas Georgescu-Roegen (Harvard University Press, 1971).

[5] It is not entirely neglected by regulators and the EU landfill directive of 1999 (1999/31/EC) and the Waste Electrical and Electronic Equipment (WEEE) Directive (2002/96/EC and 2003/108/EC) of 2002 and other similar initiative are examples how we are beginning to see increasing amounts of legislation in the area.

[6] But if I give you my apple I no longer have an apple, making the apple 'rivalrous'.

[7] That would violate the second law of thermodynamics. If when you use energy you always waste some then the batteries would eventually run out i.e. it is impossible to build a perpetual motion machine.

[8] In the words of Richard Stallman, founder of the Free Software Foundation.

[9] Though initiatives like the Ndyio project at Cambridge may help in the longer term, http://www.ndiyo.org. Ndiyo, pronounced 'nn-dee-yo', is the Swahili word for 'yes'. Ndiyo! is a project based in Cambridge and set up by John Naughton and Quentin Stafford-Fraser to foster an approach to networked computing that is simple, affordable, open, less environmentally damaging and less dependent on intensive technical support than current networking technology. The large tech industry have also decided that energy savings might be marketable and Sun Microsystems now sells servers with a low-power 'CoolThreads' microprocessor that uses less power than an average light bulb, according to their promotional materials. Of course an average light bulb tends to use an excessive amount of power compared with a low energy light bulb but that is another story.

[10] Or at least the process of storing (packaging?), transporting and accessing that information, without which that information could not exist. See also *The Economy of Ideas: Selling Wine Without Bottles on the Global Net* by John Perry Barlow.

[11] Quoted by Matthew Yi in the *San Francisco Chronicle* at http://www.sfgate.com/cgi-bin/article.cgi?f=/c/a/2006/01/31/BUGO0GVTT11.DTL.

[12] James Boyle, *The Second Enclosure Movement and the Construction of the Public Domain*, (2003) http://www.law.duke.edu/pd/papers/boyle.pdf.

[13] Uphoff is the Director of the Cornell International Institute for Food, Agriculture and Development (CIIFAD) and of the International Program Agriculture, College of Agriculture and Life Sciences and Professor, Department of Government, College of Arts and Sciences, at Cornell University. The paper was *Local Institutions and Participation for Sustainable Development* and was part of the International Institute for Environment and Development, Gatekeeper Series. It was partly based on *Local Institutional Development: An Analytical Sourcebook, with Cases* by Norman Uphoff (Kumarian Press, Library of Management for Development, 1986). See also the IIED website at: http://www.iied.org/index.html.

[14] A specialised agency set up by the United Nations in 1967 and "dedicated to developing a balanced and accessible international intellectual property (IP) system". At the time of writing it has 183 member states.

[15] *Free Culture* by Lawrence Lessig (Penguin, 2004), p86. Actually the first printing privileges appeared in the 15th-century; by the mid-16th-century, printers and booksellers in Venice had gained monopolies in exchange for acting as agents of censorship. There had also been Crown granted monopoly printing privileges in England since the mid-1500s, in exchange for the publishers' agreement to censor heretical or seditious works. As tools of monopoly and censorship these early intellectual property laws were severely criticised by free trade advocates. The aim of the Statute of Anne was to control publishing monopolies. Lyman Ray Patterson *Copyright in Historical Perspective* (Vanderbilt University Press, 1968) pp3–19, 143–179 and 222–230 has a clear and very convincing exposition of the intention behind and subsequent confusion generated by the Statute.

[16] *The Law of International Copyright* by William Briggs (London, Steven and Haynes, 1906) pp36–38.

[17] Its equivalent in the international patent and trademark arenas is the 'Paris Convention for the Protection of Intellectual Property' originally agreed in 1883. This has also seen a number of significant revisions over the years, the most recent being in 1967 and 1979. Both the Berne Convention and the Paris Convention are administered by the World Intellectual Property Organisation, WIPO.

[18] The title of this sub-section is an explicit nod to a wonderful account of the emergence of TRIPS written by Peter Drahos and John Braithwaite which was based on personal interviews conducted with many of the individuals involved in shaping the process. If you really want a comprehensive understanding of how DDM in intellectual property happens in international forums, then *Information Feudalism: Who Owns the Knowledge Economy?* by Peter Drahos with John Braithwaite (Earthscan, 2002) is absolutely *essential* reading.

[19] Previously known as the General Agreement on Tariffs and Trade (GATT), this was originally an international trade agreement first signed in 1947 and became an international forum to encourage free trade between states party to the agreement. It was succeeded by the WTO in 1995.

[20] *Information Feudalism: Who Owns the Knowledge Economy* by Peter Drahos with John Braithwaite (Earthscan, 2002) is the definitive account. *The TRIPS Agreement: Drafting History and Analysis* by Daniel Gervais (Sweet & Maxwell, 1998) describes the negotiating history of each part of the TRIPS agreement. *Integrating Intellectual Property Rights and Development Policy*: *Report of the Commission on Intellectual Property Rights* (London, September 2002) considers "how national IPR regimes could best be designed to benefit developing countries within the context of international agreements, including TRIPS; how the international framework of rules and agreements might be improved and developed – for instance in the area of traditional knowledge – and the relationship between IPR rules and regimes covering access to genetic resources; the broader policy framework needed to complement intellectual property regimes including for instance controlling anti-competitive practices through competition policy and law" and is also recommended reading. The full report runs to 235 pages of A4 print but is surprisingly readable. Even if intellectual property is not a major area of interest for you, the executive summary (which runs to about 30 pages) is well worth skim reading. It can be found at http://www.iprcommission.org/graphic/documents/final_report.htm.

[21] He likes black pudding but refuses point blank to go anywhere near a beef burger.

[22] It was signed as part of the Final Act of the Uruguay round of GATT talks in 1994 after eight years of negotiations and came into force officially at the beginning of 1995. It is administered by the WTO.

[23] Given the systemic complexity and the often tightly coupled nature of these organisational structures and Charles Perrow's warnings about the ripple effects of problems and changes, it is [almost] remarkable that some of them function as well as they do.

[24] In an opinion piece for the *New York Times* on 9 July 1982 entitled *Stealing from the Mind* a senior executive at Pfizer even accused WIPO of "trying to grab high technology inventions for underdeveloped countries" and attempting to "confer legitimacy on the abrogation of patents". WIPO were also severely criticised for having no dispute resolution or enforcement process whereby transgressors of international standards in intellectual property could be brought to heel. Developing countries led by Brazil and India had also been making efforts through WIPO to reduce the impact of intellectual property restraints, such as patents on pharmaceutical products, on their developing economies. WIPO had a one nation one vote policy which meant that the US and Europe could not wield the kind of commanding influence they were used to in other international forums

[25] See Drahos op.cit. p108.

[26] The chairman of the main TRIPS negotiating group, Lars Anell, later brought the Director General of WIPO, Arpard Bogsch, in to observe the negotiations and act as an expert adviser.

[27] Again this is not necessarily a direct criticism of the politicians but just another example of C.P. Snow's idiom that the "most important choices about a nation's physical health are made... by men who normally are not able to comprehend the arguments in depth".

[28] A formally legally constituted committee set up under US trade law in 1974 to give the private sector a direct input to trade policy.

[29] http://www.heritage.org/ whose mission, as it says on their website "is to formulate and promote conservative public policies based on the principles of free enterprise, limited government, individual freedom, traditional American values, and a strong national defense".

[30] http://www.brook.edu/. Less conservative than the Heritage Foundation, it is "a private non profit organization devoted to independent research and innovative policy solutions".

[31] In addition the US and Europe had successfully kept intellectual property off the agenda at the United Nations Conference on Trade and Development (UNCTAD), a forum in which there was significant sympathy for the view that the intellectual property rules were heavily biased in favour of the developed nations.

[32] This quote is taken from an interview conducted by Peter Drahos and John Braithwaite with the US trade representative in 1994. Drahos op. cit. p73.

[33] Council Regulation (EEC) No 2641/84. This has since been revised and replaced by Regulation (EC) No 3286/94 in 1994.

[34] *Free Culture: The Nature and Future of Creativity* by Lawrence Lessig (Penguin Books, 2004), pp68–69.

[35] The number of creative commons licences now used is in the hundreds of millions, having only been launched in 2002. See the creative commons website at http://creativecommons.org/ for more details of how these licences work.

[36] Pamela Samuelson, *Should Economics Play a Role in Copyright Law and Policy?* 1 U. Ottawa L. & Tech. J. 3 (2004) suggests that "economic analysis has had relatively little effect on copyright law and policy thus far". And that "many in the copyright field, including policymakers, have little or no economic expertise and little inclination to seek it out" since "industry professionals have been successful in getting much if not all of what they want without the aid of economics". The definitive account of the economics of intellectual property is *The Economic Structure of Intellectual Property Law* by William M. Landes and Richard A. Posner (The Belknap Press of Harvard University Press, 2003). Landes and Posner's book is actually remarkably readable given that it covers the meshing of two subject areas which themselves are complex and opaque. It should be compulsory reading for anyone who is involved in making policy in this area.

[37] See for example *Innovation and Its Discontents: How our Broken Patent System is Endangering Innovation and Progress, and What to Do About it* by Adam B. Jaffe and Josh Lerner (Princeton University Press, 2004), *Shamans, Software and Spleens* by James Boyle (Harvard University Press, 1996), *Promises to Keep: Technology Law and the Future of Entertainment* by William W. Fisher III (Stanford University Press, 2004), *Information Rules: A Strategic Guide to the Network Economy* by Carl Shapiro and Hal R. Varian (Harvard Business School Press, 1999), *The Wealth of Networks: How Social Production Transforms Markets and Freedom* by Yochai Benkler (Yale University Press, 2006), *Copyrights and Copywrongs* by Siva Vaidhyanathan (New York University Press, 2001), *Silent Theft* by David Bollier (Routledge, 2002), *The Common Thread: Science, Politics, Ethics and the Human Genome* by John Sulston and Georgina Ferry (Corgi, 2003),

DNA: The Secret of Life by James D. Watson with Andrew Berry (Alfred A. Knopf, 2003), *Steal this Idea* by Michael Perelman (Palgrave, 2002) and *The Origin of Wealth* by Eric D. Beinhocker (Harvard Business School Press, 2006).

[38] *Piracy of U.S. copyrighted works in ten selected countries: A report by the International Intellectual Property Alliance to the U.S. Trade Representative* 1985 covered Singapore, Taiwan, Indonesia, Korea, the Philippines, Malaysia, Thailand, Brazil, Egypt and Nigeria. By 1992 the report covered 28 countries and estimated losses at $4.6 billion; by 1993 it was $15 to $17 billion, $8 billion of which was accounted for by copyright losses in 36 countries and the numbers have grown alarmingly ever since.

[39] Including India, Pakistan, China, Saudi Arabia, Kuwait, Argentina, Colombia, Venezuela, Mexico, Peru, Dominican Republic, Costa Rica, Panama, Jamaica and Turkey.

[40] Though technically the formal request in the Federal Register for written evidence is not limited to the IIPA and there are other submissions. I also put the word evidence in inverted commas to emphasise the less than solid basis of the figures produced by the IIPA. An Italian government report came to the conclusion, for example, that the video piracy problem in Italy was less than a tenth as big as suggested by the Motion Picture Association. Failure to accept the US figures was subsequently used as further 'evidence' to prove that the Italians were not taking their obligation to protect US intellectual property seriously.

[41] The Uruguay GATT round had fourteen separate formal groups negotiating on 'goods', the key groups being agriculture and intellectual property (the number 11 TRIPS group). It also had a separate strand of negotiating groups on "services"

[42] Drahos op.cit, Chapters 6–9.

[43] '*Remarks of Professor John J. Jackson*' in Symposium: Trade Related Aspects of Intellectual Property, 22 *Vanderbilt Journal of Transnational Law* (1989) pp343, 346.

[44] Chief Justice Burger of the US Supreme Court said, in his ruling in the 1980 Diamond v. Chakrobarty gene patent case, that Congress had intended, when passing the Patent Act of 1952, that "anything under the sun that is made by man" should be patentable. The decision is credited with opening the floodgates on gene patenting.

[45] Drahos op.cit. p69.

[46] *The Future of Ideas: the fate of the commons in a connected world* by Lawrence Lessig (Random House, 2001) and *Free Culture: the nature and future of creativity* by Lawrence Lessig (Penguin Books, 2004) described this as a revolution facilitated by new technology followed by a commercial counter-revolution as established companies move to protect their interests in the new context.

[47] Drahos op.cit. p73. The full text of TRIPS is available at the WTO website at http://www.wto.org/English/docs_e/legal_e/27-trips_01_e.htm and in pdf form at http://www.wto.org/English/docs_e/legal_e/27-trips.pdf

[48] Ironically early in 1996 the US took action against erstwhile TRIPS ally Japan, complaining about a lack of protection for US sound recordings. The case was settled the following year. There have been numerous actions wielding TRIPS and section 301 in the years ever since.

[49] For a terrifically accessible account of the range of problems associated with DRM see *30 Days of DRM* by Michael Geist, September 2006. http://www.michaelgeist.ca/component/option,com_docman/task,doc_download/g id,8/.

[50] I know you can get multi-region DVD players but I am just making the point about restrictive DRM. There is an interesting BBC *You and Yours* report from 2004 indicating how baffling the effect of DRM is, even to hardened consumer affairs journalists, covering the story of how copy-protected CDs refused to play on new Volkswagen CD players http://www.bbc.co.uk/radio4/youandyours/ram/youandyours_20040211_1.ram. When the BBC journalist gets round to interviewing a music industry spokesman from the British Phonographic Industry (BPI), he tells her that CD standards have been around for a long time and then says the CD manufacturers have recently "enhanced CDs" with new features (i.e. copy protection). And the effect of these new features is that the CD produces silence when played i.e. doesn't work. It is a bit like Raleigh saying "we decided to take the wheels off our bikes to reduce bicycle thefts and improve our service to customers; and don't blame us that the bikes are no good for cycling, the government should have adapted the road transport infrastructure to take account of our changes". The spokesman also says "The CD player he has got in his car is not actually, initially supposed to play audio CDs." Oh you mean that road was not meant for cycling my wheel-free-enhanced bike on? Even the BPI spokesman thinks "Now that might sound a bit strange."

[51] Directive 2001/29/EC of the European Parliament and of the Council of 22 May 2001 on the harmonisation of certain aspects of copyright and related rights in the information society.

[52] Even intellectual property lawyers who work primarily on behalf of copyright and trademark owners find that the some of the technical protectionist provisions of the DMCA go too far. See *Confessions of a Copyright Enforcer* by Megan Gray http://www.mediainstitute.org/colloquium/articles/2003/article15/article.html.

[53] For a very readable account of the proposals see *The Copyright Grab* by Pamela Samuelson *Wired News* Issue 4.01, January 1996, http://www.wired.com/wired/archive/4.01/white.paper_pr.html.

[54] According to *Digital Copyright* by Jessica Litman (Prometheus Books, 2001). Litman has a comprehensive warts and all account of the development of the White Paper. Chapter 11 of *Shamans, Software and Spleens* by James Boyle (Harvard University Press, 1997), Chapter 3 *Promises to Keep* by William Fisher III (Stanford University Press, 2004) and *The Exclusive Right to Read* by Jessica Litman, *13 Cardozo Arts & Entertainment Law Journal 29* (1994) (http://www-personal.umich.edu/%7Ejdlitman/papers/read.htm) are also recommended reading. For a rich account of Lehman's later successes and failures in pushing his agenda at WIPO, you will not find a better paper than *The US Digital Agenda at WIPO* by Pamela Samuelson 37 *Vanderbilt Journal of International Law* 369 (1997). See also daily reports on the actual WIPO meetings by Seth Greenstein, originally posted on the CNI-Copyright listserv and now available on the Internet Archive at http://web.archive.org/web/19981203130003/www.hrrc.org/wiponews.html.

[55] See http://www.wipo.int/treaties/en/ip/wct/trtdocs_wo033.html#P87_12240.

[56] See The Electronic Frontier Foundation's *Unintended Consequences: Seven Years under the DMCA*, April 2006.
http://www.eff.org/IP/DMCA/unintended_consequences.php for a description of the range of worrying cases that have sprung out of the DMCA.

[57] Note I am emphatically *not* suggesting here that the strength of a law is determined by its length, just that simple provisions can sometimes turn into complex provisions in the process of being incorporated from one legal context into another. Section 1201 of the DMCA reads in part:
"(1)(A) No person shall circumvent a technological measure that effectively controls access to a work protected under this title...
 (2) No person shall manufacture, import, offer to the public, provide, or otherwise traffic in any technology, product, service, device, component, or part thereof, that–
        (A) is primarily designed or produced for the purpose of circumventing a technological measure that effectively controls access to a work protected under this title;
        (B) has only limited commercially significant purpose or use other than to circumvent a technological measure that effectively controls access to a work protected under this title; or
        (C) is marketed by that person or another acting in concert with that person with that person's knowledge for use in circumventing a technological measure that effectively controls access to a work protected under this title."
For the full text of the act see the Library of Congress website
http://thomas.loc.gov/cgi-bin/query/z?c105:H.R.2281.ENR:.

[58] Under sections 296ZA to 296ZE of the directive. The text of the directive can be found at the UK Patent Office website at:
http://www.opsi.gov.uk/si/si2003/20032498.htm#24.

[59] The *Foundation for Information Policy Research* has an excellent report on the debate which took place within various member states in advance of the directive being incorporated into national laws http://www.fipr.org/copyright/guide/.

[60] Wikipedia keeps a running check on the implementation status of the directive in all member states
http://en.wikipedia.org/wiki/EU_Copyright_Directive#Implementation.

[61] See the website of the Office of the US Trade Representative for an up-to-date list of trade agreements.
http://www.ustr.gov/Trade_Agreements/Section_Index.html.

[62] See for example the *Evatt Foundation* paper, *The FTA and the PBS* by Peter Drahos, Thomas Faunce, Martyn Goddard and David Henry, which was the authors' submission to the Australian Senate Select Committee on the US–Australia Free Trade Agreement. http://evatt.labor.net.au/publications/papers/126.html.

[63] See the Europa website for an accessible report of how the EU is supposed to work http://europa.eu/abc/12lessons/index4_en.htm.

[64] In January 2007, two more states, Romania and Bulgaria joined the EU.

[65] http://swpat.ffii.org/lisri/cnino/index.en.html#cons041215.

[66] *Dutch Parliament Considers Revoking Support for Patent Directive* Arend Lammertink http://www.osnews.com/story.php?news_id=7442. Technically they

ordered the minister to change the Dutch vote on the Council, unless the EU procedures governing these things hold open the possibility of revoking the earlier vote until the Dutch Parliament could have a substantive debate on the matter. European law allows for states to revoke an earlier vote in Council in the light of new information.

[67] Thomas Jefferson said "Constant vigilance is the price of liberty" but it seems it is also the price those opposed to software patents need to pay, if they are to avoid the long term practice of the European Patent Office of granting software patents being formally encoded in European law. That it has been the practice is one of the key arguments being used in favour of the software patent directive.

[68] See b2fxxx blog, Tuesday, 22 June 2004 http://b2fxxx.blogspot.com/2004/06/it-seems-as-if-dutch-parliament-may.html and http://wiki.ael.be/index.php/V002.ogg at AEL Association Electronique Libre.

[69] The Directive on measures and procedures to ensure the enforcement of intellectual property rights, directive 2004/48/EC http://eur-lex.europa.eu/smartapi/cgi/sga_doc?smartapi!celexapi!prod!CELEXnumdoc&numdoc=32004L0048&model=guichett&lg=en.
It was implemented in the UK in the spring of 2006 in The Intellectual Property (Enforcement, etc.) Regulations 2006 (2006 No. 1027) http://www.opsi.gov.uk/si/si2006/20061028.htm.

[70] EU policies are divided into three main 'pillars', relating firstly to economic, social and environmental issues, secondly to military and foreign policy and thirdly to fighting crime. Wikipedia has a nice outline of how the codecision procedure is supposed to work at http://en.wikipedia.org/wiki/Codecision_procedure.

[71] The criminal sanctions clauses were removed before the directive was passed and are now being re-introduced in a second intellectual property rights enforcement directive being considered in the EU at the time of writing. By the summer of 2006 this proposal on criminal measures aimed at ensuring the enforcement of intellectual property rights (COM(2006) 168 final) was encountering some procedural hurdles, with the Dutch parliament complaining that the proposal "does not comply with the principle of subsidiarity and proportionality". 'Subsidiarity' relates to the EU stepping on the sovereignty of member states and 'proportionality' is the 'don't use a sledgehammer to crack a nut' principle.

[72] Known as 'Anton Pillar' orders in UK law.

[73] Called 'Mareva injunctions'.

[74] Jean-René Fourtou. With the various acquisitions and mergers since then the company is now called Vivendi (http://www.vivendi.com/)

[75] The foundation was reportedly subject to formal investigation in France over the purchase of Vivendi bonds but investigators were satisfied there were no improprieties. See *Fourtou defends foundation's Vivendi bond purchase* by Nicola Clark in the *International Herald Tribune*, 17 May 2004.
http://www.iht.com/articles/2004/05/17/viv_ed3_.php. The Fourtou foundation is involved in charitable work in France and Morocco, including the fight against extreme poverty and it provides aid to disadvantaged children and victims of war.

[76] See also Michael Geist's blog for a critical commentary of former Canadian Heritage Parliamentary Secretary Sam Bulte's ties to copyright lobby groups. http://www.michaelgeist.ca/index.php.

[77] Robin Gross of IP Justice, Cory Doctorow of the Electronic Frontier Foundation and David Tannenbaum and Shyamkrishna Balganesh of the Union for the Public Domain tell the story in a letter of complaint to the WIPO Deputy-Director General. The text of the letter is available at: http://www.eff.org/deeplinks/archives/002117.php.

[78] See *The Future of Ideas* and *Free Culture* by Lawrence Lessig and *Shamans Software and Spleens* by James Boyle for a deeper discussion of this point.

[79] See *Information Systems: Achieving Success by Avoiding Failure* by Joyce Fortune and Geoff Peters (John Wiley & Sons, 2005).

[80] James Boyle, in an opinion piece for the *Washington Times* of 14 November 1995, discussing the Lehman White Paper that eventually led to all the DRM protection laws we have today, said "The document is dense and outrageously legalistic, denying any citizen but a member of the copyright bar an ability to comment on this crucial piece of information policy. I am a law professor and I find it hard going." Commissioner Lehman was reportedly quite angry at the criticism http://www.teleread.org/update6.htm#top. Indeed the barnacle – bolt on some more provisions when we think of them – approach to intellectual property law sometimes makes the rules incredibly difficult to follow. By the time I have read "... under section 3.1 of the 1976 Act, as amended by article 4, subsection 12.1 of the treaty, as amended by..." my head is already spinning and I have not got anywhere near what the substance of the law actually says. By the time several amendments of previous amendments are bolted on top, you have to dig down through several layers of number and paragraphs references, sometimes of laws that no longer exist, before reaching that substance. Sometimes you cannot find the substance there and have to go and look up and read the original clauses in every law or treaty referred to and try to reconstruct what all these amendments are actually saying like a jigsaw puzzle. The detailed rules of intellectual property are not for the faint hearted.

[81] James Boyle gave the report a guarded welcome in an opinion piece for the *Financial Times* in January 2006. http://www.ft.com/cms/s/99610a50-7bb2-11da-ab8e-0000779e2340.html.

[82] See *We the Jury: The Jury System and the Ideal of Democracy* by Jeffrey Abramson (Basic Books, 1994) p245.

[83] Abramson op.cit. p246.

[84] Social Learning for the Integrated Management and Sustainable Use of Water at Catchment Scale. The results of the research are published under a creative commons licence at http://slim.open.ac.uk/page.cfm?pageid=aimshome.

[85] Directive 2000/60/EC, 23 October 2000, which "aims at maintaining and improving the aquatic environment in the Community, primarily in terms of the quality of water".

[86] See SLIM Policy Briefing No. 2 *Stakeholders and Stakeholding in Integrated Catchment Management and Sustainable Use of Water* (European Commission DG research, May 2004).

[87] Just as the statistician who declares a road safe because there has never been a recoded serious accident there, can learn from the parent who is witness daily to the numerous speeding cars that pass their house.

[88] I had intended to include a case study at this point on the effects of DDM in intellectual property, but pressure of space and time mean it gets relegated to this footnote. Instead of outlining my own perspective of the story of the disagreement between Pfizer and government officials in the Philippines considering parallel imports of a Pfizer drug from India, I will therefore refer you to the following accounts by James Love and Judit Rius Sanjuan of the Consumer Project on Technology:

http://www.huffingtonpost.com/james-love/hank-mckinnell-asks-for-i_b_20071.html

http://www.cptech.org/ip/health/c/phil/

http://secondview.blogspot.com/2006/03/pfizer-is-suing-philippines.html

http://www.huffingtonpost.com/james-love/terrorism-pfizer-style_b_18290.html

http://www.cptech.org/ip/health/c/phil/philtimeline.html

See also *The Truth About Drug Companies: How They Deceive Us and What to Do About It* by Marcia Angell (Random House, 2004), *The $800 Million Pill: The Truth Behind the Cost of New Drugs* by Merrill Goozner (University of California Press, 2004) and *Intellectual Property and Pharmaceutical Markets: A Nodal Governance Approach* by Peter Drahos *Temple Law Review* Vol 77, 2004, pp401–424 for a much more detailed discussion about the issues raised by drug patents and the regulatory tactics the pharmaceutical companies engage in to maximise their income from those patents.

Chapter 9

[1] Feynman tells this story in a chapter called *Judging Books by Their Covers* in the book *Surely You're Joking, Mr. Feynman!: Adventures of a Curious Character*, Richard Feynman, Ralph Leighton (contributor), Edward Hutchings (editor), (W.W.Norton, 1985). The book was based on taped interviews that Ralph Leighton conducted with Feynman and a copy is available online at http://www.textbookleague.org/103feyn.htm.

[2] He said: "Everything was written by somebody who didn't know what the hell he was talking about, so it was a little bit wrong, always! And how we are going to teach well by using books written by people who don't *quite* understand what they're talking about, I *cannot* understand."

[3] See Feynman's letter to Dr Max Rafferty of 29 November 1965, reprinted in *Don't you have time to think?* edited by Michelle Feynman (Penguin Books, 2006), p194. The Textbook League, set up in 1989, "to support the creation and acceptance of sound schoolbooks" says the adoption of textbooks for US public schools today is no better than it was in Feynman's experience in the 1960s. http://www.textbookleague.org/103feyn.htm. See also *The Muddle Machine: Confessions of a Textbook Editor* by Tamim Ansary in *Edutopia* Magazine, November 2004 for an account of textbook production at an unnamed "major pub-

lisher of elementary and high school textbooks".
http://www.edutopia.org/magazine/ed1article.php?id=Art_1195&issue=nov_04.
[4] Not in accordance with some constrained administrative tick box scheme
[5] That is not to say it does not have problems, as for example radical ideas and approaches might not survive such a review process. See *The Structure of Scientific Revolutions* by Thomas Kuhn (University of Chicago Press, 1962).
[6] Mainly print materials.
[7] The facilities of which are hired out to the OU.
[8] I should note that summer schools are no longer a compulsory part of the OU's curriculum, unless you are interested in taking specific named degrees.
[9] The course was *T102 Living with Technology*. 1995 was the year I began to work for the OU. One of my earliest jobs was to train the tutors in how to use the communications system the course was employing.
[10] Some have already been written, *Delivering Learning on the Net: the why, what and how of online education* by Martin Weller (Kogan Page, 2002) and *Virtual Learning Environments - using, choosing and developing your VLE* by Martin Weller (Routledge, 2007) being amongst the best.
[11] As was the case with many T171 students at the turn of the century.
[12] The first third of the course was all about teaching the students to use their computers, the Internet and the FirstClass® conferencing system. This module was later replaced with one on commerce and the Internet.
[13] I did not say 'new' because Dale Spender was advocating the approach back in 1995. See *Nattering on the Net: Women, Power and Cyberspace* by Dale Spender (Spinifex, 1995).
[14] See *Mastering Communication* by Nicky Stanton (Palgrave, 4th edition, 2004) for a comprehensive discussion of the issues.
[15] Microsoft Outlook as opposed to FirstClass®.
[16] Traditional 'operational research' is the application of scientific methods to management problems and can involve the use of complicated mathematical models to predict system behaviours. Throughout this book I am using the term in a slightly looser sense than that in the DDM context in referring to experts and users building and developing a working system together.
[17] See http://en.wikipedia.org/wiki/Henry_Faulds.
[18] *On the Skin-Furrows of the Hand* by Dr Henry Faulds, *Nature* 28 October 1880.
[19] Her Majesty's Inspectorate of Constabulary (HMIC) report stated "That the mark was not made by Shirley McKie. It is (the independent experts) view that decision could have been reached at an early point in the comparison process."
[20] There are some excellent websites on the case at
http://www.shirleymckie.com/index.htm and http://www.clpex.com/McKie.htm and the Scottish Parliament's Scottish Criminal Record Office inquiry homepage http://www.scottish.parliament.uk/business/committees/justice1/ScottishCriminal RecordOfficeInquiryHomepage.htm.
[21] I appreciate that this is a fairly weak analogy as the fingerprint experts stuck to their opinion with full knowledge of the consequences for Shirley McKie and in the face of their opinion being brought into question by expert colleagues. Never-

theless I make the analogy primarily to emphasise the subsequent point about system failure.

[22] Responsible for the prosecution of crime in Scotland and the investigation of any complaints against the police.

[23] Jerry Fishenden has an interesting perspective on the impact on public confidence in forensic science such mistakes might have when biometrics begin to be widely employed. See Fishenden's blog post of 1 August 2006, *Biometrics: Enabling Guilty Men to Go Free? Further Adventures from the Law of Unintended Consequences* http://ntouk.com/?view=plink&id=169.

[24] In an open letter to the Scottish parliament one of the international experts who testified on behalf of McKie, David Grieve, eloquently spells out the consequences if we ignore this.
http://www.shirleymckie.com/correspondencePDFs/David%20Grieve%20An%20 Open%20Letter%20to%20the%20Members%20of%20Parliament.pdf.

[25] The url or web address on the Tornado system included the user's login details.

[26] See http://caselaw.lp.findlaw.com/scripts/ts_search.pl?title=18&sec=1030 for the precise text of the relevant section of the act.

[27] And Jennifer Grannick of the Stanford Center for Internet and Society, who later represented McDanel during his appeal, said the $5000 estimated damages was inflated by the company and the cost of its efforts to cover up the problem. See the Stanford website for further details of the case.
http://cyberlaw.stanford.edu/about/cases/united_states_v_mcdanel.shtml.

[28] See *The Sad Tale of a Security Whistleblower* by Mark Rasch, *SecurityFocus* 18 August 2003 http://www.securityfocus.com/columnists/179.

[29] See also Chapter 10 of *DNA: The Secret of Life* By James D. Watson with Andrew Berry (Alfred A. Knopf, 2003) for some good examples of how lawyers and scientists tend to speak entirely different languages.

[30] Like Wing Commander Grenfell at Biggin Hill who came up with the idea of using the Tizzy angle for setting a course to intercept raiding enemy aircraft. See also *The Visual Display of Quantitative Information* by Edward R. Tufte (Graphic Press, 2001). Tufte explains that ordinary people are eminently capable of understanding the message in masses of complex data, providing the data is presented in a pattern conducive to engaging the remarkable cognitive abilities of the human brain. Basically we can see a pattern in a well-presented graphic of a mass of data much easier than if the same data is presented in big lists or tables of numbers. He also points out that it is crucial for the graphic-artists to understand quantitative methods for analysing raw data; otherwise they focus on the aesthetics of the image rather than the substance of the data. The result is images which lie about what the data is really saying.

[31] There is a nice example of this kind of constrained thinking in an OU summer school context. I occasionally teach the structures modelling lab at summer school where the students build some mathematical, computer and physical models, rounding off the day by testing their model bridges to destruction. I used to see a whole range of weird and wonderful bridge designs some years ago but since we introduced the computer-aided design software, the physical models are largely restricted to the two types that can be easily set up on the computer.

[32] Such as the Tacoma Narrows suspension bridge disaster in Washington in 1940. See http://en.wikipedia.org/wiki/Tacoma_Narrows_Bridge for the details and the University of Bristol's engineering maths webpage http://www.enm.bris.ac.uk/anm/tacoma/tacoma.html which also includes some short video footage of the collapse. The University of Washington also have an excellent website on the history of the bridge at http://www.lib.washington.edu/specialcoll/exhibits/tnb/.

[33] George Lakoff explains there are not really any such things as totally free markets, though, because real markets are constructed from thousands of rules. http://www.berkeley.edu/news/media/releases/2003/10/27_lakoff.shtml.

[34] In mathematical terms, if P is the amount invested at the start, r is the rate of interest and n is the number of years you are investing for, you will earn a total sum, including your original investment of $P \times (1+r/100)^n$.

[35] In practice of course, even if a sound recording does fall into the public domain there are still multiple opportunities for the copyright owner to derive revenues from it. If the copyright expired on a Cliff Richard recording, for example, Cliff is still at liberty to record and release an end-of-copyright-celebration version of the song. Then it hardly matters that the Joe Bloggs Garage Band has recorded a version too. Cliff's new recording is still likely to achieve significant sales.

[36] Heisenberg's principle states that you cannot measure the momentum and the position of an electron simultaneously with any degree of accuracy or precision.

[37] Nicholas Georgescu-Roegen singled out economists as a generic group of experts who were particularly prone to confusing their models with reality in *The Entropy Law and the Economic Process* (Harvard University Press, 1971).

[38] http://www.ilikecurry.co.uk/?p=84.

[39] We spend far too much time emphasising differences and generating conflict and not enough embracing the differences and accepting people for who they are. A computerised multiple-choice test or a booklet cannot make someone a better person – we have to do that ourselves. See also *The Baby Lab How Elizabeth Spelke peers into the infant mind* by Margaret Talbot, in *New Yorker* magazine, September 4, 2006, where Elizabeth Spelke, whose baby psychology research has led her to believe that we are all born with the same cognitive tools regardless of race, gender or culture, is quoted thus: "Nobody should ever be troubled by our research, whatever we come to find. Everybody should be troubled by the phenomena that motivate it: the pervasive tendency of people all over the world to categorize others into different social groups, despite our common and universal humanity, and to endow these groups with social and emotional significance that fuels ethnic conflict and can even lead to war and genocide."

[40] There are various other slightly more sophisticated versions of this model which discuss taking adverse consequences of possible options into consideration and clearly the Schneier five-step test from Chapter 5 would be useful here but the steps as listed are pretty much how we teach them to OU students, albeit usually with concrete examples and numbers.

[41] Memo/06/181, 03/05/2006, available on the Internet at http://europa.eu.int/rapid/pressReleasesAction.do?reference=MEMO/06/181&format=HTML&aged=0&language=EN&guiLanguage=en.

[42] See http://trendchart.cordis.lu/scoreboards/scoreboard2005/inoutput.cfm and http://trendchart.cordis.lu/scoreboards/scoreboard2005/methodology.cfm#_ftn3.
[43] See *The Best War Ever: Lies, Damned Lies, and the Mess in Iraq* by Sheldon Rampton and John Stauber (Jeremy P. Tarcher, 2006).
[44] See *A Primer on Decision Making: How Decisions Happen* by James G. March (Free Press, 1994).
[45] Feynman op. cit.

Chapter 10

[1] *T860 Environmental Decision Making: A Systems Approach* (1996–2006) and its successor *T863 Environmental Decision Making: A Systems Approach*, presented to students for the first time in 2006.
[2] See *Redesigning the Future: Systems Approach to Societal Problems* by Russell L. Ackoff (John Wiley & Sons, 1974).
[3] See *ID cards doomed, say officials* by David Leppard, *Sunday Times*, July 09, 2006, http://www.timesonline.co.uk/article/0,,2087-2262437_1,00.html. The leaked emails written by David Foord, Mission Critical Director (ID & Defence) in the Office of Government Commerce (OGC) and Peter Smith, Acting Commercial Director of the ID & Passport Service are a fairly damning indictment of the ID card plans. They are available online at http://www.idealgovernment.com/index.php/weblog/comments/943/.
[4] See the Foord and Smith emails and *UK ID card scheme near collapse, as Blair pushes cut-down 'variant'* by John Lettice in *The Register*, Sunday 9 July 2006. http://www.theregister.co.uk/2006/07/09/st_id_cards_doomed_emails/.
[5] See *ID cards could cost less, minister says* by Lucy Sherrif in *The Register*, Monday 25 September 2006. http://www.theregister.co.uk/2006/09/25/id_card_costs/.
[6] The term 'blue-skies research' has to some degree lost its meaning in the wave of political and commercial promotional rhetoric about big initiatives that we are constantly subjected to these days. It did once mean highly innovative or creative research unimpeded by short term 'goals' or 'targets' and with possible outcomes not even conceived of at the beginning of the process.
[7] Often, as Arnold Wilkins states in the preface to his memoirs, the pressure to get things done meant that the building of the 'Chain Home' radar stations was done with home-made apparatus and there was no opportunity for development testing except in the form of live operations. See *The Birth of British Radar: The Memoirs of Arnold 'Skip' Wilkins* edited by Colin Latham and Anne Stobbs (Speedwell for the Defence Electronics History Society, 2006).
[8] See *Steal This Vote: Dirty Elections and the Rotten History of Democracy in America* by Andrew Gumbel (Nation books, 2005) and *The Best Democracy Money Can Buy* by Greg Palast (Constable and Robinson, 2003) for stories of 'hanging' and 'pregnant' chads in Florida in 2000.
[9] See for, example, *Ehrlich Wants Paper Ballots For Nov. Vote* by Christian Davenport and Ann E. Marimow, *Washington Post*, 21 September 2006.

http://www.washingtonpost.com/wp-
dyn/content/article/2006/09/20/AR2006092001356_pf.html.
[10] See the Interim Report of the Commission on Electronic Voting, April 2004,
available at: http://www.cev.ie/htm/report/view_report.htm.
First Report of the Commission on Electronic Voting, December 2004 available
at: http://www.cev.ie/htm/report/first_report.htm.
Second Report of the Commission on Electronic Voting, June 2006, available at:
http://www.cev.ie/htm/report/download_second.htm.
[11] The Electoral Commission is an independent, non-partisan public body established in November 2000 under the Political Parties, Elections and Referendums
Act 2000 (PPERA). The Commission is supposed to be directly accountable to the
UK Parliament.
[12] *The Shape of Elections to Come,* p7, available at the Electoral Commission
website
http://www.electoralcommission.org.uk/templates/search/document.cfm/8346.
[13] The three main reports were *Modernising elections: a strategic evaluation of the
2002 electoral pilot schemes*
http://www.electoralcommission.org.uk/files/dms/Modernising_elections_6574-
6170__E__N__S__W__.pdf,
Technical report on the May 2003 pilots
http://www.electoralcommission.org.uk/templates/search/document.cfm/8944,
and *Findings paper on electronic counting pilot schemes 2006*
http://www.electoralcommission.org.uk/files/dms/FindingsElectronicCounting_22
986-17173__E__N__S__W__.pdf.
[14] In fairness to the government, however, the most recent changes to UK election
law in the form of the Electoral Administration Act, passed in the summer of
2006, was broadly welcomed by the Commission
http://www.electoralcommission.org.uk/elections/eladbill.cfm. The Act itself can
be seen at http://www.opsi.gov.uk/acts/acts2006/ukpga_20060022_en.pdf. It runs
to about 150 pages and is not bedtime reading unless you suffer from insomnia.
[15] There are already many, many books, academic papers and websites that cover
such techniques. Amongst the best are the Open University's *Systems Thinking
and Practice* series of materials: *T551 Systems Thinking and Practice: A Primer,
T552 System Thinking and Practice: Diagramming* and *T553 Systems Thinking
and Practice: Modelling.* A useful starting point, though is the Open2.net website
on *Systems Practice: Managing Complexity* at http://www.open2.net/systems/.
[16] For what it is worth, the ones I find most useful for making sense at the early
stages of the framework are systems maps, mind maps, influence diagrams, multi
ple cause diagrams, stakeholder analysis and a version of the boundary setting
questions from *Critical Heuristics of Social Systems Design* by Werner Ulrich,
European Journal of Operational Research, 31 pp276–283, 1987. For the later
stages, in the area of accounting, cost benefit analysis, statistics, mathematical and
computer modelling, vast areas of the British Library's shelf space are devoted to
volumes on just these subjects. Yet in the crucial area of intellectual property
none of this collected wisdom seems necessary as policy is based on the claims
and dubious numbers of influential interested parties.

[17] The description is not mine but that of my friend and colleague, Bernard Coen, who has read full early drafts of the book and in thinking about how he would describe it to a third party came up with this.

[18] The World Trade Organisation, the World Intellectual Property Organisation, the US Congress, the various bilateral and multilateral trade forums and the decision making institutions of the European Union.

[19] I am assuming a starting point here of the Diamond v Chakrabarty US Supreme Court decision in 1980, which opened the floodgates on genetic patenting. The decision is available online at http://caselaw.lp.findlaw.com/scripts/getcase.pl?court=US&vol=447&invol=303. U.S. Supreme Court, *Diamond v. Chakrabarty.* 447 U.S. 303 (1980).

[20] Their European patents, however, covering the diagnostic methods for detecting the BRCA1 gene mutations, were revoked or amended to exclude the diagnostic tests in 2004. The company are appealing the decision. WIPO Magazine had a short article on the controversy in August 2006. http://www.wipo.int/wipo_magazine/en/2006/04/article_0003.html.

[21] See *DNA: The Secret of Life* by James D. Watson with Andrew Berry (Alfred Knopf, 2003) pp313–316.

[22] *Drug firms' lobby tactics revealed* by Rob Evans and Sarah Boseley, *The Guardian*, Thursday 28 September 2006. http://politics.guardian.co.uk/publicservices/story/0,,1882582,00.html.

[23] Incidentally the lack of access to AIDS drugs in Africa and other needy parts of the world is also a story of how one or a small group of committed individuals can make a difference on a global scale. The attention of the Western/Northern media and policy makers was largely drawn to the impact of intellectual property laws on plight of AIDS sufferers in South Africa through the work of James Love and his small group of colleagues at the *Consumer Project on Technology* (soon to be known as *Knowledge Ecology International*). See http://www.cptech.org/.

[24] It is an article of faith in the pharmaceutical industry that patents are critical to encourage innovation and investment in research and development of drugs. That may well be the case, but there is a genuine question about whether the patents are encouraging the right kind of innovation. Various academic studies suggest that although thousands of new drugs have been produced, the industry has not really developed very many novel treatments over the past thirty years. See *The Truth About Drug Companies: How They Deceive Us and What to Do About It* by Marcia Angell (Random House, 2004). Drug companies are commercial entities driven primarily by the profit motive so they are only going to sell drugs that make money. They have more incentive to develop drugs to cure baldness (hair restorer and baldness treatments are big markets in the West) than treatments for neglected diseases that are rampant in parts of the developing world, where the communities lack the means to pay for them. It is not just the developing world that loses out. The system encourages development of drugs that will sell rather than those that meet important health needs. Yet if the system was re-shaped to include lucrative incentives to develop responses to these needs, the pharmaceutical sector, as rational commercial actors, would pursue those kinds of treatments.

So the process of vacuuming up raw biotech and genetic data in patent portfolios creates an even wider concern than the usual ethical, moral, religious objections along the lines 'you can't own a gene' because the common heritage of life 'should not be commoditised'. It means that fundamental knowledge about the human genome and possible health benefits will be locked away unless there is an expectation that they can be commercially exploited. This depends on the current distribution of wealth and people's ability and willingness to pay.

[25] Pharmaceutical tourism in North America, where US citizens cross the Canadian border to buy cheaper versions of the same drugs has been a source of angst for US politicians and drug companies for some time. See, for example: *Cheap Drugs From Canada: Another Political Hot Potato* by Gardiner Harris, *New York Times*, 23 October 2003.

[26] See also *Stop Making Pills Political Prisoners* by Lawrence Lessig *Wired* Magazine Issue 12.02, February 2004.

[27] See *The Economic Structure of Intellectual Property Law* by William M. Landes and Richard A. Posner (Harvard University Press, 2003), *Information Rules: A Strategic Guide to the Network Economy* by Carl Shapiro and Hal R.Varian (Harvard Business School Press, 1999), *Innovation and Its Discontents* by Adam B. Jaffe and Josh Lerner (Princeton University Press, 2004).

[28] See Chapter 1 and *Adomnan's Life of Columba (Oxford Medieval Texts)*, (Clarendon Press, 1991) by St. Adomnan translated and edited by Alan Orr Anderson and Marjorie Ogilvie Anderson.

[29] Professor of Law & Legal History at Columbia Law School and General Counsel of the Free Software Foundation.

[30] *The DotCommunist Manifesto: How Culture Became Property and What We're Going to Do About It* by Eben Moglen, November 2001. A video of the talk is available at http://www.ibiblio.org/moglen. The italicised words are my attempt to capture Moglen's rhythm and emphasis from the video of his talk. My perspective, you might say.

[31] *Science and Corporate Strategy: Du Pont R and D, 1902–1980* by David A. Hounshell and John Kenly Smith Jr (Cambridge University Press 1988) p302.

[32] Pellegrino Research Professor in Entomology for the Department of Organismic and Evolutionary Biology at Harvard University, Wilson is a world renowned scientist best known for his environmentalism and the espousal of ethics, reason and justice as the three overriding factors that should guide our decisions in life. He remains one of science's great communicators.

[33] *The Diversity of Life* by Edward O. Wilson (Penguin Books, 2001), p306. Bernard Coen points out that there is also an argument to be made that familiarity breeds contempt and when we take things for granted we do not pay enough attention to preserving them. See, for example, *Easter's End* by Jared Diamond, August 1995 at http://www.mnforsustain.org/easter_island_diamond_j.htm and *The Lessons of Easter Island,* an extract from *A Green History of the World: The Environment and the Collapse of Great Civilizations* by Clive Ponting (Penguin Books, 1993) at
http://www.mnforsustain.org/ponting_c_the_lessons_of_easter_island.htm. The

complexity of the interaction of understanding and preservation would suggest there is no simple pattern which will apply in all contexts.

[34] See *Intellectual Property, Education and Access to Knowledge in Southern Africa* Report for the Trade Law Centre for Southern Africa (with the support of the ICTSD-UNCTAD Project on IPRs and Sustainable Development) by Andrew Rens, Achal Prabhala and Dick Kawooya. From the report: "Andrew Rens is legal lead of Creative Commons South Africa, a fellow of the Stanford Centre for Internet and Society, and researches IPR issues at the LINK Centre at the University of the Witwatersrand, Johannesburg. Achal Prabhala coordinated the Access to Learning Materials Project in Southern Africa in 2004/2005, and researches IPR issues in association with the Alternative Law Forum, India. Dick Kawooya is a PhD Candidate at the School of Information Sciences, University of Tennessee, and founding member of the Africa Access to Knowledge Alliance formerly Africa Copyright Forum". Note: ICTSD is the International Centre for Trade and Sustainable Development and UNCAD is the United Nations Conference on Trade and Development. It is a fascinating document which runs to 70 pages and at the very least the two-page executive summary is well worth a read. See also http://b2fxxx.blogspot.com/2006/06/intellectual-property-education-and.html.

[35] This is based on a version of my *Unfinished wish list for government in the area of education* first published on William Heath's Ideal Government website in October, 2004. See http://www.idealgovernment.com/index.php/weblog/unfinished_wish_list_for_government_in_the_area_of_education/.

[36] Messy in the Ackoff sense but also in the sense of untapped potential.

[37] See *The Economy of Ideas: Selling Wine Without Bottles on the Global Net* by John Perry Barlow http://www.eff.org/~barlow/EconomyOfIdeas.html.

[38] And still relatively cheaply for those of us who have access to it, though if my thoughts on the impact of the impending energy crisis, in Chapter 8, have any resonance this state of affairs may not continue even in the affluent West.

[39] See also *Information, Systems and Information Systems* by Peter Checkland and Sue Holwell (John Wiley & Sons, 1998), Chapter 5 *The Information System Which Won the War*, for the authors' crucial lesson about the difference between information systems and information technology.

[40] See *The Birth of British Radar: The Memoirs of Arnold 'Skip' Wilkins* edited by Colin Latham and Anne Stobbs (Speedwell, Defence Electronics History Society, 2006).

[41] MIT OpenCourseWare http://ocw.mit.edu/
Open2.net http://www.open2.net
The BBC Creative Archive http://creativearchive.bbc.co.uk
Utah State University http://ocw.usu.edu/Index/ECIndex_view
Johns Hopkins School of Public Health http://ocw.jhsph.edu/
Carnegie-Mellon http://www.cmu.edu/oli/
TESSA (Teacher Education in Sub-Saharan Africa) http://www.tessaprogramme.org
Japan OpenCourseWare Alliance http://www.jocw.jp/
Open Door http://www.open.ac.uk/idc/news/current/opendoor.html

Rice University Connexions Content Commons http://www.cnx.rice.edu
The Foothill-De Anza Community College Sofia Project http://sofia.fhda.edu/
Tufts University http://ocw.tufts.edu/
ParisTech OpenCourseWare project http://graduateschool.paristech.org/
China Open Resources for Education (CORE) Project (A network of 156 Chinese
universities by the autumn of 2006) http://www.core.org.cn/en/index.htm
Fulbright Economics Teaching Programme OpenCourseWare project in Vietnam
http://ocw.fetp.edu.vn/home.cfm
The Learning Matrix http://thelearningmatrix.enc.org/
SMETE Digital Library http://www.smete.org/smete/
iLumina Educational Resources for Science and Mathematics http://www.ilumina-dlib.org/
HEAL National Digital Library http://www.healcentral.org/
MERLOT http://www.merlot.org/
JORUM online repository service http://www.jorum.ac.uk/about/index.html
These are just some of the bigger initiatives, not to mention the tremendous work
of individual scholars like Peter Suber
http://www.earlham.edu/~peters/hometoc.htm
http://www.earlham.edu/~peters/fos/fosblog.html
Just as this book is about to go to press the Creative Commons folks are setting up
a new division, CC Learn, to promote networks of open educational resources and
interoperability among existing repositories and portals.
[42] http://oci.open.ac.uk/index.html. It is my hope that the Open University's near
40 year experience of producing self-contained, pedagogically sound, open self-
learning materials will help to drive these initiatives to a new level.
[43] Brewster Kahle, the Max Planck Society and many others have extensively articulated the benefits, so I will not repeat all that here. Eben Moglen casts it as a
moral or ethical issue. For a comprehensive perspective of Kahle's point of view
see his luminary lecture at the Library of Congress in November 2002
http://www.loc.gov/rr/program/lectures/kahle.html. Note the webcast of this lecture is about an hour and a half. A much quicker overview can be had from the
following *Wired* and *Guardian* articles and many like them on the Web,
http://www.wired.com/news/business/0,1367,60948,00.html
http://www.guardian.co.uk/online/story/0,3605,946511,00.html.
The Max Planck Society *Berlin Declaration on Open Access to Knowledge in the
Sciences and Humanities* is available at: http://www.zim.mpg.de/openaccess-
berlin/berlindeclaration.html.
[44] Even if they receive their funding from governments or large charitable or be
nevolent foundations.
[45] See *Piracy is Progressive Taxation, and Other Thoughts on the Evolution of
Online Distribution* by Tim O'Reilly
http://www.openp2p.com/pub/a/p2p/2002/12/11/piracy.html. As O'Reilly says:
"Publishing is not a role that will be undone by any new technology, since its existence is mandated by mathematics. Millions of buyers and millions of sellers cannot find one another without one or more middlemen who, like a kind of step-
down transformer, segment the market into more manageable pieces."

[46] The latter is such a common, superficial and irritating approach to 'e-learning' that I will not bore you with my long rant on it. I will just say that if I want a student to learn to draw a graph, the thinking processes involved in getting to grips with the appropriate mathematical principles are significantly different to the thinking processes involved in finding out how many colours the graphics software on your computer allows you to use, in producing something that looks vaguely like a graph on screen.

[47] See Martin Weller's blog at
http://nogoodreason.typepad.co.uk/no_good_reason/2006/10/love_technology.html.

[48] The OECD (http://www.oecd.org) issued a Final Communiqué on 30 January 2004, supporting open access to publicly funded research data available at http://www.oecd.org/document/15/0,2340,en_2649_33703_25998799_1_1_1_1,00.html.

[49] See the open letter of 25 Nobel Prize winners to the US Congress on 26 August 2004 at http://www.public-domain.org/?q=node/60.

[50] The umbrella body for UK research councils, in requiring researchers in receipt of government grants to make the results of their research openly available, was not necessarily supported by the UK government who were concerned about the possible impact on publishers of academic journals.

[51] *Study on the Economic and Technical Evolution of the Scientific Publication Markets in Europe* Final Report, January 2006, Commissioned by DG-Research, European Commission, undertaken by Mathias Dewatripont, Victor Ginsburgh, Patrick Legros and Alexis Walckiers, ECARES, Université libre de Bruxelles; Jean-Pierre Devroey, Marianne Dujardin and Françoise Vandooren, Library Department, Université libre de Bruxelles; Pierre Dubois, Jérôme Foncel and Marc Ivaldi IDEI, Université des Sciences Sociales, Toulouse; Marie-Dominique Heusse Library Department, Université des Sciences Sociales, Toulouse.

[52] T*he Common Thread: A Story of Science, Politics, Ethics and the Human Genome* by John Sulston, Georgina Ferry, published by Black Swan, 2003. I realise that this open publication sets all kinds of hares running, from the immediate potential impact on the income of academic journal publishers to that on the organisations wishing to patent the fruits of publicly funded research. But to get into a detailed discussion of these is beyond the scope of the book at this stage.

[53] The very existence of various organisations' 'e-learning strategies' often leads me to wonder whether they're distracted by the 'e' and focused on technology rather than the purpose and the system.

[54] The most readable and practical accounts of this work are in Martin Weller's books, *Delivering Learning on the Net: the why, what and how of online education* (Kogan Page, 2002) and *Virtual Learning Environments: Using choosing and developing your VLE* (Routledge, 2007). Anyone with any responsibility for the incorporation of 'e-learning' in whatever context or scale should be made to read Martin's work. I can recommend lots more literature but these are the easiest, most accessible, comprehensive guides to the subject, all gathered between the covers of two books.

[55] Policymakers need to understand why the Net and peer-to-peer technologies are significant in education. This is another vast subject about which I will just say two things. Firstly, these are 'many to many' network technologies, that put people in touch with people. Secondly, read Chapters 1 and 2 of Martin Weller's *Delivering Learning on the Net* where he gives a nice overview of the subject and some 'e-learning myths'.

[56] http://www.blackboard.com/company/press/release.aspx?id=887622 Blackboard is the same company that sued two students who found security holes in their campus IS card system. See Chapter 3 and Jennifer Jenkins' terrific account of the case at http://www.chillingeffects.org/weather.cgi?WeatherID=383.

[57] US Patent no. 6,988,138.

[58] To determine the precise claims, however, it is essential to view the original text of the patent and consult several intellectual property lawyers

[59] http://www.alt.ac.uk/docs/ALT_Blackboard_20060823.pdf.

[60] Blackboard sued Desire2Learn within weeks of the patent being granted in the US.

[61] I failed miserably to interest my colleagues in another patent saga involving a company called Acacia in the US, which has a patent on audio and video streaming technologies over the Internet and successfully sued pornography companies in a prelude to attempting to get universities and colleges in the US to licence this patent, if they were using the Internet in their teaching. I believe the cheapest licence they offered was $5000 per annum. There are lots of web reports on these cases, one of the easier to negotiate sites being http://www.streamingmedia.com/patent/.

[62] The educational technology community do not really move in the same circles as the digital rights community which has been exorcised about intellectual property for some years. Maybe they should talk? Put people in touch with people and they might learn a thing or two.

[63] See, for example, *What Is Web 2.0: Design Patterns and Business Models for the Next Generation of Software* by Tim O'Reilly at http://www.oreillynet.com/pub/a/oreilly/tim/news/2005/09/30/what-is-web-20.html and the World Wide Web Consortium (W3C) website at http://www.w3.org/.

[64] TCP/IP protocols.

[65] See *The Digital Promise: Using Technology to Transform Learning* by Michael Feldstein in the Association for Computing Machinery's *eLearn* magazine http://elearnmag.org/subpage.cfm?section=articles&article=39-1.

[66] There's a project in San Francisco, *Just Think!* (http://www.justthink.org/aboutus/mission.html), which operates from two buses full of multimedia technology, to teach kids what the director, Dave Yanofsky, calls "media literacy", a much maligned term. Yanofsky defines media literacy as "the ability to understand, analyse, and deconstruct media images. It's aim is to make kids literate about the way media works, the way it's constructed, the way it is delivered and the way people access it." There is a growing collection of academic literature on this subject covering things like the notion of kids learning to 'write' (communicate) with multimedia technologies. The notion of writing

through multimedia opens a whole new world to people who have not benefited from a sound education or who have experienced barriers (e.g. dyslexia) to assimilating traditional written educational materials.

[67] Having said it is wishful thinking, though, there are increasing numbers of publicly funded municipal wi-fi networks springing up in various parts of the world, even in US cities. Singapore has made a commitment to offer a free wireless broadband service in public areas from 2007 with a plan to put 5000 wireless hotspots in place over a period of two years. See also *The Future of Ideas* by Lawrence Lessig (Random House, 2001) pp79–83 on the wireless spectrum in Tonga.

[68] Like that being created by the Ndiyo project http://www.ndiyo.org/.

[69] See *Libraries fear digital lockdown* by Ian Youngs, BBC News, 3 February 2006 http://news.bbc.co.uk/2/hi/technology/4675280.stm. See also my blog entries at http://b2fxxx.blogspot.com/2006/09/groklaw-british-library-gets-it-on-drm.html and http://b2fxxx.blogspot.com/2006/05/british-library-and-drm.html.

References

Abramson, J (1994) We the Jury: The Jury System and the Ideal of Democracy. Basic Books, New York

Ackoff R (1974) Redesigning the Future: A Systems Approach to Societal Problems. John Wiley & Sons, New York

Ackoff R (1978) The Art of Problem Solving: Accompanied by Ackoff's Fables. John Wiley & Sons, New York

Ackoff R (1999) Ackoff's Best: His Classic Writings on Management. John Wiley & Sons, New York

ACLU v NSA (2006) US District Court Eastern District of Michigan Southern Division Case No. 06-CV-10204 Filed 08/17/2006

Adams J (1995) Risk. Routledge, Abingdon

Agre P et al (2004) An Open Letter to the U.S. Congress Signed by 25 Nobel Prize Winners. Union for the Public Domain

Agreement on Trade-Related Aspects of Intellectual Property Rights (1994), GATT Uruguay Round

Anderson C (2006) The Long Tail: How Endless Choice Is Creating Unlimited Demand. Random House Business Books, New York

Anderson AO, Anderson MO (translators & eds) (1991) Adomnan's Life of Columba (Oxford Medieval Texts). Clarendon Press, Wotton-under-Edge

Angell M (2004) The Truth About Drug Companies: How They Deceive Us and What to Do About It. Random House, New York

Ansary T (2004) The Muddle Machine: Confessions of a Textbook Editor. Edutopia Magazine

Baird Z, Barksdale J (2006) Mobilizing Information to Prevent Terrorism: Accelerating Development of a Trusted Information Sharing Environment. Markle Foundation, New York

Barbour V, Chinnock P, Cohen B, Yamey G (2006) The impact of open access upon public health. Bulletin of the World Health Organization (BLT), Volume 84, Number 5, May 2006, pp337–424

Barlow JP (1992) The Economy of Ideas: Selling Wine Without Bottles on the Global Net.

Beinhocker E (2006) The Origin of Wealth: Evolution, Complexity, and the Radical Remaking of Economics. Harvard Business School Press and Random House Business Books, Boston

Benkler Y (2006) The Wealth of Networks. Yale University Press, New Haven

Berners-Lee T (2000) Weaving the Web. Textere LLC, London

Bickers RT (1990) The Battle of Britain. Salamander Books, Baltimore

Bignell V, Fortune J (1984) Understanding Systems Failures. Manchester University Press, Manchester

Birkenhead Earl (1962) The Professor and the Prime Minister. Riverside Press and Houghton Mifflin Company, Cambridge

Blackmore et al (2006) T863 Environmental Decision Making: A Systems Approach. Open University course.

Bollier D (2002) Silent Theft: The Private Plunder of Our Common Wealth. Routledge, New York

Bollier D (2005) Brand Name Bullies: The Quest to Own and Control Culture. John Wiley & Sons, Hoboken

Bowen LJ (1903) McQuire v. Western Morning News [1903] 2 KB 100

Boyle J (1997) Shamans, Software and Spleens: Law and the Construction of the Information Society. Harvard University Press, Cambridge

Boyle J (2003) The Second Enclosure Movement and the Construction of the Public Domain. In: 66 Law and Contemp. Probls. Vol. 66, nos. 1&2: pp33–74

Bradley I (1996) Columba: Pilgrim and Penitent. Wild Goose Publications, Iona

Brands S (2000) Rethinking Public Key Infrastructures and Digital Certificates: Building in Privacy. MIT Press, Cambridge

Brazile D Chairman (2005) Democracy at Risk: The 2004 Election in Ohio. Democratic National Committee Voting Rights Institute

Briggs W (1906) The Law of International Copyright. Steven and Haynes, London

Brockman J Ed. (2006) Intelligent Thought: Science versus the Intelligent Design Movement. Vintage, New York

Brown I et al (2003) Implementing the European Union Copyright Directive. Foundation for Information Policy Research

Brown L (1999) A Radar History of World War II: Technical and Military Imperatives. Institute of Physics Publishing, Bristol

Brundtland GH (1987) World Commission on Environment and Development Report: Our Common Future

Buderi R (1996) The Invention that Changed the World: The Story of Radar from War to Peace. Simon & Schuster New York

Bungay S (2001) The Most Dangerous Enemy: A History of the Battle of Britain. Aurum Press, London

Caro RA (1974) The Power Broker: Robert Moses and the Fall of New York. Knopf, New York

Checkland P, Holwell S (1998) Information, Systems and Information Systems: Making Sense of the Field. John Wiley & Sons, New York

Chomsky N (1992) Deterring Democracy. Vintage, New York

Churchill, WS (1985) The Second World War, Volume 1: The Gathering Storm. Penguin, London New York

Churchill, WS (1985) The Second World War, Volume 2: Their Finest Hour. Penguin, London New York

Clark RW (1965) Tizard. Methuen, London

Collier B (1962) The Battle of Britain. Batsford, London

Coleman R, Carlin M (2001) Hacker With A White Hat. Gibney Anthony & Flaherty LLP, New York

Colum P (1936) The Legend of Saint Columba. Sheed and Ward, London

Consumers International (2006) Copyright and Access to Knowledge: Policy Recommendations on Flexibilities in Copyright Laws. Consumers International & Open Society Institute Development Foundation (OSI) & International Development Research Centre (IDRC), Kuala Lumpur

Conyers J, Miller A Ed. (2005) What Went Wrong in Ohio: The Conyers Report on the 2004 Presidential Election. Academy Chicago Publishers, Chicago

Coogan TP (1991) Michael Collins. Arrow, Dublin

Coogan TP (1996) The Troubles. Arrow, Dublin

Corrigan R (2004) Harry Potter, Armoured Car DRM and the Lawyers. IEEE International Symposium on Consumer Electronics

Corrigan R, Naughton J (2004) T182 Law, the Internet and Society: Technology and the Future of Ideas. Open University

Dayton BW (2004) Managing Crises in the Twenty-First Century. International Studies Review Vol.6, pp165–194

Dawkins R (1976) The Selfish Gene. Oxford University Press, Oxford

Deffeyes KS (2001) Hubbert's Peak: The Impending World Oil Shortage. Princeton University Press, Princeton

Deighton L (1977) Fighter: The True Story of the Battle of Britain. Alfred A Knopf, New York

Department of Transport (2000) The Future of Aviation – Consultation on Air Transport Policy. UK Department of Transport

Department of Transport (2003) The Future of Air Transport. UK Department of Transport

Dewatripont M et al (2006) Study on the Economic and Technical Evolution of the Scientific Publication Markets in Europe Final Report. European Commission Directorate-General for Research Information and Communication Unit, Brussels

Diamond v. Chakrabarty. 447 U.S. 303 (1980)

Directive 96/9/EC of the European Parliament and of the Council of 11 March 1996 on the legal protection of databases

Directive 2001/29/EC of the European Parliament and of the Council of 22 May 2001 on the harmonisation of certain aspects of copyright and related rights in the information society

Directive 2004/48/EC of the European Parliament and of the Council of 29 April 2004 on the enforcement of intellectual property rights

Drahos P (2004) Intellectual Property and Pharmaceutical Markets: A Nodal Governance Approach. Temple Law Review Vol 77, pp401–424

Drahos P, Braithwaite J (2002) Information Feudalism: Who Owns the Knowledge Economy. Earthscan, London

Drahos P, Faunce T, Goddard M, Henry D (2004) The FTA and the PBS. Evatt Foundation, Sydney (Submitted to Australian Senate Select Committee on the US-Australia Free Trade Agreement)

Drexler E (1987) Engines of Creation: The Forthcoming Era of Nanotechnology. Anchor, New York

Drout M (2004) Wrong About Almost Everything: Editing J. R. R. Tolkien. Medieval Academy of America, Cambridge

Duncan F (1990) Rickover and the Nuclear Navy: The Discipline of Technology. Naval Institute Press, Annapolis

Duncan F (2001) Rickover: The Struggle for Excellence. Naval Institute Press, Annapolis

EFF (2006) Unintended Consequences: Seven Years under the DMCA. Electronic Frontier Foundation

Election Science Institute (2006) Memorandum to Ohio Election Officials: Report on the Cuyahoga County May 2 Primary Election. Election Science Institute, San Francisco

Faulds H (1880) On the Skin-Furrows of the Hand. Nature, 28 October

Feldstein M (2006) The Digital Promise: Using Technology to Transform Learning. Association for Computing Machinery eLearn Magazine

Felten E, Feldman A, Haldermann A (2006) Security Analysis of the Diebold AccuVote-TS Voting Machine. Center for Information Technology Policy Princeton University

Ferry G, Sulston J (2003) The Common Thread: Science, Politics, Ethics and the Human Genome. Corgi, London

Feynman R (2001) The Pleasure of Finding Things Out. Penguin, London

Feynman R, Feynman M Ed. (2006) Don't You Have Time to Think? Penguin Books, London

Feynman R, Leighton R, Hutchings E Ed. (1985) Surely You're Joking, Mr. Feynman!: Adventures of a Curious Character. W.W.Norton, New York

Fisher A (2001) Critical Thinking: An Introduction. Cambridge University Press, Cambridge

Fisher D (2006) A Summer Bright and Terrible: Winston Churchill, Lord Dowding, Radar and the Impossible Triumph of the Battle of Britain. Shoemaker & Hoard, London

Fisher WW (2004) Promises to Keep: Technology Law and the Future of Entertainment. Stanford University Press, Palo Alto

Fortune J, Peters G (2005) Information Systems: Achieving Success by Avoiding Failure. John Wiley & Sons, Chichester

Franklin B (1753) Method of Deciding Doubtful Matters. Letter to Joseph Priestley

Geist, M (2006) 30 Days of DRM. Michael Geist, Ottowa http://www.michaelgeist.ca/daysofdrm

Georgescu-Roegen N (1971) The Entropy Law and the Economic Process. Harvard University Press, Cambridge

Gervais D (1998) The TRIPS Agreement: Drafting History and Analysis. Sweet & Maxwell, London

Goozner M (2004) The $800 Million Pill: The Truth Behind the Cost of New Drugs. University of California Press, Los Angeles

Gray M (2003) Confessions of a Copyright Enforcer. The Media Institute Copyright Colloquium

Greenberg K Ed. (2005) The Torture Debate in America. Cambridge University Press, Cambridge

Gumbel A (2005) Steal this Vote: Dirty Elections and Rotten History of Democracy in America. Nation Books, New York

Harris B (2003) Black Box Voting: Ballot Tampering in the 21st Century. Pan Nine Publishing, High Point NC

Higham C (2004) Howard Hughes: The Secret Life. St. Martin's Griffin & Virgin Books, New York

Holland J (1975) Adaptation in Natural and Artificial Systems: An Introductory Analysis with Applications to Biology, Control, and Artificial Intelligence. University of Michigan Press, Mitchigan

Holland J (1998) From Chaos to Order. Perseus Books, New York

Hounshell DA, Kenly Smith J (1988) Science and Corporate Strategy: Du Pont R and D, 1902–1980. Cambridge University Press, Cambridge

Hursti H (2006) Diebold TSx Evaluation: Critical Security Issues with Diebold TSx. Black Box Voting

IIPA (1985) Piracy of U.S. Copyrighted Works in Ten Selected Countries: A report by the International Intellectual Property Alliance to the U.S. Trade Representative. International Intellectual Property Alliance

Irish Commission on Electronic Voting (2004) Interim Report: Secrecy, Accuracy and Testing of the Chosen Electronic Voting System. Commission on Electronic Voting, Dublin

Irish Commission on Electronic Voting (2004) First Report: Secrecy, Accuracy and Testing of the Chosen Electronic Voting System. Commission on Electronic Voting, Dublin

Irish Commission on Electronic Voting (2006) Second Report: Secrecy, Accuracy and Testing of the Chosen Electronic Voting System. Commission on Electronic Voting, Dublin

Jackson JJ (1989) Remarks of Professor John J. Jackson in Symposium: Trade Related Aspects of Intellectual Property, 22 Vanderbilt Journal of Transnational Law

Jaffe A, Lerner J (2004) Innovation and Its Discontents: How our Broken Patent System is Endangering Innovation and Progress, and What to Do About it. Princeton University Press, Princeton

Johnson S (2001) Emergence. Penguin Books, London

Jonas J, Rosenzweig P (2005) Correcting False Positives: Redress and the Watch List Conundrum. Heritage Foundation Homeland Security Legal Memorandum #17

Jones DW (2001) Problems with Voting Systems and the Applicable Standards. Testimony before the U.S. House of Representatives' Committee on Science, Washington DC, May 22, 2001

Jones RV (1998) Most Secret War. Wordsworth Editions, Ware

Kelly K (1995) Out of Control: The New Biology of Machines, Social Systems, and the Economic World. Perseus Books, New York

Kohlers P ed. (1980) Processing of Visible Language 2. Plenum Publishing Corporation, New York

Kohno T, Rubin A, Stubblefield A, Wallach D (2003) John Hopkins University Information Security Institute Technical Report TR-2003-19, July 23, 2003

Kuhn T (1962) The Structure of Scientific Revolutions. University of Chicago Press, Chicago

Lakoff G (2004) Don't Think of an Elephant: Know Your Values and Frame the Debate. Chelsea Green Publishing Company, White River Junction

Landes WM, Posner RA (2003) The Economic Structure of Intellectual Property Law. The Belknap Press of Harvard University Press, Cambridge London

Lasica JD (2005) Darknet: Hollywood's War Against the Digital Generation. John Wiley & Sons, Hoboken

Latham C Ed, Stobbs A Ed (2006) The Birth of British Radar: The Memoirs of Arnold 'Skip' Wilkins. Speedwell, Reading

Lessig L (1999) Code and Other Laws of Cyberspace. Basic Books, New York

Lessig L (2001) The Future of Ideas: The Fate of the Commons in a Connected World. Random House, New York

Lessig L (2003) Free Culture: The Nature and Future of Creativity. Penguin, New York

Lessig L (2004) Stop Making Pills Political Prisoners. Wired Magazine Issue 12.02

Levy S (2000) Crypto: Secrecy and Privacy in the New Code War. Allen Lane The Penguin Press, London

Lipstadt D (1994) Denying the Holocaust: The Growing Assault on Truth and Memory. Penguin, London

Litman J (1994) The Exclusive Right to Read. 13 Cardozo Arts & Entertainment Law Journal 29

Litman J (2001) Digital Copyright. Prometheus Books, New York

LSE Identity Project (2005) The Identity Project: An Assessment of the UK Identity Cards Bill and its Implications

Macaulay (1841) Speech to the House of Commons. Hansard 5th February 1841

Macaulay (1842) Speech to the House of Commons Committee on Copyright Term Extension. Hansard 6th April 1841

March J (1994) A Primer on Decision Making: how decisions happen. The Free Press, New York London Toronto Sydney

Mayfield M (2006) Thinking for Yourself: Developing Critical Thinking Skills Through Reading and Writing, 7th Edition. Thomson Heinle & Heinle, Boston

Medvedev G (1991) The Truth About Chernobyl. Basic Books, New York

Menzies L (1992, originally published 1920) Saint Columba of Iona. Llanerch Press, Llanerch

Mercuri, R (1992) Physical Verifiability of Computer Systems. 5th International Computer Virus and Security Conference

Mosley L (1977) Battle of Britain. Time Life Books, London

MGM v Grokster 545 US 125 (2005)

MGM v Grokster (Lieber v Consumer Empowerment BV) US District Court Central California (September, 2006)

Mould RF (2000) Chernobyl: The Definitive History of the Chernobyl Catastrophe. Institute of Physics Publishing, Bristol

Mulvihill M (2003) Ingenious Ireland: A County-By-County Exploration of the Mysteries and Marvels of the Ingenious Irish. TownHouse & CountryHouse, Dublin

Naughton J (1999) A Brief History of the Future: The Origins of the Internet. Weidenfeld & Nicolson, London

Norden L Chairman (2006) The Machinery of Democracy: Protecting Elections in an Electronic World. The Brennan Center for Justice: Task Force on Voting System Security, New York

O'Donnell M (1532) Betha Colaim Chille

O'Harrow R (2005) No Place to Hide. Free Press, New York

O'Kelleher A, Schoepperle G (translators, eds) (1918) Betha Colaim Chille: Life of Columcille, compiled by Maghnas Ó Domhnaill in 1532. University of Illinois Press, Chicago

O'Reilly (2002) Piracy is Progressive Taxation, and Other Thoughts on the Evolution of Online Distribution. O'Reilly P2P article

OECD (2004) OECD Science Ministerial "Declaration on Access to Research Data from Public Funding." OECD Committee for Scientific and Technological Policy at Ministerial Level

Overton S (2006) Stealing Democracy: The New Politics of Voter Suppression. W.W. Norton & Company, New York

Palast G (2003) The Best Democracy Money Can Buy. Constable and Robinson and Pluto Press, London

Pannick D (1992) Advocates. Oxford University Press, Oxford

Parker M (2001) The Battle of Britain, July – October 1940. Headline Book Publishing, London

Patterson LR (1968) Copyright in Historical Perspective. Vanderbilt University Press, Nashville

Perelman M (2002) Steal this Idea: Intellectual Property Rights and the Corporate Confiscations of Creativity. Palgrave, New York

Perrow C (1999) Normal Accidents: Living with High Risk Technologies. Princeton University Press, New Jersey

Ponting C (1993) A Green History of the World: The Environment and the Collapse of Great Civilizations. Penguin Books, New York

Price A (1998) The Hardest Day: Battle of Britain, 18 August 1940. Cassell Military Classics Series, London

Price A (2005) Instruments of Darkness: The History of Electronic Warfare 1939–1945. Greenhill Books and Stackpole Books, London PA

Rampton S, Strauber J (1995) Toxic Sludge is Good For You: Lies, Damn Lies and the Public Relations Industry. Common Courage Press, Monroe

Rampton S, Strauber J (2006) The Best War Ever: Lies, Damned Lies, and the Mess in Iraq. Jeremy P. Tarcher, New York

Rauhofer J (2006) Defence against the Dark Arts: How the British Response to the Terrorist Threat is Parodied in J K Rowling's "Harry Potter and the Half

Blood Prince". GIKII Workshop VI Computer Law World Conference, Edinburgh

Ray J (2000) The Battle of Britain: Dowding and the First Victory, 1940. Cassell Military Paperbacks Series, London

Rens A, Prabhala A, Kawooya D (2006) Report for the Trade Law Centre for Southern Africa: Intellectual Property, Education and Access to Knowledge in Southern Africa. Trade Law Centre for Southern Africa, Stellenbosch

RIAA v. Diamond Multimedia Systems, Inc., 180 F.3d 1072 (9th Cir. 1999)

Rockwell T (1992) The Rickover Effect: How One Man Made a Difference. Naval Institute Press, Annapolis

Rosen J (2000) The Unwanted Gaze: The Destruction of Privacy in America. Random House, New York

Royal Commission (1998) 21st Report Setting Environmental Standards. Royal Commission on Environmental Pollution

Rubin A (2006) Brave New Ballot: The Battle to Safeguard Democracy in the Age of Electronic Voting. Morgan Road Books, New York

Rudmin F (2006) The Politics of Paranoia and Intimidation: Why does the NSA engage in mass surveillance of Americans when it's statistically impossible for such spying to detect terrorists? Counterpunch

Samuelson P (1996) The Copyright Grab. Wired News Issue 4.01

Samuelson P (1997) The US Digital Agenda at WIPO. 37 Vanderbilt Journal of International Law 369

Samuelson P (2004) Should Economics Play a Role in Copyright Law and Policy? 1 U. Ottawa L. & Tech. J. 3 2004

Schneier B (1995) Applied Cryptography: Protocols, Algorithms, and Source Code in C. John Wiley & Sons, New York

Schneier B (2000) Secrets and Lies: Digital Security in a Networked World. John Wiley & Sons, New York

Schneier B (2003) Beyond Fear: Thinking Sensibly about Security in an Uncertain World. Copernicus Books, New York

Schneier B, Ferguson N (2003) Practical Cryptography. John Wiley & Sons, Chichester

Schroter S (2006) Importance of Free Access to Research Articles on Decision to Submit to the BMJ: Survey of Authors. BMJ 2006 332: 394–396. (18 February)

Senge P (1992) The Fifth Discipline: Art and Practice of the Learning Organization. Random House, New York

Shapiro C, Varian HR (1999) Information Rules: A Strategic Guide to the Network Economy. Harvard Business School Press, Cambridge

Sharpe R translator (1995) Adomnán of Iona: Life of St Columba (Penguin Classics) Penguin Books, London

Shirky C (2000) Content Shifts to the Edges. www.Shirky.com

Simon H (1957) Models of Man. John Wiley & Sons, New York

Singh S (2000) The Code Book: The Secret History of Codes and Code-breaking. Fourth Estate, London

Skrebowski C (2004) Joining the Dots. The Energy Institute's Oil Depletion: No Problem, Concern or Crisis conference

SLIM (2004) SLIM Policy Briefing No. 2 Stakeholders and Stakeholding in Integrated Catchment Management and Sustainable Use of Water. The SLIM Project for the European Commission – DG Research

Snow CP (1960) Science and Government. Oxford University Press, Oxford

Solove D (2004) The Digital Person: Technology and Privacy in the Information Age New York University Press, New York

Spender D (1995) Nattering on the Net: Women, Power and Cyberspace. Spinifex, Melbourne

Stanton N (2004) Mastering Communication 4th edition. Palgrave, Basingstoke

Sunstein C (2005) The Laws of Fear. Cambridge University Press, Cambridge

Sunstein C (2002) Risk and Reason: Safety, Law, and the Environment. Cambridge University Press, Cambridge

Talbot M (2006) The Baby Lab: How Elizabeth Spelke Peers into the Infant Mind. The New Yorker September 5, 2006

The Max Planck Society (2003) Berlin Declaration on Open Access to Knowledge in the Sciences and Humanities. The Max Planck Society, Berlin

The President's Commission on the Accident at Three Mile Island (1979) The Need for Change: The Legacy of TMI. US Government Printing Office (GPO), Washington, DC

The President's Commission (1986) Report to the President by the Presidential Commission on the Space Shuttle Challenger Accident. US Government Printing Office, Washington DC

The Stationery Office (2006) The Intellectual Property (Enforcement, etc.) Regulations 2006. Her Majesty's Stationery Office and Queen's Printer of Acts of Parliament

The Stationery Office (2006) Electoral Administration Act 2006. Her Majesty's Stationery Office and Queen's Printer of Acts of Parliament

Townsend P (2000) Duel of Eagles: The Struggle for the Skies from the First World War to the Battle of Britain. Phoenix Press, London

Tufte ER (1990) Envisioning Information. Graphics Press, Cheshire

Tufte ER (1997) Visual Explanations: Images and Quantities, Evidence and Narrative. Graphics Press, Cheshire

Tufte ER (2001) The Visual Display of Quantitative Information. Second Edition Graphics Press, Cheshire

Tufte ER (2003) The Cognitive Style of PowerPoint. Graphics Press, Cheshire

UK Electoral Commission (2002) Modernising Elections: A Strategic Evaluation of the 2002 Electoral Pilot Schemes

UK Electoral Commission (2003) The Shape of Elections to Come: A Strategic Evaluation of the 2003 Electoral Pilot Schemes

UK Electoral Commission (2003) Technical Report on the May 2003 Pilots.

UK Electoral Commission (2006) Findings Paper on Electronic Counting Pilot Schemes 2006

Ulrich W (1987) Critical Heuristics of Social Systems Design. European Journal of Operational Research, 31 pp276–283

Uphoff N (1986) Local Institutional Development: An Analytical Sourcebook, with Cases. Kumarian Press, Bloomfield

Uphoff N (1992) Local Institutions and Participation for Sustainable Development. International Institute for Environment and Development, London

US Directorate of Defence Trade Controls, US International Traffic in Arms Regulations. US Government Printing Office (GPO)

Vaidhyanathan S (2001) Copyrights and Copywrongs: The Rise of Intellectual Property and How it Threatens Creativity. New York University Press, New York

Vaidhyanathan S (2001) The Anarchist in the Library: How the Clash Between Freedom and Control is Hacking the Real World and Crashing the System. Basic Books, New York

Vaughan D (1997) The Challenger Launch Decision: Risky Technology, Culture and Deviance at NASA. University of Chicago Press, Chicago

Vickers G (1970) Freedom in Rocking a Boat: Changing Values in an Unstable Society. Penguin Books, Harmondsworth

Watson JD, Berry A (2003) DNA: The Secret of Life. Alfred A Knopf, New York

Weller M (2002) Delivering Learning on the Net: The Why, What and How of Online Education. Kogan Page, London

Weller M (2007) Virtual Learning Environments: Using, Choosing and Developing Your VLE. Routledge, London

Wilson EO (2001) The Diversity of Life. Penguin Books, London

Wood D (2003) The Narrow Margin: The Battle of Britain and the Rise of Air Power, 1930–1940. Pen and Sword Books, Barnsley

Woodgate MV (1969) St. Columba. St Paul Publications

Wright R (1969) Dowding and the Battle of Britain. MacDonald.

Yaroshinskaya A (1995) Chernobyl: The Forbidden Truth. University of Nebraska Press, Nebraska

Index